REVOLUTIONARY IRAN

Other Works by the Author

The Middle East and the European Common Market (1964)

The Northern Tier: Afghanistan, Iran, and Turkey (1966)

The Foreign Policy of Iran, 1500–1941:
A Developing Nation in World Affairs (1966)

The Persian Gulf: Iran's Role (1972)

Iran's Foreign Policy, 1941–1973:
A Study of Foreign Policy in Modernizing Nations (1975)

Beyond the Arab-Israeli Settlement:
New Directions for U.S. Policy in the Middle East (1977)

The Persian Gulf and the Strait of Hormuz (1977)

Security of Access to Persian Gulf Oil Supplies in the 1980's (1982)

The United States and Iran: The Patterns of Influence (1982)

The Gulf Cooperation Council: Record and Analysis (1988)

Revolutionary Iran

CHALLENGE AND RESPONSE IN THE MIDDLE EAST

R. K. Ramazani

The Johns Hopkins University Press

BALTIMORE AND LONDON

Originally published, 1986
Second and third printings, 1987
Johns Hopkins Paperbacks edition, 1988

The Johns Hopkins University Press
701 West 40th Street
Baltimore, Maryland 21211
The Johns Hopkins Press Ltd., London

∞ The paper used in this publication meets the minimum requirements of American
National Standard for Information Sciences—Permanence of Paper for Printed Library
Materials, ANSI Z39.48-1984.

Library of Congress Cataloging-in-Publication Data

Ramazani, Rouhollah K., 1928–
    Revolutionary Iran.

    Bibliography: p.
    Includes index.
    1. Near East—Foreign relations—Iran.   2. Iran—
Foreign relations—Near East.   3. Near East—Politics
and government—1945–   4. Iran—Foreign relations—
1979–   I. Title.
DS63.2.I68R36   1986   327.56055   86-45440
ISBN 0-8018-3377-9 (alk. paper)
ISBN 0-8018-3610-7 (pbk.)

Maps on pages 56 and 146 reprinted with permission of Current History, Inc., 1985.
Map on page 2 reprinted with permission of Rand McNally and Co.

Inspired by Thomas Jefferson's precept that here at the University of Virginia *"we are not afraid to follow truth, wherever it may lead, nor tolerate any error so long as reason is left free to combat it,"* this book is dedicated to his legacy.

Contents

Foreword

Professor Ramazani's ambitious and comprehensive study can be appreciated from three different perspectives. First, it offers a sweeping analysis of the challenge represented by Khomeini's ideological vision and by Iran's fundamentalist revolution, as well as of the multiple ways in which Iran's neighbors have tried to deal with so formidable a ferment. There is no other volume that covers so much ground; indeed, the book could have been called "Coping with the Iranian Revolution." Ramazani describes both the effects it has had—mainly but not exclusively on the Shi'ites—in various Middle Eastern countries, and the different strategies of containment, of which the bloodiest is the Iraq-Iran war. He analyzes the motives of Iraq's attack on Iran with persuasive subtlety. No reader of this volume will again feel bewildered or lost amid the complexities, twists, and turns of Middle Eastern politics.

A second perspective is U.S. policy in that part of the world. Ramazani is critical of past and current American attitudes and moves, which, he believes, have fostered anti-American resentment by associating Washington with an often shaky political status quo. He is also critical of Washington's "tilt" toward Iraq. He advocates a policy that would go beyond the containment of Iran and entail an important diplomatic ingredient, not only toward Syria and Iran but also in the Iraq-Iran war and in the Arab-Israeli conflict, whose perpetuation has allowed Iran to become a complicating factor in an already explosive and tangled situation. At a time when the United States is obsessed by the apparently unconquerable phenomenon of terrorism, this plea for a more flexible, better-informed, highly active policy attuned to the currents and storms of the area is likely to be controversial.

This is so, especially, because of the third aspect of the book. In no way can Professor Ramazani be mistaken for an apologist of the Iranian revolution, but both his empathetic attempt to present its origins and above all his belief that it has become somewhat more pragmatic and less extreme in recent months result in a picture that is assuredly more benign than that which most Americans have in their minds. They tend to look at Khomeini as a fanatic Satan, guilty of atrocities at home and of exporting terror. Ramazani's view is more complex. Above all, it is rooted in the conviction that, given Iran's importance in the region, hostility between Iran and the United States is not in America's long-term interest, and that Americans must not become complacent about oil supplies, despite the present glut. Even those who may disagree with some of his evaluations ought to hear Professor Ramazani's call for U.S. policy toward Iran that would take its inspiration from the mutual self-restraint observed by Iran and by many of the "moderate" or traditional Middle Eastern states, a policy that would also try to understand the "demand for spiritual and moral values" that underlies anti-Western movements in that part of the world.

STANLEY HOFFMANN
Harvard University

Preface

Ever since the Iranian Revolution, the United States has made revolutionary Iran the "Great Satan" of the Middle East. Having destroyed the friendly Shah's regime and the longtime American power and influence in Iran, the revolutionary regime first seized the American hostages and then launched an ideological crusade against American strategic interests in "pro-American" countries stretching from the western shores of the Persian Gulf to the eastern coasts of the Mediterranean. Allegedly as a result, "pro-Iranian" terrorists have wreaked havoc on American life and property in the Middle East and, by refusing to negotiate peace with Iraq, the "Iranian fanatics" threaten to spread the war to friendly Gulf states and to disrupt the flow of Gulf oil supplies to world markets, especially the Western democracies and Japan. In response, the Reagan administration has sought, if not in words, then certainly in deeds, to pursue a rigid containment policy toward revolutionary Iran.

This book is published in the hope of setting the record straight. To fail to do so would be to shirk the intellectual duty of exploring the subject as objectively as reason can guide our search for truth. Furthermore, there is the danger that such a failure would perpetuate the current misassessment of the entire Middle Eastern situation, which could lead to more mistaken U.S. policies. In *The United States and Iran: The Patterns of Influence* (New York: Praeger, 1982), I showed that our poor understanding of the Iranian situation, particularly our overidentification with the Shah's mistaken policies, in effect made us part of the Iranian problem, and to that extent, we contributed to the very eruption of the Iranian Revolution. In this book, I try to show that our flawed policies, including the stern containment of "Shi'ite radicalism, Moslem fundamentalism, and Iranian agitation" in the region advocated by Henry Kissinger, have already made us part of the larger Middle Eastern problem, as exemplified by the debacle in Lebanon, and can contribute to cyclic indigenous sociopolitical convulsions of even more disastrous consequences for American life and interests.

In this book, I do not present an exhaustive narrative of the policy of revolutionary Iran toward every other regional state. Nor do I confine this study to an analysis of Iranian regional policies. Rather, I focus on the challenge posed by Iran and the response of other governments in the area to that challenge during the first half-dozen years following the Iranian Revolution. My concept of the challenge-response process, however, is dialectical rather than linear. For example, Iran's revolutionary crusade provoked the Iraqi invasion of Iran, which in turn prompted the Iranian incursion into Iraqi territory.

A more important concept is that both the challenge and the response of governments must be understood in the broader context of the history, society, and culture of the Middle Eastern peoples. The disregard of this imperative is largely responsible for our depiction of revolutionary Iran as the engineer of all the calamities that have befallen the United States and its friends, as though the Middle East was a tabula rasa before the Iranian Revolution. The Shia protest movement is as old as Islamic history. The Arab-Israeli conflict, the Lebanese crisis, the Palestinian problem, and the like all have their own indigenous roots. In this book I try to emphasize this broader context, which I hope will be taken into account in formulating future U.S. policy in the Middle East.

Without the support of the University of Virginia, this book would not have been published, which is the reason I am dedicating the book to the legacy of the university's founder, Thomas Jefferson. Research for this book in effect dates back to 1979, when I first received support from the Energy Policy Studies Center, for which I wrote the monographic study *Security of Access to Persian Gulf Oil Supplies in the 1980's.* I am indebted to Professor Fred D. Rosi, who was then its director, for his patience. The Center for Advanced Studies also supported my research, and I gratefully acknowledge its support, with special thanks to its director, Professor Dexter W. Whitehead. I also would like to thank my research assistants, Drs. Bahman Bakhtiari, Tawfiq Hasou, Joseph Kechichian, and Farhang Rajaee, all former graduate students who taught me more than I could possibly teach them.

In reading the book manuscript, Professor Bruce R. Kuniholm of Duke University recognized its place in the existing literature on the

Middle East and made many helpful suggestions, for which I am thankful.

In introducing this volume, Professor Stanley Hoffmann of Harvard University identified incisively the perspectives from which the reader may appreciate my analysis of the complexities of Middle Eastern politics. I am grateful for his contribution.

I owe special thanks to the Johns Hopkins University Press: to its director, J. G. Goellner, for his enthusiastic interest in the manuscript; to its managing editor, Barbara Lamb, for her innovative idea about the title of the book; and to the staff of the Press, for their courtesy. Jackie Wehmueller's work surpassed my expectations for truly competent editing.

I am grateful to my wife, Nesta, for helping me every step of the way in the course of my work on this book as unfailingly as she did in the course of all my other publications over more than three decades.

Without repeated visits to the Middle East from 1979 to early 1986 for on-site interviews, conversations, and observations, it would have been impossible for me to complete this book. Doing so would have been equally impossible without the help of the many Middle Eastern acquaintances who shared their insights with me but who wish to remain anonymous. This accounts for the absence of source citations in a number of instances. While the generous—and always gracious—help of these leaders, officials, academicians, businessmen, media leaders, and individuals belonging to various religious and political groups was indispensable to my search for information and indigenous perceptions, my casual conversations with ordinary people in the streets, suqs, and bazaars of the Middle East have inspired what I have had to say about their frustrations over their fate and their aspirations for a better life.

Author's Note, 1988

Revolutionary Iran was published just before the disclosure of the U.S.-Iran secret arms deals. The new epilogue examines the Iranian side of these deals, or what I call Iran's "America initiative." This initiative reflected factional domestic politics; pragmatic revolutionaries built it up, and xenophobic revolutionaries tore it down.

Yet, what precipitated the conflict between Tehran and Washington in the Persian Gulf was not the revelations of Iran's arms purchases from the "Great Satan." For months after the revelations first broke, Iran's pragmatic leaders retained the option of resuming relations with the United States despite a chorus of denials. It was only after the

Reagan administration began its naval escorts of reflagged Kuwaiti oil tankers that this option was suspended.

I would like to thank my son, Jahan, for his incisive critique, Andrew T. Parasiliti for his research assistance, and Anne Whitmore for her able editorial help.

Part One

THE NATURE OF CHALLENGE AND RESPONSE

1

The Geostrategic Balance

Both the challenge of revolutionary Iran and the response of the other Middle Eastern states to Iran's challenge are multidimensional. An exclusive emphasis on the military, ideological, or political aspects of these phenomena will not adequately explain them. Nor can any a priori combining of these and other factors help. An inquiry into the intimate and dynamic interplay of the actors involved does provide insight, however, especially when the behavior of the governments is considered within the wider context of their countries' geography, history, culture, and society.

In this chapter we shall see how such factors as geographic location, size of population, and the sites of oil fields, oil lanes, oil terminals, and oil installations in the Persian Gulf region influence the Iranian challenge and the response of the other Gulf states to it. The combination of these factors tips the geostrategic balance in favor of Iran, even though its military power, particularly its air power, has been weakened over the past half-dozen years while that of other nations has grown stronger.

IRAQ

The Iranian challenge to Iraq is, in a sense, nothing new. The territories that were carved out of the disintegrated Ottoman Empire as a basis for the modern Iraqi entity immediately placed the nascent state at a disadvantage vis-à-vis Iran. Iraq is less than a third the size of Iran. Combined with its smaller and more heterogeneous population, Iraq's relatively small size has always placed Iraqi regimes at a great disadvantage. None of these factors, however, is as critical to Iraq as its geographic location. Situated along the entire eastern shore of the Persian

Gulf, Iran enjoys easy access to the high seas through Gulf waters. It also abuts the Gulf of Oman and the Arabian Sea, and it dominates the strategic Strait of Hormuz at the entrance to the Persian Gulf. But no other Gulf Arab state is located so disadvantageously as is Iraq; its gulf coastline (only ten nautical miles) is at least fifty times less extensive than Iran's.

Iran's free access to Gulf waters is not the only locational problem for Iraq, however. The two neighboring countries' proximity to each other is another factor in Iran's ability to challenge Iraq. They share some 550 miles of boundaries, including a river boundary (120 miles), the Shatt al-Arab. This river, which is vitally important to Iraq's access to Gulf waters, is formed by the confluence of the Iraqi Tigris-Euphrates river system with the Iranian Karun (the largest tributary), Upper and Lower Zab, Dialeh, and Kabur rivers. The land and river boundary lines have been disputed between the two countries since the birth of the modern state of Iraq. Given that the Shatt al-Arab River is Iraq's main access route to the open seas, it has always been vitally important to the Iraqi economy, and hence to Iraqi security, regardless of who was ruling the country.

Iranian demographic features also influence the concerns of Iraq (see appendix A, table 5). Iran's population is approximately thrice that of Iraq. The peoples of neither country are homogeneous, but two factors place Iraq at a disadvantage. First, although both countries have large Kurdish populations, Iraq has a larger percentage (25 percent) than Iran (11 percent). In fact, Iraq has the largest percentage of Kurds of any Middle Eastern country, including Turkey and Syria. Second, the majority of the Iraqi people (about 60 percent) are Shia Muslims in a country that is ruled by the Sunni minority, whereas the Shias of Iran (about 95 percent) are governed by fellow Shias. The sociopolitical implications of this difference for the Iranian challenge to Iraq will be examined in greater detail later, but we should note here that the accident of the concentration of most Iraqi Shias in areas close to the Iranian southwestern frontiers, especially the strategic port city of Basra, compounds the challenge Iran presents to Iraq. The fact that Arabic-speaking Iranians also live close to the Iraqi frontiers in the oil-rich province of Khuzistan does not quite tip the scale of demographic advantage toward Iraq; the Arabic-speaking peoples of Iran are partly Shia and have also been relatively well integrated into the larger Iranian society. Never in modern times have they rebelled in unison against the central government in Iran as have, for example, the Kurds, the Baluchis, and the Turkomans.

The challenge Iran presents to Iraq reflects more than the relatively favorable size and location of the Iranian territory and the size and composition of its population. It also stems from the ways these factors combine with the oil factor in the two countries. The oil-rich areas of the two nations, including their major oil fields, oil terminals, pipelines, and other petroleum-related facilities and structures, happen to be located in dangerous proximity to each other. Foremost, Iraq's limited access to the Gulf waters makes Iraq extremely dependent on two existing pipelines for oil transportation to world markets, one through Syria and the other through Turkey (see appendix A, table 4). Three prospective pipelines were being considered in 1984, through Jordan, Turkey, and Saudi Arabia. This basic Iraqi desideratum was never more graphically demonstrated than in the course of the current protracted Iraq-Iran war. I would like to suggest here that this Iraqi predicament, more than any other single factor, has contributed to Iraq's desperate military acts, causing an oil spill, destroying civilian as well as strategic targets, using chemical weapons, and attacking oil tankers. Granted the Iraqis would have been able to export more oil through the Trans-Syrian pipeline had it not been for the Syrian-Iranian axis that led to the closure of the system after 10 April, 1982, it is essentially Iraq's geography that puts it at a disadvantage.

This disadvantage has an important bearing on the vital question of oil transportation. Given Iran's extensive Gulf coastline, it was possible for the Shah's regime to change the longtime patterns of Iran's oil transportation. For nearly half a century, oil products had been shipped from the Abadan port down the forty-two-mile channel of the Shatt al-Arab to the mouth of the Gulf and then to world markets. But in the postwar era, the river port's inability to handle effectively the loading of tankers larger than 16,000 deadweight tons, in addition to repeated disputes with the Iraqi revolutionary regime, resulted in the Shah's decision to shift the functions of the Abadan port to Mah Shahr on the Khor Musa inlet, where he built a modern oil terminal capable of receiving oil tankers with capacities of up to some 50,000 deadweight tons. Thereafter, the oil terminal facilities were no longer in point-blank range of Iraqi artillery, a not insignificant development.

Iran's geographic advantage also made it possible for the Shah's regime to construct the gigantic oil terminal at Kharg Island, which the current war has made almost a household word. The terminal has been the most highly valued target for the Iraqi military since the war began. Located 150 miles south of the oil refinery at Abadan and 25 miles off the Iranian mainland, the island can receive oil tankers with up to 500,000 tons loading capacity. Throughout the war Iraq has claimed "direct and effective hits" on the island's shipping installations, but even during the unprecedented escalation of armed hostilities as a result of the intensified tanker war in 1984 and damaging air raids on the Kharg Island oil terminal in 1985, the Iraqis were neither able nor, perhaps, willing to destroy Iranian oil exports.

The bristling defense of the island is made possible by the island's favorable location and the massive antiaircraft missile armory placed in and around it. Thus far, Iraq has only been able to hit the Kharg oil terminal ineffectively. It also has attacked, and sometimes damaged, hundreds of oil tankers within an imposed fifty-mile war zone around Kharg Island, but that strategy has not been as successful as it appeared at first. Even seven weeks after the start of the tanker war, its adverse impact on Gulf oil exports was "marginal," and Iranian exports, which dropped drastically for a very short time, increased rapidly to 1.6 million barrels a day, the level maintained before the tanker war began. Even during the momentary cutoff, some 200,000 barrels of Iranian oil were being shipped daily to world markets, because Iran has access to Gulf waters through other ports, Sirri and Lavan, to the south of the Kharg Island terminal.

The Iranian geostrategic situation in terms of oil transportation contrasts graphically with Iraq's predicament. Almost from the start of the war, Iraq completely lost its capacity to export its oil through the Gulf channels because of its geographic vulnerability. Its principal oil terminals are within easy reach of Iranian fire power. On 23 September 1980, the day after the war began, Iraq attacked Iran's oil refinery at Abadan, and Iran attacked Iraqi oil terminals in retaliation. Iranian ships and jet fighters struck the deep-water Iraqi terminals at Khor al-Amaya and Mina al-Bakr that day, and later they attacked Fao, an oil port and terminal. Thus, early in the war, Iran completely stopped Iraq's oil exports through the Gulf (see appendix A, table 3). The combatants did not spare other strategic targets, but Iranian attacks on vital Iraqi oil cities did not devastate Iraq financially, whereas Iran's destruction of Iraq's vital oil terminals did. Iraq's oil exports dropped dramatically, from 3 million barrels a day to less than 1 million barrels at first. And when the Trans-Syrian pipeline was also closed, exports sank further, to a mere 700,000 barrels a day beginning in April 1982. But as a result of improved oil exports by pipeline, by late 1985 Iraq was able to export about 1.5 million barrels a day and expected to reach its prewar level in two years.

Implicit in the foregoing analysis is the geostrategic challenge of Iran to Iraq as a consequence of the interaction among geographic, demographic, economic, military, and technical factors, but at this point the military factor should be spelled out in greater detail. There is no need here for a comparative description of Iraqi and Iranian military hardware as a means of indicating their relative military strength. Those interested in comparing the raw military forces in the Gulf region may refer to appendix A, table 9. It is relevant here, however, to mention the interrelationship between the military and other forces underlying the Iranian geostrategic challenge to Iraq.

First, on balance, Iran clearly enjoyed a superior military power before the revolution, and the Iranian navy was superior to Iraq's even after the revolution and after the war began, but the strength of Iran's ground and air forces relative to Iraq's was not clear when the war started. Five years after the war began, however, there seemed to be a general consensus among military analysts that the Iraqi air force was clearly superior to Iran's because of the latter's lack of spare parts and inadequate maintenance as well as its combat losses. Estimates placed Iranian air strength at only "60 to 70" combat planes capable of flying, whereas 444 planes were listed as "combat-ready" during the Shah's regime. According to the respected London-based Institute of International Strategic Studies, for example, 77 U.S.-made F-14 fighter planes were in Iranian possession in 1984, but according to other estimates, only 11 or 12 of these aircraft could be flown.

Second, even if Iraq's air superiority is granted, the overall military balance does not diminish substantially the Iranian military threat to Iraq. Iran's manpower is far superior to Iraq's, and Iranian ground forces continued to pose a major threat to Iraq despite the repeated postponement of the Iranian "final victory" after the important offensives in February 1984. Following the "spectacular" Iranian capture of parts of the oil-rich Majnoon Islands inside southern Iraq, 300,000 to 500,000 Iranian troops had reportedly been assembled along the border, seemingly for a final push toward the vital Basra-Baghdad Road. But in a surprise offensive in February 1986, other forces captured the port city of Fao. Thus, Iranian armed forces and Revolutionary Guards were able to maintain pressure on Iraq despite the military stalemate after they recovered Khorramshahr (May 1982). These developments corroborated earlier research findings which suggested that, contrary to general opinion, the Iranian armed forces had not been "decimated" as a result of revolutionary purges and executions, as previously suspected.[1] They also showed that the Revolutionary Guards and the Mobilization Forces created after the Shah's fall added to Iran's military strength in spite of the potential for a division between the regular and the paramilitary forces.

Third, the Iranian Revolution did not wipe out overnight either Iranian native ability or the effects of the longstanding American military training. Both factors have been influential in the unexpected performance of the Iranian armed forces. On the contrary, the revolution seems to have strengthened overall Iranian military power in two interrelated ways. The new paramilitary Islamic Revolutionary Guards Corps (IRGC) that was created worked side by side with the regular Iranian Islamic armed forces to make the so-called human wave offensives possible, and the indoctrination of all Iranian forces added an unprecedented element of ideological commitment that is partly responsible for the relatively high morale of Iranian combat forces.[2]

SAUDI ARABIA

Iran's geostrategic challenge to the kingdom of Saudi Arabia also involves interaction among geographic, demographic, economic, and military conditions in the two countries. In terms of sheer size of territory, Saudi Arabia, the largest Gulf state, is only about 1.3 percent larger than Iran. Generally, overall Saudi access to open seas compares favorably with Iran's, but the Saudi access is divided between the Persian Gulf and the Red Sea. In fact, the Saudi coastline on the Red Sea is about five times longer than its coastline on the Gulf, where Iran's coastline is about twice as long as Saudi Arabia's. Unlike Iraq, Saudi Arabia shares no land or river boundaries with Iran, and the state enjoys some distance from Iran across the wider section of the Persian Gulf. The two nations have resolved territorial claims to Gulf islands and jurisdictional disputes regarding the continental shelf, although the Saudi-Iranian air dogfight in June 1984 raised some questions about the territorial water of the Saudi island of Al-Arabiyah.

Yet, Saudi Arabia's relatively favorable geographic position vis-à-vis Iran, as contrasted with Iraq's, does not necessarily provide the kind of protection against Iran desired by Saudi rulers. The gigantic Saudi oil industry is located on the Gulf side of the desert kingdom, rendering its vital oil installations and terminals more vulnerable to Iranian threats in three major ways. First, the hub of the Saudi oil industry, at the Ras Tanura terminal, is about sixteen minutes from Bushehr via Iranian Phantom jet. Second, the center of the Saudi oil industry also happens to be the region in Saudi Arabia inhabited largely by Shia Muslims, who are susceptible to Iranian revolutionary agitation. Third, the bulk of Saudi oil exports still has to be shipped through the Iran-dominated Strait of Hormuz. In 1984, for example, when the Saudis exported about 4.8 million barrels of oil daily, only about 1.5 million barrels a day passed through the Saudi pipeline to Yanbu on the Red Sea (see appendix A, table 4). The relatively higher cost of transporting oil by pipeline than by ship through the Strait of Hormuz largely accounts for the limited use of the pipeline.

Were it not for the Iranian Revolution and the Iraq-Iran war, these sources of Iranian geostrategic challenge to Saudi Arabia would probably have remained dormant. But these two interrelated developments have changed all that. As we shall see in chapter 3, Shia Muslims in Saudi Arabia have already staged a couple of uprisings, and Iran and Saudi Arabia have fought an air battle (chapter 7). In addition, the Iranian threat to close the Strait of Hormuz looms large in the Saudi mind. Iran's potential geostrategic challenge to Saudi Arabia entered an active phase on 5 June 1984, when Saudi planes jumped Iranian fighters as they prepared to attack two ships. An Iranian F-4 fighter plane was shot down by a Saudi F-15 aircraft—with the intelligence aid of American AWACS aircraft—near the Saudi island of Al-Arabiyah, about sixty miles northeast of Jubail. The Iranian attempt was part of the expanding tanker war between Iraq and Iran which began in earnest on 26 April 1984, when, ironically, the Iraqis destroyed a Saudi tanker with an Exocet missile fired from a French-made Super Etendard plane. A brief standoff between eleven other Iranian F-4s and eleven Saudi F-15s also occurred on 5 June, when the Iranian fighters decided to withdraw.

What seems remarkable about this first and, so far, only Iranian air challenge to Saudi Arabia is the two states' mutual restraint. Both sides seemed anxious to avoid a direct military confrontation. The Saudis did not at first report the fight, and when they did, they merely said they had destroyed an "aerial target," while the Iranians surprised almost everyone by confining themselves to a mild diplomatic protest and continued criticism of the Gulf Arab states, especially Saudi Arabia, for aiding Iraq against Iran (chapter 5). In 1984, before the tanker war and the aerial fight, there was much talk in Gulf Arab circles about the prospects of Iran expanding the war into the Gulf before and after the war with Iraq. Iran would probably have preferred to avoid a full-scale armed conflict with any other Gulf Arab country, either before or after the war, unless its oil exports were stopped altogether for at least six months. The subsequent demonstration of restraint on the part of Iran seems to confirm that view.

Iran's geostrategic restraint vis-à-vis nonbelligerent Gulf Arab states reflected, I believe, a complicated mix of both internal and external considerations. Domestically, factional divisions within and between the Revolutionary Guards and the regular armed forces, political friction among the ruling clerics, and mounting economic woes due to the war were influential factors. The increasing unpopularity of the protracted and bloody war, the worsening ethnic insurgencies, and the necessity of doing something about the oft-repeated promises of a better life for the "oppressed" masses also were considerations.

Externally, the fear of American military intervention in favor of Saudi Arabia—with or without the help of other Western powers—and the reluctance to weaken Iranian armed strength further were major factors. Soviet military presence in Afghanistan, the ever-present threat of direct Soviet intervention, and the diplomatic pressure of Syria, Turkey, and Pakistan also militated against a full-scale Iranian invasion of Saudi Arabia. Political tensions between the Iranians and the Saudis are, of course, another matter and will be considered later (chapters 6–9).

Saudi Arabia's own military power can also be considered a major deterrent to military action by Iran. For all practical purposes, Saudi Arabia has surpassed prerevolutionary Iran in acquiring advanced weapons systems and sophisticated training as a means of building a credible deterrent against perceived adversaries. Today, principal among these is revolutionary Iran, although Israel as well as the Soviet Union and its surrogates in and around the Arabian peninsula rank high as potential threats to Saudi Arabia. Even Iraq is not overlooked as a potential threat to the kingdom. Iran's military power surpassed those of both Saudi Arabia and Iraq before the Iranian Revolution and the Iraq-Iran war, but in terms of air power, Saudi Arabia and Iraq probably surpass Iran today, at least insofar as military hardware is concerned. Despite its longstanding security relationship with the United States, only since the Iranian Revolution and especially since the start of the Iraq-Iran war has Saudi Arabia begun to build a credible military deterrence in earnest (chapter 7). This buildup demonstrated the kingdom's unprecedented concern with the protection of its Gulf ports, oil fields, and shipping against possible attacks by Iranian bombers. Saudi Arabia's 185 combat aircraft in 1985 made its air force the largest of any Persian Gulf state.

Once the tanker war extended the war perimeters from the upper to the lower part of the Gulf, and closer to Saudi Arabia, the Saudis began to plan to establish a protected zone, running from the Strait of Hormuz at the mouth of the Persian Gulf along the western side of the Gulf at least as far north as Ras Tanura. Later on—after the 5 June 1984 air fight with Iran—the Saudis established the Fahd Line, an "air defense interception zone" that extended beyond the commercial traffic control zone and the twelve miles of territorial waters. A second zone, known as "the flight information for commercial flights," was also established. Saudi aircraft were empowered "to take a look" at unauthorized planes entering the first zone, to see if shipping was being threatened, but they were under orders "to shoot on sight" aircraft that actually invaded Saudi airspace by entering the second zone.[3] Saudi Arabia and its Gulf Cooperation Council (GCC) partners also worked out, in late June 1984, the details of an air-cover plan. Kuwait, more than any other GCC member, was considered to be vulnerable to an Iranian attack. The United States offered at the time to provide Kuwait with virtually instantaneous intelligence from American AWACS aircraft on duty in Saudi Arabia to monitor the Gulf.

The Iranians knew, as did the Saudis, that the successful Saudi dogfight in the air did not terminate the overall Iranian geostrategic challenge to Saudi Arabia; the Saudis still did not control the skies over the Gulf. The continuing Iranian geographic and demographic advantages aside, any consideration of Saudi air superiority in the Gulf should take into account the challenge of the battle-tested Iranian pilots as opposed to the inexperienced pilots of Saudi Arabia and its GCC partners. The Saudis knew that, although their military capability had improved greatly since the Iranian Revolution, they still offered the Iranians vulnerable targets in the form of desalination, gas, and electricity plants, as well as the main oil facility at Ras Tanura (although the reported installation of ground-to-air missiles around this giant terminal by the Raytheon Company may offer protection).[4]

THE OTHER GCC STATES

Other facts and all fantasies aside, the Gulf Cooperation Council was established primarily as a response to the challenge of the Iranian Revolution (see chapter 8). The oft-cited concern with the adverse spillover effects of the Iraq-Iran war can be considered a secondary impetus for the establishment of the organization. The concern of the GCC states with the Soviet Union and Israel cannot be denied; nor can the significant "tradition of cooperation" among the GCC states. But insofar as the Iranian challenge is concerned, the revolution and the war were the main security concerns when the GCC states established their organization for cooperation in "all fields." The Iranian geostrategic challenge to the member states of the GCC differs from country to country, although the sheer size of Iran, in terms of both territory and population, its location, its competitive oil resources, its dominance at the Strait of Hormuz, and like factors concern them all generally. Despite the notion of *Khalij* (Gulf) geostrategic identity among the six Gulf monarchies, the Iranian challenge is individualized.

Iran presents the most serious geostrategic challenge to the small state of Kuwait. The fact that, diplomatically, Iran maintains better relations with the sheikhdom than with most other Gulf states does not sufficiently counter Kuwait's geostrategic disadvantages. Iran is about one hundred times larger than the tiny city state of Kuwait, which is the size of New Jersey. Iran's access to Gulf waters is far superior to Kuwait's, its coastline on the Gulf is about six times longer than Kuwait's, and, most important, Iran is located closer to Kuwait than to any other GCC state. Demography as well as geography favors Iran enormously: its population is about twenty-seven times larger than that of its small neighbor at the head of the Gulf. More important, about a quarter of the Kuwaiti *citizen* population (about half of Kuwait's total population is noncitizen) are Shia Muslims, a fact that underpins Iran's sociopolitical challenge to Kuwait (see chapter 3).

Kuwait, as the second major paymaster of Iraq after Saudi Arabia, has also earned the wrath of Iran. Kuwait's logistical aid to Iraq throughout the war has been the primary cause of Iran's warning air attacks on Kuwait. Twice in November 1980, once in June 1981, and again in October of that year the Kuwaitis bore the brunt of Iranian "accidental" air attacks. In addition, the Iranians were blamed for "sponsoring" the terrorist group responsible for multiple bomb attacks against American and other targets in Kuwait in December 1983. Vehement denials by some Iranian officials were seemingly contradicted by statements other Iranian officials made. Saudi Arabia and Kuwait were the only GCC states to suffer from Iranian attacks on their oil tankers when the tanker war began in earnest in April 1984.

The Iranian challenge to two other GCC nations should be considered briefly. These are Bahrain and Oman. Since the Iranian challenge to Bahrain presents itself more in sociopolitical than in geostrategic terms, it will be taken up in detail in chapter 3. About four times the size of Washington, D.C., Bahrain has reason enough to feel intimidated by its giant revolutionary neighbor. The main Iranian challenge to Bahrain, however, is based on historical and social factors. Prerevolutionary as well as revolutionary regimes in Iran have claimed the Bahraini archipelago as an integral part of Iranian territory. And the Shia citizen population of the tiny sheikhdom makes up the single largest percentage (about 72%) of Shia Muslims in any Arab Gulf state (see appendix A, table 5), a fact that has far-reaching implications for the Iranian sociopolitical challenge to Bahrain. While other small GCC states have tiny air forces, Bahrain has no combat planes at all. Saudi F-15 jets fly over Bahrain as a show of support against the perceived Iranian threat. Presumably, the construction of the long-awaited, eighteen-mile, five-hundred-million-dollar causeway between Saudi Arabia and Bahrain will afford the Bahrainis even greater physical protection vis-à-vis Iran, although the liberal-minded Bahrainis have qualms about being embraced too closely by the conservative Saudis. Yet, at the moment, security considerations rather than ideology govern the relationship between the governments in Manama and Riyadh. The Bahraini business community, however, seems divided about the economic advantages of the causeway, which is expected to be opened in November 1986.

In a sense, the Iranian geostrategic challenge to Oman is unique. Omani shorelines (1,005 nautical miles) lie mainly outside the Persian Gulf, but the isolated 51-mile Omani enclave that lies within Gulf waters looks Iran straight in the eye across the strategic Strait of Hormuz. The Iranian challenge to Oman, therefore, interconnects uniquely with the Iranian challenge to all Gulf states at the Strait of Hormuz. The Iranian Revolution turned Tehran's previously friendly relations with Muscat around. The Shah had been an admirer of Sultan Qabus for all sorts of reasons, including the sultan's implicit acquiescence to the preeminent Iranian position at the strait in return for the Shah's unreserved military support for the Omani regime against the Dhofari rebellion. The "joint Iranian-Omani patrol of the Strait of Hormuz" that had been set up by the two monarchs was scrapped by the revolutionary regime, resulting in Oman undertaking unilateral military efforts—with the help of the United States—to keep a watchful eye on the strategic waterway. Since the Iranian Revolution, the Omanis have attached even greater importance to security at the Strait of Hormuz. Immediately after the Iranian Revolution, there was no visible military activity in Khasab, on the tip of the strategic Musandam Peninsula. Only the British enjoyed a small presence. A few years later, however, the village was earmarked as the site of one of the air bases to be used by the Omani air force and by the United States Central Command (formerly the Rapid Deployment Force, RDF) in a contingency situation for the purpose of keeping the strait open in the face of the Iranian threat to close it under certain circumstances.

THE STRAIT OF HORMUZ

Iran's greatest potential geostrategic challenge to the world community of states is at the Strait of Hormuz. The strait, which is 104 miles long along the median line, connects the Persian Gulf, a semienclosed sea, and the Gulf of Oman, an open sea, and is geographically dominated by Iran in three major ways. First, the entire length of Iran's eastern shore abuts the strait. Second, the Iranian Larak Island sits on top of the narrowest navigable channel (about 20 nautical miles wide) of the strait, facing the Quoins Islands on the Omani side. Third, all vessels traveling to and from the head of the Gulf proceed between the Iranian-occupied island of Great Tunb and the Iranian-owned island of Forur in close proximity to a cluster of other Iranian-occupied islands (Little Tunb and Abu Musa) and another major Iranian-owned island (Sirri).

Elsewhere, I have characterized the strait as "the global chokepoint" because of its obvious economic and strategic importance not only to the Gulf states and the industrial nations, especially Japan, but also to some sixty Third World countries which also depend on Gulf oil supplies.[5] Oil tankers en route between world markets must traverse this vital strait before sailing through the Eastern Mediterranean and the Pacific Ocean. All other sea lanes through the Strait of Bab al-Mandab and the Suez Canal to the east and the Strait of Malacca to the west would be of no use to Gulf-bound oil tankers if the Strait of Hormuz was closed to shipping.

The Iranian challenge at the strait, as elsewhere in the Gulf, is a function of Iran's revolution and its war with Iraq. True, prerevolutionary, as revolutionary, Iran considered the strait its single most strategic asset, but the revolution and the war have increased its value to Iran (chapters 2 and 4). As a result, only in recent years has Iran threatened repeatedly to close the strait in retaliation for Iraq's threats to cripple Iran's oil exports from Kharg Island.

Iran at first only hinted at a threat to close the strait in order to discourage the Arab Gulf states from aiding and abetting Iraq by military means at the start of the war. But Iraq's threats to cripple Iran's oil exports completely, first made earnestly in the summer of 1983, elicited the more specific counterthreats. Saddam Hussein then threatened to use Exocet missiles fired by French-made Super Etendard aircraft. At the time, matters were looking increasingly desperate for Iraq because of its mounting financial problems, which were due to its vastly diminished oil exports. Even before the French planes were delivered in October 1983, Iranian leaders minced no words about their determination to retaliate by closing the Strait of Hormuz if the Iranian oil exports were stopped. Ayatollah Khomeini was the first Iranian to issue a warning:

> I warn the regional states as well as countries which make use of oil in some way, that the Government of Iran exercising its utmost power will oppose this aggression and is determined to block the Strait of Hormuz thus obstructing the passage of even a single drop of petroleum from there, should such an aggression be actualized. The French Government will bear the responsibility for all the consequences thereof.[6]

It was not clear from this statement, or from what other Iranian leaders said subsequently, under just what circumstances Iran would attempt to carry out its threat; the ambiguity was deliberate. The threat was made more specific only after the French delivered the planes to Iraq. Hojatolislam Hashemi-Rafsanjani, the Speaker of the Iranian *Majlis* (parliament), used a sermon on Friday, 14 October 1983, to spell out in detail exactly what Iran intended to do and under what circumstances. The key passage in his long statement was:

> We will block the Strait of Hormuz when we cannot export oil. Even if they [the Iraqis] hit half of our oil, it will not be in our interest to block the Strait of Hormuz. When we do not have oil, when we are unable to export oil, the Persian Gulf will be of no use to us since we will have no money, and the Strait of Hormuz will be of no use to us. That is when we will enter the arena and do what we like, although I consider such an eventuality to be very unlikely.[7]

Despite the fact that this was the most authoritative statement on the subject made by Iran, the world press did not take sufficient note of its contents to understand completely the rather restrained Iranian position. Foreign newspaper correspondents seemed to assume that Iranian leaders were irresponsible and adventurous, rattling the saber at the Strait of Hormuz. The facts in this instance, however, pointed to a different conclusion. First, no observer denied that, despite the rhetoric, Iran had in practice "impeccably" observed the freedom of navigation through the strait throughout the war. And, second, Iran's declaratory policy clearly indicated that no attempt would be made to close the strait unless Iranian oil exports were cut off. Rafsanjani specifically said that even if half of Iran's oil exports were stopped, it would be contrary to Iran's interests to block oil traffic through the strait. In fact, his full statement seemed to suggest that Iran would tolerate even total loss of its oil exports for as long as six months before it would resort to closing the strait (see appendix D).

This worldwide inattention to the actual Iranian position lay behind the surprise of many observers in the spring of 1984 when Iran refrained from trying to close the Strait of Hormuz despite the fact that Iraq's stepped-up attacks on oil tankers near Kharg Island caused a considerable drop in Iran's oil exports for a short period of time. Instead, Iran adopted a strategy of restrained response in kind; it retaliated by hitting oil tankers. One unidentified foreign correspondent, for example, told Speaker Hashemi-Rafsanjani at the height of the tanker war crisis that it seemed that Iran had "given up its threat to close the Hormuz Strait." The correspondent's remark revealed the persistence of foreign misperception. Rafsanjani tried to correct this widespread misperception by saying:

> It would not be correct to say we have given up. We are still firmly backing what we said in the beginning. We never said we would simply close the Strait of Hormuz, nor do we wish to have it closed, because if the Strait were to be closed it would harm us, too, and we would incur losses. Therefore, we have always emphasized that we would close the Strait of Hormuz if the Persian Gulf became unusable for us. And if the Persian Gulf becomes unusable for us we will make the Persian Gulf unusable for others. This has been our policy, and if the day ever comes, then our threat will still be good and we will act in accordance with it. Nevertheless, we hope that the world will be sufficiently wise to prevent such a day, and we think it highly unlikely that such a day will come. We are serious in this respect.[8]

More important than the Iranian intention, of course, was its capability to carry out such a threat. There had never been a consensus among private specialists on the subject, and I do not intend to enter into the inconclusive debate here. One point, however, needs mentioning briefly: perhaps more important than the question of the Iranian capability to close the strait and keep it closed long enough to jeopardize the interests of Gulf producers and oil consumers alike by sinking ships within the strait channels is the psychological impact of such an attempt on shipping.[9] The fact that even at the height of the tanker war the oil tankers continued to use the Gulf does not necessarily suggest that they would continue to do so if a number of tankers were in fact sunk in the waters of the strait itself by Iranian mines or other destructive means.

There is enough independent evidence to suggest that, in desperation, Iran would undoubtedly try to carry out its threat. It is already deploying the Revolutionary Guards on Larak Island and is also feverishly engaged in economic and military activities on its large Qeshm Island on the strait as well as in its nearby ports on the mainland, perhaps in preparation for launching and supporting amphibious operations in the strait region were such a course of action to become necessary. Certainly the Pentagon seemed to take Iranian preparations seriously in January 1984, when it rushed Stinger antiaircraft missiles to U.S. Navy ships off the coast of the Arabian Sea, apparently as a deterrent to the threat, as perceived by American intelligence sources, of kamikaze-style attacks by bomb-laden Iranian jets, light planes, or helicopters.[10]

The best Iranian estimate of its own capability was made by Speaker Hashemi-Rafsanjani. In his October 1983 sermon, he left no doubt that

Iranian leaders believed they could effectively carry out their threat to close the Strait of Hormuz if they had no other choice. He scoffed at the idea expressed in some Western quarters that it would be necessary to sink a large number of ships to close the Strait of Hormuz, an operation presumably beyond Iran's capability. Instead of making such a silly attempt, he said, Iran

> would create a wall of fire over the Strait of Hormuz twice a day. On the island of Qeshm, we are very near the strait. Larak Island is right on the strait. Even from Bandar 'Abbas itself, we can use our 175-mm guns with a range of 48 km. Who would be able to approach the strait if we were to shell it with such guns from Bandar 'Abbas? You yourselves [the Americans] know that our planes are armed with many air-to-sea missiles. Our underground depots are full of such missiles, which we have not yet used. The Americans themselves know; the Americans are aware that we have not yet even used the planes that they gave us in the shah's era.[11]

Are the Iranian leaders unaware of the consequences of such a drastic course of action for Iran itself? After all, as the most populous country in the region, Iran is more dependent on the Strait of Hormuz than any other Gulf state not only for its oil exports, but also for vast quantities of imported food, capital goods, and arms. Despite all the efforts of the revolutionary regime to increase overland trade with the rest of the world through routes traversing the Soviet Union, Pakistan, and Turkey, the bulk of Iran's trade continues to be dependent on its lifeline through the Strait of Hormuz. In the first three months of the Iranian year 1363 (beginning 21 March 1984), the total volume of Iranian imports amounted to five million tons, of which nearly three million were imported via the Gulf ports. Since the start of the war, Iranian oil exported through the strait has acquired an unprecedented value—it is the principal source of financing for the war. The Shah used to call oil a "noble commodity," and Speaker Hashemi-Rafsanjani dubs it a "divine blessing" and "the foundation of the revolution."

Speaker Hashemi-Rafsanjani admits, as do other Iranian leaders, that the closing of the Strait of Hormuz would cause "hardship" for Iran, but "our nation is prepared," he claims, "to put up with six months of hardship if necessary." To be sure, such a closing would cause "economic and financial austerity" for Iran, but it would be "even worse" for Western consumers of oil and for Japan. They should expect the price of one barrel of oil "to reach 100 dollars" should the strait remain shut for that length of time. He believes, however, that such a hardship would *not* be "suicidal" for Iran, as the Western media contend, because "we are not like you. We are a nation that follows the line of Imam Husayn [Hussein, the martyred Imam of the Shia Muslims] and Karbala [the site of Imam Hussein's tomb in Iraq]. We are a people who have planned our lives and revolution on the basis of the model left to us by Imam Husayn."[12] In Western terminology, this would take us into the realm of "ideology," and in the context of the Iranian revolutionary creed, this would carry us to the mystique of "faith power." In either case, a discussion of this "Karbala epic" at the Strait of Hormuz would fit best the analysis of the ideological crusade of revolutionary Iran in the next chapter.

2

The Ideological Crusade

Given the broad geostrategic balance in favor of Iran in the Persian Gulf, the ideological crusade of the Khomeini regime makes the Iranian challenge even more formidable. More than any other single factor, it is this crusade that has kept Iran's war machine churning in spite of the country's massive losses of men and equipment in five and a half years of conflict. The brunt of the war has been borne by the ideologically committed *Pasdaran* (IRGC, the Revolutionary Guards) and the *Baseej* volunteers (mobilization force), whose young bodies, in "human waves," prepared the way for the forward march of the regular army.

The religiously inspired ideological-psychological complex of factors influencing Iranian behavior has remained unexamined by most observers, who have simplistically viewed the behavior as nothing but Islamic "fanaticism." Even those observers who do allow for the influence of factors other than "fanaticism" on political behavior find the Iranian behavior incomprehensible—not to mention the purists of the "power politics" school of thought. If they fail to acknowledge, for example, the religious influence of the Calvinist cast of mind on Woodrow Wilson's concept of world order, how can they possibly understand Khomeini's concept of an Islamic world order? There is no better way to begin to examine this concept than to remind ourselves of Raymond Aron's sage dictum: "No one understands the diplomatic strategy of a state if he has not studied the philosophy of those who govern it."[1]

KHOMEINI'S ISLAMIC WORLD ORDER

The key to understanding Khomeini's concept of Islamic world order is the idea of the *vilayat-e faqih* (rule of the leading jurisprudent). The concept of *hukumat* (government) in his political thought is rooted in

19

that of *vilayat* (rulership), a rulership that belongs to God, to the Prophet Muhammad, to the infallible Imams (*ma'sumin*), and, by extension, to the learned and pious *faqih*. To the *faqih* belongs temporal as well as spiritual authority, which he should exercise in the absence of the Twelfth Imam, who will appear (*zuhur*) ultimately as the *Mahdi* (Messiah) or the *Sahib-e Zaman* (master of the age) to establish just and equitable rule.[2]

The rule of the *faqih* during the waiting period, or before the appearance of the *Mahdi*, is preparatory to the ultimate establishment of "Islamic world government" by the *Mahdi*. In other words, the *faqih* paves the way for the *Mahdi*'s eventual creation of just and equitable government throughout the world. But where will the way be paved for the fulfillment of that divine promise? In Khomeini's own words, "the way will be opened for the world government of imam mahdi . . . once the governments of the meek will be [are?] established."[3] But in Khomeini's view and in that of his disciples so far, "the government of God" has been established only in one country, and that is Iran, as a result of the Iranian Revolution. It has been established, in Khomeini's words, in "a country which wishes to establish divine justice in the world, first of all in Iran itself."[4] It is more than implicit in the views of Khomeini and his close adherents that because of this unusual rule of the *faqih,* it is Iran that is uniquely qualified as a nation to pave the way for the ultimate founding of world government by the expected *Mahdi*.

Since the virtuous government is in the process of being established in Iran, it is Iran that has become, as it were, the "redeemer nation." As such, it is Iran that aspires to spread justice throughout the world and, to borrow Prime Minister Mir-Hussein Musavi's words, to make possible "the liberation of mankind." In Khomeini's words, "Islam is a sacred trust from God to ourselves and the Iranian nation must grow in power and resolution until it has vouchsafed Islam to the entire world." According to Khomeini's disciples, "this magnificent fact [the rule of the *faqih*] has only come to reality in the Islamic country of Iran, and Imam Khomeini . . . has accepted the responsibility for the political leadership, formation of the Islamic Government as well as the Commander in Chief of the Armed Forces."[5]

From the perspective of this essentially chiliastic and simultaneously particularistic and universalistic view of the world, the current international system is basically flawed. As early as World War II, Khomeini rejected in his *Kashf-i Assrar* the very idea of the nation-state on the ground that it is the creation of man's "weak mind."[6] In other words, in Khomeini's ideal Islamic world order there would be no room for the modern secular post-Westphalia conception of the international system.

The present international system must be transformed into the abode of humankind and, above all, the home of the "oppressed masses of the people" (*mustaza'fin*). The current state system based on a congeries of artificially created territorial states should ultimately disappear. This emphasis on the concept of the "meek" or the disadvantaged masses of the people, which is said to be borrowed from 'Ali Shariati—reputedly the ideologist of the Iranian Revolution—adds a militantly populist tinge to Khomeini's own essentially traditionalist, elitist, and chiliastic world view. Contrary to Shariati's perspective, Khomeini's view accords the leadership of Iran to the clerical class.

"NEITHER EAST, NOR WEST, ONLY THE ISLAMIC REPUBLIC"

No refrain is better known to the students of Iranian affairs than the slogan Neither East, nor West, only the Islamic Republic (*nah sharq, nah gharb, faqat jumhuri-i islami*). But this is more than a mere slogan. The Khomeini view of the international system clashes with the role the superpowers play in world affairs. In Khomeini's words, "We must settle our accounts with great and superpowers, and show them that we can take on the whole world ideologically, despite all the painful problems that face us."[7] Such a conflict between the Islamic Republic and the superpowers, he believes, is inevitable; they have arrogated all the worldly power (*qudrat*) to themselves at the expense of the exploited, dispossessed masses of the people everywhere.

The Khomeini doctrine of "neither East, nor West, only the Islamic Republic" should be understood in terms of the above-mentioned tenets and not in terms of the irrelevant notions of "equidistance," "nonalignment," and the like as these terms are ordinarily understood. In Khomeini's view, in fact, no nonaligned state could be truly nonaligned. As applied to Iran itself, this tenet turns on its head Muhammad Musaddiq's idea of "negative equilibrium" (*muvazinih-ye manfi*), let alone the Shah's Western-oriented "positive nationalism." These ideas of Musaddiq and the Shah are basically secular and this-worldly, allowing the lesser powers to enter the game of great power politics, while Khomeini's religiously based, millenarian view rejects the global role of both superpowers. To Khomeini, the superpowers are "illegitimate players"; they dominate (*tahmil*) the international system.

The rejection of the role of the superpowers is not a matter of balancing or playing off one power against the other; it is, rather, an aspect of the unyielding insistence on the doctrine of "Islamic self-reliance." It is fundamentally a reflection of the ultimate goal of establishing an Islamic world order. According to Prime Minister Musavi, the addition of "the

Islamic Republic" to the words "neither East, nor West" is intended to emphasize that Iran will not "under any circumstances" allow itself to slide toward the East or toward the West. But this is not all; he adds that the Iranians "want to establish a new system of values, independent of East and West in their own country; to expand it, and under the all-round cover of this new system of values—which stems from ideology, Islam—to continue their own way, organize their lives, organize their relations with other countries, nations and liberation movements."[8]

In other words, Khomeini's Iran rejects "nonalignment," "equidistance," and similar doctrines in foreign policy altogether, because theoretically these are predicated on the acceptance of the reality of the existing international system. As we have seen, Khomeini rejects the existing system not only because he considers it to be philosophically flawed, but also because he believes that the superpowers dominate it politically. This they do at the expense of the suffering and deprived masses of the people, most of whom happen to live in Muslim and other Third World nations. His deep skepticism concerning nonalignment as it is usually understood finds expression, for example, in these words: "The governments of the world, except Iran's . . . belong either to the Eastern bloc or to the Western bloc publicly, or secretly. Don't believe that even the nonaligned countries are truly independent; if there are really any nonaligned governments they are very rare indeed."[9] Khomeini's reputedly "moderate" foreign minister, Ali Akbar Velayati, emphasizes the inadequacy of nonalignment in these words: "Neutrality vis-à-vis these two arrogant powers [the superpowers] cannot serve as a motive for nations to come together and free themselves from their domination; rather a power that can stand up to theirs must be created. The Islamic Revolution [ary] experience has proved that the weapon that has maintained its cutting edge against the superpowers' weapons is the weapon of faith."[10]

The preceding discussion, in addition to illustrating the Khomeini regime's skepticism toward the very idea of nonalignment, should also clarify the doctrinal basis of Khomeini's characterization of the United States as the "Great Satan" and the Soviet Union as the "Lesser Satan." These views are not simply a matter of "Persian xenophobia." Nor are they exclusively a reflection of Iran's unhappy historical experience with the superpowers. The influence of these factors must be taken into account, but the doctrine on which they are based should not be overlooked. No matter how crude the theoretical formulation of the regime's antisuperpower orientation may appear to Western minds, Khomeini and his disciples can effectively manipulate the symbols associated with it in the conduct of Iranian foreign policy. This point is particularly relevant to our analysis of the Iranian ideological challenge to the Gulf Arab states, because Khomeini's ideological crusade against the regional leaders never fails to portray their association with the superpowers as being contrary to authentic Islamic self-reliance.

"MINISATANS AND THE TRIUMPH OF THE MEEK"

Two interrelated tenets of Khomeini's ideology combine to provide the basis of the doctrinal challenge of Iran to the Arab Gulf states. First, given his ideological hostility toward the superpowers, Khomeini is totally opposed to a close link or association between the Gulf states and Moscow and Washington. Whether the Gulf Arab governments are viewed as being dependent on the Soviet Union, like Iraq, or on the United States, like Saudi Arabia and most of the other GCC states, because of their alleged subservience to these superpowers, according to Khomeini, they have become "minisatans" of the Gulf region. In addressing the leaders of the Gulf Arab states on 18 September 1983, Khomeini said:

> What America expects from you is oil and profit; it wants you to remain a market for it. The same thing applies to the Soviet Union; there is no distinction. They want to take advantage of you; they want to make use of the resources given you by God; they want you to be [a] servant for them. But if you encounter difficulties, then none of them will respond to your cry for help. Do you not know them? This is the situation concerning those who think of themselves and their own world. They cooperate with those who serve their interests. However, as soon as they realize that this no longer applies, then they reject them.[11]

Khomeini's doctrinal opposition to the alleged servile identification of the Gulf Arab states with the superpowers has a significant bearing on his concept of the requirement of security in the Gulf region, as we will see. But when this opposition is combined with his potential ideological appeal to the disadvantaged groups in Gulf societies, the perceived threat of revolutionary Iran to the Gulf Arab leaders becomes very significant. From the perspective of the populist dimension of the Khomeini ideology, the powerless, disadvantaged masses of the people (*mustaza'fin*) who are presently exploited by the great superpowers constitute the camp of the oppressed. This camp confronts the camp of the "oppressors" (*mustakberin*), a camp that includes both the United States and the Soviet Union. The capitalist and the socialist components of this camp join hands with other oppressive elements, including the "Zionists, Fascists, Phalangists, and Communists." In the worldwide struggle between these two camps, it is the camp of the oppressed that will eventually, and inevitably, succeed. In Khomeini's Qura'nic-inspired dictum: "The disposessed must triumph over the dominant elements" (*Bayad mustaza'fin bar mustakberin ghalabeh kunand*).

This view of the world is compatible with the Shia cultural tradition. The conflict between the camp of the oppressors and that of the oppressed resembles significantly the classical theme of conflict between right and might as enshrined in the Shia epic battle at Karbala (A.D. 681) between the martyred forces led by Imam Hussein and others led by the oppressor Yazid. It is also a view that is similar to such basic Shia notions as *zalim* (tyrant) and *mazlum* (tyrannized) and the related ethos of *masa'ib* (sufferings), *najat* (salvation), and, especially, the ancient Shia quest for *adl* (justice). Khomeini's view of the world, it seems to me, also reflects the pre-Islamic Iranian cultural tradition, a tradition that insists on the incessant struggle between the forces of good and evil and the inevitable triumph of the former.

EXPORT OF THE "ISLAMIC REVOLUTION"

The most familiar aspect of the Iranian ideological challenge is the notion of the export of the Islamic revolution, but this aspect is not necessarily well understood in relation to Khomeini's overarching concept of Islamic world order. The universalistic claim of this concept, like its populist and chiliastic features, makes the export of the Islamic revolution a matter of international, rather than regional, concern. But given Iran's geostrategic challenge to the Gulf Arab states, nowhere else in the world does Iran's export of the Islamic revolution concern political leaders of other countries as much as it does in the adjacent Persian Gulf region.[12] As if Iran's geographic advantages and putative power were not enough, the Khomeini regime's mission to spread Iran's brand of Islamic revolution first to the neighboring Gulf states is perceived by the leaders of these countries as a potential threat to their own regimes.

Khomeini believes that the export of revolution is obligatory. In his words: "We should try to export our revolution to the world. We should set aside the thought that we do not export our revolution, because Islam does not regard various Islamic countries differently and is the supporter of all the oppressed peoples of the world. On the other hand, all the superpowers and the [great] powers have risen to destroy us. If we remain in an enclosed environment we shall definitely face defeat."[13] Simply stated, Iran must export the Islamic revolution both to pave the way for the ultimate establishment of an Islamic world order when the

Mahdi appears and to meet the more immediate, short-term need to make the Iranian regional environment safe for Iran's power and for its new revolutionary ideology.

What is not so clear, however, is the means that Khomeini's ideology considers legitimate for exporting revolution. On numerous occasions, he has declared categorically that "swords" should not be used. Note, for example, this dictum: "It does not take swords to export this ideology. The export of ideas by force is no export."[14] Or this statement: "When we say we want to export our revolution, we do not want to do it with swords."[15] But what does this mean? Does it mean that the use of force is prohibited? No clear answer has been given so far on the more specific meaning of such a prohibition. Hence, I will explore this important question briefly within the context of Khomeini's view of the use of armed force in war in general, and Khomeini's view of nonforcible interference in the internal affairs of other nations.

In Khomeini's view, the use of armed force in war is permissible only in self-defense. This view is fully compatible with Shia legal thought as well as the principles of modern international law. The *faqih,* to put it differently, has the authority to fight a "defensive war" (*jang-e difa'i*); he is prohibited from waging an offensive war, because such a war, *jihad,* is the prerogative of the infallible Imam. Generally, Khomeini's concept of self-defense presents the same problem that Article 51 of the Charter of the United Nations does: What constitutes self-defense? But a closer examination reveals that Khomeini's concept is potentially even more troublesome; his concept of the Islamic world order basically rejects the validity of the very notion of the territorial state which is the principal subject of the modern law of nations. This is why, throughout the long and inconclusive war with Iraq, he has repeatedly spoken of "the defense of Islam" rather than of Iran. He told the representatives of the Islamic Conference Organization (ICO) that their guide to action should be the Qur'an, which prescribes what may be called a kind of Islamic concept of "collective self-defense." He told them that they should side with Iran instead of trying to mediate in the war. The relevant Qur'anic verse, he declared, requires that "if one tribe invades the other then all others are obliged to defend the latter in war, until they obey God. Once they obey God, then make peace with them."[16]

Ambiguity also surrounds the question of nonforcible interference (*dikhalat*) as a means of exporting revolution, and the reason for the lack of clarity is the same. According to the Iranian Constitution, interference in the internal affairs of other states is prohibited, except in "self-defense." In admonishing the Gulf Arab leaders for aiding and abetting the Iraqi war effort, he assured them that Iran had "neither ambition in,

[nor] right to, any country, unless it is solely a matter of self-defense."[17] But what constitutes self-defense is as ambiguous with regard to interference as it is with regard to war. Iran has been accused in practice of all sorts of acts of subversion, terrorism, and interference, and obviously such statements as Ayatollah Montazeri's characterization of the suicide bombings in Kuwait as acts in the "performance of Islamic duty" do not help dissipate the widespread suspicion that Iranian authorities incite, if they do not actually sponsor, such violent acts as a means of exporting revolution.

Is it any more clear what peaceful means are preferable, in Khomeini's ideology, for exporting revolution? Generally, the answer is yes. Two major instruments for export of revolution stand out prominently. One is the example of the "Islamic behavior" of Iranians. On one occasion, for example, Khomeini encouraged the Iranian athletic students traveling abroad to export revolution. He instructed them that "our way of exporting Islam is through the youth who go to other countries where a large number of people come to see you and your achievements. You must behave in such a way that these large gatherings are attracted to Islam by your action. Your deeds, your action, and your behavior should be an example; and through you the Islamic Republic will go to other places, God willing."[18] On another occasion, he told the Iranian ambassadors and chargés d'affaires, "We shall have exported Islam only when we have helped Islam and Islamic ethics grow in those countries. This is your responsibility and it is a task which you must fulfil . . . this is a must."[19]

Khomeini's concept of spreading the revolution by the example of Islamic behavior, of course, includes many methods and techniques. Publicity and propaganda are most highly valued. Many thousands of Iranians, for example, go annually on the pilgrimage to Mecca in Saudi Arabia, where they have used the religious occasion to propagate Khomeini's brand of Islam (see chapter 6). Another example is the use of government-controlled media, such as the radio station established on Kish Island, to broadcast Iranian propaganda to the Gulf region in general, and to Saudi Arabia, Egypt, Jordan, and the Sudan in particular. According to President Ali Khamene'i, the new 800-kilowatt transmitter would perform a service for nations "eagerly awaiting revolutions."[20]

The other principal peaceful instrument of export of revolution is missionary work by both Iranian and sympathetic foreign *ulama* (religious scholars). Given the importance of the sermon in the Shia cultural tradition in general and its powerful role in the Iranian revolutionary process in particular, it has not received the attention it deserves. On the Islamic sabbath (Friday), the Imams of Friday prayers frequently deliver not only religious sermons, but also what amounts to serious policy statements on public issues. Sometimes these sermons are broadcast in Arabic for the Gulf Arabs, as well. For example, Speaker Rafsanjani has delivered more far-reaching policy statements on the Gulf during Friday sermons than he has in the halls of the Iranian *Majlis.*

More important for the export of revolution, Khomeini and his disciples attach a great deal of value to the role of foreign *ulama* in propagating the Khomeini brand of revolutionary Islam. Quite apart from receiving Sunni and Shia clerics from all over the Muslim world, especially from the Gulf region and Afghanistan, Khomeini and his named successor, Montazeri, have been keen on sponsoring conferences of clerics in Iran, as exemplified by the meeting of some five hundred religious leaders in May 1984. Khomeini told the members of "the second global congress of the world Friday prayer leaders" on the thirteenth of that month: "You should discuss the situation in Iran. You should call on people to rebel as Iran did" (*da'vat kunid mardum ra bih-inkih nazir-i iran qiam kunand*).[21]

IRAN'S CONCEPTION OF SECURITY IN THE PERSIAN GULF

The most serious aspect of the ideological challenge to the Gulf Arab states, of course, is Iran's revolutionary conception of security in the region. Yet neither in Khomeini's own policy statements nor in those of his disciples is there to be found a concrete composite description of the concept. Against the backdrop of the foregoing analysis, however, a description can be fashioned by gleaning relevant information from literally hundreds of pertinent statements made by Khomeini and his officials between the dawn of the Iranian Revolution and the present. The analysis that makes up the rest of this chapter, therefore, begins with this question: What is revolutionary Iran's conception of security in the Persian Gulf region? To put it more concretely, what seem to be the principal requirements of security in the Gulf region as envisaged by Iranian revolutionary leaders?

To start with, one of the most frequently encountered phenomena in the policy statements of Iranian leaders is the way they use the term *security* with respect to the Gulf region. It is seldom, if ever, used by itself; it is almost always preceded by such adjectives as *real, true,* and *genuine.* The implication of this usage for the Gulf Arab leaders should be obvious: it means that in the eyes of the present revolutionary leaders of Iran, the existing Gulf political order is not secure or stable. But what may not be so obvious, at least at first, is that revolutionary Iran seems to prescribe a remedy to make the Gulf region truly secure and stable.

"True Independence"

Iranian leaders seem to require "true independence" for all the Gulf states as a condition for "true security" in the entire region. The Khomeini conception of Islamic world order insists on ideological confrontation with "the camp of the oppressors." In the more colorful language of psychological warfare, the "Great Satan," the "Lesser Satan," and the "minisatans" all occupy the camp of the oppressors. The "camp of the oppressed," on the other hand, is presumably led by the Islamic Republic of Iran as the self-appointed redeemer nation.

From such a perspective, the Gulf Arab leaders have placed their states in the camp of the oppressors by aligning themselves with the Soviet Union or the United States. But since they are neither willing nor powerful enough to resist the control and influence of foreign powers, they are perforce the servants of the Soviet Union and the United States. The corollary of this perception is that one of the basic requirements of real security in the Gulf region is the severance of all ties of servitude between the Gulf states and the superpowers, a severance that can take place only with the rise of "Islamic consciousness." In a blistering statement directed at the Gulf Arab leaders' alleged servility, Khomeini described what he wanted leaders of the Gulf states to do:

> It is hoped that the heads of these governments, some of whom are indulging in sensuality, some preoccupied with their debaucheries, some embroiled in clashes with their brethren, and some . . . emasculated by their fear of the United States, will be awakened [by my warnings] into an Islamic humanitarian consciousness, thus putting an end to their sordid states. [They must] reject all superpowers, just as our heroic nation has done.[22]

"True Islamic Government"

For the Gulf region to become "really secure," the Gulf Arab leaders should not only terminate their servile dependent relations with the superpowers, as Iran has, but also try to establish a "true Islamic government" in their societies. What does it take to have such a government? First, and perhaps foremost, a monarchy cannot be truly Islamic. According to Khomeini, Islam is "fundamentally opposed to the whole notion of monarchy," and, he adds, "anyone who studies the manner in which the Prophet established the government of Islam will realize that

Islam came in order to destroy these palaces of tyranny. Monarchy is one of the most shameful and disgraceful reactionary manifestations" of political life.[23] The implication of this categoric indictment of the institution of monarchy for the conservative Gulf Arab monarchies is obvious. Although on the basis of his own writings and statements before his exile by the Shah in 1964, Khomeini seemed to favor a political system based on a form of "limited monarchy," he now is in fact a latter-day antimonarchist.[24]

Second, in a true Islamic government, the clerical class controls power. It is not at all clear from the pronouncements of Khomeini and his close disciples whether in other Muslim states the clerics are required to rule exactly as they do in Iran. Nevertheless, two kinds of evidence would support the proposition that the clerical rule should be "similar" to rather than "identical" to Iran's model. First, Khomeini himself has repeatedly used the term *similar.* Second, the Khomeini regime's attitudes toward prospective governments in Afghanistan and Iraq seem to confirm this proposition. Iran's November 1981 proposal for the establishment of an Islamic government in Afghanistan does not insist on a duplication of Iran's present type of government, in which one religious leader, the *faqih,* rules.[25] With respect to a desirable prospective Islamic government in Iraq, Iran's support of Hojatolislam Baqir al-Hakim does not necessarily mean that Iranian leaders prefer that one *faqih* rule in every country. Even in Iran itself it was conceded that Khomeini's powers would have devolved on a committee of three to five clerics (*fuqaha*) if the so-called Assembly of Experts (*Majlis-i Khibrigan*) had failed to agree on the election of a single successor to Khomeini. (The assembly did agree on Montazeri as the successor to Khomeini, finally, in November 1985.)

The third prerequisite of a true Islamic government is that the clerically ruled republic be populist. This requirement, of course, does not mean that there ought to be a representative form of government based on majority rule. That would be a "popular" form of government, which would be quite different from what Khomeini calls "the government of the oppressed" (*dawlat-i mustaz'afin*). Because the clerical class is given the right and the power to know what is good for the whole Muslim community, only a government that is controlled by one or more clerics can help the dispossessed masses "to inherit the earth."

The Gulf "Security Umbrella"

Finally, the "real security" of the Persian Gulf region cannot be achieved without the religious and political primacy of Iran throughout the entire region, particularly at the Strait of Hormuz. Too many observers jumped to the conclusion that the Iranian Revolution put an end to the Iranian claim to political preponderance in the Gulf region. They were perhaps misled by the categoric statement of the Shah's last prime minister, Shahpour Bakhtiar, who declared that Iran would no longer play the role of the Gulf "policeman." He meant, of course, on behalf of the United States. The revolutionary forces' opposition to the role of Iran as an "American policeman" had nothing to do with the ancient Iranian perception of its political primacy in the Gulf region.[26] The nationalist foreign minister Karim Sanjabi viewed Iran's role as "central" in the whole Gulf area, just as the Shah had before him. The disciples of Khomeini have followed suit, except that they have added the new claim of religious leadership to the old claim of political primacy in the Gulf area. The Khomeini regime has not only kept the Shah-captured islands of Abu Musa and the two Tunbs, claimed by the Arabs, but it has also revived Iran's ancient claim to Bahrain (see chapter 3).

The new revolutionary leaders have added what they call their "faith power" to the Shah's political power in the Gulf region. The combination is a potent recipe for regional security. The Shah used to insist on the preservation of Iran's expanding "security perimeter" (*harim-e amniyyat*), and the Khomeini regime insists on spreading Iran's "security umbrella" (*chatr-e amniyyat*) all over the Gulf region. The influential Speaker Hashemi-Rafsanjani, who has introduced this new concept, sounds just like the Shah when he says, for example, that the security of the region has been "the responsibility of our valiant and courageous Navy. We declared once again that the security of the Persian Gulf is more important to us than any other party, and we will strive to maintain the Gulf's [security] as much as we can."[27] Khomeini's Iran, like the Shah's Iran, considers its role in maintaining Gulf security as superior to, but not exclusive of, the role of other Gulf states, because Iranian leaders tend to believe that their country is primus inter pares.

Above all, this perception of Iran's superior role in the Gulf region applies to the strategic Strait of Hormuz. In his celebrated sermon during the Iraqi threat to strike at Iran's main oil terminal at Kharg Island in October 1983, Speaker Hashemi-Rafsanjani declared: "He who holds the key to the Strait of Hormuz is in fact strangling the enemy and he will press on the enemy's throat when it is in his interest to do so." In a less colorful way, other Iranian leaders also addressed the vital interest of Iran in the Strait of Hormuz. For example, Defense Minister Colonel Muhammad Salimi said that the strait "with its special situation is by itself our biggest defensive element in the region."[28] In fact, throughout the war Iran has played the strait "card" to counter Iraqi threats by threatening to close it to all oil shipments.

Yet at the Strait of Hormuz, as elsewhere in the Gulf region, the Iranian national interest is fused, in the thinking of the Khomeini regime, with the regime's religiously inspired ideological interest. For example, when Speaker Hashemi-Rafsanjani invoked the "epic of Karbala" with reference to the Iranian defense posture at the strait, he was not just rationalizing the Iranian national interest in the strategic waterway or simply trying to mobilize the Iranian forces for its defense. He was also trying to signal the depth of the commitment of "martyr-nurturing" Iranians to the preservation of the "Islamic revolution."

Even this combination of national interest and Islamic ideology, or political power and faith power, cannot adequately explain the complex nature of the Iranian challenge in the Persian Gulf region. We need to examine yet a third dimension of the phenomenon.

3

The Sociopolitical Explosion

The Arab leaders of the Persian Gulf perceive revolutionary Iran as a threat for reasons other than regime interest and Islamic ideology. Neither the putative power of Iran nor the ideological crusade of the Khomeini regime separately or together would pose a great threat to their regimes were it not for the possibility of the contagion of revolutionary fundamentalist Islam within their own societies. To be sure, the destruction of the Shah's regime sent shudders down the spines of all Arab monarchies. They feared that their days might also be numbered. But the fear of the contagion of revolutionary fundamentalist Islam has not been confined to monarchies of the Persian Gulf. The potential contagion has been just as much a source of concern to revolutionary Iraq as it has been to conservative Arab monarchies, and the concern is clearly evident across the globe—from Manama in Bahrain to Marawi City in the Philippines, and beyond.

And yet, the threat of revolutionary fundamentalist Islam has been perceived to be the greatest in the Middle East, in the Persian Gulf and in Lebanon. In this chapter we shall take up the developments in the Gulf region. In the Gulf, Iran is the center of power for this ideology; not only is Iran in close proximity to the Arab states, but it has the largest population of Shia Muslims of any country in the world. Neither of these factors, however, would necessarily be perceived as a threat to the Gulf Arab leaders were it not for critical sociopolitical and psychological conditions within their own societies. These conditions affect the Arab leaders' perception of the Iranian threat in two major ways.

First, every Arab regime's awareness of its own domestic political fragility has increased as a result of the Iranian revolutionary upheaval. After all, despite its multiple ethnic, linguistic, and other societal divisions, Iran is, comparatively, a cohesive society. Revolutionary Iraq and a number of conservative Arab monarchies have been plagued by far greater threats to their social cohesion than Iran has. To the primordial problems of tribal, dynastic, and sectarian divisions has been added the presence of millions of expatriates, which has aggravated the problem of nation building in the Gulf area. Paradoxically, in order to overcome their primordial problems through modernization, the sparsely populated, oil-rich Arab monarchies have imported foreign labor. The number of Arab (Egyptian, Palestinian, Syrian, and other) and non-Arab (Indian, Pakistani, European, American, and other) foreign nationals in most Gulf Arab monarchies has gradually increased, and foreigners now outnumber citizens in these countries. The foreign populations in Qatar (73.2 percent of total population), the United Arab Emirates (69.0 percent), and Kuwait (61.2 percent) are most significant, but those of other countries are by no means insignificant (see appendix A, table 6).

Second, this overall problem of social and political fragility could, of course, be useful to any dissident group, but it is the threat of dissident elements within various Shia communities that concerns the Arab leaders most. Iran is the single largest Shia-inhabited country in the world. And because Shia communities exist in all Gulf Arab countries as well as in Iran, the Gulf region is in fact the world's Shia heartland (see appendix A, table 5). The large foreign populations in these countries skew the statistics; the percentages of Shia Muslims *among citizens* are actually very large. For example, Bahrain's Shia community composes 49 percent of the state's total population, but it composes almost 72 percent of its citizen population, because more than 32 percent of the total are foreign nationals. Using one set of statistics, an extreme example is the United Arab Emirates (UAE), whose Shia community composes only 11.53 percent of the total population, but 41.39 percent of its citizenry, because fully 69 percent of its inhabitants are foreign nationals (see appendix A, table 5, note b). The Shia communities in Iran, Bahrain, and Iraq constitute the majority of citizens. In some countries the addition of Iranian expatriates to native Arab Shias increases the Arab leaders' fear of the potential threat of "Shia-Iranian fifth columnists." In Kuwait and Qatar, Iranians account for 5.12 and 23.29 percent of the foreign populations, respectively.

There is no simple correlation between the Arab leaders' perception of the Shia threat and the size of the Shia and Iranian communities in Arab states. The perception is determined by experience. For example, according to one source, Qatar has the largest percentage of Shia Muslims (80 percent) of any Gulf Arab state, and yet it has not experienced the Shia unrest that has taken place in Bahrain, Iraq, and Saudi Arabia.

Qatar also has the largest percentage of Iranians (23.29 percent) of any Gulf Arab state, yet it has not experienced the kind of Iranian agitation that Kuwait has. Because the perception of the Shia threat depends on the kind of experience Arab leaders in each country have had with Shia dissidents, the best way to examine the problem is through case studies.

Before the case studies are presented, however, three interrelated aspects of the Shia revolutionary potentials in the Arab Middle East as a whole should be mentioned. First, by and large, most Shias consider themselves socially and economically deprived (*mahroomin*), politically powerless, and generally treated as second-class citizens, regardless of where they live. This is generally true, not only in countries where they constitute small minorities, but also in countries where they constitute great majorities. Recent government efforts in various countries to ameliorate the Shia human conditions have no doubt been important. There is not yet a common perception among Shias, however, that past socioeconomic grievances have been sufficiently redressed. More important, regardless of such efforts, intense complaints about the Shias' lack of political power and participation persist. To be sure, there are many well-to-do Shia merchants, bankers, businessmen, and others, but this does not necessarily translate into support for incumbent Sunni-dominated regimes. For example, it is rumored that some rich Shias in Dubai surreptitiously subsidize pro-Khomeini and antiregime political activities, and it is alleged that some Shia bankers exert considerable influence on Sheikh Sultan al-Qassimi, the ruler of Sharjah, because he is heavily indebted to them. Having failed to acquire needed funds from the UAE president, it was rumored, the sultan simply flew to Iran in April 1984 and returned home loaded with Iranian money! But in a discussion with this ruler-scholar in February 1986, I discovered that these rumors were baseless; the sultan said that he had not visited Tehran since the Iranian Revolution.

Second, anti-Shia sentiments among Sunni Arabs have been rife historically, and they have increased in recent years as a result of unprecedented acts of political violence by the Shias in the Middle East. Shia terrorists, for all practical purposes, have been their own larger community's worst enemy, although this larger community has genuine grievances that have yet to be redressed. The cycles of death and violence have not produced the desired results. Nevertheless, not all Sunnis nurture prejudices against the Shias. For example, in spite of heavy pressures from the Iraqis, the ruler of Dubai, where Iranians compose 10 percent of the population, and of Sharjah, whose banking and aid provide it with important ties to Iran, have been reluctant to clamp down indiscriminately on the Shias and Iranians. Furthermore, not all Shias are free from anti-Sunni sentiments. In reality, the emotional and doctrinal animosity is mutual.

Third, the Shias have proved to be far more susceptible than the Sunnis to Islamic fundamentalist appeals. In fact, Islamic extremism has in recent years been more prevalent among the Shias than among the Sunnis. The "Shia international" now cuts across state boundaries in the Gulf region and all the way to the Eastern Mediterranean in Lebanon. The crucial and controversial issue of the Iranian "state sponsorship" of Shia terrorism will be discussed in the context of each case study that follows. This issue, however, should not overshadow the ancient and bona fide social, economic, and political grievances of the Shia community throughout the Middle East.

THE SHIA SUBVERSIVES OF IRAQ

Apart from being one of the major powers of the Persian Gulf region and being involved in an inconclusive war with Iran, Iraq has the single largest Shia population in absolute terms (about 8 million) of any Arab state in the Middle East. There are discrepancies in statistics on Shia populations (see appendix A, table 5, note b), but it seems that only Bahrain's Shia population composes a larger percentage of its citizen population (about 72 percent) than Iraq's does (60 percent). Furthermore, Iraq happens to be the site of the holiest Shia shrines. Karbala, Najaf, and Kazemain are names that are powerful symbols of faith for millions of Shia Muslims in the world. But here we are concerned primarily with the Shia problem as the principal aspect of the perceived sociopolitical threat of Iran to Iraq, a threat that partly underpins the Iraq-Iran war.

For all the Gulf Arab nations, the pro-Iranian Shia challenge began to loom menacingly large after the fall of the provisional government of Mehdi Bazargan in the wake of the seizure of the American embassy in Tehran by the militant revolutionary elements (4 November, 1979). But the trauma to the regime of Saddam Hussein was the most intense. Organized Shia political opposition was more serious in Iraq than in any other Arab country in the Middle East. The Iraqi Shia revolutionaries themselves trace the beginnings of their main political party, the *Da'wa,* to "after the 'revolution' of 1958," which destroyed the monarchy in Iraq. This view of the origin of the party is that of Ayatollah Sayyid Mahdi al-Hakim, a son of the founder of the party, although Hana Batatu, an acknowledged authority on the subject, dates it back to the late 1960s.[1] "The main objective of the party," according to Mahdi al-Hakim, "is to establish an Islamic state." "The leaders of the *Da'wa* party," he continues, "had also consulted the leaders of Ikhwanul Muslimin, who broadly agreed that the objective of establishing an Islamic state constituted the best programme of cooperation between the Shi'i and Sunni Muslims." Hence, even before the exile of Khomeini to Iraq in 1964, the Iraqi Shias had had their own ideas on establishing an Islamic state, and had possibly formed some rudimentary groups, as well. It was only on the less-influential Iraqi-Shia dissident group, the *al-Mujahidin* party, which was established much later in 1979, and not on the *Da'wa,* that Batatu says the Iranian Revolution had a strong impact.

Yet, it is the originally Ikhwan-inspired *Da'wa* that today cooperates closely with the revolutionary regime in Iran, especially since the outbreak of the Iraq-Iran war. The leading personality in this cooperation is Hojatolislam Baqir al-Hakim, another son of the founder of the *Da'wa,* the late Muhsin al-Hakim. (Hojatolislam is the title Khomeini prefers for him; Khomeini does not use the higher title of Ayatollah, which Batatu and others have used for Baqir al-Hakim.) He lives in Iran, as do many other Iraqi Shia dissidents, who began to arrive in Iran in large numbers after the Iraqi regime executed Ayatollah Sayyid Muhammad Baqir al-Sadr, "the most respected Iraqi *'alim'*" (religious leader), and his sister in April 1980. These executions reverberated throughout the Gulf and caused Shias to immigrate to Iran more than to any other Gulf country.

The outbreak of the Iraq-Iran war in September 1980, however, was responsible for the largest flow of anti-Hussein Shia revolutionaries to Iran. By late 1984, there were over 350,000 such Shias in Iran, including those who were expelled by the Iraqi regime at the outset of the war, refugees from various countries, and Iraqi prisoners of war. No one seems to know precisely how many anti-Hussein Shia Iraqis in Iran actively oppose the Iraqi regime and seek to overthrow it. But some Shia dissidents from Iraq have organized themselves, under the leadership of Baqir al-Hakim, in an Iran-based group called the Supreme Assembly of the Islamic Revolution in Iraq (SAIRI). Al-Hakim has personally paid heavily for collaborating with Iran against Saddam Hussein; for example, the Ba'thist regime executed members of al-Hakim's family. Al-Hakim divulged on 17 June, 1983 that six of them had been put to death in Iraq; other sources indicate that three of them may have been his brothers.

The nature of the relationship between the SAIRI and the *Da'wa* is not entirely clear. Whether there is an organizational link between the two pro-Iranian insurgent groups or not, it seems to me that the *Da'wa* does support SAIRI activities. In March 1984, for example, when Iranian President Khamene'i called on all Iraqi revolutionary forces to rally around the SAIRI in its efforts to overthrow the Iraqi regime, the *Da'wa* responded immediately. It was "its religious duty," it believed, to uphold and further activate the assembly (SAIRI) so that the party's members could take "pride in defending Islam and in liberating suppressed masses in Iraq who are denied their civil rights under the Ba'thists' rule in that country."[2]

There is little doubt that SAIRI supporters operate underground within Iraq, but it is not clear whether they work through, or with, the Islamic 'Amal Organization. (Although the English transliteration of the name of this organization and the Lebanese *Amal* is the same, the two groups should not be confused. The Iraqi 'Amal group claims that it is a different Shia faction; its name in Arabic actually means "action," whereas the Lebanese *Amal* means "hope.") The Iraqi Islamic 'Amal has claimed responsibility for a number of antiregime attacks, including the suicide attacks in Baghdad against Iraqi Airways offices, an Iraqi newspaper print room, and the security police in 1983. In May 1984 the group also claimed responsibility for an explosion in the offices of Iraqi Airways in Nicosia, Cyprus, and similar attacks in 1980 and 1982 against the Iraqi embassies in Paris and Rome. Al-Hakim announced on 25 June, 1984 that the SAIRI had decided, in a session attended by Iranian President Khamene'i, to step up its military operations inside Iraq.

Khomeini publicly expressed unequivocal support of SAIRI on 20 September 1983. He instructed the members of the organization as follows: "You should aim to form an Islamic government and to implement God's commands." "God willing," he added, "you will be successful in your efforts to be a mujahid (warrior) along the path of God. God willing, you will return to Iraq, where we too will join in the shrine of Imam Husayn, peace upon him. God bless you all."[3] In practice, the Iranian support includes hosting SAIRI and its branch offices in Iranian cities, training its supporters in paramilitary camps, and dispatching *mujahidin* (warriors) to the war front to fight on the Iranian side against the Iraqi forces, as evidenced by the *mujahidin's* large-scale participation in the Iranian advance to Hajj 'Umran in the northern front.

Revolutionary Iran's active, high-level, and persistent support of SAIRI activities inside Iraq is designed to undermine the Hussein regime and pave the way for the establishment of an Iranian-type Islamic government in Iraq. Although Iranian officials have declared time and again that the Iraqi people, not Iran, should decide their future, there are indications that the Iranians would play a big part in that decision should the time come. First, Iran has made the removal of Saddam Hussein the principal objective of the war with Iraq. Second, al-Hakim and his organization have been in constant communication with Iranian leaders. Al-Hakim, in fact, reports annually to Speaker Hashemi-Raf-sanjani about the functions of SAIRI in general and its subversive activities inside Iraq in particular. Iranian leaders have promised to be very supportive of a new Islamic government in Iraq, should SAIRI-supported subversives succeed in overthrowing the Ba'thist regime. In July 1984, for example, Speaker Hashemi-Rafsanjani said: "After 4 years [of war], our aim is to save the people of the region from the evils of the Iraqi regime. If the matter were to reach the stage whereby the Iraqi people took their fate into their own hands, we would not ask for any reparations [about $150 billion] from the Iraqi people, and in addition we would be prepared to use our own manpower and financial resources to assist the Iraqi people to continue on the path of Islam."[4] No doubt, SAIRI has been groomed since the start of the war exactly for that purpose. After the fall of the Hussein regime, al-Hakim would be the Iranian candidate for the leadership of an Islamic Republic in Iraq.

The effects of the Iranian-sponsored Shia challenge to Iraq have been limited for two reasons. First, the susceptibility of the Iraqi Shias to the Iranian revolutionary appeal was probably greater before July 1982, before Iran carried the war into Iraqi territory. Khomeini's appeal at that time to the Iraqi masses to rise up against the Hussein regime fell on deaf ears, and subsequent reports indicated improved morale among the Iraqi armed forces, including the ground forces, which are composed mostly of Iraqi Shias. The Iraqis were fighting on their own soil, regardless of their sectarian loyalty.

Second, Hussein's strategy has so far contained the threat of SAIRI-supported subversive acts inside Iraq. He has pursued a carrot-and-stick policy. The Hussein government has ruthlessly clamped down on all violent manifestations of opposition sponsored by the *Da'wa* and other Shia dissident groups. Ayatollah Muhammad Baqir al-Sadr and his sister were executed because of charges that they were plotting to assassinate Tariq 'Aziz, currently Hussein's foreign minister, just as the "executions" of members of the al-Hakim family were carried out on charges of antistate activities.

Saddam Hussein has also enforced relentless surveillance of the loyalty of suspected Shias to his government. Arbitrary arrests, harassment, and police brutality have been features of his reign of terror. Finally, he has used government funds to improve the lot of the Shias and to co-opt and appease their leaders, despite the taxing costs—more than $500 million a month—of the war. Shia holy cities in particular have been chosen as sites for government activities designed to pacify Shias, including housing projects, playgrounds, water and sewage works, and electrification. The golden-domed shrines at Najaf, where Khomeini prayed at the tomb of the first Shia, Imam 'Ali, during fourteen years of exile, and at Karbala, the site of the martyred Shia Imam Hussein, have been refurbished, and loyal Shia mullahs and others have been given key posts in the Shia establishment.[5] This threefold strategy of Saddam Hussein's seems so far to have blunted the Iranian-sponsored Shia challenge, which Hussein considers to be the most dangerous internal threat to his regime (the other threats are the Kurdish nationalists and the communists). But the overall success of his response will depend, ultimately, on the outcome of the war. The success of the Iranian offensives launched on 9 and 25 February 1986 increased the morale problem in Iraq and aggravated the threat of the guerrillas of the Kurdish Democratic party to the stability of the regime of Saddam Hussein.

THE SHIA UPHEAVAL IN SAUDI ARABIA

Revolutionary Iran's sociopolitical threat to Saudi Arabia is quite different from its threat to Iraq. First, the Saudi Shias form a small minority of the population. Some put the number of Saudi Shias at 115,000, and others estimate there are 200,000 to 350,000 Shias in the state. Saudi Shias probably compose between 5 and 10 percent of the population. Second, there is no organized Saudi Shia opposition inside the kingdom or in Iran, although the existence of individual Saudi Shia dissidents inside and outside the country cannot be denied, as evidenced by the involvement of discontented Saudi Shias in the coup plot in Bahrain. In comparison to the Shia "threat" in Iraq, that in Saudi Arabia is minimal; it is largely a sociopolitical protest, and it is only a *potential* threat to the House of Saud.

Yet, from the Saudi perspective, the Shia challenge is the single most troublesome sociopolitical problem facing the royal family today. The Shias are concentrated in the oil-rich al-Hasa Province, where they constitute between 40 and 60 percent of the work force in the nation's vital oil industry. But this fact, which is so often paraded by analysts, cannot in itself explain the pervasive Saudi sense of vulnerability. It is the age-old and festering social, economic, and political grievances of the Shias resulting from both private and official discrimination that underpins the Saudi fear of Iranian agitation among their Shias. No Saudi official, to my knowledge, has ever denied the existence of Sunni bias against grass-roots Shia Muslims, although this bias is generally considered to be part of the past. But that is not necessarily the way the Shias see it. "You must keep the dog hungry so that it will follow you" is the kind of adage that some Saudi Shias believe characterizes the Sunnis' attitude toward them. "The Shias suffer," said one person, "not so much from an empty stomach, as from a sense of injured dignity." The bias, however, is mutual, and the Saudi government is trying to help the Shias.

It is no wonder that a cry for "justice" (*adl*) symbolized the two major Shia uprisings in Saudi Arabia. The first Shia disturbance, in the Eastern Province in late November 1979, was no doubt inspired by the Iranian revolutionary upheaval. Some 90,000 demonstrators defied the government ban on the Shia religious commemoration of the martyrdom of Imam Hussein on *'Ashura*, the tenth of the month of *Muharram*. During the ensuing riots a number of people were killed, and several national guard soldiers, who are perceived generally among the Shias as the agents of Saudi repression, were among those killed. The second Shia unrest also took place in the Eastern Province, in February 1980, when demonstrators demanded, inter alia, that oil remain in the ground since the revenues from its sale did not help alleviate the sufferings of the oil workers, who are largely Shia Muslims.

It is enlightening to examine these two disturbances from the perspective of the Saudis. One reliable source in Saudi Arabia recounted:

> The revolution in Iran which was led by a religious leader stirred up emotions [in Saudi Arabia] and struck a responsive chord in Qatif. The religious factor, however, was not the only reason for the disturbances. Until 10 years ago, all villagers in the Kingdom suffered from a lack of basic services. Basic services were not getting to them. The situation in the cities and urban centers was far better than it was in the villages. This created a climate, a fertile soil, for disgruntlement, contributing to the response in Qatif to the events in Iran. Note that no disturbances occurred in al-Hasa, because it is more of an urban area. But in the villages, the situation was different. Villagers felt they were deprived of benefit and saw themselves as "oppressed."

While this account by a Saudi Sunni intellectual emphasizes the social and economic roots of the Shia unrest, it clearly skirts the problem of anti-Shia sentiment among the Sunni majority, which is precisely what the Shias complain about. Furthermore, the Saudi Sunnis downplay the problem of a political grudge among the Shias; this grudge is often expressed in terms of the fact that not a single cabinet-level position in the Saudi government today is held by a Shia Muslim. But the political alienation of the Shias from the Sunni government, in addition to the Shias' economic and social alienation, it seems to me, forms the foundation of the Al-Saud's sense of vulnerability vis-à-vis the Iranian ideological, political, and propaganda agitation from across the Gulf.

Saudi Sunnis have an anti-Shia bias, but the Sunnis are no less the object of Shia bias. Saudi Shias, to be sure, lash out at the Sunnis, whom they pejoratively call the "*Wahhabis,*" for treating them as second-class citizens. Two factors deepen the Sunni-Shia conflict. One is the well-known doctrinal differences between the two sects. These differences are as old as the history of Islam. The other is the new "Islamic consciousness," which is pervasive among Sunnis and Shias alike, but which in reality reinforces the old sectarian conflict.

The Saudi government is trying to cope constructively with the Shia problem. The recent expenditure of billions of dollars demonstrates clearly that the Saudi government is determined and able to alleviate the sources of Shia grievances. Even some critics of the Saudi government readily acknowledge its various efforts for the betterment of Shia living conditions. They point out, for example, the late King Khalid's meeting with Shia leaders in Qatif in the wake of Shia disturbances. One individual optimistically predicted that the Shias in Qatif were "immune to Iranian influence" because of the government extension of social services to them and because of the improved attitude on the part of Saudi officials toward the Shia minority. Another person pointed out that perhaps the government had overdone a good thing. He said:

There are now people [in Saudi Arabia] who believe that attention to Qatif [by the Saudi government] far exceeds that given to other villages. Yesterday [7 March, 1984] the cabinet decided to build 600 villas in Qatif, but only 400 in al-Hasa, although al-Hasa is bigger and larger. In fact, Qatif now ranks fourth in the government's priorities, after Riyadh, Jidda, Damman and al-Qasim. The [last] is being overlooked despite its half a million people. All this is congruent with the need to eliminate any climate which would be conducive to injustice.

The emphasis of the Saudi strategy for dealing with the Shia problem has thus far focused on redressing the economic disadvantages of the Shia community. The rising and growing Shia middle class will probably continue to judge the efforts of the Saudi government largely in terms of opportunities for political participation and freedom from foreign domination—both of which bridge the Shia-Sunni division. The lower-class Shias, however, will continue to be vulnerable to Iranian propaganda as long as they do not perceive an improvement in their living conditions. The seemingly contradictory attitudes of the Saudi authorities is also a source of Shia confusion. For example, the predominantly Ja'fari Shia inhabitants of Qatif in the Eastern Province were pleased with the change of the chief of police, but some Shia intellectuals elsewhere in Saudi Arabia were concerned about the Sunni officials' allegedly restrictive policy regarding the admission of Shia students into universities.

THE SHIA BOMBINGS IN KUWAIT

The Shia challenge in Kuwait reflects an extraordinary combination of circumstances that place it in a class unique among the Gulf Arab states. First, the tiny city state faces two largely Shia-populated neighbors (Iran, 95 percent, Iraq, 60 percent), which are too large, too close, and too threatening for comfort. At the nearest point, Iran, a hundred times larger than Kuwait, is only twenty miles away, and irredentist Iraq abuts Kuwait's mainland and covets its islands. Second, while revolutionary Shia Iran seeks to export its "Islamic revolution," revolutionary Iraq's persecuted Shia Muslims menacingly infiltrate the neighboring skeikhdom. Third, as if having more than 25 percent of its citizenry composed of Shias is not a sufficient source of anxiety, another 14 percent are Iranians, and, to top it off, there are a considerable number of pro-Iranian elements among the large Palestinian expatriate population.

Fourth, the Kuwaiti parliament has been the most coveted object of political control by various groups, including the Shias. This is not a rubber-stamp assembly. Although still largely a traditional and tribal country, Kuwait has been a relatively open society by Middle Eastern standards. The ancient, indigenous institution of *diwaniya* (private gathering) has kept alive a tradition of political discussion. In addition to serious political issues, gossip and rumors are discussed in the *diwaniyas,* and in this respect they remarkably resemble the Iranian *dowrehs* (private gatherings). The *diwaniyas,* however, perform two additional functions. First, being relatively open gatherings, they tend to temper the divisions between the Shias and the Sunnis and the haves and have-nots. Second, the ruling family uses them as a sounding board for policy initiatives before making policy decisions.

At this time, however, the revived parliament seems to rival the *diwaniyas* as a nationwide forum for political debate and for criticism of government policies. In 1981 there was much doubt among Kuwaiti political activists that the suspended parliament would reopen. They thought that the al-Sabah ruling family would keep the parliament suspended out of fear that the Muslim fundamentalists and pro-Iranian elements might gain strength in the elections. Elections were held, however—both then and again in 1985. Even more important, so far the parliamentarians have given government officials such a hard time that some Kuwaitis suspect that the ruling family might again suspend the assembly, while others believe that the emir is determined to keep it in session as long as he rules, although there might be some opposition to the parliament within the ruling family.

Insofar as the threat of Islamic fundamentalism in the parliament is concerned, none has materialized so far. In 1981 only a half-dozen Sunni and Shia fundamentalists were elected for the first time, although some believed that their strength was greater than their numbers, as they were able to muster much support for their legislative proposals. In the 1985 elections, the leaders of the *Salafi* and the *Jama'at Islah,* the two main Sunni fundamentalist groups, lost their seats, but the first group won two seats, and the second claimed to have won eight seats (which seems doubtful). The Shia community retained the three seats it had won in 1981, and the pro-Khomeini *Jama'at Saqafah* won one seat.

Fifth, the decline of oil revenues has been accompanied by the demand of the trading families for greater influence in politics. The traditional influence of the trading families in the political process diminished with the flow of ever-increasing oil revenues to the coffers of the royal family in the 1970s, but dwindling oil income in the 1980s has whetted the appetite of the trading families for the renewal of their traditional political influence. There are limits, however, to the amount of influence they might be able to recover, because, despite falling oil revenues, the royal family continues to control the purse strings, thanks largely to income derived from investments.

Sixth, regardless of the real strength of the Shias in the political process, the rise of Islamic fundamentalism has tended to polarize Kuwaiti Muslims between secular-liberal and religious-conservative social and political orientations. The influence of the conservatives, Sunni and Shia alike, is increasingly felt in legislative and administrative acts presumably intended to make the Kuwaiti society "more Islamic," a trend that is deeply resented by the Westernized Kuwaiti intelligentsia. My own guess is that the Kuwaiti commitment to political pluralism will eventually prevail over ideological dogmatism.

Seventh, and finally, given the Kuwaiti vulnerability to these internal pressures, the Kuwaiti rulers fear that an Iranian victory in the war with Iraq would ignite a Shia rebellion, a scenario that is not envisioned by most Kuwaiti Shias. The rulers have supported Iraq, albeit reluctantly, to prevent that eventuality. Paradoxically, this support has subjected Kuwait to Iranian attacks, including several "accidental" air raids on the city state and its supertankers. The Shia bombings in Kuwait on 12

December 1983, according to some Western analysts, were another indication of Iran's wrath at Kuwaiti support of Iraq. This Western view clearly implicates Iran in the incident, whereas Iran vehemently denies responsibility.

The multiple explosions in Kuwait, which killed five and wounded eighty-six persons, have been the most violent Shia protest in the Gulf region to date. The bombings were apparently part of a grand plot to assault the American embassy and seven other targets: the headquarters building of American Raytheon Company, which at the time was installing a Hawk missile system in Kuwait; an apartment house occupied by Raytheon's employees; the control tower at the international airport; the Kuwaiti Ministry of Electricity and Water; the Kuwaiti Passport Control office; the French embassy; and a major petrochemical and refining complex at the port of Shuaiba. As it did in the truck bombings of the American Marines and the French paratroopers (23 October, 1983), the "Islamic Jihad" (probably a fictitious cover name rather than a real Shia faction) claimed responsibility. There were speculations about various motives for the operation, but above all it was seen as another effort to frighten the Americans and the French, who were then deeply involved in the Lebanon crisis, and as another move on the part of Iran to alarm the Gulf Arab states that support Iraqi war efforts.[6]

Iran was implicated in the plot by Western sources primarily through a reconstruction of bits and pieces of evidence. First, the evidence "beyond doubt" showed that most of the plotters "entered Kuwait from Iran" by boat, and not only with stocks of explosives for the bombings, but also with such conventional weapons as rocket-launched grenades, machine guns, rifles, pistols, and detonators.[7] Second, it was established that the "final approval" for the operation "came directly from a message carried to Kuwait by a courier from Iran and that planning for it took place in Switzerland and [the] Bekaa Valley of Lebanon."[8] Third, it was established that of the twenty-two men initially known to have been involved, eighteen were native-born Iraqis, all of whom were members of the *Da'wa* party.

The Iranian authorities not only vehemently denied responsibility, but tried to offer their own explanations. The day after the incident, the spokesman of the Iranian Ministry of Foreign Affairs said: "These attacks have no connection whatsoever with the Islamic Republic. Attributing them to Iran is part and parcel of a comprehensive plot by the United States and its agents against the Islamic Revolution."[9] One day later, President Khamene'i tried to explain away the Iranian implication in the plot by blaming the United States, adding, "While we deny any connection between these events and the Islamic Republic of Iran, at the same time, we regard it a foolish and stupid lie. We do not expect the propaganda loudspeakers dependent upon America and Israel to stop engaging in such foolish lies and allegations."[10]

Other Iranian officials, however, rejected the charges by the United States and offered other explanations. Some attributed the bombings to a larger and wider authentic protest movement against alien domination. For example, Foreign Minister Velayati told the foreign diplomatic community in Tehran on 15 December:

> The suicide movements, contrary to futile claims, do not stem from Iran or other countries; neither are they confined to 100 or 1,000 self-sacrificing Muslims in Lebanon or elsewhere. Rather, they stem from the depth of hatred and rancor of such deprived nations as Lebanon and Palestine, whose lands have been usurped and whose interests have been transgressed. It is axiomatic that no country, not even Iran, can direct the destiny of a self-generating movement against the interests of the hegemonists.[11]

Such an analysis seems to make sense; the underlying malaise suggested by such a statement at least partly stems from a deep-felt sense of foreign domination, just as the Iranian Revolution itself erupted partly because of the perceived domination of Iran by the United States. Furthermore, it can be argued that the Western case against Iran was at least partly based on circumstantial evidence. It is still difficult to establish that the Iranian government "directed" the Kuwaiti operation. Iran's "direct" responsibility cannot be established because "deniability" safeguards are generally built into state-sponsored terrorist operations. The Western case against Iran is based on conjecture more than on hard evidence.

Yet, there is little doubt that Iran aids and abets Iraqi Shia dissidents and guerrillas, including the *Da'wa* and the SAIRI, as discussed earlier. Also, there is no doubt that most of the perpetrators of the Kuwaiti plot belonged to the *Da'wa*. Western suspicion of Iran's direct responsibility is fueled not only by Iran's proven moral and material support of the SAIRI and the *Da'wa*, the Islamic Amal, the Lebanese Fadlallah group, and the *mujahidin*, but also by statements by Iranian leaders such as Ayatollah Montazeri, who stated that the perpetrators were performing their "Islamic duty." Any reasonable person noting the freewheeling support of the SAIRI in and by Iran over the years and the latter's "resolution" about the perpetrators in Kuwait (see below) cannot escape the impression that revolutionary Iran's behavior invites Western suspicion.

Witness, for example, the fanfare reaction in Tehran of the SAIRI to the Kuwaiti bombings. On 24 December, 1983, only twelve days after the bombings in Kuwait, SAIRI devotees staged a massive demonstration, carrying portraits of both Khomeini and the late Sayyid Muhammad Baqir al-Sadr. They were led by Hojatolislam al-Hakim and other Iraqi dissident clerics to the Kuwaiti embassy in Tehran. The resolution read in front of the "Iraqi *mujahidin*," who, the resolution said, "have the right to take their revenge on the United States because it is America which strengthens and supports Saddam and which sends military equipment to him day and night," demanded the "release of all arrested prisoners" and threatened that if this demand was not met, they would "not stand back and be witness to the oppression imposed on [their] nation."[12]

In the two years following the bombings it was amply demonstrated that the Shia dissident extremists would indeed "not stand back," and that they would resort to terrorist acts for "the release of all arrested prisoners." On 27 March, 1984 a Kuwaiti court sentenced the twenty-five accused men. Five were acquitted of being involved in the bombings, six (three of them tried in absentia) were sentenced to death, seven (four of them tried in absentia) were sentenced to life imprisonment, four were sentenced to fifteen years; one to ten years; and two to five years. If the emir of Kuwait ratified the sentences, the three who were sentenced to death and were in custody would be hanged.[13] Fully one year after the sentences had been handed down, they were not yet ratified. In the meantime, Shia demand for their release sparked terrorist acts, two of which should be mentioned briefly.

For six days in December 1984, a group of Shia hijackers demanded the release of their fellow Shias after hijacking a Kuwaiti airliner to Tehran. According to Iranian sources, the plane, which had 155 passengers and 11 crew on board for a flight from Dubai to Karachi, landed in Mehrabad airport on 4 December. Opposed to hijacking, the Iranians had sent up a fighter plane in order to stop the hijacked airliner from entering Iranian airspace. But then the airliner was permitted to land because its pilot told the Iranians that he was running out of fuel. The Iranian foreign minister condemned the hijacking and the killing of two Americans on board the plane. Finally, Iranian soldiers stormed the plane, captured the hijackers, and freed the remaining passengers on 9 December. Foreign Minister Ali Akbar Velayati said on the same day: "As we have repeatedly announced, we are violently opposed to such acts, under whatever name, or by any group or individual, because these are opposed to religious and humanitarian norms."[14] On 18 December, the Tehran public prosecutor, Hojatolislam Mir-Emadi, said that the hijackers would be "tried in accordance with the penal law of the Islamic Republic of Iran."[15] And on 29 December Iran's chief justice, Ayatollah Abdol-karim Musavi-Ardabili, said that hijacking was a crime punishable under Iranian laws, that the hijackers could receive a prison sentence ranging from three to fifteen years, and that "other criminal acts of the hijackers could result in additional time being meted out to them"[16]

In spite of this chorus of condemnation of the hijacking by Iranian officials, as well as the Iranian-negotiated release of most of the passengers and the military rescue of the others, and the Iranian promise that the hijackers would be tried and punished, the Western media almost universally suspected Iran of "some degree of complicity." For example, although the *Economist* (London) said that its own accounts did not necessarily prove that the Iranians were "in with" the hijackers from the beginning, it seemed likely that, at the very least, they found themselves tugged in two opposite directions: "On the one hand, they must have increasingly felt during the six days that the hijack was causing Iran harm. On the other, they presumably felt some fellow-Shia sympathy for the hijackers, and wanted to avoid alienating their Shia supporters around the Gulf."[17] Other observers who suspected Iran of complicity rather simplistically attributed the eventual "rescue" to international pressures. Indeed, the leaders of many Third World countries, including King Fahd of Saudi Arabia on behalf of the GCC, requested Iran to end the crisis peacefully.

What was completely overlooked by outside observers was the ongoing feud within the Iranian policymaking community between the "hawks" and the "doves," or between the *maktabi* and the *hojatti* tendencies, in the unfinished revolutionary process. The conservative tendency had increasingly asserted itself in Iranian domestic and foreign policy, as evidenced by the opposition to the nationalization of foreign trade, to the redistribution of large tracts of land, and to the top-priority status accorded the export of the "Islamic revolution" in Iranian foreign policy. Probably caught between these two opposite tendencies, the decision-making machinery slowed down until the differences were finally resolved in favor of storming the hijacked plane. This resolution was perfectly compatible with an increasingly pragmatic trend in Iran's foreign relations. It is dubbed by revolutionary leaders an "open-door" foreign policy.

In the second terrorist act, a group of Shia kidnappers threatened the lives of the Americans they held in Lebanon in February 1985. On the sixteenth of that month, a person who said he represented the Islamic Jihad telephoned a Western news agency in Beirut to say that one of the

American hostages had been sentenced to death. A month earlier, a similar anonymous caller had said that the Americans would be put on trial. Six Americans had been abducted within the previous year, but before 16 February, one television correspondent had escaped. The call prompted Secretary of State George P. Shultz to warn the Iranians through the Swiss government, which represented U.S. interests in Iran, that Iran would suffer consequences if Americans held in Lebanon were executed.[18] Neither the exact wording nor the date of the secretary's message was revealed, and the news of the message was only made public on 1 April.

On 25 March, however, Robert C. McFarlane, the president's national security adviser, explicitly linked Iran to the Shia extremists in Lebanon. He said that there was "sufficient evidence that radical Shiite terrorists are responsive to Iranian guidance for us to hold Tehran responsible for such attacks against the United States citizens, property, and interests."[19] He also said that the United States "should be prepared to direct a proportional military response against bona fide military targets in a state which directs terrorist actions against us." Reports from London said that the U.S. warship *Texas* was poised in the Persian Gulf to attack Iranian oil export installations if the American hostages were harmed.[20]

The day after the news of the secretary's message was made public, the Iranians reacted to the American threat. With an eye to the London report on the USS *Texas,* Prime Minister Hussein Musavi warned the United States on 2 April against precipitating another American hostage crisis with Muslim revolutionaries in the Middle East. He also said that Iran was committed to a policy of "reciprocal treatment," whether "the enemy is the United States or Iraq."[21] While threats and counterthreats between Tehran and Washington continued, the Shia extremists in Lebanon used yet another means of focusing attention on their demand for the release of the convicted Shia terrorists in Kuwait. The Shia captors allowed the reporters of the Kuwaiti daily newspaper *Al-Watan* to visit with four of the Americans. The Shia kidnappers told the Kuwaiti reporters that, before they freed the Americans, they wanted the "people jailed in Kuwait for the known bombings" to be released.[22]

THE SHIA UNREST IN BAHRAIN

Bahrain lies at a greater distance from Iran (and Iraq) than does Kuwait, but this is no source of comfort. The Sunni rulers of the island state confront a large Shia population. About 49 percent of the total population, and almost 72 percent of Bahraini citizens, are Shia Muslims. But the Shia challenge to the Al-Khalifah ruling family stems from far more serious sources than geographic proximity to Iran and demography. First, Bahrain is the only Gulf state whose sovereign independence has been historically challenged by the Shia state of Iran; second, the country has had an unhappy history of Shia unrest. In 1981 it was also the object of a coup plot.

The Iranian Revolution revived the ancient Iranian claim to Bahrain. The Shah's regime had unequivocally relinquished the claim, and the Iranian government was the first to recognize the independence of Bahrain. A leading Iranian clergyman, Ayatollah Sadeq Ruhani, announced in 1979 that he would lead a revolutionary movement for the "annexation" of Bahrain unless its rulers adopted "an Islamic form of government similar to the one established in Iran."[23] The threat was qualitatively quite different from the ancient Iranian claim. Before, Iran had claimed Bahrain on the ground that Iran had historically exercised an "uncontested sovereign right" over Bahrain. But the Ruhani claim was the first example of the revolutionary claim to religious primacy in the Gulf region.

The threat by this extremist cleric caused the Bazargan government in Iran considerable embarrassment. The moderate prime minister had been trying to maintain "equitable" relations with the superpowers and close ties with the neighboring Gulf states. He blamed Ruhani's "unauthorized" statement regarding Bahrain on the revolutionary and chaotic conditions in Iran at the time, which, he repeatedly complained, had a "thousand chiefs." Bahraini officials, however, would not let the matter go at that; they embarked on a feverish diplomatic exchange with other Arab leaders, who joined them in a chorus of sympathetic support. This collective diplomatic démarche paid off handsomely. Bazargan's ambassador to Riyadh, Muhammad Javad Razavi, declared: "We respect other nations' sovereignty and Iran has no claims or ambitions of any sort on any part of the Gulf," and Bazargan's deputy, Sadeq Tabataba'i, went to Bahrain to ease the mounting tensions between Tehran and Manama.[24] He assured leaders in Bahrain that Ruhani's statement did not represent the "official position" of the Iranian government. He also told the correspondent of the Kuwaiti newspaper *Al-Qabas* that the whole thing had been a "misunderstanding." No Iranian revolutionary leader has repeated the claim to Bahrain, and considering the revolutionary extremists' seizure of power in November 1979 and the resultant hardening of Iranian foreign policy, this Iranian restraint is significant. Even at the height of its ideological crusade, the revolutionary regime has not overlooked practical considerations.

Granted the ever-present potential threat of Iran, the basic reasons for the Bahraini rulers' sense of vulnerability are internal. Even the allegedly Iranian-supported coup plot should be viewed in the context of indigenous Bahraini Shia ferment. In Bahrain, as in other Gulf Arab nations, the unrest of the Shias is rooted at least partly in their relatively disadvantaged human conditions. But in all fairness, the Sunni rulers of Bahrain treat Shia citizens far better than the rulers in other Gulf countries do, despite the fact that Bahraini financial resources relative to the oil-rich states are quite limited.

The first major indigenous Shia unrest in Bahrain occurred in the wake of the Iranian Revolution in 1979. It apparently was not instigated by the Iranians, but was part and parcel of the year's general Islamic ferment, which spread throughout the area as far as Pakistan. The leader of the uprising, Muhammad 'Ali al-'Akri, was arrested and incarcerated.

The second major Shia unrest in Bahrain was not instigated by Iranians, either. It was triggered by the January 1980 arrest of the regionwide respected Shia religious leader Ayatollah Sayyid Muhammad Baqir al-Sadr in Iraq. It is widely believed that Saddam Hussein executed him and his sister, Bint al-Huda, in April. The ensuing Shia demonstrations in Bahrain were directed against the Iraqi embassy and bank in Manama, and not the Bahraini government. At the time, Bahraini police arrested a Shia leader named Jamil 'Ali, better known among Bahrainis as *Al-Thawr*. According to Shia sources, he was subsequently "beaten to death," but Bahraini authorities claimed that he "died in custody." Later that year, in November, during the *'Ashura* processions, Shia mourners carried a picture of the "mutilated body" of *Al-Thawr* bearing the inscription Martyred by the Pharaonic Regime.

In the following year, the coup plot sent shock waves throughout the Gulf Arab states, although it was essentially a quixotic affair. The facts of the clumsy affair are being still debated, but the event unfolded basically as follows. The Bahraini government announced on 13 December 1981 that it had arrested a group of "saboteurs," allegedly trained in Iran. Subsequently, the Bahraini interior minister charged that the group had planned to assassinate Bahraini officials; that it belonged to the Islamic Front for the Liberation of Bahrain, which is headquartered in Tehran, and that its "sixty" members were all Shia Muslim. The group in fact had seventy-three members, including sixty Bahrainis and eleven Saudis, as well as an Omani and a Kuwaiti national. No Iranians were involved, just as none were in the Kuwaiti bombings discussed earlier. In the 1981 incident, five unidentified armed men reportedly presented a written memorandum to the Bahraini embassy in Tehran in which they claimed responsibility for the group arrested in Bahrain. At the time, Bahrain asked Iran to recall its chargé d'affaires. After a long, drawn-out investigation and trial, the plotters were finally sentenced in May 1982; their jail sentences ranged from seven years to life imprisonment.

Further details have emerged over time. First, Arab officials seem absolutely convinced that the arrested Shia dissidents had been both trained and armed by Iran. Second, Saudi officials seem to have been closely involved in the process of investigation through consultation and the exchange of intelligence information. Third, Arab officials, and also media representatives, believe what the secretary-general of the GCC said in February 1980; "What happened in Bahrain was not directed against one part of this body [GCC] but against the whole body." Plainly put, in addition to the Bahrain government, other Arab governments, including the Saudi government, were the objects of the coup plot. Fourth, the plotters were apparently "trained" in Iran's holy city of Qom by Hojatolislam Hadi al-Modaressi, presumably an Iraqi Shia who carried a Bahraini passport; he could also be a *Da'wa* member. Fifth, and finally, the ploters got such "light sentences" either because Iran quietly "threatened revenge" if they were executed or because the Iran-supported Liberation Front for Bahrain threatened to "punish members of the Bahraini royal family if the court handed down death sentences."

The panicky reaction of GCC leaders to the coup plot at the diplomatic level has blurred the deeper meaning of the crisis. Grass-roots Bahraini Shias constituted the bulk of the plotters, and they, like most other Arab Shias who live in the economically depressed areas of their own societies, must have nurtured social, economic, and political grievances. Considering that even some educated and powerful Bahraini Shias in the government complain of their lot, this conjecture about the grievances of the plotters seems reasonable. According to my calculations, 30 percent of the members of the coup plot were disaffected young Arab students, and 17 percent were unemployed. This alone should indicate something about the nature of the deeper problem. But the response of a reliable Bahraini Shia to a question about the Shia view of the Bahraini government is even more revealing. He said:

> We don't say the ruler of Bahrain should be a Shia because the majority of the people [citizens] are, but we want to have more say in our government; the present Shia membership in the cabinet does not include important ministries; it is a kind of tokenism.
>
> We want freedom of the newspapers. We also want a parliament; you know we used to have one, but we don't have one now. On the whole, we want more participation.

An Islamic government could help all this. It could give our children more Islamic education.

Such grievances lie at the root of the fanciful perception of the Shia Arabs of the conditions in revolutionary Iran. The Iranian appeal feeds on indigenous frustrations. In answer to a question about his view of Iran, one Bahraini Shia enthusiastically offered the following account without ever suggesting that Bahrain should have an Iranian type of Islamic government:

The only Muslim country in the world that dares to successfully defy both the East and the West and maintain its independence is Iran.

The Iranian government is the only oil-rich government in the Arabian Gulf that distributes wealth among the people equitably.

It is only the wealthy in Iran who do not like Ayatollah Khomeini.

Who says freedom is squashed in Iran? Even Sunnis and Christians can talk and act freely!

Should Iran win the war against the 'Aflaqite regime in Iran, Bahraini Shia muslims, like all others, will be delighted.

The universal game of reward and punishment is also played in Bahrain as a strategy for dealing with Shia discontent. Given the facts that, unlike Iraq, it cannot fight Iran; unlike Saudi Arabia, it cannot create a military deterrence; and unlike Kuwait, it cannot scramble feverishly to strengthen its own military capability, Bahrain must continue to seek, as it has in the past, Saudi protection, and to strengthen its own defensive capability against external threats. But internally, Bahrain, like all other Gulf Arab states, has tried to improve the human conditions of its Shia citizens, in spite of its very limited financial resources. The pattern seen in other Gulf Arab states—of building new mosques, schools, houses, and other amenities and grooming Shia mullahs—is evident in Bahrain, as well.

More important, it is believed that Sheikh Isa bin Abdullah al-Khalifa, the ruler of Bahrain, receives Shia leaders during his *Majlis* meetings. Although this traditional avenue of dialogue between the ruler and the ruled seems to satisfy some Shias, many Shia intelligentsia consider it to be anachronistic in the modern age and demand the reopening of the suspended parliament. Unlike in Kuwait, the reopening of the parliament in Bahrain could pose a threat to the ruling family, who are Sunnis, whereas the majority of Bahraini citizens are Shias. The composition of any future parliament in Bahrain will have to reflect this critical fact if political power is to be retained by the Sunni ruling family.

The tightening of internal security in Bahrain also follows the pattern established elsewhere, particularly since the discovery of the coup plot. Bahraini authorities today consider the Shia Islamic Guidance Society (*Jam'iyyat al-Taw'iat al'Islami*) "an illegal political organization." The society was established "as early as 1972," although it "began its activities in 1976." Bahraini authorities charge that the society's Central and Ideological Committee (CIC) has "foreign links" and receives "its orders from foreign quarters," which are not named. The president of the society, Ibrahim Mansur Ibrahim, better known in Bahrain as Ibrahim al-Jufairi, was arrested in February 1984, eleven days after another member of the society, Muhammad Abdallah Muhammad Hussein, was arrested. This man reportedly "confessed to possessing pistols, ammunition, and a rocket-propelled grenade." Muhammad Hussein was arrested in the nearby village of Al-Markh, where he had hidden arms and ammunitions, perhaps left over from the clandestine preparations for the coup plot in 1981. Both men were to be jailed for fifteen years.

THE CHALLENGE OF INSTABILITY

Enough has been said in the first part of this book to extract four points. First, the cutting edge of Iran's challenge to the other states of the region is not its geostrategic advantage or its alleged superior ideological message, or a combination of these. Rather, Iran's strength is derived from the sociopolitical fragility of its neighbors, a fragility rooted not only in the festering Shia grievances but also in the overall inability of the ruling elites to meet the mounting demands of their people for a better standard of living and for social justice and political participation.

Second, just because most Middle Eastern rulers use Islamic symbols to try to legitimize their regimes, as do many political dissidents to protest their abysmal human conditions, this should not be construed to mean that Islam has replaced nationalism as the focus of identity. They coexist and compete.

Third, sociopolitical instability poses equal challenges to both revolutionary and conservative regimes and, hence, permeates such issues as war, peace, security, alignment, nonalignment, subversion, terrorism, and the threat of disruption of oil supplies, which will be analyzed in the context of the subjects covered in the next three parts of this book.

Fourth, the tension between sociopolitical change and continuity that underpins endemic political instability throughout the area constitutes the central feature of the Middle Eastern situation. Thus, the traditional American tendency to define stability largely in terms of preserving the status quo vis-à-vis the Soviet Union is outmoded and, hence, U.S. policy in the entire area requires new guidelines if it is to become more relevant to the realities of the Middle Eastern situation, as I shall suggest in the fifth and final part of this book.

Part Two

THE PERSIAN GULF

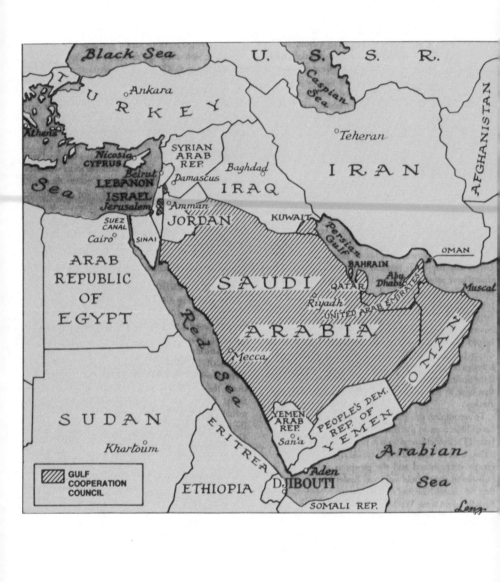

4

The Causes of the Iraq-Iran War:
Containment and Aggrandizement

The Iraq-Iran war began as Iraq's response to the perceived threat of the contagion of the Khomeini brand of Islamic fundamentalism. But it also reflected the ambition for power of Saddam Hussein. Contrary to conventional wisdom, his ambition was not whetted simply by the power vacuum in the Persian Gulf that emerged after the Shah's regime fell. The Iraqi sense of opportunity in the Gulf region coincided with the rise of Iraqi economic power. Iraq had replaced Iran as the Gulf's second-leading oil producer after Saudi Arabia. The emergence of Iraqi political power as a result of the demise of Egyptian power and influence in the Middle East after Egypt signed the peace treaty with Israel, and the rise of a new tide of hostility between Iraq and Syria in the "Eastern Front," also fueled Saddam Hussein's ambition.

BAZARGAN, KHOMEINI, AND SADDAM HUSSEIN

It is doubtful whether there would have been a war between Iraq and Iran at all if the nature of the Iranian Revolution had not changed drastically. For all practical purposes, the war may be said to have been prompted by Iran's "second revolution." Iraq's response to the revolutionary regime in Iran before the outbreak of the war in September 1980 can be broken down into two major phases. The first phase began when the revolutionary forces seized power, on 11 February 1979, and ended when the provisional government of Prime Minister Mehdi Bazargan fell, on 6 November 1979, two days after the takeover of the American embassy in Tehran. The second phase, which began in November 1979, ended at the start of the war, on 22 September 1980.

The eruption of the Iranian Revolution did not at first destroy the prerevolutionary rapprochement between Baghdad and Tehran which followed the signing of the Algiers agreement in 1975. In addition to other issues, the agreement settled the longstanding dispute between Iran and Iraq over the boundary in the border river, the Shatt al-Arab. The agreement essentially reflected a quid pro quo between the two countries. The Shah's regime would withdraw its support for the Kurdish insurgents fighting the Iraqi central government in return for the Iraqi acceptance of the *thalweq* as the boundary line in the river. Considering that hostilities between the two countries had nearly erupted into full-scale armed conflict in 1974, after years of border skirmishes, the agreement was hailed by the Arab states, the superpowers, and, of course, the parties themselves. After the settlement, relations between Baghdad and Tehran improved dramatically. Saddam Hussein and the Shah went so far as to consult each other on issues of mutual concern, including the problem of regional security in the entire Persian Gulf. In keeping with this overall rapprochement, Saddam Hussein acceded to the Shah's request that he expel Ayatollah Khomeini from Iraq, where he had been in refuge for fourteen years.

Against the backdrop of improved relations between the two countries, both Saddam Hussein and Mehdi Bazargan seemed disposed to continue good relations in spite of the Shah's fall. More important, the two leaders did not clash head-on ideologically. Bazargan's moderate Islamic modernism was a far cry from Khomeini's militant Islamic fundamentalism. Secular Ba'thists hardly felt threatened by the technocratic provisional government of Bazargan. Rather, they welcomed the National Front influence in the Bazargan government. For example, when the Bazargan government formally withdrew from the pro-Western Central Treaty Organization (CENTO), the Iraqi government took the opportunity to compliment the Iranian foreign minister and National Front leader, Karim Sanjabi, for Iran's "independent foreign policy" and to offer Iraqi support should Iran seek to join the Non-Alignment Movement (NAM).[1] To cite another example, President Ahmad Hassan al-Bakr personally sent a message to Khomeini on the occasion of the establishment of the Islamic Republic of Iran (1 April 1979) to offer his "best wishes for the friendly Iranian people" and to express his hope that "the new republic will offer more opportunities for the friendly Iranian people to enhance Iran's role in serving peace and justice, and [for] establishing the closest ties of friendship and neighbourhood with the Arab countries in general, and Iraq in particular."[2] In addition, as late as July-August 1979, Iraqi authorities extended an invitation to Bazargan to visit Iraq with the aim of improving bilateral relations between the two countries, and, according to then Foreign Minister Sa'a-doun Hammadi, Bazargan was receptive to the idea. "I should say for the record," Hammadi said subsequently, "that Mr. Bazargan was also cooperative and tried to strengthen relations between the two countries."[3]

The Iranian revolutionary process, however, began to take its toll on Iraq-Iran relations even before the fall of Bazargan. Tensions between Baghdad and Tehran began to increase partly because of chaotic revolutionary conditions. But the animosity of the Islamic militants toward the Ba'thist regime was a major factor. Armed pro-Khomeini factions roamed the country and, in defiance of the Bazargan government, assaulted the security forces of the provisional government, which sought to protect foreign interests, including Iraqi interests, in Iran. Most of all, the Revolutionary Guards took the law into their own hands and harassed and attacked Iraqi interests, including schools, consulates general, and other institutions in Tehran and particularly in the port city of Khorramshahr.

Yet, it was not until after the fall of the Bazargan government that relations between Tehran and Baghdad began to deteriorate seriously, and only beginning in April did their relations take a serious turn for the worse. In justifying their invasion, Iraqi authorities charged that Iran violated Iraqi air space 69 times and attacked Iraqi targets 103 times before the war. All of these incidents took place between April and September 1980. Iranian support of the Shias inside Iraq offers the best explanation for the sequence of events.

The principal event that touched off rapid deterioration of Iranian relations with Iraq coincided with the first anniversary of the establishment of the Islamic Republic of Iran. According to the Iraqi Foreign Ministry, "The most cruel terrorist act was the throwing of bombs at a huge student . . . gathering at al-Mustansiriyah University in Baghdad, . . . where an attempt was made to assassinate Mr. Tariq Aziz," a member of the Revolutionary Command Council and a deputy prime minister. An attempt was subsequently made on the life of the prospective minister of culture and information. These and other "terrorist acts" were all committed, according to Iraqi sources, by "Iranians" in Baghdad, where allegedly "some Iranian diplomats" also took part in throwing bombs at "innocent" people.[4]

The Iraqi Foreign Ministry attributes all these acts to a decision made by the *Da'wa* party leaders at Qom in Iran "to overthrow the Iraqi Government, through subversion, sabotage, and terrorism by the so-called Jondi el Imam', i.e., the Imam's soldiers." The reference to the Imam here is to Khomeini, under whose "auspices and with [whose] blessings" the meeting at Qom was allegedly held. A few days after the 1 April incident, Saddam Hussein characterized Khomeini as a "Shah dressed in religious garb" and reportedly also said that "Iranians should look for a change of Bani-Sadr and Khomeini the rotten."[5] Mutual recrimination followed. The Iraqis sought to link the *Da'wa* subversive acts to the Khomeini regime. For example, the *Baghdad Observer* managed to report an interview with a former member of the *Da'wa*, Abdul Hamid al-Mansouri. The report was intended to show that a close relationship existed between Ayatollah Muhammad Baqir al-Sadr and Ayatollah Khomeini and to link them both to *Da'wa*. Whether this report was valid or not, by the end of April 1980 the ideological and psychological warfare between Baghdad and Tehran was in full swing. The respected Iraqi religious leader and his sister were executed in the same month by the Hussein government. Years after this event, Shia communities everywhere in the Gulf remembered Saddam Hussein's brutal act.

The escalation of tensions and border skirmishes, like the psychological warfare, started in April. According to Arab diplomats in the Gulf, it was in that month also that Saddam Hussein began to prepare for the war that he finally began on 22 September. On that day, Iraq launched "air raids on at least 10 major Iranian military installations, thus widening the theater of operations in its conflict with Iran and expanding the border fighting between the two states into an undeclared war."[6] This statement is not from Iran; it is from an official American source.[7] By this time, an estimated 50,000 Iraqi troops, comprising a third of the country's total military strength, had been assembled along the border with Iran. By this time also, Saddam Hussein had abrogated the Algiers agreement (on 17 September 1980). The Iraqis, however, charged that Iran had started a "total war" (*harb al-shamilih*) by announcing general mobilization and closing Iranian airspace, "thus affirming [that the Iranians] have expanded the circumference of the military conflict and brought the situation to a total war."[8] This reasoning, of course, contradicts Arab diplomatic reports stating that Iraq had begun planning the border attacks about six months previously, when it mobilized 50,000 of its troops.[9]

How did Saddam Hussein explain the critical Iraqi decision to abrogate the Algiers agreement? In addressing an extraordinary session of the Iraqi National Assembly on this decision, he said:

Since the rulers of Iran have violated this agreement as of the beginning of their reign by blatantly and deliberately intervening in Iraq's domestic affairs by backing and financing, as did the Shah before them, the leaders of the mutiny [Kurdish leaders], which is backed by America and

Zionism, and by refusing to return the Iraqi territories, which we were compelled to liberate by force, I announce before you that we consider the 6 March 1975 agreement as abrogated from our side, also. The RCC has made a decision to this effect.

Thus, the legal relationship concerning Shatt al-Arab should return to what it was before 6 March 1975. This Shatt shall again be, as it has been throughout history, Iraqi and Arab in name and reality, with all rights of full sovereignty over it.[10]

In light of the preceding discussion, this explanation seems to constitute a rationalization of Saddam Hussein's grave decision to go to war. First, Iran's support of the Kurds who followed the Barazani sons was matched by Iraq's widely reported supply of arms and other support to the Arabic-speaking inhabitants of Khuzistan.[11] Second, and more important, the territorial issue that Iraqi authorities emphasized as a cause of war was neither new nor unresolved. The Iraqis themselves said that even before the revolutionary regime took power in Iran, the land the Iraqis claimed under the 1975 agreement had not been returned to them by the Shah, a fact that seemed not to have disturbed them for a year and a half after the Shah's departure, much less to have been cause for war.

Furthermore, Saddam Hussein said that Iraq had already recovered the territories it claimed "by force." In fact, his staff general, 'Adnan Khayrallah, had declared: "On 7 September, we began to regain the first area, called Zayn al-Qaws. On 10 September, we regained the second area, that of Sayf Sa'd." Khayrallah added: "I believe that on 12 or 13 September we regained five border posts which had been trespassed upon. *Thus we have regained all the land areas which have been trespassed upon by the Iranian side and have settled our dispute with Iran concerning the land differences.*"[12] If so, then how could the territorial claim be a valid basis for the abrogation of the Algiers agreement four days later? Further, how could it be a bona fide ground for the escalation of hostilities to a full-scale war ten days subsequent to the recovery of all the lands that Iraq had claimed?

Neither President Hussein nor his officials made a convincing case for the abrogation of the treaty or the invasion of Iran. There is no doubt that the Iraqis had been provoked, as, indeed had all the other Gulf Arab states. The Khomeini regime did pose a geostrategic, ideological, and socio-political threat to the Iraqis, but it is highly doubtful that the threat was sufficient cause for either the abrogation of the treaty or the launching of the war. Every Iraqi charge of treaty violation could be matched by a charge by the Iranians. Saddam Hussein may not have liked the

Algiers agreement he signed in 1975, but he had managed not to complain for years. In fact, although in his abrogation speech he explained the difficult "circumstances" under which he had signed the treaty, he never invoked those circumstances as a ground for annulling it. On the contrary, he said that the signing of the agreement had been "a courageous and serious decision" that had "saved Iraq from real dangers," dangers that were threatening "its unity, security and future." He added that the agreement had "helped the Iraqi revolution and the process of reconstruction and development."[13]

To avoid entering into a detailed legal discussion here, I would like to say, simply, that the Iraqi response—invasion—far exceeded the undeniable Iranian provocation. In the jargon of international law, the Iraqi action failed to pass the test of "proportionality." To argue the opposite, the Iraqi Foreign Ministry asserted that "its direct preventive strikes against military targets in Iran" were in accord with the well-known *Carolina* case, which prescribed "a necessity of self-defense, instant, overwhelming, leaving no choice of means and no moment of deliberations." Even if Iraqi actions were in accordance with the *Carolina* case during the first days of the war, the accordance became highly questionable as time wore on. U.S. President Jimmy Carter, who had been reluctant to speak up because of the hostage crisis, finally did. "We would like to see any invading forces withdrawn," he said, because (as he explained it) the Iraqi forces had surpassed the war goal set by Saddam Hussein himself.[14]

The central point of the preceding analysis is that the Iraqi legal rationalization sheds no light either on the root causes of the war or on the calculations that led the Iraqis to launch the war. Iraq, like other states, desires to justify its behavior in legal terms, but even a better case by Iraqi officials would have been inadequate as a basis for probing the deeper reasons, motives, and circumstances that underpinned the Iraq-Iran conflict. The Iraqi leaders' decision to resort to war to achieve their objectives would remain unexplained by legal reasoning, as well. To be sure, both root causes of the conflict between the two states and explanations for the Iraqi decision to go to war will be debated for years to come. But neither issue seems to have been subjected sufficiently to objective analysis. Oversimplifications abound, and the issues are far more complex than has been realized. Iran's threats and Iraq's ambitions are an integral part of the Iraq-Iran conflict.

IRAN'S THREATS

From the perspective of the Hussein regime, the security of Iraq had been threatened by revolutionary Iran. In the light of the previous discussion, there is little doubt that Iraq's fear was justified. As a virtually landlocked country, Iraq is at a tremendous geographic disadvantage vis-à-vis Iran. In fact, Iraq has more geographic liabilities than any other Gulf state. Historically, this has been the primary cause of Iraq's sense of insecurity, compelling all the state's leaders since the birth of modern Iraq after the disintegration of the Ottoman Empire to insist on the preservation of Iraqi interests in the Shatt al-Arab.

Since 1958, Iraqi revolutionaries have been as concerned about this geographic predicament of Iraq as was the Iraqi monarchy before them. In the wake of every change of regime in Iraq, Iraqi leaders have tried to assert control over the Shatt al-Arab and have been thwarted by Iran, sometimes by means of a demonstration of military force, as in the 1968–69 and the 1974–75 crises. The Algiers agreement, which ended the latter crisis, embodied, for the first time in the history of Iraq, the consent of its leaders to the principle of *thalweg* as the basis for drawing the boundary line in the Shatt al-Arab, a principle on which Iran had always insisted and which Iraq had always rejected. In return, however, Saddam Hussein got what he wanted above all: the survival of his regime in his fight against the Shah-supported Kurdish rebels. The civil war had cost the Hussein government dearly. Between March 1974 and March 1975, according to Hussein, the "Iraqi Army lost more than 16,000 casualties" and the total losses of civilians and military personnel "amounted to more than 60,000 between martyred and wounded." The Kurdish war had also cost the Ba'thist government 4 billion dollars. Above all, the Ba'thist government was threatened with Kurdish control of the oil-rich regions of Iraq, the economic backbone of the Hussein regime.

It is no wonder that the Algiers agreement and the related protocols included such elaborate provisions for the preservation of "security"—not merely the security of the Iraqi and Iranian states, but, mainly, the survival of the regimes. A major technical problem was the failure of the parties to establish safeguards and institutions to prevent future border clashes. Even more critically, they failed to devise mechanisms to preempt subversive acts, one of the principal security issues attended to in the Algiers agreement. Both the Shah and Saddam Hussein must have realized that the demarcation of boundary lines on land and the agreement on the *thalweg* line in the river were inadequate safeguards for the security of their respective regimes. The quid pro quo at the time seems to have satisfied both leaders' sense of regime security, but, as it turned out, neither citadel could withstand the onslaught of revolutionary change.

The challenge of revolutionary Iran no doubt intensified the ancient Iraqi sense of insecurity, but, more to the point, it threatened Saddam

Hussein's personal rule, the Ba'th party, and Ba'th ideology. Khomeini must have nursed a sense of personal resentment for having been expelled from his longtime exile in Najaf. But it is doubtful that anti-Khomeini feelings entered in a major way into Saddam Hussein's decision to go to war.

As seen from Baghdad, Khomeini's ideology was a basic threat to the Iraqi regime in two major ways. First, his religious conception of an Islamic world order and his commitment to the export of the Islamic revolution on the Iranian model were perceived to be inimical to the secularist, socialist, and Pan-Arab tenets of Ba'th ideology. Second, Khomeini's conception of security in the Persian Gulf, especially its unequivocal claim to Iranian political and religious superiority throughout the region, collided with the Ba'thist regime's conception of regional security. Although the Iraqi conception of security has historically centered on the protection of Iraqi interests in the Shatt al-Arab, the Pan-Arab tenet of the Ba'th ideology has also interjected the notion of Iraqi leadership of the "Arab Nation" in the entire Gulf region.

In reality, the Iraqi invasion aroused Iranian patriotic feelings against Iraq. The surge of nationalist sentiment gripped pro- and anti-Khomeini elements alike. But Khomeini expressed the Iranian rage in the only language he knew. He characterized Saddam Hussein as an "infidel" who "is corrupt, a perpetrator of corruption and a man who resembles the Shah." He told the Iranian people at the outset of the war that they

> should never have any fear of anything. You are fighting to protect Islam and he [Saddam Hussein] is fighting to destroy Islam. At the moment, Islam is completely confronted by blasphemy, and you should protect and support Islam. . . . Defense is something that is obligatory to all. Every person should defend Islam according to his ability. They [the Iraqi forces] have attacked Islam and we have to defend Islam. There is absolutely no question of peace or compromise and we shall never have any discussions with them. . . . Our weapon is faith, our armoury is Islam and with the weapons of faith and Islam we shall succeed and we will win.[15]

Regardless of how repugnant Khomeini's brand of Islamic fundamentalism was to Saddam Hussein, Hussein saw Iran's greatest threat to his regime in its sponsorship of Shia subversive acts. The Iraqis have never tired of citing the connections between the Khomeini regime and the *Da'wa* party as the principal source of Iranian provocation and the principal cause of war. His brutal execution of the Shia leader Ayatollah Muhammad Baqir al-Sadr and his sister illustrated the depth of Saddam Hussein's fear of the Iranian-inspired, if not -sponsored, Shia threat to his regime's stability. The Iranian provision of refuge for *Da'wa* members and sponsorship of the Supreme Assembly of the Islamic Revolution in Iraq during the war have been cited by the Iraqi regime as conclusive evidence of the prewar linkage between the *Da'wa* and the Khomeini regime which was centered in the holy city of Qom. In terms of this study, however, the conjunction of the ideological crusade of the Khomeini regime and the wider Shia revolution provided the foundation for the Iraqi perception of the Iranian threat, was a major cause of the war, and is one source of the war's durability.

IRAQ'S AMBITIONS

To suggest that Saddam Hussein launched the war in order to contain the threat of Khomeini's revolutionary fundamentalist Islam against the security of Iraq would be another oversimplification. The evidence at hand reveals other factors at work. In the dramatic downfall of the Shah, Saddam Hussein saw an extraordinary opportunity to project the emerging Iraqi power into the Persian Gulf. In the perceived power vacuum of the region, he suddenly saw an opportunity to realize the ancient Iraqi dream of gaining complete control of the Shatt al-Arab River. Had the Shah not forced his way on Hussein for years by making the ships traveling through the river fly the Iranian flag? Had the Shah not fueled the Kurdish war for years, sometimes with American, Israeli, and Turkish help? Had the Shah not appointed himself the "policeman" of the Persian Gulf region, with full British and American backing, for an entire decade?

Saddam Hussein was fanning the flames of resentment over the past but he was also aspiring to a great future for his regime and for Iraq, ideologically and politically. Ideologically, as heir to Michel Aflaq's Ba'thism, he placed "Arabism" at the center of his Pan-Arab, socialist, and secularist ideology. He lashed out at Khomeini's Islamic revolution and hailed the Arab revolution. Long before the war, for example, in an interview with a correspondent from *Al-Mostaqbal,* he boasted that the "Arab Revolution has the task of effecting a qualitative change in the society in all fields, to recover the glorious past of the Arabs in new concepts and in a new movement, and to place the Arab Nation in a position whereby it can defend itself, reconstruct itself and . . . achieve justice." He then cautioned that the "Islamic Revolution should be friendly to the Arab Revolution; any revolution that calls itself 'Islamic,' but contradicts the Arab Revolution would not be Islamic at all."[16]

In practice, Hussein has tried to show that he carries the burden of what he calls "Pan-Arab responsibility." Shortly before and after the start of the war he appointed himself the spokesman of the Arab Nation and made the return of the Gulf islands of Abu Musa and the two Tunbs to Arab possession one of the main objectives of his regime, an objective that he has since, presumably, relinquished. At that time he also appointed himself the spokesman of the Arabic-speaking Iranians of Khuzistan, or "Arabistan," in their demand for autonomy. Early in the war, in fact, he undertook to speak for all the minorities seeking autonomy in Iran, including the Baluchi tribesmen. And throughout the war he has claimed to fight on behalf of the Arab Nation, especially the Gulf Arab countries, which would face "catastrophic" consequences if Iraqi war efforts failed and the Iranians won the war. Just as Khomeini claims to fight "in the defense of Islam," Hussein fights "in the defense of the Arab Nation."

In addition to a self-appointed Pan-Arab role for Iraq in the Gulf region, Hussein's Ba'thism has two other characteristics. First, its "Arabism" is antithetical to Iranian nationalism, which Hussein repeatedly characterizes as both racist and imperialist. No wonder he terms his war the second battle of Qadisiyah, or "Saddam's Qadisiyah" (the first one was fought by the Arabs against the Persians in A.D. 637). In justifying the war, for example, he told the Iraqi people on 28 September 1980: "We had to unsheath the swords of 'Ali, Khalid, Sa'd and Al'Qa'qa' [Muslim leaders who fought the Romans and the Persians in early Islam] in order to strike this tyrannical clique and teach it a new historical lesson like that of the glorious Al-Qadisiyah battle which destroyed Khosrow's arrogance, raised the banners of Islam and eliminated infidelity, ignorance and aggression in the region. This was also done by our brave army in Zayn al-Qaus and Sayf Sa'd."[17]

Second, Hussein's Ba'thism challenges Khomeini's ideology on the ground of the superior Arab claim to Islam itself. This is neither a gimmick to appeal to the Iraqi Shias nor a claim contradictory to the central tenet of Ba'thism, that is, Arabism. It is a view that is fully compatible with the mainstream Arab cultural tradition, a tradition that has extolled the superior claim of the Arabs to Islam on the basis of the "Arabness" of the prophet Muhammad, the Arabic language of the Qur'an, and the location of Islam's principal holy sites in Arab lands. It is a Ba'thist claim that is inspired by the Arab preeminence in Islam as far back as the rule of the Umayyad dynasty. Saddam Hussein claims not only the Sunni Arab heroes, but the Shia first and third Imams, as well. He says: "We are the grandsons of 'Ali and Al-Husayn."[18]

Politically, it was not simply the fall of the Shah's regime that whetted the ambition of Saddam Hussein to fill the power vacuum in the Persian Gulf region; greater ambitions were also at work. The demise of

Pax Iranica coincided with two other major changes in the Middle Eastern balance of forces. First, the Hussein government felt particularly confident about Iraq's emergence as a great regional power. Politically, it believed itself to be more stable than ever: the Algiers agreement had effectively ended the debilitating, prolonged Kurdish war. Economically, it also felt stronger: by the start of the war, Iraq had emerged as a leading oil producer—in fact, as the second-largest Gulf oil producer after Saudi Arabia. Its foreign currency reserves were more than $31 billion when the war began.

Second, Egyptian leadership in the Arab world waned as a result of the signing of the Camp David Accords and the Egyptian-Israeli peace treaty, and Saddam Hussein perceived that the Arab world and even the Third World were beckoning for Iraqi leadership. Hussein believed that the Persian Gulf region could be the center of a wider bid for Iraqi power. He hosted an Arab summit meeting (November 1978) and an Arab foreign ministers conference (March 1979) in Baghdad with all the fanfare and prestige that would naturally accompany Iraq's emerging prominent role in the Arab Middle East. Having established his credentials with the Saudis through his effective mediatory role in the border war between North and South Yemen and through his condemnation—despite his longstanding close relations with Moscow—of the Soviet invasion of Afghanistan, Hussein saw his own star rising in the Arab world, particularly during the tumultuous March conference. The habitually cautious Saudis reluctantly went along, finally, with tough sanctions against Sadat's Egypt largely as a result of the hard line taken by Iraq. Even the radical PLO, Syria, and Libya seemed to follow Baghdad's new leadership. Saddam Hussein, who at that time was vice-president, haughtily told the conference members on 27 March 1979 that there was no longer any room for neutrality concerning Egypt, and that "anyone who collaborates with Sadat is a collaborator with the Zionist enemy."[19]

MOTIVES AND CONDITIONS

Thus, the causes of the war were more complex than is generally realized. The apologists for Iraq tend to reduce Iraqi motives to the preservation of Iraqi "security," while the apologists for Iran reduce Iraqi motives to the greed for power of Saddam Hussein. Monistic analysts are no less guilty of oversimplification. They tend to attribute the war to such single factors as a personality conflict between Khomeini and Saddam Hussein; the failure of the Shah to return to Iraq certain border areas as specified in the Algiers agreement; Saddam Hussein's resentment of the Shah's imposition of the agreement on him; the Sunni-Shia mutual antagonism; and the Arab-Iranian racial, or cultural, conflict.

In conclusion, four points need to be considered. First, the Iraq-Iran war was not an inevitable result of the eruption of the Iranian Revolution. Had the second revolution, against the Bazargan government, not occurred, there is every reason to believe that the two revolutionary regimes would have been able to settle their differences peacefully. But after the fall of Bazargan and the ascendancy of Khomeini's brand of Islamic fundamentalism, tensions began to rise dramatically. The second revolution drastically hardened the orientation of Iran's foreign policy; Khomeini's attitude toward Iraq was no exception. It is not surprising that the relations between the two countries began to deteriorate rapidly only after the fall of Bazargan.

Second, Iraq's own sociopolitical conditions made the Khomeini regime's ideological crusade appear even more ominous. Saddam Hussein feared that Khomeini's militant message might fall on the receptive ears of the restive Shia community in Iraq. Extremist elements within that community had, long before the Iranian Revolution, opposed the Ba'thist secular rule, and the *Da'wa* party on its own had advocated the establishment of an Islamic republic in Iraq after the Iraqi Revolution in 1958. Thus, the fateful events of April 1980, which led to the murder of the respected Shia leader and his sister, had precedents. They could not be blamed entirely on Iranian provocations. Regardless of how pervasive Khomeini's influence on it was, the Shia anti-Ba'thist movement provided fertile ground for Iranian propaganda. No wonder Saddam Hussein's war plan was set in motion when it was.

Third, it is doubtful that Saddam Hussein would have launched the war solely to contain the Iranian-inspired Shia upheaval in Iraq. His own ambitions got the best of him. He saw the rising economic power of Iraq in the Third World and beyond as a result of the country's position as the second-largest Gulf oil producer. He saw, at the same time, the growing political clout of Iraq in the Arab world and the Persian Gulf after the demise of Sadat's Egypt and the Shah's Iran. And, finally, he witnessed the revival of Iraqi-Syrian hostility with a vengeance in the wake of the collapse of a plan for an Iraqi-Syrian merger on the "Eastern Front" against Israel, allegedly because of a Syrian-instigated coup attempt against him (see chapter 12).

Fourth, and summarily, a complex combination of Saddam Hussein's need to contain the effects of the Iranian Revolution inside Iraq and his desire to project Iraq's power into the Gulf region and the Arab world joined with an extraordinary conjunction of circumstances in the entire

Middle East region to unleash the forces of war. The miscalculations that made war appear to be the best means to those ends contributed not only to the "causes" of the war, but also to its persistence. It is already the longest, the costliest, and the bloodiest war in the contemporary history of the Middle East.

5

Persistence of the Iraq-Iran War

Whatever the causes of the war, it has been the war's persistence that has wreaked havoc in the lives of the combatants and has kept the entire region of the Persian Gulf in a state of chaos. A feat like the Egyptian "Suez crossing" was not in Saddam Hussein's cards when he started the war. The Iraqi forces could not cross the Karun River. Such a feat has not been in Khomeini's cards, either, although the Iranian forces have acquired an important foothold in the Fao Peninsula. Military stalemate alone, however, cannot adequately explain the persistence of the war. To be sure, the mutual military incompetence of the combatants has contributed to the prolongation of the war. Iraq cannot end the war that it started, and Iran cannot impose peace on its own terms. But the persistence of the war also reflects the nature of the Iraqi war decision, the obduracy of the Iranians, and the aid of foreign powers to the war efforts of the belligerents.

IRAQ'S WAR DECISION

The Iraqi decision to go to war involved two sets of miscalculations which have contributed to the country's inability to end the war. One consisted of Iraq's miscalculations about its own war capacity. The other consisted of Iraq's miscalculations about the capacity of its adversary, Iran. The first set resulted from a geostrategic miscalculation, an initial miscalculation of forthcoming Soviet military aid, and uncertainty concerning the strength of Arab support.

Perhaps the most serious Iraqi miscalculation was of its own geostrategic conditions. Iraq grossly misperceived the disadvantage at which it would be placed in a war by virtue of being almost completely landlocked. Given Iraq's limited physical access to Gulf waters, its proximity to Iranian fire power, and its experience with Iran's ability to impose its will on Iraqi navigation, it is incomprehensible that Iraqi leaders did not foresee Iran's ability to cripple with impunity their oil exports to world markets through the Gulf at the outset of the war. To be fair, Iraq, like other nations, underestimated the strength of the Iranian armed forces after the fall of the Shah. Only years later were there assessments to the effect that, contrary to the general view, the Iranian armed forces had not "largely ceased to exist" or been "decimated."[1] Before the war, however, such assessments were unavailable.

Inaccurate prewar assessments, however, largely concerned the conditions of the Iranian army and air force, not the Iranian navy. It was widely known that the army and air force had been subjected to frequent purges and executions. The role of the relatively intact and rather powerful navy, therefore, must have been grossly underestimated. Nevertheless, Iraq's miscalculation about the extent of its own geostrategic vulnerability has probably cost Iraq more than any of its other miscalculations. Even a severely weakened Iran, one could have foreseen, would be able to jeopardize Iraqi seaborne oil exports. Iran crippled Iraq's oil exports early in the war, and once the Trans-Syrian pipeline was closed (10 April 1982), Iraqi oil exports were reduced from more than 3 million barrels a day to as few as 700,000 barrels. In 1984 Iraq was planning to diversify its outlets away from the Gulf by means of three new pipelines overland, one to the Mediterranean through Turkey, and two to the Red Sea, one through Jordan and the other through Saudi Arabia. If all goes as projected, by 1987 Iraq should be able to export 3 to 4 million barrels a day, but in the meantime, it will have to bear the enormous economic and strategic burden of its initial miscalculation.[2]

Iraq's second miscalculation about its own war capacity seems to center on a faulty assessment of Soviet willingness to provide whatever arms the Iraqis believed they needed for their war effort. Given the longstanding Soviet-Iraqi friendship treaty of 1972, and especially the less well known Moscow-Baghdad arms delivery agreement of December 1978, the Iraqis no doubt had expected to receive the arms necessary to wage their war against Iran. But from the very beginning it became evident that the Iraqis had overestimated the Soviets' willingness to supply arms on demand. To Iraq's great dismay, the Soviets adopted a posture of "neutrality" and proved reluctant to comply with the Iraqi request for arms.

Could Iraqi leaders have reasonably expected this Soviet reluctance? On the basis of two facts, well known to them before the war, yes. First, the Soviet attitude toward the Hussein regime before the war was far from cordial, partly because of Hussein's policies. He had tried to steer a nonaligned and pragmatic course as a means of asserting Iraqi leadership in both the Arab world and the Third World. Hussein's clampdown on communists in Iraq, his tilt toward Saudi Arabia and other conservative regimes, and his condemnation of the Soviet invasion of Afghanistan, among other factors, had irked Soviet leaders.

Second, it was common knowledge that Soviet leaders were trying their best to woo the Khomeini regime. Before the war, Iraqi leaders had seen ample evidence of Soviet attempts to please the Khomeini regime. Specifically, Iraqi leaders were well aware that as early as June 1980 the Iranian ambassador to the Soviet Union, Muhammad Mokri, was seeking a Soviet decision to halt, not just reduce, Soviet arms supplies to Iraq. The prewar Soviet foot-dragging on arms supplies to Iraq led to the reduction of Soviet arms to Iraq for a year and a half into the war.

The third, and final, ingredient of this set of Iraqi miscalculations was the uncertainty surrounding what Iraq could expect from its new Arab friends. Saddam Hussein may well have imagined that he could pull off a "Suez crossing" feat in Iranian Khuzistan: he would cross the Karun River into the oil refinery city of Abadan, and his new Arab friends would bow to his leadership. But the lack of Iraqi tactical skills prevented this. "Iraq consistently failed to concentrate its armor in the initial stages of the war and consistently lost the advantages of time and space," one observer noted.[3]

More important, there is no indication that prior to the war Iraq had been able to forge an Arab coalition even faintly resembling, for example, the Egyptian-Syrian axis before the 1973 October war. Although Saddam Hussein unfurled the banner of his Arab Charter as early as 8 February 1980, the Iraqi bid for leadership did not have many takers. This cautious, if not suspicious, Arab attitude toward Hussein's bid for leadership should have alerted Hussein to the limits of the Arab leaders' willingness to cooperate with him. Many factors appeared to favor his bid for leadership. These included the fall of the Shah; the disappointment of the conservative Gulf states in the Carter administration's perceived failure to "stand by the Shah"; the Soviet invasion of Afghanistan; the Iranian-inspired agitations in Kuwait and Bahrain; the seizure of the Great Mosque in Mecca; and the Shia uprising at Qatif, all in 1979. Although these factors resulted in an unprecedented flurry of diplomatic activity among the Gulf Arab states, there is no indication that any Gulf Arab state would commit itself to military cooperation with Iraq against Iran in advance of a war, despite the well-known concern of the Gulf Arab regimes with the threat of the Iranian Revolution.

That Baghdad and Riyadh discussed security issues, there can be no doubt. The Saudi interior minister hailed the "special agreements" for security cooperation between Saudi Arabia and Iraq as early as April 1979. But he said the agreements concerned civil defense, police, extradition, and similar security issues; there was no indication that the Saudis promised wartime support—or even logistical aid, which they later provided.[4] During the war, the Saudis quietly allowed light vehicles and arms to be transshipped through three Red Sea ports, Iraqi planes to land on Saudi airfields, and to fly through Saudi airspace to Oman.[5] But just because this and other Arab aid to Iraq took place after the war broke out, a prewar Arab commitment to aid Iraq cannot be inferred. Probably the Arab states were prompted to support Iraq by the course of the war, but even then, the Arab leaders who helped Iraq were not prepared to do so totally, even in the area of logistics. One indication of their cautious approach was their reaction to the opposition of the United States to greater Arab involvement in the war. The Saudis and the Omanis pulled in their horns when President Carter opposed any attack on Iran by Iraqi planes from Saudi or Omani airfields.[6]

The Iraqis also underestimated the ability of their adversary, a point that was implicit in the foregoing analysis. Iraqi leaders overestimated the implications of the Shah's fall for Iran's military and ideological prowess. Overconfident about the Iraqi capacity to take on Iran in a full-scale war, they magnified Iranian weaknesses.

Militarily, as mentioned, the Iraqis should have realized that the general assessment of the Iranian armed forces as having been "decimated" did not apply to the Iranian navy. But the size of Iran's military manpower, well known before the war, should alone have given Iraqi leaders pause. Iran's active army before the war was figured at 150,000 (Iraq's, 200,000); Iran's reservists numbered 400,000 (Iraq's, only 250,000); its air force numbered 70,000 (Iraq's, 28,000); and its navy numbered 20,000 (Iraq's, 4,250).[7] The crucial factor, of course, as the Iraqi armed forces belatedly discovered, was the sterling performance of the Iranian armed forces, for which two major explanations were subsequently offered. One emphasizes "the Iranians' ability to learn . . . on the anvil of battle."[8] The other view, held by U.S. Secretary of Defense Harold Brown and others, gives credit to American military equipment and training.[9] Another element that was well known before the war and was more significant than military hardware was the Islamic Revolutionary Guards Corps, which proved to be a formidable new aspect of Iranian military power. Even before the war the corps numbered more than 100,000 ideologically committed men.

Ideologically, the Iraqis grossly underestimated the Iranian capacity to resist their attacks in two ways: First, by exaggerating Iranian political and ethnic divisions, they failed to anticipate the Iranian patriotism that a conquest of Iranian soil would generate. The same Arabic-speaking Iranians on whom Saddam Hussein had counted to rise up against the central government did everything except flock to the banner of Saddam Hussein's "Arabism." (Khomeini made the same kind of mistake in July 1982, when he expected Iraqi Shias to rise up.) In retrospect, the Iraqi attack on Iran, perhaps more than any other single factor, gave the Khomeini regime a new lease on life.

Second, the Ba'thist leaders of Iraq underrated the force of Islam, mainly because of their secularist bias against "the forces of tradition." Iranian nationalists and other modernists had failed to appreciate adequately the hold of Islamic religious symbols on the Iranian masses, and now Ba'thist modernists viewed Khomeini and his followers with contempt. Perhaps Iranian modernists, nationalists and monarchists in exile filled the ears of Iraqi leaders with what they wished to hear about the internal divisions and weaknesses of the Khomeini regime. Shahpour Bakhtiar and others are believed to have done exactly that.

Finally, Iraqi leaders seem to have grossly misread the domestic Iranian political process. The Iraqis were quite right in believing that the Iranian government was gravely divided, but they failed to realize that the division was significantly reduced after the fall of Bazargan and the gradual consolidation of power by the militant forces. While it is true that the militant forces succeeded in monopolizing power largely after the fall of president Bani-Sadr (June 1981), they clearly had begun to amass power as early as almost a year before the start of the war. Iraq invaded Iran only after the usefulness of the hostage crisis to the Khomeini regime had almost disappeared, and thus, ironically, Iraqi leaders provided new strength to the very regime they wanted to destroy. The Khomeini forces were then able to use the war as a primary instrument of consolidation of control.

IRAN'S OBDURACY

Why has the war lasted as long as it has? Miscalculations by Iraqi leaders provide a partial explanation. The stance taken by Iran, however, is perhaps a more significant factor in the prolongation of the war. Iran has refused to negotiate a peace settlement with Iraq. Iran began to turn the tide of war against Iraq in September 1981, when it managed to halt the Iraqi siege of the vital oil refinery city of Abadan. More important, on 24 May 1982, Iran finally recovered the port city of Khorramshahr, the only major Iranian city Iraqi forces had succeeded in conquering between the start of the war on 22 September 1980 and that time. With its back against the wall, the Hussein government withdrew most Iraqi forces from Iranian territory by the end of June, but Iranian forces continued to fight and finally carried the war into Iraqi territory on 13 July 1982. Between then and July 1985 Iranian forces launched six major offensives, all purportedly intended to lead to "the final victory" (fath-i naha'i).

This "military stalemate" has been no source of comfort to Iraq. In fact, the reduced Iraqi oil exports resulting from the Iranian destruction of Iraqi oil terminals at the beginning of the war has threatened the Iraqi economy. Iraq's foreign currency reserves of $31 billion at the start of the war were reduced by more than 90 percent in less than four years. This fundamental Iraqi predicament lies behind Hussein's desperate, and often questionable, war strategy (which is discussed in chapter 14).

What is the "final victory" that Iran is seeking? Statements made by its leaders between the recapture of Khorramshahr and the initial fighting in Iraqi territory provide the best clue. Contrary to speculations at the time, there does not seem, at least in public, to have been any disagreement between the military high command and the leading clerics about taking the war into Iraqi territory. For example, Defense Minister Muhammad Salimi said on 6 July that "a push into Iraqi territory has become inevitable," and two days later Air Force Chief Colonel Monipoor called for an all-out offensive as "the only way" to ensure "final victory."[10]

Although Ayatollah Khomeini said that he wanted to "deliver the Iraqi nation from this accursed party," other Iranians revealed that the destruction of the Ba'th party was not the only Iranian objective in the drive toward final victory. Speaker of the Iranian parliament Hojato-lislam Hashemi-Rafsanjani said: "We will get the last bit of our rights and our greatest right is the toppling of Saddam."[11] Instead of calling for the overthrow of the Iraqi president, however, Foreign Minister Velayati said that one of the conditions for peace with Iraq would be "the convening of an international tribunal to try Saddam Husayn for his aggression against our people."[12] President Khamene'i also called for a trial. The difference between the two prescriptions for treating Saddam Hussein may well prove to be important in the future, but at this writing, "final victory" may mean the overthrow of Hussein or his trial or the destruction of the Ba'th party or the establishment of an Islamic republic in Iraq or any combination of these.

Against the backdrop of the ideological stance of the Khomeini regime and the preceding statements, it may too readily be concluded that the prolongation of the war reflects the transformation of the war from an armed conflict between Iraq and Iran to a "sacred mission." Students of international affairs know that such a stance makes a compromise solution between warring parties virtually impossible. While that much must be granted, the stubborn persistence of this war cannot be entirely explained by Khomeini's ideological crusade or by Saddam Hussein's resilience. In addition to the will to persist on their course, Iran and Iraq have had the means to do so; the acquisition of the means of war is another factor in the combatants' capacity to prolong the conflict.

That capacity reflects an extraordinary web of relationships that Iraq and Iran have spun throughout the war with a wide variety of nations. Rather than solely the arms component, these relationships encompass almost every aspect of the foreign relations of the two countries. The acquisition of foreign arms for the conduct of the war is clearly important, but the war effort of each combatant requires other forms of aid, as well. An indication of the nonmilitary as well as the military forms of foreign aid going to Iraq and Iran can be gleaned from the following discussions of sample relationships.

FOREIGN AID TO THE IRAQI WAR EFFORT

Iraq's war effort has been aided financially and logistically in part by regional friends. The principal paymasters of Iraq are well known; they are Saudi Arabia and Kuwait. Despite the reduced oil income of all OPEC producers in recent years (resulting largely from a major drop in demand for oil supplies), and not discounting occasional reports about Kuwaiti difficulties in contributing further to the Iraqi war chest, Arab "loans" to Iraq are estimated at about $35 billion so far. The Iranians contend the loans amount to more like $45 billion, while the Iraqis have complained in the past that they received less than $20 billion. Regardless of the exact amount, Arab money is obviously a major source of support for the Iraqi war effort. In addition, Iraq "borrows" 350,000 barrels of oil daily from Saudi Arabia and Kuwait to buy both arms and merchandise.

Saudi Arabia and Kuwait have also been two of the major providers of logistical support, although their activities are shrouded in secrecy. For example, early in the war the Saudis quietly made available three Red Sea ports for the transshipment of military equipment to Iraq, guns, and ammunition.[13] Subsequently it was revealed that these shipments included about one hundred Soviet-made T-54 and T-55 tanks from Eastern Europe. Washington officials, who confirmed the reports about the shipment of the tanks, believed that the tanks were insufficient to tilt the balance of military power in the war.

Kuwaiti, rather than Saudi, ports have been a wartime lifeline for Iraq. The Iranians, who have always maintained that the Gulf Arab states signed secret military agreements before the war, have managed to conduct several "accidental" raids on Kuwait. Twice in November 1980, once in June 1981, and again in October 1981, the Kuwaitis bore the brunt of Iranian attacks. The last one destroyed part of the Kuwaiti oil installation at Umm al-Aish, north of Kuwait City.[14] Some observers believe that the truck bombings in Kuwait in December 1983 were also part of the price the Kuwaitis have paid for continuing to aid Iraq logistically.

The importance of Saudi and Kuwaiti logistical aid to Iraq should not be exaggerated. Neither country is comfortable with its logistical support of the regime of Saddam Hussein, a regime that each country distrusts for its own reasons. Yet, in view of the perceived large threat posed by Iran, neither country can afford to bow out. Even with respect to Iran, the wartime policies of Kuwait and Saudi Arabia are not as straightforward as they may seem. The Saudis have tried cautiously to communicate to Iran, both by words and by action, the limits beyond which they would not tolerate an Iraqi defeat. For example, in October 1982, they called for "quick and serious" Arab aid to Baghdad. A radio broadcast also warned Iran that if the Iranian forces broke through the Iraqi line, they would face a war "with the whole Arab world"; never have the Saudis gone farther from the position of official neutrality.[15]

Of the nations outside the Gulf region, Jordan has supported Saddam Hussein's war effort most. King Hussein's wartime aid to Iraq has been motivated by a variety of considerations, including Hafiz Assad and King Hussein's deepening rift in the past over the Syrian suspicion that Jordan is offering covert assistance to the anti-Assad Moslem Brothers; King Hussein's own distaste for the Khomeini revolutionary government; King Hussein's moderate conservative affinity with the Gulf Arab monarchies; and last, but not least, generous Iraqi economic aid to the king's coffers.

King Hussein's open support of the Iraqi war effort has so far taken primarily two forms. First, the Jordanian port of Aqaba on the Red Sea has been made available to Iraq for seaborne transportation while Iraq-bound cargo ships have been unable to use Iraqi ports in the Gulf. For years now food, building materials, (possibly) military spare parts, and Soviet military equipment stockpiled in South Yemen and Ethiopia have been shipped to Iraq through Aqaba.[16] Iraqi transport planes have also occasionally been allowed to use Jordanian airfields. The Iranians claim that the Jordanian air base near the Iraqi border at Mafraq has been completely turned over to the Iraqis.[17] Second, since early 1982 Jordan has been recruiting other Arab as well as Jordanian volunteers for combat duties in Iraqi war fronts. Perhaps as many as three thousand Jordanian volunteers have been fighting alongside the Iraqi army.[18]

Egypt has also aided the Iraqi war effort. That Iraq has warmed up to Egypt is mainly a function of the war. Iraq must fuel the war machine by whatever means possible, and to this end, Saddam Hussein did an about-face after the war began. He turned to Egypt with no qualms after having condemned it not too long before for its "treason" in signing the Camp David Accords and the peace treaty with the "Zionist enemy."

The Egyptian desire to help out Saddam Hussein is a different matter. First, Sadat's death made it easier for Egypt to respond to Iraq's overture. Second, President Mubarak has been interested in returning Egypt to the Arab fold, and Egypt's aid to Iraq can endear Cairo not only to Iraq, but also to all Arab supporters of Baghdad. Third, and finally, Mubarak and Saddam Hussein share an antipathy toward the Khomeini regime and its brand of Islamic fundamentalism.

Egypt's support of the Iraqi war effort has been twofold. First, as a longtime recipient of Soviet arms, Egypt has been able to sell the Iraqis the kind of military equipment they can use. Egyptian arms sales to Iraq have included Russian-made equipment worth about $1 billion. Although publicly Egypt and Iraq did not strengthen their political, military, and commercial ties until July 1983, apparently "for years" the two countries had been in "covert and close relationship."[19] Second, Egypt has been extremely helpful to Iraq in supplying manpower, which the Iraqis have badly needed. Some 15,000 Egyptian "volunteers" have served in the Iraqi army, mostly in logistical jobs, but also as "combat troops."[20] No less important, some 1.5 million Egyptian workers in Iraq have helped Iraq cope with the war drain on its manpower for economic development. (As a matter of interest, Egypt's friend and neighbor the Sudan has bragged about aiding the Iraqi war effort; as early as 3 October 1982, the Sudanese government had announced a high-sounding decision to dispatch combat troops to the Iraqi battle front.[21] As of early 1986, however, no major Sudanese aid had been given.)

The Iraqi war effort also entangles the superpowers. The Soviet Union has been the principal supplier of Iraqi arms, especially since the spring of 1982. Hiding behind the facade of "neutrality" for opportunistic reasons, Moscow either reduced or halted supplies of large-scale arms to Iraq before then. On the day the war began, the Iraqi delegation, led by Foreign Minister Tariq 'Aziz, left Moscow empty-handed after having been rebuffed in its demand for Soviet arms.[22] The Iraqis tried all along to pressure the Soviets for arms, but to no avail. They continually invoked the friendship treaty of 1972 and the arms agreement of

December 1978. Once the tide of war clearly turned against Iraq with the Iranian offensive of March 1982 (*Fath al-Mubin*) and the decisive follow-up Iranian victory at Khorramshahr in May, Soviet arms supplies to Iraq were stepped up and continued afterward.

Although the Soviets resumed supplying to Iraq, Iraqi criticism of Soviet conduct continued at least into the fall of 1982. Then the Iraqis complained about the delivery of Soviet arms to Iran through Syria and Libya. For example, Foreign Minister Tariq' Aziz criticized Moscow for having permitted such a delivery—as evidenced, he contended, by the supply of sixty-two tanks, 130-millimeter guns, and AK-47 automatic rifles.[23] From the Iraqi perspective, this was one of the reasons compelling Saddam Hussein to complain that Iraqi-Soviet relations, which had prospered under the 1972 treaty before the war, had "not worked" during the war. Some observers reported that the Iraqis had gone so far as to hint at abrogating the treaty. Considering Iraq's arms needs, this hint must have been more in line with Iraqi pressure tactics against Moscow than anything else. Well into 1984, the Iraqis kept saying that they had obtained new weapons of "mass destruction" which would be used against Kharg Island and other Iranian targets. There were also reports that the Soviets had given the Iraqis SS12 surface-to-surface missiles with a range of 500 miles, but these reports could not be confirmed at the time.[24]

Despite the fact that Iraq is handicapped by a legacy of acrimonious relations with the United States, it has sought to do what it can to influence America in favor of the Iraqi war effort. From the Iraqi perspective, the strategy of wooing Washington has been a success. Baghdad has, above all, complained of the supply of American arms to Iran directly or through neutral countries, whereas the United States has repeatedly said that it does not provide arms to Iran or Iraq. The United States claims that it tries to discourage the sale of arms to the combatants by other arms suppliers, and points out that it cannot control the black market in arms. In addition to pressure tactics, the Iraqis have tried more positive tactics, including lobbying for their cause in Washington, dangling the prospects of "normalization" of Baghdad-Washington relations before American eyes, and propagating the theme of the importance of Iraq's success in the war not only to America's Arab friends in the Gulf region, but also to the industrial democracies. For example, Saddam Hussein claimed in November 1982 that Iraq had considered how best to resume relations with the United States, while at the same time his foreign minister, Tariq 'Aziz, was saying: "We all know that if Iraq falls, it will be a catastrophe for the Persian Gulf states. We are fighting on their behalf."[25]

The United States has finally "tilted" toward Iraq, but the tilt has been rather limited. The Reagan administration, to be sure, has said that it opposes the defeat of Iraq in the war.[26] It has also taken Iraq off the list of countries aiding terrorism and has allowed Boeing and Lockheed to sell airliners and (possibly) transport planes to Iraq.[27] It has also established diplomatic relations with Baghdad. But various factors militate against the establishment of a relationship. Iraq's implacable hostility toward Israel, and anti-Iraqi sentiment in congressional circles, are two factors, although these may change over time. The most important reason for keeping the tilt limited is the need to preserve the option of improving relations with Iran in the future.

Other Western nations have been generous in supporting the Iraqi war effort. France has been Iraq's biggest Western arms supplier. In addition to supplying a stream of tanks, artillery, missiles, and aircraft, it has furnished five Super Etendard aircraft, which arrived in Iraq in October 1983. These were apparently put to use for the first time in the spring of 1984 during the tanker war. Before acquiring these aircraft, the Iraqis had used helicopter-carried Exocet missiles against Iranian oil targets, but to no great effect, whereas their own oil exports through the Gulf had been crippled at the beginning of the war. There had been much talk about the devastating effect on shipping of the radar-evading Exocet missiles, which had been used successfully against British ships in the war in the Falkland Islands. But American officials suggested in June 1984 that the Iranians seemed to have "fooled" the Exocet missiles by building and launching a number of small floating structures designed to deflect Iraqi Exocet missiles.[28] The Iraqis, however, kept threatening to knock Iran out of the war by using new weapons of "mass destruction." In the meantime, Exocet missiles proved to be rather ineffective against oil tankers. They were also incapable of destroying the large Kharg oil terminal. So far, Iran has successfully defended the vital terminal by means of a formidable antiaircraft armory in and around the island.

FOREIGN ASSISTANCE TO THE IRANIAN WAR EFFORT

Iran has also tried to maintain its war-waging capability through an intricate web of relations with other nations. Severely handicapped by its need for American spare parts that it cannot obtain directly from the United States, Iran has reportedly developed relations with some forty countries not only for arms and spare parts, but also for capital goods and food. For various reasons, Iran refuses to divulge its sources of foreign aid. North Korea is believed to be its most important arms

supplier, but little specific information is available. Iran has only recently begun to break out of international isolation, which it entered into
during the hostage crisis. Iran's ruffled relations with major arms suppliers such as France are due to this and other factors. The fact that
France granted political asylum to the Iranian forces opposed to the
Khomeini regime has poisoned relations between Paris and Tehran for
years, while Paris has conducted brisk military and economic deals with
Baghdad.

Syria may be the single most important contributor to Iran's overall
war effort. Two major agreements marked the beginning of a formalized
Syrian-Iranian axis. Between 13 and 16 March 1982 the two countries
signed a ten-year economic agreement and a closely related oil "sale"
accord.[29] There was no official indication of how the Syrians would pay
for 9 million tons of Iranian oil each year, but this amount far exceeded
the amount the Syrians could barter for. Almost a year later, Western
sources divulged that Syria was receiving 20,000 barrels per day of
Iranian oil free, a further 10,000 barrels per day in a barter deal, and
100,000 barrels per day at the low price of $28 a barrel, when the official
price of OPEC oil had not yet been reduced from $34 to $29.[30] The
Iranian parliament has continued to approve the free oil delivery to
Syria. Is there a connection between this Iranian "generosity" and the
flow of arms to Iran from Syria?

Reportedly, Iranian Foreign Minister Velayati signed a "secret arms
accord" with his Syrian counterpart. There were also reports that, beginning in early April 1982, Syria sent several shiploads of heavy war
supplies to Iran from its northern ports of Tartus and Latakia. Later
reports said that several planeloads of lighter weapons arrived in Iran
from Syria. The weapons included 130-millimeter field artillery pieces,
ZSU-23 aircraft guns, and crates of ammunition and tank engines. The
Iranians were apparently eager to obtain the Soviet tank engines for the
many Soviet-made Iraqi tanks they had captured in the war. Although
Syria had been sending Soviet arms to Iran sporadically since the war
began, the shipments were accelerated after the secret agreement on
arms. It is no coincidence that Iran was able to turn the tide of the war
decisively against Iraq in May, when Iran captured the oil port city of
Khorramshahr. The deal with Syria must have helped to some extent.
The Syrian-Iranian axis has so far been held together primarily by the
common enmity of Hafiz Assad and Khomeini toward Saddam Hussein,
although ideological and political differences do divide Tehran and Damascus.

Another important facet of Syria's contribution to the Iranian war
effort is indirect. The Iranian geostrategic stranglehold over Iraqi oil

exports through the Gulf would have been much less ominous for Iraq had Assad not closed the Trans-Syrian pipeline. Only weeks after signing the Syrian-Iranian agreements in Tehran, the government in Damascus closed the Syrian border with Iraq, and more crucially on 10 April 1982, it also shut off the pipeline that until then had carried oil from pumping stations in northern Iraq to terminals on the Mediterranean. Iraq was left, as a result, with only the Trans-Turkey pipeline, which then had capacity of a mere 500,000 barrels a day. Theoretically, Saudi Arabia and Kuwait could use their annual financial aid (over $1 billion each) to Hafiz Assad to pressure him to allow the flow of Iraqi oil exports through the pipeline, but it is doubtful that this would work. The Syrian leader considers his current economic and political axis with the Khomeini regime to be more beneficial to Damascus than Arab aid.

Considering the blistering ideological and propagandist attack by revolutionary Iran against Israel, Iran's acquisition of Israeli arms surprised most observers. The Iranians, of course, vehemently denied the deal. The reports of the arms sale were "absolutely false," they said, intemperately calling both the United States and Israel "bloody liars."[31] Apparently there is a correlation between the embarrassment of being found out and the vehemence of the denial! The sale was "a symbolic supply," said Ariel Sharon, and was made through a third party.[32] American officials estimated the sale at about $27 million. It apparently included some 250 Israeli retread tires, other tires, spare parts for U.S.-made F-4 Phantom jets, and (possibly) some "munitions." The sensational news about the deal and the American-Israeli public controversy over whether the United States had or had not been told about it in advance certainly seem to have far surpassed its importance. The Israeli concern over the Jews in Iran must have been an important consideration. In addition, the Israeli view that Iraq is a major adversary of Israel in the Middle East (Israel destroyed an Iraqi nuclear reactor on 7 June 1981) and the traditional Israeli perception of the strategic importance of Iran must have influenced the Israelis' decision. It is possible that the deal never had the approval of high-level Iranian authorities. In the chaotic conditions of the time, the order for the purchase originated secretly in Isfahan rather than in Tehran. Furthermore, this sale was in all probability only a "one-shot deal." In 1984 the Israelis apparently declined to send any new arms shipments, directly or indirectly, to Iran.

Has the United States aided Iran's war effort? If Iran could deal with the "Zionist offspring" of America, why could it not do the same with the "Great Satan"? To Western observers the distinction between direct and indirect aid may appear unimportant, but to Iranian ideologues it is extremely important, because it makes room for ideological flexibility.

There is no doubt that Iranian authorities have behaved completely in keeping with their ideological tenets; they have not made any arms deals with the United States directly. As an indication, when the hostage negotiations with the United States were finally in progress, the Iranians did not press, according to Defense Secretary Harold Brown, for the five hundred and fifty million dollars worth of spare parts to which they are entitled, the Shah having already paid for them.[33]

There is no doubt, however, that Iranians have bought American arms and other military equipment on the black market. More recently, relatives of the Speaker of the parliament, Hashemi-Rafsanjani, were charged with illegally exporting millions of dollars worth of arms to Iran through Britain and Switzerland. One of the Hashemis pleaded guilty, and the other was indicted in New York (18 July 1984).[34] American officials maintain that American-supplied spare parts for U.S.-made civilian aircraft, vehicles, and oil field equipment "indirectly support the Iranian war effort."[35] Others have argued the U.S. exports to Iran (1983 exports were about double those of 1982) and U.S. purchases of about 30 million barrels of Iranian oil in 1983 (which are obtained through uncontrollable international markets) have necessarily redounded to Iran's advantage. Neither Iranian ideological purity nor American political purity ("neutrality" in the war) seems to have overcome the imperatives of necessity.

Finally, has the Soviet Union aided the Iranian war effort? The answer to this question lies in two matters apart from the frequently reported supply of Soviet-manufactured arms and other military equipment to Iran through Syria, Libya, and North Korea. One concerns direct Soviet arms supplies to Iran. The other pertains to Iranian pressure on the Soviet Union to cease supplying arms to Iraq. Too much has been made of a secret protocol signed between Tehran and Moscow in July 1981, which provided for technical military aid to Iran through the service of Soviet advisers in Iran as well as for the training of Iranians in the Soviet Union.[36] This agreement has not noticeably affected the Iranian war effort, which is our concern here. Whatever other effect it may have had has already been neutralized by the deteriorating relations between Tehran and Moscow, especially since the Soviets resumed supplying arms to Iraq in the spring of 1982. Furthermore, early in the war (when the Soviets had high hopes of wooing the Iranians) the Soviet ambassador in Tehran reportedly offered arms to Prime Minister Muhammad Ali Raja'i (5 October 1980). But, taking note of the prime minister's negative reaction, the Soviets quickly denied that they had ever made any such offer.

Instead of getting arms from the Soviets directly, the Iranians have concentrated on trying to pressure Moscow to stop supplying Iraq with arms. In fact, they were making such efforts as early as June 1980, months before the outbreak of the war. Shortly after the war began, the Iranian ambassador in Moscow said that he had asked the Soviets not simply to reduce the quantity of arms supplied to Iraq, but to "stop [supplying arms] altogether."[37] Even before the Soviets stepped up their arms supplies to Iraq in the spring of 1982, the Iranians nagged them about the issue, to Moscow's great annoyance. At one point, for example, the Soviet defense minister snapped back angrily in public: "It is not true that the Soviet Union is delivering arms and sending military advisers to Iraq." He called on Iran to stop making "unfounded accusations."[38]

THE "BORROWED CAPACITY"

Monistic theories about the war are equally inadequate regarding its persistence and its causes. Blaming the continuity of the war on Khomeini's "fanaticism" or on the "nature of his regime" means disregarding the influence of pragmatic interests in the Khomeini regime's foreign policy. As noted, Khomeini's ideological crusade has not prevented Iranian leaders from cuddling up to the "atheistic" Ba'thists of Syria or purchasing arms from the "Israeli enemy" or acquiring Soviet- and American-manufactured arms wherever they could. The Khomeini regime's persistence in waging the war reflects not only an ideological commitment, but also an assessment of Iran's capacity to continue to fight. Iranian leaders believe that the balance of power, if not that of military equipment, will ultimately swing in their favor.

That, of course, can prove to be a faulty assessment, for two principal reasons. First, foreign support for Iran's war effort, as for Iraq's, might diminish because of changes in the interests of Iran's wartime allies. For example, the Khomeini regime cannot indefinitely count on Syrian support. Iran and Iraq's capacity for fighting each other is essentially a fleeting one, because it is so heavily dependent on foreign support. It is what may be called a "borrowed capacity."

The second, and more critical, reason is that the all-important internal capacity of the combatants has definite limits. After five years of war, signs of the public's war weariness are mounting. Antiwar demonstrations are no longer a matter of foreign fabrication, as charged by the Iranians, but a reality. The death of nearly a quarter of a million people in the battlefields, severe economic and social dislocation, and massive physical destruction (amounting to more than five hundred billion dollars worth of damage), in addition to the physical and mental agony of enduring a revolutionary process for six years, have taken their toll. All the "borrowed capacity" in the world could easily be destroyed by a new internal explosion in Iran or, for that matter, in Iraq. Neither combatant is immune to such an occurrence. Therein lies the Iranian fear that might finally move Iran toward a negotiated peace—if an ingenious face-saving device can be found, either before or after Khomeini.

Therein also lies the principal threat to Iraqi staying power. Military pundits have characterized the armed conflict as the war of attrition, which neither combatant can win, and economic purists predict that the side that makes the most money from selling oil may win the war. Both schools of thought miss the central point. This war is essentially political in nature, because it involves the survival of the two regimes, especially that of Saddam Hussein. The Khomeini regime is waging what may be called a "nibbling war," designed to bring down the Iraqi regime by gnawing at Iraqi territory, as evidenced by the successful Iranian capture of parts of the Majnoon Islands in February 1984 and the oil port of Fao in February 1986. Combined with the Iranian-supported rebellion of the guerrillas of the Kurdish Democratic party, these effective forays into Iraqi territory in early 1986 called into question Iraq's stamina for the first time.

6

Containment by Conciliation: Saudi Arabia

Saudi Arabia's response to the challenge of revolutionary Iran has been containment. Like Iraq, Saudi Arabia has sought to contain the effects of the Iranian Revolution, but, in addition, Saudi Arabia has sought to contain the Iraq-Iran war. Saudi Arabia's response to the Iranian Revolution has been different from Iraq's in one other major respect: although Saudi Arabia has always wished to spread its protective wing over the Arabian Peninsula, it has not seen an opportunity in the Iranian Revolution for the aggrandizement of Saudi power in the Persian Gulf region, as revolutionary Iraq has.

No less important, Saudi Arabia's twofold containment response to revolutionary Iran has differed dramatically from Iraq's response in terms of preferred means. Iraq has chosen war as the instrument of its policy vis-à-vis Iran, whereas Saudi Arabia has opted for a strategy of conciliation and deterrence. Although each face of the Saudi response to the challenge of revolutionary Iran has in reality been indistinguishable from the other, for purposes of analytical clarity the two faces will be examined separately, conciliation in this chapter, and deterrence in the following chapter.

THE LEGACY OF ACCOMMODATION

In contrast to the legacy of acrimony between Iraq and Iran, relations between the House of Saud and the Pahlavi Shah were, on the whole, correct if not always cordial, partly because of Saudi accommodation. In the tumultuous decade between the British decision (January 1968) to withdraw forces from the Persian Gulf region by the end of 1971 and the outbreak of the first signal revolutionary uprising at Qom in Iran (January 1978), the two large states had managed to weather their differences. They settled peacefully such bilateral disputes as the controversy over the continental shelf and the ownership of the islands of Farsi and Arabi, and they did not let other disagreements poison their relations. King Faysal's disagreements with the Shah over Iran's claim to Bahrain (1968–69), over the Iranian occupation of the Gulf islands of Abu Musa and the two Tunbs (1971), and over the Shah's longstanding "discreet alliance" with Israel are among the better-known disagreements. But it is less well known that the two kingdoms also disagreed about the usefulness of Islam as a source of regional security. Contrary to the conventional wisdom that the Shah was simply jealous of Saudi leadership in the Muslim world, the truth is that the Shah did not believe that "Muslim solidarity" could be an effective means of achieving regional peace and security.

The two kingdoms' differences, however, were outweighed by mutual interests. As monarchies oriented toward the status quo, they opposed Soviet ambitions in the Middle East, whether the ambitions were pursued directly or through such perceived Soviet surrogates as South Yemen and Ethiopia. Considering the Iraqis pro-Soviet, Pan-Arab, socialist subversives, the Saudis and the Iranians did not trust them. As modernizing, pro-Western—especially pro-American—monarchies, however, Saudi Arabia and Iran both welcomed a "special relationship" with the United States. From the perspective of the United States, these two friendly states were the "twin pillars" of U.S. security policy in the Persian Gulf region.

This legacy of Saudi-Iranian accommodation was reflected in the way Saudi leaders reacted to the revolutionary developments in Iran before the revolutionary forces seized power. The House of Saud watched with intense concern the gathering revolutionary storm. Like most other states, however, Saudi Arabia seems to have underestimated the gravity of the Iranian revolutionary situation. For example, Prince Sultan praised the Shah, in an interview in August 1978, for doing a great deal for his country and people. He blamed "international communism" for the threat to stability in the region, and called on the Arab countries "to support the Shah in his struggle with his opponents in Iran."[1] The prince's interview reveals that he saw the Iranian upheaval in the light of the perceived gains by the Soviets and the Marxists in Afghanistan and, especially, South Yemen. Even a year later, Saudi leaders did not seem to comprehend fully Iranian revolutionary dynamics. Crown Prince Fahd, for example, said in an interview in January 1979, shortly before the Shah fled Iran, that Saudi Arabia supported "the rule of Shah Muhammad Reza Pahlavi, Emperor of Iran," because his rule was based on the Islamic law, "al-Sharia'h al-Qanuniyyah." He also hoped that the Iranians would end the crisis, a crisis that "is in the interest of the enemy [the Soviet Union?]." "This situation," he said, "does not create or help to create stability in the Middle East region."[2]

After the Shah left Iran, on 16 January 1979, Saudi leaders made no public statements on the Iranian situation. The Saudi press, however, continued to sound the basically optimistic pro-Shah theme. On 1 February 1979, the day Ayatollah Ruhollah Khomeini triumphantly arrived in Tehran, *Al-Riyadh* called for a dialogue between "the legitimacy represented by the Prime Minister Bakhtiar and the religious opposition leader Khomeini." In calling on the Iranians to reason together in order to avoid civil strife, the editorial considered the absence of the Shah, the return of Khomeini from exile, and the "continuity of legitimacy" to be factors that "might lead the way out of the vicious circle in which Iran lives today."[3] On 12 February 1979, the day after the revolutionary forces seized power, *Al-Riyadh* was still writing about the Iranian situation in terms of Bakhtiar, "who represents the legitimacy," and Khomeini, "who represents the opposition," without, apparently, having an inkling that the "legitimacy" of the Shah's rule was being challenged by the forces of the opposition.[4]

Saudi leaders welcomed the appointment of the provisional government under Prime Minister Mehdi Bazargan. Crown Prince Fahd immediately congratulated him, adding: "I am confident that the fraternal relations between our two countries, which are based on friendship and cooperation, will continue to serve our two countries and peoples and to serve our Islamic community."[5] This hopeful note was repeated by King Khalid on 2 April 1979, the day after the Islamic Republic of Iran was officially established. The king congratulated Khomeini and said that his proclamation of the event "echoed well throughout the Kingdom," adding that "it gives me great pleasure that the new republic is based on Islamic principles which are a powerful bulwark for Islam and Muslim peoples who aspire to prosperity, dignity, and well-being. I pray the Almighty to guide you to the forefront of those who strive for the upholding of Islam and Muslims, and I wish the Iranian people progress, prosperity, and stability."[6]

Prince Abdallah, like King Khalid, either did not realize that Khomeini's Islam was not quite the Islam the Saudis would prefer, or found it diplomatically practicable to play down the grave differences between the two brands of Islam. In an interview, the prince said that the new system in Iran removed "all obstacles" that had stood in the way of cooperation between Saudi Arabia and Iran, and that Saudi-Iranian relations would no longer be based on "material interest and political geography." Rather, said the prince, they would be based on "religious sources," and hence he was "very optimistic about the future of the relations" between the two countries. Prince Abdallah also said: "This is a new beginning because it [makes] Islam, and not arms or materialism, the regulator of cooperation and the source of dialogue." He ended his interview on Iran by saying: "The truth is that we are very relaxed toward the Iranian Islamic Republic."[7]

Whatever sense of optimism about the Iranian Revolution might have in fact existed among the members of the Saudi royal family began to evaporate quickly after the fall of the Bazargan government on 6 November 1979. The unhappiness of the al-Saud with the perceived failure of the United States to support the Shah during the revolutionary crisis was compounded by its fear of American military intervention in Iran in the wake of the hostage crisis. Prince Saud al-Faysal denied that his country was involved in mediation between Tehran and Washington over the hostage imbroglio, and he cautioned both sides to observe self-restraint in resolving the dispute.[8] Alarmed by the militancy of the Iranian action, however, the prince did not hesitate to state publicly his opposition to the seizure of the American embassy. He said that it was "contrary to Islamic principles and international law and conventions," although Saudi Arabia "supported Iran's sovereignty, territorial integrity and political independence."[9] This well-worn diplomatic language was intended to parry any accusations of collusion between Saudi Arabia and the United States. More in keeping with the low-key style of Saudi foreign policy, the Saudis were trying to maintain a dialogue with the new militant wielders of power in Tehran.

Regardless of their real concerns, in public the Saudi leaders scoffed at any suggestion that a similar revolutionary fate might be awaiting their kingdom. Crown Prince Fahd's view of the so-called contagion of the Iranian revolution was shared by all Saudi leaders. When asked about such a possibility, the prince wondered aloud on what basis such a question was "even asked." What similarities could possibly exist, he asked, between "the former ruling system in Iran and the ruling methods in Saudi Arabia?" The prince then pointed out that the situation in Saudi Arabia was quite different from that in Iran, where the revolutionaries called for "the rule to be based on Islamic principles." Islamic principles have been "the basis of rule in Saudi Arabia since" its foundation, according to the prince. Furthermore, relations between the people and the authority structure in Saudi Arabia are "harmonious, like a family," the Saudi government works to satisfy the "people's needs," and the king always "allows days in the week to see the *ulama* and the ordinary people."[10]

THE NATURE OF THE SAUDI-IRANIAN CONFLICT

Generally speaking, as seen from Riyadh, the fall of the Shah's regime presented both an opportunity and a threat. It presented an opportunity to increase Saudi influence in the smaller Gulf Arab states on the west coast of the Gulf, the states that abut the Arabian Peninsula. Essentially, there was nothing new about the Saudis' view of the pivotal importance of the peninsula to the kingdom or about the Saudis' protective attitude toward the nearby small sheikhdoms; these attitudes are as old as Saudi history. Even during the Shah's regime, although they got along rather well, the two countries clashed, especially when there was any sign of Iranian encroachment on the west coast of the Gulf. King Faysal, for example, opposed the Shah's claim to Bahrain in 1968–69, just as in 1979 King Khalid objected when Ayatollah Sadeq Ruhani, a militant cleric, wished to "annex" Bahrain to revolutionary Iran. The Saudi rulers' discovery that the 1981 coup plot in Bahrain was allegedly backed by Iran also caused problems between the two countries. The extension of Saudi peninsular influence beyond Bahrain, to the smaller states of the lower Gulf, interested Saudi Arabia as much during the Shah's regime as it has since the Iranian Revolution. In the Shah's days, King Faysal supported, from the beginning to the end, the formation of a federation that is now the United Arab Emirates, while the Shah at first opposed it on the basis of his claim to Bahrain. And although he dropped his opposition to the federation after the Bahrain settlement, the Shah soon thereafter landed his forces on the islands of Abu Musa and the two Tunbs—to the consternation of the Saudi rulers, who were just as protective then as they are now with respect to any extension of Iranian power to the west coast of the Gulf.

There is, of course, a vast difference between the opportunity Saudi leaders perceived and the opportunity Iraqi leaders perceived in the fall of the Shah. Saddam Hussein wanted Iraq to fill the power vacuum he saw in the entire Gulf region after the Shah's departure, partly to provide a base for Hussein's bid for leadership in the larger Arab world, a bid that contributed, as seen, to his decision to invade Iran. No such desire animated the Saudi leaders; they had neither the requisite motive nor the power to exert control in the region; their ends and means were limited. Their only desire was to maintain the status quo, at least on their side of the Gulf, in the face of the revolutionary shock waves emanating from Iran. In fact, the Saudi leaders' desire to draw closer to the smaller sheikhdoms stemmed from their need to protect themselves as well as their weak associates against not only Iran, but also the still-suspect Ba'thist revolutionary regime. They were concerned about Hussein's ambitions before the Iraq-Iran war. Even after the outbreak of the war in 1980, when the Saudis' concern with the threat of the spread of the war to their shores increased, the Saudi rulers continued, in private, to be wary of Iraqi adventurism. Sarcastically, one of the senior Saudi princes said about the Ba'thists in Iraq: "There is something novel about a regime that tries to introduce socialism through dynastic Takriti rule."

The essentially defensive posture of Saudi Arabia has continued over the years since the Iranian Revolution, despite the fact that both Saudi opportunity and Saudi capability have improved considerably. Egyptian isolation, which lasted for years after Egypt signed the Camp David Accords (1978) and the peace treaty with Israel (1979), on the one hand, and the preoccupation of Iraq and Iran with their inconclusive war, on the other, propelled Saudi Arabia into the forefront of Middle Eastern diplomacy. At the same time, Saudi air power surpassed the air power of both Iraq and Iran. Yet, in the face of severe Iranian provocation, Saudi rulers have maintained a policy of what may be called "conciliation without appeasement." While they have consistently sought to build a credible military deterrence, they have viewed military strength only as a complement to their patient and pragmatic diplomacy.

To the Saudi rulers, neither the unsettled revolutionary conditions in Iran nor the Iranian preoccupation with the war has been a source of comfort. On the contrary, both of these factors have tended to intensify the Saudis' concern. Despite the advent of the Khomeini regime, Saudi Arabia continues to regard Iran as an important buffer against Soviet threats to the region. Saudi leaders fear that the Soviets might exploit the essentially unstable revolutionary conditions in Iran and that destabilization in the region caused by the Iranians will ultimately redound to the interests of Moscow. Although they have aided Iraq in the war with Iran, the Saudis do not necessarily consider the Iranian preoccupation with the war a blessing. The advantages of seeing Iran's hands tied up in the war may be offset by the ever-present possibility that the escalation of hostilities will invite foreign intervention or lead to an Iranian victory. Neither of these eventualities is welcomed by the Saudis. Even an Iraqi victory would not necessarily be welcome. The deep Saudi distrust and longstanding suspicion of the Ba'thist revolutionaries persist unabated.

However, from the viewpoint of the Saudi leaders, the threat of revolutionary Iran to Saudi Arabia stems primarily from a complex combination of geostrategic, ideological, and sociopolitical conditions. Neither the putative power of the Iranian state nor Khomeini's hostile ideology poses a very formidable threat to the House of Saud. The Saudis have long been adept at the game of power politics at every level: tribal, national, regional, and global. In fact, Saudi power politics have at times been pragmatic to a fault. Saudi leaders have skillfully played the game of power politics with Iran both before and after the revolution. Khomeini's brand of Islamic fundamentalism cannot seriously challenge the Saudis, either. Saudi Arabia was founded partly on the basis of an Islamic ideological and political movement. In some ways, the Saudi movement was even more pristine and revolutionary for its time than Khomeini's is for his time. The real sources of the Iranian threat to Saudi Arabia are more complicated than these factors.

First, the Saudis consider their vital oil fields, terminals, and other facilities to be too exposed geographically to potential Iranian attacks. They are also concerned about the safety of their oil exports. The bulk of their oil shipments to world markets must still pass through the Iranian-dominated Strait of Hormuz. Second, the Saudis believe that the Islamic basis of the legitimacy of their state and rule has been challenged. Khomeini's Islamic world order prescribes the establishment of a new Gulf political order based on an intolerant conception of "true Islamic government," "true independence," and "true security" for all the Gulf states. Third, the Saudis recognize the threat of Iranian exploitation of the social, economic, and political grievances of their own Shia minority. This last aspect of the Iranian challenge is the cutting edge of the Iranian threat to all Gulf Arab states, including Saudi Arabia.

To formulate these multifaceted threats to the House of Saud in purely theoretical terms, two conflicting brands of Islam can be envisaged: the Saudi *muwahhidun* Islam versus the Iranian *mustaza'fin* Islam. The latter denotes Khomeini's revolutionary, populist, and chiliastic Islam, although the term *"mustaza'fin"* technically has a more limited meaning ("dispossessed"). The former describes the conservative, elitist, and pragmatic Saudi Islam. The term *"muwahhidun"* is a more authentic rendition of the Saudi brand of Islam than is the popular term *"wahhabism."* The juxtaposition of these two kinds of Islam includes the following principal elements: clericalism versus monarchism; populism versus elitism; regionalism versus peninsularism; Shiaism versus Sunniism; and anti-Westernism versus pro-Western nonalignmentism.

First, *muwahhidun* Islam began as a revolutionary force and became a conservative legitimizing formula for the House of Saud over time. The historical coalition between the religious reformer Muhammad ibn Abd al-Wahhab and the local ruler Muhammad ibn Sa'ud formed the basis of not only an Islamic state, but also an essentially royal political system. On the other hand, Khomeini's *mustaza'fin* Islam in its earliest form accepted the rather conservative concept of "limited monarchy" and became, over time, a radical antimonarchical and proclerical formula for the legitimacy of the *faqih*. Second, *muwahhidun* Islam is headed by the House of Saud and is endorsed by the conservative religious establishment, while *mustaza'fin* Islam claims, contrary to the reality of clerical elitism, that it embraces "all strata" of society. Third, *mustaza'fin* Islam claims not only political primacy, but also religious supremacy, throughout the Gulf region, while *muwahhidun* Islam confines its claim to political primacy on the Arabian Peninsula and its immediate vicinity. It also limits its claim of religious leadership to the guardianship of Islam's holiest sites, at Mecca and Medina on Saudi territory. Fourth, Shiaism, as the official ideology of the Iranian state, can threaten the Sunni rulers of Saudi Arabia principally because it inspires the discontented Shias to rebel against their perceived "oppressors." Fifth, *muwahhidun* Islam's "special relationship" with the United States is assailed by *mustaza'fin* Islam partly on the ground that the Saudi brand of Islam, in Ayatollah Montazeri's words, is a "superficial, empty and U.S.-style Islam."[11]

Although this theoretical formula may lead to a general understanding of the nature of the Saudi-Iranian conflict, it is not by any means a complete reflection of reality, as will be seen. In order to capture that reality more fully, the recurrent dispute between Iran and Saudi Arabia over the behavior of Iranian pilgrims on Saudi territory, which illustrates the difference between theory and practice in the relations of Iran and Saudi Arabia, will be examined next.

THE PILGRIMAGE DISPUTE

No single issue has been as persistent, and potentially as challenging to Saudi domestic and international legitimacy, as the Saudi-Iranian controversy over the pilgrimage of thousands of predominantly Shia Iranian pilgrims to Saudi Arabia. To the House of Saud, the hajj institution is vitally important. As the guardian of the holiest sites of Islam, at Mecca, where Islam was born as a religion and a state, and Medina, whence Islam spread to the rest of the world, the House of Saud is burdened by the security requirements and other responsibilities deriving from the pilgrimage to Saudi Arabia of some two million pilgrims from all over the world. In 1984 it appeared that the longtime Saudi-Iranian frictions over the basic philosophy of the hajj and logistical and political differences were subsiding. But philosophical, logistical, and political problems continued to cause concern among Saudi officials.

Within Khomeini's conception of Islamic world order, it may be recalled, export of the Islamic revolution is a "divine obligation." Providing an example of Iranian "Islamic behavior" and disseminating propaganda are among the preferred means of export, and therefore the annual Iranian pilgrimage provides a unique opportunity for propagating Khomeini's brand of Islamic fundamentalism. Khomeini is adamant about the importance of the pilgrimage to the Islamic revolution. In a message to the Iranian Hajj Congress in 1983, for example, he said: "The focus of this [Islamic] appeal and propaganda should be the eminent Mecca . . . something that was begun by Abraham and the prophet Muhammad and which will be followed up in the day of judgment by the hidden [Imam]." In the same message, he assailed the Saudi *ulama* as "mercenary clergy" and expressed the hope that the Saudi government would "ignore the temptations [offered] by these ungodly clergymen" and cooperate with the Iranian pilgrims, "who have no intention but to express their grievance against ruthless oppressors"—namely, the United States, the Soviet Union, Israel, and Iraq.[12] Also in 1983, Prime Minister Musavi told a group of Iranian pilgrims that they were "true ambassadors of the Islamic Revolution among Muslim nations" and that their "behavior play[ed] an important role in exporting the Islamic Revolution."[13]

The Saudis have opposed Khomeini's conception of the hajj. The best illustration of their view is to be found in a frank exchange of messages between the late King Khalid and Khomeini. The king complained to Khomeini on 10 October 1981 that the Iranian pilgrims "indulged in activities which not only were contrary to your aims but were also contrary to the aims of pilgrimage and the honor of holy places." He suggested that such activities "will damage Iran's credibility and prestige," and he expressed his hope that Khomeini would "issue orders to the Iranian pilgrims . . . to merely perform the pilgrimage ceremonies for which they have gone to the House of God." Khomeini, replying on the same day, vehemently rejected the king's suggestion that the pilgrimage was merely a religious ceremony and should not be mixed with politics. He not only questioned the king's account of the crisis events that precipitated the exchange between the two leaders, but also dogmatically stated the view that the hajj was a "religio-political ceremony," a ceremony that the Saudi government would do well to put to "political and Islamic use" so as to "have no need of America, AWACS planes, or other superpowers."[14]

The Saudi rulers have annually faced a serious dilemma over the hajj issue. They oppose political agitation by the Iranian pilgrims on their soil not only on the grounds of religious impropriety, but also for reasons of concern with internal security. That concern has two dimensions.

First, given the large numbers of Iranian pilgrims, their political agitation may play into the hands of other pilgrims from such radical regimes as Libya's. Second, the Saudis are wary of the effect firebrand Shia Iranians might have on their fellow Shia Muslims in Saudi Arabia. Any attempt on the part of Saudi authorities to curtail drastically the number of visas granted Iranian pilgrims would be turned by the Iranians into propaganda against the al-Saud. It could also neutralize the effects of Saudi efforts to redress social and economic grievances of the Shia community in the Eastern Province. Saudi authorities, therefore, have tried to walk a tightrope between allowing Iranian pilgrims to enter Saudi Arabia and preventing them from causing political agitation. Furthermore, they have patiently tried, albeit not always successfully, to regulate the pilgrims' behavior, sometimes by agreement with the Iranian officials before the arrival of the pilgrims on Saudi territory.

Tensions between the two countries, however, have surfaced as a result of various incidents over the years. For example, in September 1982, three demonstrations by Iranian pilgrims waving Khomeini posters took place in the cities of Jidda and Medina, despite the Khalid-Khomeini exchange of messages during the preceding year's crisis over similar Iranian activities. One of these demonstrations was broken up by the Saudi police, who reportedly arrested and deported 21 Iranians.[15] The demonstration was led by Hojatolislam Musavi Kho'ini, Khomeini's representative and the supervisor of Iranian pilgrims, the same cleric who had led the Iranian "students" in occupying the American embassy in Tehran. At least one source reported that Saudi authorities expelled 100 Iranians, including their leader, in the 1982 hajj incident.[16]

In some ways, the hajj crisis of 1983 seemed more serious than the crisis of the preceding year. Iranian authorities charged that the Saudis were biased against the Iranian pilgrims, and an Iranian delegation to Saudi Arabia protested against the alleged difficulties that the Saudis had created for the Iranian pilgrims in regard to securing lodging and visas. These complaints were followed by a chorus of critical statements from Iranian leaders. Speaker Hashemi-Rafsanjani warned the Saudi authorities against obstruction and said that they should note that the *Ka'bah* (house of God) belonged to "all Muslims," and that preventing 100,000 Iranian pilgrims from going on the hajj pilgrimage would precipitate "very grave repercussions."[17] Prime Minister Musavi hit the Saudis where it hurts them most, namely, in the guardianship of the holy sites. He averred: "Basically, Mecca and Medina must not be governed by such a regime but must be governed under supervision of forces belonging to all Muslim nations."[18] Khomeini would not lag behind his disciples in such a controversy. With unusual forcefulness, he reiterated his doctrinal view of the nature of the hajj, which he had first expressed to King Khalid two years earlier:

> Those palace-appointed preachers in the region and elsewhere who say that hajj should be separated from its political content are denouncing the prophet of God, the Islamic Khulafa [Caliphs] and God's saints. They do not realize that hajj is for that purpose, for Muslims to understand and solve one another's problems. Islam's political aspects are several times greater than its aspects relating to the act of worship, for political aspects are related to acts of worship. . . . The fundamental aspect of the hajj philosophy lies in its political dimension. Criminal hands from all corners of the globe are busy attacking this aspect.[19]

In keeping with their cautious attitude, Saudi officials were tight-lipped about their difficulties with Iranian political demonstrations in 1983, despite Iranian provocations. The Iranians charged Saudi officials with "harassment," "detention," and even "injury." They complained that a number of Iranian pilgrims had been physically assaulted by the Saudi security police. Hojatolislam Kho'ini vehemently denounced the "savage onslaught" by the Saudi police on the Iranian pilgrims. He hailed the large number of non-Iranian as well as Iranian pilgrims who participated in the demonstrations, and he asserted that the huge Mecca march showed that the "Islamic force" was in the process of growing, proving "the fact that 1,000 million Muslims are gradually waking up and are going to impose the truth of their main objectives."[20]

SIGNS OF A THAW

Unlike all previous hajj seasons since the Iranian Revolution, the 1984 hajj got off to a good start. By this time Saudi-Iranian tensions had passed their peak of June 1984, when Saudi planes shot down an Iranian jet fighter at the height of the tanker war. Saudi authorities agreed to allow the largest-ever number of pilgrims from Iran to enter Saudi Arabia. In 1982, for example, they allowed 85,000, and in 1983, 100,000, but in 1984, they allowed 150,000.

This conciliatory gesture was reciprocated by Iran. Considering Prime Minister Musavi's criticism of the Saudi guardianship of the holy cities in Mecca and Medina in 1983, the remarks of Speaker Hashemi-Rafsanjani in 1984 must have been music to Saudi ears. On 10 July 1984 he categorically stated: "We have no intention of controlling Ka'ba and Mecca. Ka'ba and Mecca are located in your country, so that the people can realize the goals of the Koran and their great holinesses Ebrahim and Isma'il, at Ka'ba. But if you are not capable, then invite scholars and ulema of other Islamic countries to assist you in your planning."[21]

These earliest mutual gestures of conciliation on the hajj issue reflected the beginnings of a slowly emerging thaw in tensions between Tehran and Riyadh for the first time since the Iranian Revolution. On 14 July 1984 the Iranian supervisor of the pilgrimage organization conveyed to Speaker Hashemi-Rafsanjani the invitation of Saudi officials for him to visit Saudi Arabia on a pilgrimage to Mecca. The Speaker reportedly said, "Such approaches can be useful for bilateral relations."[22] The Kuwaiti newspaper *Al-Watan* hailed the news and interpreted it to mean that "the dialogue is still going on, contacts are continuing, and that there is some hope of finding a way to end the Iraqi-Iran war."

The first clear sign of a breakthrough in Saudi-Iranian relations occurred on 18 May 1985, when Saudi Foreign Minister Prince Saud visited Iran, becoming the first Saudi minister to visit Iran after the Iranian Revolution.[23] The visit was in response to an invitation by Iran's foreign minister, Ali Akbar Velayati, with whom Prince Saud held two major discussions; in addition, the prince met with Iranian President Khamene'i, Prime Minister Musavi, and Speaker Hashemi-Rafsanjani during his two-day official visit to Tehran.

Foreign Minister Saud's visit to Iran startled the world. What prompted it? It is difficult to say at this writing, because of both its recency and the secrecy surrounding it, but the existing evidence leads to speculations. On the one hand, the visit may reflect the GCC's initiative of two months earlier, when its Ministerial Council announced that the organization would "intensify endeavors to put an end to this devastating war, including sending a delegation to Tehran and to Baghdad to discuss without any delay the quickest way to stop the war."[24] On the other hand, it may reflect an Iranian initiative: Iranian Foreign Minister Velayati issued the invitation to Prince Saud. But in the light of this study, the possibility that both GCC and Iranian initiatives in turn reflected the convergence of two previous developments seems likely. First, the tension between Iran and Saudi Arabia had eased as early as July 1984. Second, the Iranian position began to soften somewhat because of the clear signs of antiwar sentiment in Iran after the so-called war of cities and the failure of yet another Iranian land offensive in March 1985.

Regardless of what precipitated the visit, the visit was significant for what it symbolized. In addition, the six themes that surfaced in Prince Saud's meetings with the four principal Iranian leaders were revealing. Considering that Iran had been more confrontational than Saudi Arabia since Iran's second revolution in November 1979, President Khamene'i's clear call for coexistence between the two great Gulf powers was unprecedented. He reportedly told Prince Saud on 19 May that "the Islamic Republic offers a friendly hand to all her neighbours as well as all the Muslims throughout the world and proposes to coexist with them in a spirit of unity and friendship."[25] The other themes were the Iraq-Iran war, Israel, the United States, regional problems, and Islam. The two countries' desire to stress mutual interests in improving bilateral relations and protecting regional peace and security was apparent.

Regarding the main objective of the visit, however, Iranian leaders seemed as immovable as ever. Their principal condition for peace remained the same. For example, Speaker Hashemi-Rafsanjani said: "About the war, as we have said, before the punishment of the [Iraqi] Ba'th Party which is responsible for this war and before the fulfillment of the legitimate rights of the Iranian people no other alternative would be acceptable by us."[26] If, as some reports indicated, Prince Saud had timed his visit to Iran to coincide with the beginning of the holy month of *Ramadan* in the hope of persuading the Iranians to cease armed hostilities during that month, then the visit failed to achieve its purpose. But whether or not this was the visit's intended purpose, Prince Saud found the visit "useful." In his own words, the visit was a "precious opportunity" for the exchange of views with the Iranian foreign minister. He added, "I can state that my talks with them all were frank, clear, serious and, I hope, constructive." In addition to explaining to the Iranian leaders "the immutable principles" on which Saudi Arabia's foreign policy had been based from the inception of the kingdom, the prince also "discussed with the Iranian officials the critical and sensitive conditions in the region, especially the destructive Iraq-Iran war, Iranian-GCC relations, and Iranian-Saudi relations." He expressed his hope that the talks on these issues would "open the way for building new relations based on understanding, good-neighborliness, and work in the interest of the region and in the interest of security, progress, and stability of its people."[27]

There have been indications that this visit will not be an isolated event. Prince Saud invited Foreign Minister Velayati to visit Saudi Arabia in the future, and the Iranian minister accepted. Furthermore, Velayati seemed to share the hope that "the continuation of these visits between the two countries would give suitable and practical results in the future."[28] Saudi and Iranian hopes concerning the future were echoed in the newspapers of both countries but were best expressed by *Al-Rayah,* which said: "The visit to Tehran will open a new door for peace to the region and to end this war which has lasted long, . . . it will be a beginning for peace negotiations between Iraq and Iran, and [it will] end a long period of estrangement because of the war."[29]

Hopes soared again when Foreign Minister Velayati visited Saudi Arabia on 7 December 1985. The official Saudi radio station reportedly said that Saudi Arabia was making progress in its efforts to end the Iraq-Iran war and insure good relations between Iran and its Arab neighbors in the Gulf. There was also speculation that Prince Saud was trying to secure assurances from Iran that it would not begin a new offensive against Iraq.[30] The GCC's conciliatory stance on the war—as revealed at the end of its sixth summit meeting in Muscat on 6 November—and Iran's overwhelmingly positive acknowledgment of the perceived change in the GCC attitude toward the war significantly improved the diplomatic connection between Tehran and Riyadh. Only days before Foreign Minister Velayati visited Saudi Arabia, President Khamene'i expressed again the Iranian leadership's pleasure with the GCC stance. He said that "the member-countries of the Persian Gulf Cooperation Council also changed their stance toward the Islamic Republic of Iran. We welcome this stance by the member-countries of the Persian Gulf Cooperation Council and wish their statements to be translated from words into deeds and cooperation!"[31]

Velayati's visit to Saudi Arabia was no more successful in ending the war than Saud's visit to Iran in May 1985 had been, but the fact that these visits were taking place at all—for the first time since the Iranian Revolution in 1979—is important. For the Saudis, to be sure, the first priority was to persuade the Iranians to negotiate a peace settlement with Iraq, but Prince Saud was under no illusion that the Iranian position had changed since his visit to Iran—or that it would. Saud was quoted by sources in Riyadh as saying: "We really did not sense any development in the Iranian position that would imply a positive move toward ending the Iraq-Iran war."[32] Nevertheless, according to Saudi sources, "the door of hope for the hoped-for progress in the Iranian position on the conflict with Iraq remains open to efforts to end this conflict by a peaceful solution."[33]

As important as keeping the hope for a peaceful settlement alive was the ability of the two sides to agree on the need for improving bilateral relations and following up these visits with greater efforts for dialogue in the future. The Iranian chargé d'affaires in Saudi Arabia, Muhammad Hoseyn Tarmi, called the visit of Velayati to the kingdom "a turning point on the road of developing and reinforcing relations between the two countries."[34] According to Foreign Minister Velayati, he and Prince

Saud discussed "an expansion of relations in the political, economic, trade, and cultural fields. . . . It also was agreed that further trips should take place in both directions."

Of even greater importance for the future was the emphasis both sides placed on the principle of regional security by regional powers. According to Velayati, both sides agreed that "foreign powers should not be allowed to have a presence in the region under any circumstances or for whatever reasons."[35] If it is true that Saudi Arabia has told the United States that it will allow American military forces to use its bases in case of Soviet "aggression" or if Saudi Arabia is unable to handle a Persian Gulf crisis on its own,[36] then Velayati's sweeping interpretation of Saudi Arabia's agreement with Iran against any foreign presence is a potential source of discord. But, despite the report about this confidential U.S.-Saudi understanding, the Saudis continue to refuse to allow the United States to engage in joint planning for such contingencies and will in all probability rely solely, if possible, on their own military deterrence, at least as far as the spillover of the Iraq-Iran war is concerned. This brings us to a consideration of the other face of the Saudi containment policy.

7

Containment by Disapprobation and Deterrence: Saudi Arabia

The Iraq-Iran war has caused more tension in the relations between Saudi Arabia and Iran than any other single issue. Even the recurrent hajj dispute and the continued Saudi-Iranian conflict over oil price and production issues, separately or together, have not caused as much concern in Riyadh. Nor has any other issue contributed as much to the determination and efforts of Saudi Arabia to build up its military deterrence. To be sure, Saudi leaders perceive the Soviet Union and its proxies and Iran, Iraq, and Israel as potential threats to their security. But the threat of the spillover of the war to the territory of Saudi Arabia and its GCC partners has been mainly responsible for the intensification of the longtime Saudi resolve to create a credible military deterrence based on the strength of the Saudi Royal Air Force.

Only once in five years of war has Saudi Arabia tried to demonstrate its military might to Iran, and it did so only after being seriously provoked. Even then, the Saudis acted with the utmost restraint. In coping with the Iranian challenge, Saudi Arabia has, on balance, accorded conciliation the highest priority, and when that approach has failed, it has used diplomatic disapprobation. Military force has been reserved for use in the case of a direct encroachment on the security of Saudi Arabia itself.

DIPLOMATIC DISAPPROBATION

During the first five years of the Iraq-Iran war, the Saudi response went through five major phases. The first started with the outbreak of the war in September 1980 and lasted until September 1981, when for

101

the first time the tide of war began to turn against Iraq as a result of Iran's success in lifting the year-long Iraqi siege of the oil refinery city of Abadan. Despite its prewar rapprochement with Iraq, especially after the Camp David Accords and the Egyptian-Israeli peace treaty, Saudi Arabia declared official neutrality in the war. Prior to the outbreak of the war, Saudi Arabia had allowed some Iraqi planes to land on its airfields and had permitted others to fly through its airspace to Oman.[1] Four days after the start of the war, Admiral Turner, director of the CIA, sent a message to U.S. National Security Adviser Brzezinski to the effect that "Saudi officials feared an imminent attack on Saudi oil fields by Iranian fighters."[2] At President Carter's suggestion, Riyadh and Muscat requested that Iraq withdraw its planes from both Saudi and Omani airfields. The Iranians had warned that they would retaliate against any country aiding Iraq, and the U.S. president did not wish to see the war spread as a result of these countries' involvement.

Saudi concern about Iran during the first phase was evident, but Riyadh was no less wary of a successful Iraqi offensive. Only a few months after the war began, it became clear that the old mistrust of Ba'thist Iraq was very much alive. Should Saddam Hussein succeed in his bold armed adventure against Iran, the Saudis feared at the time, he might be emboldened and return with a vengeance to his previous subversive acts in the Gulf monarchies. The long-term attitude of the Saudis toward the warring countries was this: "A plague on both your houses." Nevertheless, there was little doubt that it was the Iranian threat that concerned the Saudis most.

It is no wonder that the final push for the creation of the Gulf Cooperation Council came at this time. Reluctant to include Iraq in the organization, the GCC founding members appeared to be excluding both belligerents from the nascent body because they were fighting each other. During this earliest phase of the conflict, the GCC relied primarily on the Islamic Conference Organization and other third parties to seek an end to the war.

Saudi concern over the threat of the spread of the war soared during the second phase, September 1981 to August 1982. Along with the success of the Iranian forces at Abadan in September, four other major events contributed to the Saudis' alarm during this phase. First, the coup plot in Bahrain in December 1981 appeared to frighten the Saudis more than it did their junior GCC partners. Second, the Syrian cutoff of Iraqi oil exports through the Trans-Syrian pipeline (10 April 1982) was viewed by Riyadh as a serious blow to the Iraqi war effort. Third, the impressive Iranian offensive (*fath al-mobin*) of March 1982 was crowned by the spectacular recovery of the port city of Khorramshahr on 24 May.

Fourth, the alarm bell that in May rang all the way from the Gulf Arab capitals to Washington, D.C., was followed by near-panic less than two months later, when, for the first time, Iranian forces carried the war into Iraqi territory (13 July 1982).

The fear that intensified during these events subsided in the third major phase of Saudi concern over the war, between August 1982 and February 1984. Khomeini's call on 14 July—the day after the Iranian counterinvasion began—to all the Iraqi people to rise up and revolt against Saddam Hussein's rule fell on deaf ears, just as had the Iraqi leader's call on the Arabic-speaking Iranians of Khuzistan in the wake of the Iraqi invasion of Iran less than two years earlier. Furthermore, the surprisingly stiff resistance of the Iraqi forces—now fighting on their own soil—was a source of relief to Riyadh. The so-called war of attrition thus began to set in.

But Saudi relief was short-lived. In fact, during the fourth phase, between February and July 1984, Saudi concern over the war reached its peak. Two developments were principally responsible for this unprecedented escalation of Saudi alarm. First, Iran launched a new offensive against Iraq on 24 February 1984. Unlike the four previous offensives, this fifth offensive, the so-called operation before dawn (*walfajr*), was a success. On that day, Iranian forces seized parts of the artificial oil islands of Majnoon ("madman") inside the Iraqi marshlands north of Basra, the vital Iraqi port city inhabited mostly by Shias. The islands sat atop 7 billion barrels of oil; in addition, strategic Basra-Baghdad could be used as a springboard for an offensive against the highway, located six miles away. Speaker Hashemi-Rafsanjani did not miss the opportunity to declare that Iran would keep the islands' oil wealth as "war reparations."

The second development in this crisis phase took place at sea. The Saudis' alarm, initially caused by Iran's seizure of the Majnoon foothold inside Iraqi territory, was intensified when the continually escalating tanker war finally spread to Saudi and Kuwaiti oil tankers. For three years before April 1984, the Iraqis had attacked most of the "more than 60 ships [involved up to that time], two-thirds of them commercial vessels from nations not involved in the war," according to Lloyd's Shipping Intelligence.[3] But in April the Iraqis used French-made Super Etendard planes, instead of helicopters, to fire Exocet missiles at oil tankers in the Persian Gulf. They had received these planes as early as October 1983, but first used them in April 1984 to try to cripple Iranian oil exports and thereby force Iran to the negotiating table.

Ironically, the Iraqis hit two Saudi oil tankers that were near the Iranian oil terminal at Kharg Island, around which Baghdad had declared a fifty-mile war zone. The first Saudi oil tanker, the *Safina al-Arab,* was struck on 25 April, and the second one, the *al-Ahood,* on 7 May. Iranian oil exports dropped considerably for a short time before picking up again. Iran, which earlier had threatened to close the Strait of Hormuz as an act of desperation if it was forced to, did not consider the disruption of its exports to be serious or prolonged enough to require retaliation. Instead of tampering with navigation through the strait, Iran chose to retaliate by hitting oil tankers. Even then, it struck the oil tankers on the west side of the Persian Gulf only sporadically. Iran's first retaliatory air strike was near Bahrain, against the Kuwaiti oil tanker *Umm Casbah,* on 13 May. Its second, on the Saudi oil tanker *Yanbu Pride* on 16 May, visibly angered the Saudis.

Against the background of this ever-increasing Saudi concern over the tanker war, the 5 June downing of an Iranian fighter plane by the Saudis might appear to have been an act of Saudi retaliation. But it was not. The Saudi action was a response to the perceived Iranian encroachment on Saudi territorial waters. According to authoritative Saudi sources, "The Saudi early warning systems located a target moving toward the coast of the Saudi Kingdom. When this target got beyond international waters and entered the Saudi territorial waters heading toward its coast, aircraft of the Saudi Royal Air Force intercepted it, engaged it, and downed it."[4]

The following day, the Iranians protested the destruction of their F-4 jet fighter by the Saudi F-15 planes. The Saudi chargé d'affaires in Tehran was told by Iranian Foreign Ministry officials the "several aircraft of the Saudi Royal Air Force attacked an F-4 aircraft of the Air Force of the Islamic Republic of Iran in *international waters* while it was guarding the security of the Persian Gulf."[5] The Saudis, however, contended that they had exhaustively explained that the Iranian plane had been shot down in "Saudi *territorial waters.*"[6] Neither side has made its case public. The conflicting versions of the location of the incident may reflect divergent interpretations of the Saudi-Iranian agreement of 24 October 1968, which provided 12-mile territorial waters both for the Saudi island and for the Iranian island.[7] Since the Iranian plane was shot down "near" the Saudi island of al-Arabiyah, Saudi Arabia claimed that its territorial waters had been violated, whereas Iranians may have based their protest on the ground that the incident took place outside the territorial waters of the Saudi mainland.

The Saudi demonstration of military force against Iran in the fourth phase was preceded by an unprecedented Saudi campaign of diplomatic disapprobation against the Khomeini regime. The campaign was triggered by the Saudis' uncharacteristic agitation over Iran's seizure of parts of the Majnoon Islands. Seldom had there been a flurry of high-level diplomatic activities in the Gulf like the one that followed this success of Iranian arms. Led by the Saudis, the GCC foreign ministers met in Riyadh on 11 March 1984 to map out their strategy, and immediately thereafter, on 14 March, they joined their counterparts in Baghdad in response to the Iraqi call for an emergency conference of the Arab League. This meeting of the twenty-one-member league—the first one ever to be held exclusively on the subject of the war—called on all states "to refrain from any measures that would contribute directly or indirectly to the continuation of war between both parties." The wording was aimed particularly at countries that had furnished arms and spare parts to Iran. Although Iraq sought to have the league call on all nations to join an economic boycott of Iran to exert pressure on it to negotiate an end to the war, and Saudi Arabia was prepared to compensate the countries that would go along, this move floundered because it was unacceptable to Iran's "neutral" Arab friends such as South Yemen and Algeria.[8]

The Saudis put their strategy of diplomatic disapprobation of Iran into high gear, however, only after the attack on the Saudi oil tanker *Yanbu Pride* on 16 May. After the Iranians attacked this oil tanker while it was sailing only sixty miles northeast of the vital Ras Tanura oil complex, an unidentified source in the Saudi Information Ministry announced the ministry's regret over the incident, adding: "The Kingdom of Saudi Arabia denounces these repeated aerial assaults on Gulf tankers and condemns acts of violence and violations of international law."[9] This same source stressed that the Saudis were determined "to put an end to these infringements" in consultation with their GCC partners.

The opportunity for collective diplomatic disapprobation of Iran came only a few days later, on 20 May 1984, during a meeting of the Arab League in Tunis. The Saudi-GCC success in convincing the Arab League members of the need to take a tough diplomatic stand against Iran was all the more remarkable because Syria and Libya, who had not been at the 14 March meeting in Baghdad, were present at this meeting. In a rare departure from its usual public unanimity, the league overruled Syrian and Libyan objections to a strongly worded resolution against Iran. The resolution expressed the ministers' "extreme concern over the Iranian aggression against Saudi and Kuwaiti oil tankers in the territorial waters and maritime routes of the Gulf nations, far from the declared zone of military operations." The resolution also called on the United Nations Security Council to take "firm and clear action." Also, in a rare departure from its usual use of cautious diplomatic language, Saudi Arabia minced no words in speaking out against Iran at this time. "The Iranian aggression," said Saudi Defense Minister Prince Sultan to reporters after the league meeting, "has become so serious and so dangerous that the Arab League has no choice but to take action."[10]

Armed with the Arab League's unusual show of support, Saudi Arabia and its GCC partners took their strategy of diplomatic disapprobation of Iran to the wider forum of the United Nations Security Council. Although the anti-Iranian tone of the proposed Arab resolution on the war behavior of Iran was somewhat softened by Iran's Third World friends, Security Council Resolution 552, dated 1 June 1984, represented a clear diplomatic triumph for the GCC states over Iran. Approved by a vote of thirteen to zero (Nicaragua and Zimbabwe abstained), the resolution reaffirmed "the right of free navigation and commerce in international waters and sea lanes." But it confined that right to "shipping en route to and from all ports and installations of the littoral States that are not parties to the hostilities."

A clear victory for collective GCC diplomacy, the resolution nevertheless provided additional ammunition for Iran's repeated charges of bias against the United Nations Security Council. Iran had boycotted the council's meetings because the council had failed to condemn Iraq after it invaded Iran. In this instance, Iraq had started the tanker war, but the resolution was interpreted as saying that Iraq's use of Exocet missiles to cripple Iranian shipping was within the limits of acceptable behavior by a country at war, whereas Iran's bombardments of oil tankers were not. The council's justification for its dissimilar treatment of the belligerents was that the Iraqis had attacked oil tankers within the fifty-mile war zone near Kharg Island, whereas the Iranians had attacked vessels going to and from Kuwait and Saudi Arabia.

This resolution presumably reaffirmed United Nations Security Council Resolution 540 of 31 October 1983 on the central question of the freedom of navigation, but a comparison of the two resolutions reveals that the language of the earlier resolution was more objective. It affirmed "the right of free navigation and commerce in international waters" without confining that right to shipping to and from neutral countries, and it called "on all States to respect this right" and on both belligerents "to cease immediately all hostilities in the region of the Gulf, including all sea-lanes, navigable waterways, harbour works, terminals, offshore installations and all ports with direct or indirect access to the sea, and to respect the integrity of the other littoral States."[11] The absence of an all-encompassing affirmation of the right of navigation in resolution 552 lent credence to the Iranian charge of "one-sidedness."

The fifth, and latest, phase of the Saudi response to the war began in July 1984 and continued through September 1985, the fifth anniversary of the beginning of the war. This phase was marked mainly by a mixture of despair and hope. The Saudis, like all those who had hoped for a peaceful settlement, were deeply disappointed in the breach of the hard-won, United Nations–sponsored moratorium of 12 June 1984 on attacks on civilian targets. This, the sole agreement between the belligerents, was destroyed on 4 March 1985, when Iraq attacked an unfinished nuclear plant at Bushehr and a steel plant in Ahwaz in Khuzistan. Never keen on making war on civilian targets, Iran retaliated by shelling Basra; Iraq then hit a number of Iranian cities, including Tehran. Thus began the war of cities in 1985, while the 1984 tanker war continued. Reckoning it had an advantage on the ground, Iran also attacked across the Hawr al-Hawziah marshes, just north of Al-Qurnah, a town on the Basra-Baghdad highway. This attack was not Iran's repeatedly prom-ised and postponed "final offensive," but a response to Iraq's goading, which nearly backfired. At one point, the Iranian forces managed to advance within striking distance of the highway. As they had in 1984, the Iraqis used chemical weapons in this battle. About two months later, a flicker of hope appeared for Saudi Arabia when Saudi Foreign Minis-ter Saud al-Faysal visited Tehran.

MILITARY DETERRENCE

The Saudi response to the Iranian military challenge has involved a great range of efforts. In fact, the current defense and deterrence capa-bility of Saudi Arabia largely reflects the impact of the Iranian Revolu-tion and the Iraq-Iran war. Saudi Arabia's military modernization, like that of the Shah's Iran, had its roots in the 1940s and 1950s. The Saudis were also aided primarily by the United States in their modernization effort, which accorded the highest priority to air defense enhancement. Yet, by the time Saudi air defense buildup picked up momentum in the 1970s, the Shah's Iran provided air security for Saudi Arabia in most of the Gulf region. Gulf security, it was often tactfully said, had been maintained by Saudi Arabia as well as Iran—the so-called twin pillars of American security policy in the region. But in reality, Saudi leaders had been neither willing nor able to police the Gulf. They had largely de-pended on the preeminent security provided by the Shah's Iran.

The Iranian Revolution did more than destroy Saudi Arabia's air security. The Bazargan government abandoned the role of policeman of the Gulf. But the Khomeini regime, emerging fully after the second revolution, vigorously set claim to providing a security umbrella (*chatr-e amniyyat*) for all the littoral states of the Gulf. Given the nature of the challenge of the revolutionary regime, the Khomeini regime's security umbrella, far from being seen as providing air security for Saudi Arabia, was seen as a threat to the security of the kingdom.

The Iraq-Iran war compounded apprehensions about the Iranian threat to Saudi security. Just as Saudi concern about the spread of the war lay behind the Saudi response of disapprobation to the threat posed by Iran, that concern also underpinned the country's unprecedented determination and efforts to build up its defense and deterrence capability. Only two years before the start of the war, in order to satisfy U.S. conditions aimed at overcoming the objections of Israel and its American supporters in Congress, the Saudis agreed not to purchase bomb racks or external fuel tanks for the F-15 interceptors it bought from the United States. Israel and its supporters contended that such equipment would enhance the F-15s' offensive capability. But when, at the very outset of the war, Saudi leaders witnessed Iraq and Iran's lack of restraint about striking against each other's vital oil terminals, installations, and facilities, the Saudis' interest in strengthening the Saudi air defense system soared.

The vital Saudi oil terminals at Ras Tanura and Jaymah, which in the early 1980's handled more than 90 percent of Saudi crude oil exports, are farther from Iranian fire power than are Iraq's major oil terminals, but this did not calm Saudi nerves. From the Iranian bases at Bushehr and Shiraz, these Saudi oil terminals could be reached by Iranian jet fighters in sixteen minutes.[12] Given Saudi Arabia's vast and exposed territory, maintaining air security for the kingdom had always presented a major problem, as, for example, when the South Yemeni air force had struck at Saudi targets in 1973. But that general problem became specific and acute vis-à-vis revolutionary Iran, which characterized all its conservative Gulf neighbors, particularly Saudi Arabia, as "glass houses." From the Saudi perspective, the kingdom and its fellow monarchies had to be defended by the most efficient and sophisticated air defense system possible. Only such a system could identify, engage, and shoot down approaching Iranian planes from across the Gulf before they could wreak havoc on the vital area of Saudi Arabia which faces Iran.

It is little wonder that the momentum for enhancing Saudi air defense picked up after the start of the Iraq-Iran war. Realizing the inadequacy of their F-15 interceptors under the 1978 conditions, and in the face of the realities of postrevolutionary Iran and the war, the Saudis accepted the deployment of four American AWACS planes on their territory beginning in September 1980. This was only a stopgap measure, however; Saudi Arabia needed to build up its own defense and deterrence capability. The momentous events that took place between the visit to Saudi

Arabia of General David Jones, chairman of the U.S. Joint Chiefs of Staff, only six days after the outbreak of the war, and U.S. Senate approval of the Air Defense Enhancement Package on 28 October 1981 resulted in the establishmeant of unparalleled foundations for the strengthening of the Saudi air defense and deterrence system.

That system, like the air defense system of the United States, is a "layered" system.[13] It consists of three "envelopes" of protection: the outer, the intermediate, and the immediate. The sixty F-15 interceptors the Saudis had purchased in 1978 had been somewhat emasculated by American sales conditions, but they were meant to provide protection in the first, or outer, layer of the air defense system. The Air Defense Enhancement Package, which included the sale of five AWACS planes to Saudi Arabia in 1981 (for delivery in 1985), would also provide protection in the first layer. The combination of the F-15 interceptors and the AWACS planes would build the Saudis' deterrent capability to a level it had never attained before.

The tanker war resulted in Saudi efforts to strengthen all three layers of the Saudi air deterrence system. The tanker war began in earnest in April 1984, but insofar as the Saudis were concerned, it peaked on 16 May, when the Saudi oil tanker *Yanbu Pride* was struck by Iranian fighter planes. This event invigorated the Saudi campaign of diplomatic disapprobation and prompted the Saudis to request American emergency military aid. The request was made to Richard W. Murphy, assistant secretary of state, on 22 May, when he was in Saudi Arabia. The Saudis asked him for an "emergency shipment of an unspecified number of Stingers."[14] The missiles were delivered to Saudi Arabia on 28 May. Before this crisis, the Saudis had requested 1,200 Stinger missiles and 400 launchers, but the shipment that arrived during the Memorial Day weekend—and immediately sparked controversy—included 400 shoulder-fired Stinger missiles and 200 launchers.[15]

There is no doubt that the Saudis requested Stinger missiles in order to discourage the Iranians.[16] In spelling out the function of these missiles as a deterrent, Major General Edward L. Tixier, deputy assistant secretary of defense for Near Eastern and South Asian affairs, told the Committee on Foreign Affairs of the House of Representatives on 11 June 1984 that the "idea of Stingers being [in Saudi Arabia] in and of itself is a deterrent. It is just no fun [for Iranian planes] coming in knowing that that rascal down there on the ground has something to blow you out of the sky with. . . . I can tell you from experience, it makes you drop your bombs a little less higher, a little less accurately, and get out faster." He also said, more specifically, that the Stinger "is good against helicopters, and that is precisely the reason we think it is important for [the Saudis] to have that capability in those coastal areas that are in range of the large number of attack helicopters the Iranians have. They have a tremendous capability in that area."[17] The Stinger could also be used to protect Saudi shipping, oil fields, and important installations such as desalinization plants against Iranian aircraft and warships.

But the emergency American aid included more than Stinger missiles. In response to the tanker war, the Saudi deterrence was also strengthened by other means. Before the tanker war and the resultant American emergency supply, the Saudi F-15s had been aided not only by the four American-owned and -operated AWACS, but also by three U.S. KC135 refueling planes that had been on assignment in Saudi Arabia since the start of the war in September 1980. By providing in-flight refueling, these planes had extended the range of the F-15s and their ability to stay on airborne patrols for long periods. The F-15 fighters could do even better with additional refueling aids, which the United States supplied in response to the crisis. A U.S. KC10, a larger aerial tanker than the KC135, was immediately added to the four KC135s already available in Saudi Arabia. During the crisis, the United States also accelerated the delivery of auxiliary tanks, called conformal fuel tanks (C.F.T.s), which the Saudis had purchased earlier. All of these refueling aids enabled the Saudi F-15s to stay aloft for long periods to patrol Saudi shipping lanes and airspace.

This improved patrol capability combined with the range and destruction capability of the Stinger missiles to enhance all three layers of the Saudi air defense system. For example, the Stinger, "as the point weapon," with a range of three miles, augmented air protection in the intermediate envelope. This more flexible weapons system supplemented the improved Hawk antiaircraft system, with a range of two miles, which the Saudis deployed in static positions in order to improve their air defense with respect to vital points. But static deployment of the T-Hawk omits the less vital areas, which the Stinger could cover. It could be deployed where the T-Hawk is ineffective as well as around Ras Tanura, airfields, and other potential targets.

From the Saudi perspective, the kingdom's improved air defense and deterrence capability would benefit its GCC partners, as well. The Saudi request for American emergency aid in 1984, like the Saudi military purchase in 1981, was couched in terms of the Saudis' intention of helping to protect all GCC countries. Saudi leaders indicated to their American counterparts in 1981 their desire "to work toward an integrated regional defense system."[18] In other words, the U.S.-Saudi air defense enhancement package was ultimately to benefit all GCC states.

From the perspective of the Khomeini regime, however, all this military buildup with the aid of the Great Satan smacked of the devil's work. Khomeini did not fail to criticize the Air Defense Enhancement Package in his 10 October 1981 message to King Khalid. During the 1984 crisis over the Saudi destruction of an Iranian fighter plane, the Iranians also went beyond simply protesting the Saudi action. They charged that the Saudi action aided "the expansion of tension in the Persian Gulf region," and they warned that Iran would "respond severely to any further attack on aircraft of the Islamic Republic of Iran."[19] They claimed that the pilots of the F-15 planes that shot down the Iranian F-4 had not been Saudis. They also charged that the United States was planning to attack Iranian oil installations with Saudi cooperation, from Saudi bases, and with U.S.-piloted aircraft. Although the Saudis refuted the Iranian allegations on 13 June 1984 by stressing that "all the pilots who work in the Saudi Air Force are sons of the Kingdom of Saudi Arabia," and that "not a single foreign pilot is among them,"[20] the fact remains that until the process of "Saudization" of the kingdom's air defense and deterrence system progresses much further, the Iranians will continue to exploit the Saudis' military dependence on the United States.

THE TWO FACES OF THE SAUDI CONTAINMENT POLICY

The containment policy of Saudi Arabia has for six years aimed at protecting the House of Saud against the contagion of Khomeini's brand of revolutionary fundamentalist Islam. For five years it has also been directed against the spread of the Iraq-Iran war. Both of these interrelated goals have been pursued through diplomacy and deterrence, the two faces of Saudi Arabia's containment policy. Neither face of this policy is complete without the other. While it prefers conciliation toward revolutionary Iran over deterrence, Saudi Arabia has kept its powder dry. In doing so it has nevertheless been anxious to make it clear that military force would be used only as a complement to diplomacy, and only when there is direct encroachment on Saudi Arabia or, possibly, one of its GCC partners.

The conflict between Saudi Arabia and Iran in the first six years of the Iranian Revolution has been reflected in a variety of issues, including, for example, the hajj problem, the Saudis' relationship with the United States, oil production and prices, and, most of all, the Iraq-Iran war. That conflict was theoretically depicted herein as a conflict between the Saudi *muwahhidun* and the Iranian *mustaza'fin* Islam. Yet we have seen that, in practice, the relationship between Riyadh and Tehran has not been an irreconcilable Manichaean conflict. Looking at this phenomenon exclusively from the perspective of Saudi Arabia, it would be easy to suggest that the conciliatory approach of Saudi Arabia to Iran reflects the cautious style of Saudi foreign policy. But this would be a simplistic interpretation. The empirical truth of the matter is that both sides have exercised restraint. This was best evidenced at the height of the tanker war and after the dogfight between Saudi and Iranian planes in June 1984. At the time, most Western observers characterized the Iranian retaliation as "underresponse" with respect to both the Iraqi attacks on oil tankers and the shooting down of an Iranian F-4 plane by the Saudis.

The mutual restraint between Saudi Arabia and Iran reflected the fact that the ideological conflict between the two countries was tempered significantly by a perceived mutuality of interest. In five major areas, the two countries' interests converged more than they diverged. First, the conflict between *muwahhidun* and *mustaza'fin* Islam was tempered by the fact that both countries shared the premise that religion constituted the central value of their states. This was the principal point made by Prince Saud in explaining the foundation of Saudi foreign policy to Iranian leaders in his historic May 1985 visit to Tehran. In this respect, Saudi Arabia has more in common with revolutionary Iran than with revolutionary Iraq. Although Islam is a cultural value in Ba'thism, the central value in Ba'thism is Arabism, as served by means of secularism and socialism, not religious fundamentalism.

Second, Saudi Arabia and revolutionary Iran both evinced an anti-Soviet and anti-communist stance. Khomeini's Iran had more grounds on which to oppose the Soviet Union than the Shah's regime did. The Soviet Union was considered by Iran to be not only a historically hostile state, but also an atheistic and aggressive power that was wrongfully occupying neighboring Afghanistan. Third, although Saudi Arabia enjoyed a "special relationship" with the United States which was opposed by revolutionary Iran, both Riyadh and Tehran opposed American intervention in the Gulf region. Fourth, although Saudi Arabia pursued the path of peaceful diplomacy vis-à-vis Israel, whereas Iran advocated armed struggle as the only way of resolving the Palestinian problem, the positions of Riyadh and Tehran on Israel moved closer together after the fall of the Shah's regime. Fifth, quite apart from the common Saudi-Iranian ideological differences with Baghdad, Riyadh and Tehran shared a basic suspicion of the Ba'thist regime's power ambitions. Sixth, and finally, Saudi Arabia and Iran both subscribed to the principle of regional security by regional powers, despite the Iranians' claim—under Khomeini as well as under the Shah—to primus inter pares among the Gulf States.

The convergence of Saudi and Iranian interests in these areas accounted for the efforts of each country to accommodate the other, even in the face of the ever-escalating tension produced, largely, by the war. The conciliatory face of the Saudi containment policy will probably become predominant after the war ends, as will a more pragmatic and accommodating stance in Iran's foreign policy.

8

Containment of Revolution:
The Genesis of the GCC

Bahrain, Kuwait, Oman, Qatar, and the United Arab Emirates have joined Saudi Arabia in creating the Gulf Cooperation Council partly in response to the challenge of the Iranian Revolution. The impact of this revolution, the threat posed by the Soviet invasion of Afghanistan, and the concern over potential American military intervention were the primary considerations in the minds of the founding fathers of the GCC. In this light, it can be seen that the conventional assumption that the Iraq-Iran war brought about the establishment of the GCC is unfounded. The war was indeed a precipitative factor at the inception of the GCC, but only later did it become a primary concern of GCC members. Furthermore, in the decade before these multiple sources of challenge to the Gulf monarchies surfaced in 1979–80, a tradition of cooperation in the Persian Gulf region had been established.

Neither the charter of the GCC nor the statements of its founding fathers sheds much light on its origins. At the GCC's summit meeting, in May 1981, the leaders of the six founding nations declared their objectives to include the promotion of "cooperation," and "integration" among the member states in a wide variety of fields, "in order to serve their interests and strengthen their ability to hold on to their beliefs and values."[1] Nowhere, however, were these interests, beliefs, and values authoritatively defined.

Comments by its supporters as well as by its detractors have contributed to misperceptions about the origins and nature of the Gulf Cooperation Council. One of the avowed enthusiasts of the GCC, for example, speaks of its raison d'être as if it were created primarily, if not solely, as an anti-Israeli alliance. The concern of all members of the organization with the Palestinian plight for reasons of both self-interest and "fellow Arab" consciousness long preceded the formation of the GCC. But there is no evidence that the perception of an Israeli threat or the concern with the Palestinian ordeal had a significant bearing on the thinking of its founders. The detractors of the organization, on the other hand, have characterized it variously as an "arm of NATO," a "tool of the United States," a "stalking horse of Saudi Arabia," and a "latter-day CENTO."

What is perhaps more unfortunate is the universal assumption that the GCC was formed solely in response to the Iraq-Iran war. That the war made the timing of the formation of the organization fortuitous there can be no doubt. And that in the war the member states had a perfect excuse for excluding the distrusted Arab state of Iraq from their company is obvious. But the war can hardly be regarded as the sole cause of the creation of the GCC, although the war did precipitate its official formation.

A TRADITION OF COOPERATION

The idea of regional cooperation among the littoral states emerged at the end of Pax Britannica in the Persian Gulf region. Benjamin Franklin's advice that it is better to hang together than to hang separately was particularly true in the Gulf region. Although the Shah of Iran was one of the earliest advocates of regional cooperation, he was suspected of using it as a cloak for Pax Iranica.[2] Because of their greater weakness, the smaller states were attracted to the idea of collaboration partly as a means of thwarting the bid for hegemony by the larger states. It is no wonder that the Dubai agreement of February 1967 marked the beginning of intensified efforts to unite the seven Trucial Coast Emirates with Bahrain and Qatar. Although these states ultimately decided to stay outside the proposed union, a new federated state, the United Arab Emirates, was formed in 1971. Composed of Abu Dhabi, Dubai, Sharjah, Ajman, Umm al Qawain, Fujeirah, and Ras al Khaimah, the UAE has survived as the sole successful experiment in Arab unity in strife-torn Arab society. Now a member of the GCC the UAE is a constant reminder of the possibility of cooperation in the Gulf region, despite rivalry among the Sheikhdoms that form the "federation."

Because Pax Iranica did insure regionwide security and stability between the departure of the British and the downfall of the Shah, a tradition of cooperation began to develop among all the Gulf states. In that decade, a multitude of old and new boundary disputes, tribal feuds, jurisdictional controversies, and the like were peacefully settled. These settlements were achieved between every Arab state and Iran; Saudi Arabia (1968), Abu Dhabi (1971), Qatar (1970), Iraq (1975), and the other Arab states all settled disputes with Iran. Peaceful settlements were also achieved among the Arab states themselves, such as the settlement between Saudi Arabia and Iraq (1975), Abu Dhabi and Saudi Arabia (1974), and Abu Dhabi and Qatar (1969).[3]

Regional leaders pressed the idea of regional cooperation beyond settling disputes amicably. Cooperation efforts gained momentum especially after the formation of the UAE and the settlement of the ancient Shatt al-Arab dispute between Iraq and Iran. During the Islamic Conference in Jidda in July 1975, only a few months after the Algiers agreement of March 1975, the Gulf foreign ministers agreed, for the first time, to hold a summit meeting to discuss mutual defense cooperation. Other major issues to be discussed included territorial integrity of all littoral states, limits on foreign fleets, freedom of navigation, a ban on foreign military bases in the Gulf, resolution of outstanding disputes, mutual aid against internal coups, and division of the Gulf waters. Less than a year later, in May 1976, Sheikh Jaber al-Ahmad al-Sabah, then prime minister and crown prince of Kuwait, called for "the establishment of a Gulf Union with the object of realizing cooperation in all economic, political, educational and informational fields . . . to serve the interests and stability of the peoples in the region." "Thus was born the idea for what later became the GCC," says an official GCC publication.[4] As I have suggested, the idea of regional cooperation had existed for some time, although some observers regard the GCC as the "brainchild" of Kuwait. Whether or not this attribution is justified, the important point is that the organization was not born in a vacuum.

Yet, it is doubtful whether the GCC would have been established without the revolutionary changes that preceded the war between Iraq and Iran. An examination of the impact of these changes on the growing common concerns of the GCC leaders, seen against the backdrop of a tradition of regional cooperation that had developed long before the Iranian Revolution, sheds some light on the origins of the GCC and the leadership role played by Kuwait and Saudi Arabia in its formation.

THE IMPACT OF THE IRANIAN REVOLUTION

The eruption of the Iranian Revolution and its immediate aftermath in the Persian Gulf region had a profound impact on the rise of common concerns among GCC leaders. We have already seen that the revolution made various Gulf Arab regimes uneasy. But the commonality of concern among these regimes can be seen in the earliest signs of concern shown by Saudi Arabia, Bahrain, and Kuwait, particularly over the threat of internal convulsion. This common concern emerged during the first year of the Iranian Revolution, before the outbreak of the Iraq-Iran war, the coup plot in Bahrain, and the multiple bombings in Kuwait.

The impact of the Iranian Revolution on Saudi consciousness about the need for closer cooperation with the smaller Arab states was three-fold. First, the downfall of the Iranian monarchy in 1979 was more traumatic for the Saudi rulers than the downfall of the Iraqi monarchy in 1958 had been—this was the second time in twenty years that a conservative monarchy had been destroyed in the Gulf region. Second, the fall of the Shah's regime was bound to have regionwide repercussions. *Pax Iranica,* in effect, had helped to insure the preservation of all conservative monarchical regimes in the Gulf region against leftist threats such as the South Yemeni–supported Dhofari rebellion in Oman and, especially, Iraqi Ba'thist subversive activities in the smaller Gulf nations. The downfall of the Shah's regime was seen in Riyadh not only as tipping the balance of forces in the area even further against the monarchies, but also as raising serious questions about Iran's traditional role as an anti-Soviet and anti-communist buffer against the nearby Soviet colossus. Before the second revolution in Iran in November 1979, Saudi rulers had feared that communist elements might gain control of the Iranian government in the course of the revolutionary struggle for power.[5]

Third, the Iranian Revolution seemed to present an opportunity for the Saudis to realize, finally, their historical goal of extending their protective power and influence throughout the Arabian Peninsula and the surrounding areas. There were three dimensions to this Saudi "peninsularism." First, Saudi Arabia would fill whatever power vacuum was created in the smaller Gulf Arab states as a result of the fall of the Shah's regime, in the light of the fact that the rulers of these weaker sheikhdoms had always cultivated a degree of Iranian support for themselves as a counterweight to Saudi Arabia's bid for hegemony in the area. Second, Saudi Arabia could help thwart any future attempts made by revolutionary Iran either to gain power and influence, as the Shah had done, or to subvert the Gulf monarchies, including Saudi Arabia itself, by exporting the Islamic revolution through the Shia communities in these countries. And third, Saudi Arabia would become the principal "balancer" in the Arab game of power politics. After the revolution, the Saudis' chances of assuming this balancing role seemed greater than ever. Fortuitously for Saudi leaders, Egypt lost its leadership role in the Arab world just as the Iranian Revolution was unfolding. The Camp David Accords, the Egyptian-Israeli peace treaty, and the ostracism of

Egypt in two Baghdad conferences all paralleled the eruption of the Iranian Revolution, the downfall of the Shah, and the seizure of power by the revolutionary forces.

The Iranian Revolution also increased the desire among the leaders of the smaller Gulf states for some kind of grouping. Revolutionary Iran seemed too hostile to be their counterweight to Saudi Arabia, which now seemed overly anxious to provide them with both protection and money. Their need for protection was dramatized by the revival of the ancient Iranian claim of sovereignty over the tiny island state of Bahrain. Ayatollah Sadeq Ruhani's threat that revolutionary Iran would "annex" Bahrain unless it adopted an Islamic government reverberated throughout the Gulf Arab states. Bahrain, like Saudi Arabia, experienced two internal Shia upheavals, one in 1979 and one in 1980. Although the seizure of the Great Mosque at Mecca in 1979, shortly before the first Shia uprising at Qatif, was not instigated by Iran or Saudi Shias inspired by Iran, the incident did contribute to the mounting sense of vulnerability, not only in the House of Saud, but among all the Gulf monarchies.

Even Kuwait, which seemed to enjoy exceptional relations with revolutionary Iran during the first year of the Iranian Revolution, began to perceive the threat of Iranian-sponsored subversion. Of all the rulers of the small Gulf states, Kuwaiti leaders had always been the most independent minded. They also had been the most conscious of the need for common action, and the revolutionary events of 1979 intensified this consciousness. The revival of the Iranian claim to Bahrain, the Shia insurrections in Bahrain and Saudi Arabia, and the seizure of the Great Mosque all mirrored Kuwait's own unhappy experience. Kuwait was the first Gulf Arab country to send its foreign minister, Sabah al-Ahmad al-Sabah, to Iran after the revolution (July 1979). He met with Khomeini and optimistically declared that his people saw "that the new Iran is proceeding along the correct path; this is reflected in its policies towards our country and Palestine. . . . We are confident that our relations will be better than today."[6] Generally, Kuwait's positive attitude toward revolutionary Iran continued at the diplomatic level, as evidenced, for example, by Kuwaiti opposition to the United Nations Security Council imposing economic sanctions against Iran during the hostage crisis.[7] The attitude was also reflected in Kuwait's "condemnation" of the American rescue mission in Iran and its denunciation of the American freeze on Iranian assets (Kuwait's fear of a freeze on its own assets in the United States inspired the latter action).[8]

But during the first year of the Iranian Revolution, the Kuwaiti ruling family also felt threatened, for the first time, by an Iranian-inspired, if not Iranian-sponsored, act to incite political unrest in Kuwait. The Kuwaiti interior minister, Nawwaf al-Sabah, personally ordered the arrest of a relative of Ayatollah Khomeini named Ahmad al-Mahri, who was accused of violating Kuwaiti laws in using mosques for "political purposes." At the time of the arrest, Nawwaf al-Sabah said that his ministry would "severely punish those who try to instigate instability in Kuwait."[9] Subsequently, the government of Kuwait revoked the Kuwaiti citizenship rights of Ahmad and his father, Abbas al-Mahri, a cleric appointed by Khomeini as a Shia Friday prayer leader in Kuwait, and expelled the entire al-Mahri family from Kuwait.

The traumatic experiences of these three larger Arab states rang the alarm bell among the three other prospective GCC states. Given Sultan Qabus's close relationship with the Shah and his regime, and Oman's strategic location at the Strait of Hormuz, the Omanis had their own reasons for being unhappy about the implications of revolutionary developments in Iran for Oman. But even the traditionally friendly Qatar and the UAE—or at least Dubai—now felt vulnerable vis-à-vis revolutionary Iran. The combination of a large number of Iranian expatriates and indigenous Shia Muslims in these tiny states seemed, under the circumstances, to pose a threat of internal convulsion to these states' rulers, as well. So soon after the eruption of the revolution, none of the GCC leaders could foresee the emergence of any pragmatism in Iranian foreign policy. Indeed, an ideological crusade was the most visible dimension of Iranian revolutionary behavior. Only later were these leaders able to see a glimmer of Iranian practical concerns, as, for example, Saudi Arabia did during 1984 and 1985. In 1979 every regional ruler felt the destabilizing tremors of the Iranian revolutionary earthquake.

THE EFFECTS OF THE SOVIET INVASION OF AFGHANISTAN

Among like-minded Arab leaders of the Gulf region, the Soviet invasion of Afghanistan augmented their sense of being threatened and their awareness that a closer association of Gulf Arab states had become a necessity. The Soviet invasion and occupation of Afghanistan produced four new major worries. First, whereas the Iranian Revolution had destroyed the region's traditional buffer against the Soviet Union, the Soviet military presence in Afghanistan added a new and closer threat to the entire Gulf region. Second, where previously they had felt threatened by the spread of Islamic radicalism on the right, Arab leaders now felt threatened by communism on the left. Both extremist trends threatened to destabilize the rule of the Arab monarchies. Third, whereas the Soviet invasion of a small Muslim country that was fighting against communist rule was disquieting to say the least, the possibility that the other superpower might plunge the entire region into conflict through military counterintervention was worrisome in the extreme. Fourth, and finally, the threat of communist encirclement of the Gulf region through South Yemen, Ethiopia, and now Soviet-dominated Afghanistan was bad enough, but the noncommittal reactions of Syria and Algeria to the Soviet invasion threatened to plunge the Middle East into a wave of Arab radicalism. What seemed of greatest concern to these radical states was that the United States might use the Soviet invasion to criticize their "friendship and cooperation" with Moscow. They failed to condemn the Soviet invasion, and South Yemen went so far as to suggest that the invasion saved "the progressive Afghan government."[10]

Saudi Arabia took the lead in opposing the Soviet invasion in every major international and regional organization, and the other Arab monarchies went along in varying degrees. Perhaps all the Saudi leaders did not perceive the Soviet threat in the same way, but their opposition to the invasion was unmistakable. Prince Fahd tried publicly to analyze the Soviet objectives in invading Afghanistan, which included, he said, the containment of the "Islamic Revolution in Afghanistan and Iran" as a means of preventing its spread among Soviet Muslims. He also cited as Soviet objectives the enhancement of Soviet access to warm-water ports of the Gulf and the Indian Ocean through Pakistan and Iran, and control of Iran's and other Gulf countries' oil resources. Whatever the Soviet objectives, Fahd said, "The invasion concerns us and affects us directly."[11] That, he said, was why Saudi Arabia initiated the call for a meeting of the Muslim countries in Islamabad, where the Soviets were roundly condemned. At that meeting, in January 1980, Saudi Arabia called for the isolation of the "Soviet-imposed regime in Kabul" through a refusal of Gulf Arab states to recognize it politically and deal with it economically. The Saudis also called for support by the Muslim world of "the Afghani people in their struggle against the Soviet occupation until the aggression forces withdraw from the Afghani lands."[12]

Saudi leaders also took the opportunity to repeat in this new context their longstanding argument that communism and Zionism are twin evils, and that the lack of a solution to the Palestinian problem endangers the entire region. In an extensive interview with the French newspaper Le Figaro, Crown Prince Fahd said: "If we want to contain Communism and the foreign influence [the Soviets] in the area, then we have to solve the Palestinian problem justly and comprehensively so that no one [the PLO] would be forced to seek help from sources which might interfere with our principles." "Don't put the cart before the horse," he admonished. "Communisn finds its way to the region through oppression, frustration and aggression."[13]

The leaders of the other five Gulf states emphasized different points in their opposition to the Soviet invasion, although the Palestinian theme engaged most of them, as well. Even Kuwait, the only nation among the six Gulf states that had diplomatic relations with the Soviet Union, did not hesitate to voice criticism. In keeping with its brand of nonalignment, however, it soft-pedaled its criticism of the Soviets by analogizing its opposition to them with its stand against the United States. The Soviets tried to explain their behavior to Kuwaiti leaders in terms of the 1978 Soviet-Afghan treaty, but Kuwait rejected the attempted justification. Foreign Minister Sabah al-Sabah told the Soviets, referring to the U.S.-Iran hostage crisis, that "while objecting to the use of force by the U.S. in the region, Kuwait also stresses its opposition to Soviet involvement in Afghanistan."[14] He also told the Soviet ambassador to Kuwait that Soviet intervention in Afghanistan "might result in sad consequences in the Gulf region," and that Kuwait would continue to assist the Afghan refugees in Pakistan with food and medicine.[15]

The best example of the impact of the Soviet invasion of Afghanistan on the thinking of the leaders of the six Gulf nations regarding the need for "regional cooperation and self-reliance," to borrow their words, emerged during an interview given to the Saudi Arabian newspaper *Al-Jazirah* by the Saudi foreign minister, Prince Saud al-Faysal. He said that the events in Afghanistan had "*confirmed the need for Gulf states to depend on themselves for the protection of their independence and resources,*" and he urged "friendly nations" to offer arms supplies to the Gulf states to help them achieve "self-reliance" for "self-defense."[16]

Prince Saud al-Faysal's statement does more than exemplify the impact of the Soviet invasion of Afghanistan on the thinking of the Gulf leaders. It also captures the fundamental nature of the general consensus that was emerging in the tumultuous days between the eruption of the Iranian Revolution and the outbreak of the Iraq-Iran war. The general consensus seemed to be that the best way to protect the six Gulf regimes from the threat of destruction by external and internal forces was to pool their strength—with the help of friendly countries. While such help would include, inter alia, arms supplies, it would definitely exclude the establishment of "foreign bases" in the territory of any of the six countries. The only country among the six that seemed willing to go beyond accepting arms supplies from friendly nations was Oman.

Sultan Qabus's eagerness to help his regime by forging closer ties with the West stemmed from unusual circumstances. His regime had long fought the South Yemeni–supported Dhofari rebellion with the help of the Shah's armed forces. Although the insurrection had been reasonably contained, it could always erupt again, especially at the instigation of the militant Marxist regime next door, in South Yemen. The sultan was keenly aware of the potential vulnerability of his country for another reason. Among the six, his country alone straddled the Hormuz Strait. Omani land, the narrow and isolated tip of the Musandam Peninsula, stuck out into the center of the strait. Sultan Qabus and the Shah had undertaken the patrol of the strait together. What was Qabus to do with the revolutionary leaders in Tehran?

Sultan Qabus, because he was faced with this predicament, was the only Arab leader among the six who tried to develop a Gulf security concept that would, partly through collaboration with the West, help protect his regime from any threat posed either by the new revolutionary regime in Iran or by the traditional enemy in South Yemen. The Omani Gulf security concept focused on the preservation of freedom of navigation through the Strait of Hormuz. It envisaged financial and technical aid from major oil-consuming industrial nations. The sultan was serious enough about his idea to dispatch Ali Habib, a former ambassador to Iran, on a mission to the other Gulf countries to sell the idea to various foreign ministries, including Iran's. Just as the envoy arrived in Tehran, in late September 1979, the Iranians announced their plan for naval maneuvers in the Strait of Hormuz. The Habib mission seemingly was aborted not only because of the Iranian preference to go it alone, but also because of a visit the Iraqis made to Bahrain and Kuwait in order to sabotage the mission. The Iraqi newspaper *Al-Thawra,* the mouthpiece of the Ba'th party, charged that the "Omani plan" was "a new imperialist alliance." The plan was suspect from the very beginning, because the sultan had a well-known preference for closely cooperating with the West in security matters. Long before the Soviets invaded Afghanistan, for example, he advised the Americans: "What we need is a clear drawing of the line against Soviet involvement in the area." "The U.S. position," he added, "should be clear without ambiguity. You should not allow the Russians to undermine your friends and, in the process, America itself."[17] Paradoxically, the sultan also seemed to share the belief of the other five leaders that the Gulf region "should be kept free from international rivalries in view of its importance as a key oil producer and its strategic location and position."[18]

The apparent anomaly of Oman reflected the fact that the sultan had, as early as 1975 "initiated" an agreement with the United States (through Henry Kissinger) which allowed the Americans to use the British-controlled Masirah Island airstrip off the coast of Oman. Despite

American military and economic "discreet assistance" to Oman afterward, further developments had to wait until after the Iranian Revolution. On 4 June 1980, Oman finally agreed to allow the United States to use certain "facilities." Although clearly unpalatable to the other five Arab leaders, this Omani-American agreement did not stand in the way of the formation of the GCC almost a year later. The overall concern with the Gulf situation and the consensus on the need for cooperation overshadowed this anomaly.

CONCERN OVER AMERICAN MILITARY INTERVENTION

The third major factor in the creation of the GCC was the fear of American military intervention in the Persian Gulf oil fields. To the six Gulf Arab leaders, this threat was quite real in the early days of the Iranian Revolution and the Soviet invasion and occupation of Afghanistan. The Arab leaders remembered their bitter confrontation with the United States in 1975. Although the Arab oil embargo had been lifted a year earlier, largely as the result of Henry Kissinger's peacemaking efforts, the menace of almost-extortionist oil prices prompted Kissinger and President Ford to hint, in their speeches to the United Nations in 1975, at linking food prices to oil prices. The Arabs universally denounced this American "intimidation." However, it was Kissinger's hinting at the possibility of American intervention in Arab oil fields in the event of "some actual strangulation of the industrialized world" that infuriated the Arabs.[19] The memory of these events was very much alive in 1979–80.

The Arab leaders knew all too well that, just as the Iranian Revolution had destroyed their Iranian buffer, it also had ruined the principal prop of American security policy in the Persian Gulf region. They knew that it had been the Shah's regime, primarily, that had served the parallel interests of Iran, the United States, and their own regimes in the security and stability of the region. With the Shah gone, they were afraid the United States might attempt to fill the power vacuum. The Soviet invasion of Afghanistan intensified that fear. Still worse, President Jimmy Carter's unilateral announcement of the American commitment to the defense of Gulf oil supplies—which he made without consulting the countries whose oil was to be protected—seemed to confirm that American military intervention was a possibility.

In his State of the Union Address, the president told Congress on the eve of 23 January 1980:

> The region which is now threatened by Soviet troops in Afghanistan is of great strategic importance. It contains more than two-thirds of the

world's exportable oil. The Soviet effort to dominate Afghanistan has brought Soviet military forces to within 300 miles of the Indian Ocean and close to the Strait of Hormuz—a waterway through which most of the world's oil must flow. The Soviet Union is now attempting to consolidate a strategic position, therefore, that poses a grave threat to the free movement of Middle East oil.

To deter this Soviet threat, the president declared:

> Let our position be absolutely clear: An attempt by any outside force to gain control of the Persian Gulf region will be regarded as an assault on the vital interests of the United States. It will be repelled by use of any means necessary, including military force.

Although the chronology of events, the text of the president's message, and most newspaper reports seemed to point to the Soviet invasion of Afghanistan as the primary reason for America's commitment to defending Gulf oil supplies by military means, it has been shown elsewhere that, on the contrary, the Iranian Revolution had prompted the assumption of this stance.[20] Long before the Carter Doctrine, for example, Saudi leaders had monitored various indications of the forthcoming American commitment and were opposed to it if it meant unilateral military intervention and a demand for bases. King Khalid, for example, warned as early as June 1979 against outside military intervention, and he repeated the favorite local idea of "regional security by regional powers" in response to the American search for bases in the Indian Ocean and the Persian Gulf. The same attitude was evident in other Saudi leaders, such as Prince Abdallah, who expressed the Saudis' concern over the transformation of the Gulf region into "an arena for rivalry among foreign powers."

Always opposed to foreign bases and unilateral military intervention in the Gulf region by the superpowers, Arab leaders regarded the Carter Doctrine as a red flag. Saudi Foreign Minister Prince Saud al-Faysal, in an interview with *Al-Jazirah,* said that Saudi Arabia would continue to strive "to keep the Arabian Peninsula and the Middle East out of international disputes" and stressed his country's "explicit" policy against providing "military bases" for any foreign country on its soil.[21] Crown Prince and Prime Minister Sheikh Sa'ad al-Sabah of Kuwait, to cite another example, said that his country was opposed to "all foreign intervention in the Gulf no matter what its origin." Responsibility for security in the region, he said, "must be assumed by the states in this region which must stay out of conflicts between the big powers."[22]

The less powerful small states of the Gulf were equally concerned about superpower rivalry and military intervention in the Gulf region. For example, the president of the UAE, Sheikh Zayed bin Sultan, attacked the American commitment under the Carter Doctrine to protect the Gulf oil supplies by military force; he said: "All is well in the Gulf and it has no need for American or any other force." He added that the "people of the world would cooperate and live in peace if it were not for the intervention of the big powers. So these powers must work to keep the Gulf region clear of their rivalry."[23] On the need for regional cooperation as a means of coping with the threat to the free flow of Gulf oil supplies, Bahrain's foreign minister, Sheikh Muhammad bin Mubarak al-Khalifa, was unequivocal. He stressed the importance of military cooperation among the oil-rich Gulf states in confronting what he termed the "most dangerous and serious menace to which the Gulf region is subjected at present."[24] He called for a "unified Gulf strategy" to ward off the competition of the big powers in the oil-rich region by assuring the world that the nations of the region would be capable of safeguarding world economic interest in the uninterrupted flow of Gulf oil supplies to world markets and their sale on the basis of the principle of supply and demand.

TOWARD A UNITED ARAB CONFEDERATION?

The preceding discussion makes it clear that the thesis positing the Iraq-Iran war as the reason for the creation of the GCC is simplistic. The birth of the organization reflected a complex conjunction of revolutionary changes, of which the challenge of the Iranian Revolution, the Soviet invasion of Afghanistan, and the threat of American military intervention were uppermost in the minds of the founding fathers of the GCC. This extraordinary mixture of circumstances within one year's time crystallized a consensus on the need for regional cooperation among the six monarchies. Although a tradition of cooperation had developed during the previous decade between Iran and the Arab regimes, as well as among the Arab leaders themselves, it was among the Arab monarchies that the closest human and material ties had been forged. The formation of the UAE also provided encouragement to the Arab countries. Subsequently, their common interest in opposing multiple external threats made the leaders of the six monarchies realize that the stability and security of their regimes could best be protected by joint efforts within the framework of a regional organization.

This prewar consensus on the need for regional cooperation evolved around a number of principles. Predicated on the central value of regional self-reliance, these principles included nonalignment in world affairs, nonintervention by outside powers in the affairs of the Gulf region, and regional security by regional powers. The prewar consensus also envisaged a variety of means, including cooperation in political, economic, social, cultural, and military spheres of activity.

Prior to the war, there were also some visionaries among the leaders of the six nations who embraced loftier goals than regional cooperation. For example, after an important conference at Taif in October 1979, nearly two years before the official formation of the GCC, the Kuwaiti foreign minister said: "We asked if we were, that is, peoples and governments, compatible so that we can move to [a] unity situation, not necessarily a full unity today, rather, a step on a long road. We said let us start by establishing the *United Arab States* so that we can have one foreign policy and unify defense and judiciary together with oil policy and economy in order to preserve our internal laws as Americans did in the United States. Let us strongly study this vital matter and try it."[25]

Nevertheless, even after the GCC was established, identifying its central objective was not easy. After the first GCC summit, held in Abu Dhabi in May 1981, Abdallah Bisharah, secretary-general of the GCC, reportedly said that the organization "is neither a confederal nor a federal one, but a cooperation council."[26] But at the time of the organization's second anniversary, in May 1983, he could say: "Although the Charter does not clearly define the political theory of the GCC, we in the Secretariat have come to the conclusion that the consensus is for a confederal structure. . . . In a nutshell, the goal is confederation. This is the objective."[27] And toward that objective, the GCC has pursued a fivefold strategy of "political coordination," "economic integration," "defense cooperation," "security complimentarity" (internal security cooperation), and "social, cultural and educational approximation."

In summary, the GCC was originally established in response to four major challenges. These were the Iranian Revolution, particularly the threat of subversion; the Soviet invasion of Afghanistan; the superpower competition, including unilateral American military intervention; and the threat of spillover from the Iraq-Iran war. Although the response of the GCC member states thus far has mainly taken the form of regional cooperation, the pre-GCC ideal of a "United Arab States" in the Gulf region is still alive. At the moment, the GCC secretariat thinks that such a united Arab states will ultimately take the form of a "confederation," because "each country wants to retain its own characteristics, legislative power and sovereign attributes." As opposed to other factors, the Iraq-Iran war acted primarily as a precipitative factor, in the establishment of the GCC. But over the past five years, the war has probably become the single most vital catalyst in the process of cooperation among the leaders of the GCC.

The next chapter will examine how these leaders, in order to preserve their regimes, have cooperated in trying to prevent the spread of the war to their countries. But those visionaries who dream about the formation of a new Arab confederation will first have to overcome the great skepticism of critics who believe that the organization is only a "decoration" or that it is essentially "cosmetic" in nature. There are other critics who believe that the GCC is a "rulers' club," put together to protect the status quo and to create a kind of "extended royal family" spreading across the six countries. Such criticisms by politically aware individuals and groups reflect the same challenges that the ruling families face in each country, namely, demands for economic and social betterment and for political participation. Considering the deeper challenge of developing a sense of national identity in individual countries, it is difficult to envisage the development of a sense of GCC identity among the people any time in the near future, whether the rulers aim at creating a confederation or something else as a vehicle for their cooperation.

9

Containment of Subversion and War: The GCC in Action

The Gulf Cooperation Council had to cope with a coup plot against one of its members in its first year, and with acts of terrorism in its third year. Both the coup plot in Bahrain and the multiple bombings in Kuwait were blamed on Iran. To GCC leaders, these incidents confirmed the wisdom of forming the GCC in the first place. Although they pressed on with cooperative activities in political, economic, and other nonmilitary fields, they had to accord internal security the highest priority after the Bahrain crisis.

Only a few months after this crisis, the concern of GCC leaders over the external defense of their countries also dramatically increased. Between the establishment of the GCC in May 1981 and the successful Iranian offensives against Iraq in the spring of 1982, the GCC had been more or less complacent. But when the tide of war clearly turned against the Iraqi forces, fence-sitting became more difficult for the GCC member states. Finally, when Iran retaliated against Iraq by attacking Kuwaiti and Saudi oil tankers, there seemed to be little left of the GCC's troubled neutrality.

In trying to contain the twofold threat of subversion and war, the GCC governments preferred to use diplomatic instruments. At the same time, they sought to strengthen their nations' capability for both internal security and external defense. They strove to forge ever-closer internal security ties and to create an integrated defense system among the six member states. During this period, despite their many differences, the GCC states and Iran somehow managed to exercise mutual restraint and to maintain a dialogue concerning their relationship.

A TROUBLED NEUTRALITY

Although the GCC as an entity officially adopted a neutral position vis-à-vis the war between Iraq and Iran, observing a strictly neutral policy proved difficult from the beginning. The difficulty was rooted in the revolutionary developments that had led to the establishment of the organization in the first place, including, of course, the threats of Iranian-inspired subversion and the spread of armed conflict to the territory of the GCC states. Three of the states—Saudi Arabia, Bahrain, and Kuwait—had shared with Iraq the fear of internal subversion in 1979–80. The Saudis had been threatened by the Sunni fundamentalist rebellion at Mecca and two Shia uprisings in Qatif. The Bahrainis, the Kuwaitis, and the Iraqis had all faced various kinds of internal Shia disturbances that had been either inspired by the Iranian revolutionary example, as in Bahrain, or instigated by a pro-Khomeini Shia leader, as in Kuwait.

Against the backdrop of this commonality of concern, the Iraqi invasion of Iran was seen for what, in part, it had been—an effort to contain the Iranian Revolution in Iraq. Saddam Hussein's claim that he was fighting Iran not only in self-defense, but also in defense of all the Arab states of the Gulf region, appeared to have some merit. Although other Arab state leaders were aware that the Iraqi leader's claim was intended to legitimize his decision to invade Iran, on the basis of their similar experiences with pro-Iranian agitations, they were not too unhappy when the war began. If the invasion of Iran could not thwart the Iranian determination to export the "Islamic Revolution," then perhaps nothing could.

At the same time, the Arab leaders who eventually formed the GCC were not necessarily happy about the Iraqi invasion. Instead of being a blessing in disguise—in the sense of containing the perceived threat of Iranian subversion in the Gulf region—the invasion could backfire in two ways if Iran won the war. First, a triumphant Iran could march against an Arab monarchy such as Kuwait. Second, even if Iran did not expand the war beyond Iraqi territory, an Iranian unconditional victory over Iraq could ignite rebellion among Sunni and Shia dissidents throughout the Gulf. In either case, Iran might then try harder than ever to dictate oil price and production levels within OPEC.

Caught between these opposing considerations, GCC leaders professed friendship for both belligerents soon after the organization was established. The day after the GCC was formally created, the president of the UAE said, on behalf of the GCC, that at the summit meeting of the leaders of the organization the hope had been expressed that the war would not continue until now. We also hoped that there would be no war. However, this is God's will. No one knows what is good or what is the alternative. The only result of war is unhappiness. It causes destruction and is against progress. In any event, we are affected by this war, as we also are by any confrontation between Islamic Iran and fraternal Iraq, because they are neighbor and brother countries . . .. We and Iran are linked by relations stemming from Islam and neighborliness. Iraq is a fraternal country. Both are our brothers in Islam and Arabism.[1]

Unofficially, however, Saudi Arabia and Kuwait have aided Iraq financially and logistically, and little UAE has shared a small part of the financial burden. Yet, given the essentially ambivalent attitude of GCC leaders toward Iraq, on the one hand, and their overall domestic and external vulnerability vis-à-vis Iran, on the other, the GCC states, unlike Jordan and Egypt, have avoided committing any troops or volunteers to the Iraqi war effort.

The discrepancy between the official GCC neutrality and the actual support of Iraq by some GCC member nations has at times led the organization to acknowledge the anomalousness of its position. For example, Secretary-General of the GCC Bisharah was reported to have told the Qatari newspaper *Al-Rayah* on 16 January 1982 that all Gulf countries have become a basic party in this war, and to have asked: "How can we be mediators in an issue in which we are a major party?"[2] This frank admission of the GCC's predicament in maintaining neutrality in practice proved irksome in some Arab circles. The newspaper *Al-Khalij* called on the GCC members "to pause and define a clearer stand on Mr. Bisharah's statement"; the newspaper declared that Bisharah's statement was "news to the council states in addition to [being] a contradiction of the [neutral] stands declared by the states at the Abu Dhabi and Riyadh summits."[3]

Both these summit meetings took place before the coup plot in Bahrain in December 1981. From the establishment of the GCC in May 1981 until then, GCC pronouncements emphasized impartiality in the war, and the organization relied on intermediaries such as the Islamic Conference Organization, the Non-Alignment Movement, and the United Nations. It also sought mediation efforts by Algeria, Syria, Japan, and other countries. In spite of mutual recriminations by Saudi and Iranian radio programs, Saudi leaders in particular went out of their way to suggest that the attitude of the GCC states toward Iran should be amicable. For example, Foreign Minister Prince Saud al-Faysal said in November 1981, only one month before the Bahrain coup plot, that the relations of the members of the council with Iran "should be excellent and based on the basic pillars of international relations, that is, relations of fraternity, religion, and neighborliness.''[4]

COPING WITH SUBVERSION

The discovery of the coup plot in Bahrain sent shock waves through the GCC states. To outsiders the clumsy plot did not warrant all the commotion it caused, but for the GCC leaders, particularly the leaders of Bahrain, Kuwait, and Saudi Arabia, the plot confirmed that the threat of pro-Iranian subversion in Arab monarchies justified the establishment of the GCC. Convinced that the Khomeini regime had had a hand in training and arming the "saboteurs," some GCC leaders dropped all pretense of neutrality and denounced the role of Iran in the coup plot. They also launched an unprecedented campaign for greater and more formal security arrangements among the GCC states as a means of protecting their own regimes against internal subversion. In fact, the incident marked a major shift of priorities among the panic-stricken conservative monarchies. Previously, the GCC had emphasized economic integration, purportedly patterning its activities on the model of the European Economic Community. After the coup plot was discovered, security was accorded the highest priority.

The ordinarily soft-spoken Saudis seemed to take the lead in launching the GCC's diplomatic offensive against the Khomeini regime. Saudi Interior Minister Prince Nayif publicly condemned the alleged Iranian complicity in the "conspiracy." He said:

We had hoped that Iran, our neighbour and friend, would not have such [conspiratorial] intentions. But after what has happened in Bahrain, our hopes have unfortunately been dashed and it has become clear to us that Iran has become a source of danger and harm to the Gulf nations and their security. At the very beginning of their revolution, the men in power in Iran said that they would not be the policeman of the Gulf [a reference to a remark by Premier Shahpour Bakhtiar]. Today they have unfortunately become the terrorists of the Gulf. Iran previously considered itself to be the policeman of the Gulf, but even in those days there did not happen what is happening today because of the actions of the men currently in power in Iran who have said that they are hoisting the banner of Islam and consider that their policy is being guided by the Islamic faith. But now we find that they have violated Islam by doing harm to Muslims.[5]

Saudi Arabia also took the initiative in arranging for much closer cooperation among the GCC states in matters of security. Reportedly, Prince Nayif flew to Bahrain with a squad of Saudi security men to interrogate the Saudi suspects.[6] It is clear that Saudi and Bahraini authorities collaborated closely during an in-depth investigation of the coup plot.

Secretary-General Bisharah's view that "what happened in Bahrain was not directed against one part [Bahrain] of this body [GCC] but against the whole body" was shared among most GCC member states. The Saudis rushed to conclude bilateral security agreements with Bahrain, Qatar, and Oman. The GCC foreign ministers held an emergency meeting in Manama on 6 and 7 February 1982, when Bahrain was praised by the organization for resisting "the acts of sabotage that are carried out by Iran." In a follow-up meeting in Riyadh on 24 and 25 February, interior ministers from GCC states reached a consensus on the need for a multilateral internal security agreement *(al-tansiq al-amni)* among all the GCC states. In advance of such an agreement, however, they declared that "intervention by any country in the internal affairs of one of the member states is considered to be intervention in the internal affairs of the GCC states."[7] The formal declaration of this principle was followed by increased cooperation in internal security matters among GCC member states.

The usually independent-minded Kuwaitis held back on signing a bilateral security agreement with Saudi Arabia. They were also the main stumbling block in the way of finalizing a multilateral security agreement among the GCC states. By the third GCC summit meeting (9–11 November 1982), the organization had before it for review a draft agreement composed of thirty-nine articles. Starting with the principle "that preservation of the security and stability of the GCC countries is the joint responsibility of the GCC countries," the draft agreement provided for security measures against not only "criminals," but also "opponents of the regime." The controversial fourth chapter of the draft agreement, regarding the extradition of "criminals," was believed to have prevented the Kuwaitis from signing the agreement. Presumably, Kuwaiti leaders found the relevant provisions incompatible with their "constitutional norms and international agreements." Other explanations were also offered. Some observers believed that the Kuwaitis did not wish to allow the pursuit of "criminals" into their territory, although those in pursuit would not be authorized to go more than twenty kilometers into the territory of the signatory states. Others believed that the Kuwaitis wished to avoid being identified too closely with the Saudis. The Saudis' tolerance of political dissidence is far lower than that of the more open and liberal Kuwaitis.

Even the multiple bombings in Kuwait in December 1983 did not seem to move the Kuwaitis any closer to signing the internal security agreement. For its part, the GCC seemed to play down the incident. The

GCC's reaction to the coup plot in Bahrain had been far more serious, at least in public. In reference to the bombings in Kuwait, GCC leaders simply said: "These incidents were expected and are expected to be repeated."[8] Strangely enough, GCC officials attributed such acts of terrorism to the frustrations of "some parties" with the organization's "success" in the Lebanon crisis and the Iraq-Iran war. And they predicted: "The GCC countries will further strengthen their cooperation to push forward the march of the GCC."[9] The incident was probably played down by design. Close observation at the time revealed that security measures were being tightened throughout the GCC area. By creating a joint military force not only for external defense, but also for internal security, the GCC states may have accomplished the main purpose of the agreement without formally signing it.

THE GCC'S DIPLOMATIC DISAPPROBATION

About three months after the coup plot in Bahrain, GCC members were confronted with new developments in the war between Iraq and Iran. The impressive Iranian offensive against the Iraqi forces in March 1982, followed by the recovery of Khorramshahr in May, ended about nine months of relative GCC complacency about the war. The specter of an Iranian victory loomed ever larger until finally, in July, the Iranian forces carried the war into Iraqi territory. At their third summit meeting, GCC leaders had to take note of these new developments. Yet, still pursuing a cautious policy toward Iran, they mildly criticized it for "crossing its international border with Iraq," and they pointed out "the greater threat which these developments pose to the safety and security of the Arab nation." They also asked Iran to respond to the peacemaking efforts of the Islamic Conference Organization, as they had done so many times before. Apparently, some GCC members had demanded that their organization as a whole take a much tougher stand against Iran at this time. For example, *An-Nahar* claimed that some GCC leaders had called for a joint decision to recall all the GCC diplomatic representatives from Tehran.

Nevertheless, most members of the GCC preferred that the organization not take a tough stand by itself. The GCC chose, instead, to convince other, larger, international organizations to go along with its strictures against Iran. The GCC leaders managed to elicit a relatively stiff Gulf War Resolution out of the Arab League at the league's Fez summit meeting in September 1982. This resolution stated at the outset that "the Arab presidents and kings have announced their readiness to carry out their commitments to Iraq in accordance with Article Six of the

Arab League Charter and Article Two of the Collective Arab Defense Pact in case Iran fails to respond to the peace efforts and continues its war against Iraq." It also warned Iran that its actions against Iraq could be viewed as "an act of war against the Arab Nation."[10]

Despite the fact that Iran paid no heed to this major Arab League resolution, the pronouncements the GCC made at its own fourth summit meeting at Doha, Qatar, on 7–9 November 1983 were, as usual, cautious and inoffensive. Sheikh Khalifah Hamad al-Thani, the emir of Qatar, simply referred to the United Nations 31 October resolution on the freedom of navigation and announced his nation's regret over the shedding of Islamic blood and the waste of human and economic resources. On behalf of the GCC, he said, "We still hope that Iran will follow Iraq's example in responding positively to endeavors to end the war."[11] At the time, the GCC continued to criticize Iran only restrainedly, mainly because Iranian forces seemed increasingly unable to win a decisive victory.

In 1984, however, when the war of attrition appeared to heat up, the GCC's diplomacy clearly went on the offensive. Nevertheless, the GCC leaders continued their favorite diplomatic practice of confronting Iran indirectly, through other international organizations. After Iran seized the Majnoon Islands inside Iraqi territory in February 1984, the GCC states began, to a degree unseen before, to marshal support for their diplomatic offensive against Iran. With unusual speed, the foreign ministers of the six nations met in Riyadh, mapped their strategy, and flew to Baghdad in March, when the Arab League tried to force Iran to the negotiating table by, in effect, calling on all countries to stop furnishing arms and spare parts to Iran.

Only after the intensification of the tanker war in April–May 1984, however, did the GCC discontinue fence-sitting altogether. It managed to convince the Arab League, during its meeting in Tunis on 20 May, to characterize the Iranian attacks on the Saudi and Kuwaiti oil tankers as acts of Iranian aggression. It also pushed its case against Iran in the United Nations Security Council, where on 1 June 1984 it successfully sponsored Resolution 552 against Iran (although Iran was not mentioned in the resolution by name).

THE GCC'S CREDIBLE DETERRENCE

The GCC rulers realized that diplomacy alone could not contain the spread of war to their lands, as evidenced by Iran's repeated "accidental" air raids on Kuwait. Just as the GCC states could augment their individual efforts toward tightening internal security against subversion through closer bilateral and multilateral cooperation, they could strengthen their individual defense and deterrence capabilities against external threats by combining their programs of military modernization. The role of Saudi Arabia, of course, was pivotal. As the largest and most powerful member of the GCC, it could spread its protective wing over its junior partners. By the time the GCC was created, Saudi-American discussions were leading toward the Air Defense Enhancement Package, through which the United States sold five AWACS and other military equipment to Saudi Arabia. The combination of these new sophisticated systems and the approximately sixty F-15 interceptors already in Saudi Arabia's possession assured a greater degree of defense and deterrence capability for Saudi Arabia's GCC partners, as well. From the very beginning of the GCC, in 1981, the Saudis had clearly indicated their desire to work toward an "integrated regional defense system."[12]

Such a system would obviously benefit the smaller GCC states. For all practical purposes, Bahrain, for example, did not have an air defense system of its own. The other GCC states were not much better off, although Oman and Kuwait had better systems than Qatar and the UAE. And yet, in the judgment of some American military leaders, such as Defense Secretary Casper W. Weinberger, under certain circumstances (for example, in thwarting attacks on its oil fields) Saudi Arabia would benefit from cooperating militarily with its junior GCC partners. The potential the six states had for building up their military capability for common defense and deterrence was, on paper at least, impressive. As the richest small group of countries in the world, the GCC had a defense budget that amounted to about $40 billion a year in the 1980s. This amounted to about half of the entire developing world's defense spending. Oman spent more than 40 percent, and Saudi Arabia about 28 percent, of its GNP on defense. Furthermore (again, on paper) the GCC states' combined air power, which included some three hundred fighter aircraft and eight hundred helicopters, was a force to be reckoned with.

Given that Iranian air power had been cut down to about one-third of its former strength by May 1981, the combined air power of the six GCC states seemed all the more impressive, but such a facile comparison omits many relevant variables. No one knew exactly how far Iranian air power had been eroded because of losses in the war, lack of spare parts, and other difficulties, and Iran still controlled the sea lanes of the Persian Gulf with its relatively more powerful navy. Furthermore, it still had a powerful fleet of helicopters, its ground forces dwarfed the combined forces of all the GCC states, and its forces had been battle tested over many years.

To view the balance of forces from another perspective, the GCC states' enormous defense budget and impressive air power (in terms of equipment) did not compensate totally for the many problems they faced in creating an integrated defense system. For example, in trying to diversify the sources of their arms so as to avoid becoming too dependent on the United States, the GCC states, individually and collectively, have come to possess a hodgepodge of weapons systems, making it difficult for them to standardize military hardware. In addition, given the large numbers of expatriates in their sparsely populated societies, the GCC governments face the problems of a dearth of manpower—they could put up only some 190,000 troops—and the presence of too many foreign nationals in their military services. For example, in the Omani military services, 700 of the 1,100 officers above the rank of captain are nonnationals. Saudi Arabia employs some 10,000 foreign soldiers, most of them Pakistanis.[13]

Yet, as seen by the rulers, there is no alternative for the GCC but to complement its preferred instrument of foreign policy—that is, diplomacy—with military strength. Toward that end, ever since 25 January 1982, when the GCC defense ministers met for the first time, the GCC leaders have pressed for the creation of an integrated defense system. After holding many unproductive meetings, the GCC states finally arranged for joint manuevers, and, in October 1983, for the first time, the armed forces of Bahrain, Kuwait, Oman, and Qatar, as well as Saudi Arabia, joined in military exercises known as the Peninsular Shield, a venture more satisfying on paper than in reality.

The tanker war in the spring of 1984 resulted in further strengthening of the Saudi air defense system and further efforts toward an integrated defense system among the GCC states. Although the United States "turned down" the Kuwaiti request for Stingers after furnishing them to Saudi Arabia, Washington took other steps to help Kuwait. Before the tanker war, the United States had allowed Saudi Arabia to share AWACS data with Kuwait on an ad hoc basis, but in June 1984 it helped to formalize the arrangement as a means of upgrading the air defense capability of Kuwait. However, the action, according to the State Department, was taken "on an intermittent basis" and was limited to "occasions when there is a clear and immediate threat of possible penetration of Kuwaiti airspace."[14] The United States also decided to upgrade the Kuwaiti air defense missile system, which was composed of improved American Hawks. The combination of the sharing of AWACS data between Saudi Arabia and Kuwait and the upgrading of the Kuwaiti missile system was believed to aid the GCC members further in their cooperative efforts.

Perhaps no less important, the tanker war goaded the GCC officials to work even harder toward developing an integrated defense system. At their meeting on 23 June 1984, the GCC chiefs of staff abandoned the GCC foreign ministers' 14 June idea for creating a sea corridor close to the shores of their states, over which would be extended a GCC "air umbrella." Instead, they took certain steps "to speed military integration," according to Secretary-General Bisharah, who also said that "the Iranian attacks on Kuwaiti and Saudi oil tankers have prompted the council's states to speed up unification of the military effort under a united command."[15]

If approved, the recommendations of the GCC chiefs of staff would bring the member states closer than ever before to the goal of an integrated defense system. First, they recommended that a grant of an estimated two billion dollars be made to Oman to upgrade its air defense system and to increase the effectiveness of its nascent radar network in the Strait of Hormuz in order "to monitor Iranian activities aimed at obstructing navigation in the Strait."[16] Second, they recommended the formation of a "semiunified command" for the armies of the six countries, presumably on the assumption that the early-warning stations that had recently been established would work in coordination with the AWACS planes operating in Saudi airspace. Such a network for sharing data would require American permission, as had the Saudi-Kuwaiti arrangement mentioned above. Third, they recommended the formation of "a Gulf rapid deployment force."

Although after the meeting of the GCC chiefs of staff, the Saudi air force reportedly began flying almost continuous patrols over the western Persian Gulf to protect oil tankers from Iranian attacks, it was not at all clear how far the Saudis would go in defending them. Would they defend Saudi shipping in international waters as well as in Saudi territorial waters? Would they defend the shipping of the other GCC states in both the upper and the lower parts of the Persian Gulf? So far, it is difficult to say. For example, only five days after Saudi Arabia shot down an Iranian F-4 fighter plane, Iran attacked from the air the Kuwaiti supertanker *Kazimah* in the southernmost part of the Gulf. But not a single GCC plane tried to protect the tanker from the attack, despite the fact that the Iranian plane was known to have had the oil tanker under surveillance for four hours.

THE DIALOGUE BETWEEN THE GCC AND IRAN

The foregoing discussion may present the distorted impression that the relationship between Iran and the GCC has continually been a life-and-death struggle. That is far from the truth. Although harsh words have been exchanged during crises, such as the discovery of the Bahrain coup plot or the Iranian seizure of parts of the Majnoon Islands at the height of the tanker war, the fact remains that both the GCC states and Iran, despite these very difficult circumstances, have managed to maintain a dialogue. In the spring of 1983, for example, at the height of the crisis brought on by the Iraqi-created oil spill in the Gulf region, the Kuwaiti and UAE foreign ministers went to Tehran on behalf of the GCC in the hope of mediating between Iraq and Iran.[17] They hoped to use the oil spill as a means of achieving a limited cease-fire between the two belligerents which could then be extended into a negotiated peace settlement. Behind the scenes, the GCC countries tried to improve relations between Iraq and Syria in the hope of weakening the Tehran-Damascus axis and hence putting pressure on Iran to go to the negotiating table. At one point, the GCC states also hinted at their willingness to provide financial aid to cover the material losses of the combatants and to help with the reconstruction of "vital establishments." Reportedly Saudi Arabia convinced the Syrians to go to Tehran at the height of the tanker war in order to persuade the Iranians to stop hitting oil tankers.

The Iranian attitude toward the GCC has been equally restrained. From the Iranian perspective, Iran had no alternative other than retaliating in kind when the Iraqis began the tanker war. Yet, by all impartial accounts, Iran's response was by and large an "underresponse"—apparently the Iranians demanded "one eye for two" rather than "an eye for an eye." Considering that it was well known that Saudi Arabia and Kuwait were aiding Iraq financially and logistically, the "accidental" air raids on Kuwait were clearly seen by GCC officials for what they were—warnings to Kuwait to stop aiding Iraq.

More important, although the Iranians have launched propaganda attacks, Iranian leaders have seldom condemned the GCC outright. Hojatolislam Hashemi-Rafsanjani, Speaker of the Iranian *Majlis,* set the tone by saying that the Iranian attitude toward the nascent organization would depend on whether it served the interests of its own members or those of foreign powers. To be sure, the Iranian ambassador to Kuwait once referred to the GCC as a "satanic gathering," but this did not reflect the attitude of the Iranian leaders. The Iranian government's reservations about the GCC have been voiced mainly with respect to two issues. First is the issue of Oman's close military relations with the United States. Deputy Foreign Minister Ahmad 'Azizi said in an interview in August 1983: "Unfortunately, it should be said that the presence in the Gulf Cooperation Council of some countries such as Oman, [with] its strong ties with America and the attempts it makes to expand these ties and to expand American military presence in the Sea of Oman, . . .

poses a big question mark over the aims of that council in the region."[18] But this is not too harsh a criticism of the GCC, considering that the GCC member states themselves have reservations about the Omani-American relationship. In fact, Foreign Minister Saud al-Faysal found Omani participation in the American Bright Star military exercises in November 1981 objectionable because it contradicted the principle of nonalignment, which, he said, was "accepted by all member countries of the Gulf Cooperation Council."[19]

The second, and the more important, issue that strains Iran-GCC relations, of course, is the Saudi and Kuwaiti logistical and financial aid to Iraq. From the outset of the war, while Iran has repeatedly warned the GCC rulers against getting involved in the war, it has also assured them that it has no territorial or other designs on their countries. Thus, after the Saudis shot down an Iranian F-4 plane in June 1984, President Ali Khamene'i told the Arab Gulf states:

> If you find that after all the help you have given it, Iraq refuses to listen to you [about halting attacks on oil tankers], then stop helping it. Stop making available your ports, your money, your propaganda. Get out of this war . . . we have nothing against you. If you continue, then we will have the right to act with firmness against all who oppose us . . .. We do not want to fight Saudi Arabia, Qatar, Bahrain and others . . . but this is on condition that they do not get mixed up in this war.[20]

What is the explanation for Iran's tolerant attitude toward the GCC's "tilted neutrality" in the war? There are three major factors to consider. First, Iran would have even less of a chance of winning the protracted, costly, and bloody war with Iraq if Iran allowed its dwindling air power to be diverted to new Arab fronts. Second, in spite of all their tough, defiant rhetoric about taking on the United States if need be, Iranian leaders are well aware of the so-called Reagan corollary of the Carter Doctrine. They know that the United States would probably intervene militarily in the Gulf region if the security and stability of the House of Saud were jeopardized by war or other means. Third, revolutionary Iran, like all other Gulf states, wishes to avoid a situation that could lead to a confrontation between the superpowers in the Gulf region. Iran would be the first victim of Soviet counterintervention against any American military intervention in the Gulf region.

In spite of the war, the GCC countries and Iran share a number of principles and interests. First, the Islamic bond between them is stronger than that between Iraq and the GCC states, even though they subscribe to different brands of Islam. To revolutionary Iran and conservative GCC states alike, the secular, socialist tenets of Ba'thism are unacceptable. Second, GCC leaders and Iranian leaders share an abiding suspicion of the Ba'thist regime, despite the current marriage of convenience between the GCC states and Iraq. The expectation that the Ba'thist regime will return to its prewar pattern of subversive activities in the Gulf region is prevalent on both sides of the Gulf. Third, although the Iranians claim a right to leadership in the Persian Gulf region, both GCC leaders and Iranian leaders believe in the principle of regional security by regional states. The Iranian claim to primacy in the region is nothing new to the GCC rulers. They lived with it during the Shah's days, and they can live with it now.

The convergence of Iran's principles and interests with those of the GCC states is best exemplified by UAE-Iran relations. UAE officials, for example, remember that the Iraqis are suspected of murdering the UAE minister of state for foreign affairs, Said Ghobash. The presence of a large number of Iraqi opponents of Saddam Hussein in Abu Dhabi reinforces anti-Iraqi and pro-Iranian sympathies in the UAE. At the same time, the presence of a large number of Iranians in Dubai (composing about 10 percent of its population) combines with a brisk re-export trade between Iran and Dubai and the shiekhdom's longstanding friendliness toward Iran to favor relations between the UAE and Iran. Iran-Sharjah economic ties also favor the development of good relations between the UAE and Iran. The UAE is probably the only GCC member state ever to have been considered by revolutionary Iran to be a "progressive country led by wise men."[21]

By May 1985, Iran was establishing good relations with other GCC countries. The breakthrough in Saudi-Iranian relations as a result of Foreign Minister Saud al-Faysal's visit to Tehran on 18 May was partly initiated by the GCC Ministerial Council. More important, this breakthrough was expected to lead to an improved dialogue not only between Saudi Arabia and Iran, but also between all the GCC member states and Iran. According to reliable sources, the GCC officials had prepared "comprehensive mediation proposals" aimed at ending the Iraq-Iran war.[22] They had also offered "assistance to Baghdad and Tehran to rebuild institutions destroyed in the war between the two countries." The same sources also indicated that Saud al-Faysal's visit to Iran would be followed up by the visit to Tehran of a GCC ministerial delegation, probably made up of three GCC ministers.

Whether or not the GCC succeeds in ending the war, Iran and the GCC states have managed to maintain a dialogue. That dialogue will expand, especially after the war. Iran would probably support the GCC states if their rulers were to build an Arab confederation friendly toward Iran. The war has introduced complications into its relations with the

GCC, but Iran has at least maintained correct relations with the GCC. Just as the Shah's Iran managed to welcome the formation of the United Arab Emirates, revolutionary Iran will probably welcome the creation by the six GCC members of an Arab confederation that will acknowledge Iran's primacy in the Gulf.

Regarding the immediate relations between the GCC and Iran, a subtle change for the better occurred in November 1985. On 6 November the leaders of the GCC concluded their sixth summit meeting, held in Muscat, Oman, by issuing a communiqué that was interpreted to indicate a move by the GCC toward a "more neutralist position" on the Iraq-Iran war.[23] Although the final communiqué referred to the stance assumed by the Supreme Council at its fifth session, in November 1984, the language of the new communiqué seemed to be more conciliatory, especially in one respect. It emphasized "the need of the GCC states [to be ready] to continue their endeavors with the parties [Iraq and Iran] concerned to end this destructive war *in a manner that safeguards the legitimate rights and interests of the two sides* in order to bring about the establishment of normal relations among the Gulf states."[24] This stated concern of the GCC with the "legitimate rights" of Iran triggered an unprecedented show of Iranian approval for the GCC's stance. Speaker Hashemi-Rafsanjani praised the GCC, reportedly saying: "For the first time they [the GCC states] did not praise Iraq, and did not say that Iran does not want peace but Iraq does. Rather, they emphasized that they must better their relations with Iran. And this is a sort of realism which has emerged in the GCC."[25] Subsequently, on 18 November, he claimed: "We have believed all along that the countries supporting Iraq will change their policies and give up their support when they lose hope in the Baghdad government."[26] During the entire month of November, the Iranian media conducted an unheard-of chorus of praise for the GCC's new stance. Even *Jomhuri-ye Eslami,* which usually takes a hard line, interpreted the GCC communiqué as "the first indirect criticism of the Saddamist regime's policy in this region" and as "the first step on the correct path of closer ties with Iran"; its Arabic article concluded with this statement: "The absence of support for Iraq by the GCC is considered a break with the general framework of decisions which the GCC is accustomed to adopting, as the previous GCC meetings had conveniently supported Iraq in the war it imposed on Iran."[27]

The GCC and Iran attributed the change in the GCC's stance to different factors. Other Iranian leaders subtly gave themselves credit for the change in the GCC's attitude on the war, but Prime Minister Musavi bluntly said: "These changes have naturally taken place in the light of our firm stands."[28] Such an interpretation was not welcomed in the GCC countries. The *Khaleej Times,* for example, revealed the offended Arab sensibilities more than a month later, stating in an editorial titled "Gulf Countries and Iran" that the Iranian prime minister "has gone so far as to imply that it is only Tehran's hard line that is responsible for what he called recent positive signals from neighbouring states that they wished to improve relations with Iran." The editorial went on to say: "If Mr. Musavi was referring to the Gulf countries, and last month's AGCC summit, where a calculatedly mild resolution was adopted on the Gulf war, then he is mistaken when he sees in this vindication of the Tehran regime's intransigence." On the contrary, the *Times* contended; although the GCC states have made "no secrets of their solidarity with the brotherly Arab country of Iraq, [they] have sought to maintain a dialogue with Iran."[29]

There was an element of truth in both interpretations, but the real reasons for the admittedly "mild resolution" on the war were inadequately noted. One major reason was the concern of the GCC rulers that the war, as they characterized it, had reached a "critical stage" and threatened to spread as a result of the Iraqi escalation of air raids on the Kharg Island oil terminal beginning in August 1985 and the Iranian retaliatory strategy of searching ships suspected of carrying arms and other war materials for Iraq. The other main reason was the 25 May 1985 assassination attempt against the ruler of Kuwait. Although neither the threat of the spread of the war nor terrorism was new in the area, these two recent developments were clearly on the minds of the GCC leaders, as evidenced by their 1985 communiqué and the statements of Sultan Qabus of Oman, King Fahd of Saudia Arabia, the emir of Kuwait, and others during and after the summit meeting. They seemed determined to keep both war and terrorism from spreading across their borders through an intensified dialogue with Iran. This strategy significantly differed from the GCC's disapprobation campaign against Iran at the height of the tanker war in the spring of 1984.

One may say, therefore, that the GCC's mild position on the war was a mere ploy. Saudi Arabia and Kuwait continued their financial and logistical aid to Iraq, and the GCC communiqué called on Iran to observe not only the more neutral UN Security Council Resolution 540 of 1983, but also resolution 552 of 1984, which was an anathema to Iranian leaders. Yet, the fact remains that the GCC states have consistently opposed Iraqi efforts to destroy the Kharg Island oil terminal for fear that the terminal's destruction may well result in Iranian air strikes against their own oil installations or in Iranian efforts, as a last resort, to hamper freedom of navigation. In this context, the more balanced stance of the GCC resulted in an intensified dialogue with Iran. Preventing the spread of the war and terrorism to the GCC nations was a hope, and indicating disapproval of the Iraqi escalation of armed hostilities was an intention. Finally, as it turned out, the conciliatory attitude of the GCC toward Iran also improved the overall political atmosphere in the Gulf only weeks before the Iranian foreign minister paid his important visit to Saudi Arabia.

As long as the Iraq-Iran war continues, however, relations between Iran and the GCC states will fluctuate according to the state of the armed hostilities. The Iranian offensives launched in February 1986 seemed to mar the improved political climate that had followed the exchange of visits by the Saudi and the Iranian foreign ministers and the GCC's issuance of its mild communiqué at the conclusion of its sixth summit in November 1985. The first Iranian offensive (dubbed "Dawn 8") against the Iraqi army in the southern extremity of the front, which began on 9 February 1986, resulted in the capture of the Iraqi oil port at Fao, and the second offensive ("Dawn 9"), in the northernmost sector of the war front, which began on 25 February, resulted, according to Iranian claims, in the capture of the town of Choarta. The chorus of mutual recrimination between Iran and the GCC states following these successful Iranian offensives resembled that which had followed Iran's capture of parts of the Majnoon Islands two years earlier. On 24 February 1986, the United Nations Security Council for the first time announced that it deplored the "initial" aggression that had started the war in 1980, although it did not mention Iraq by name. But, like the GCC's November 1985 communiqué, this U.N. resolution came too late to persuade the Iranians to discontinue their nibbling war.

Part Three

THE EASTERN MEDITERRANEAN

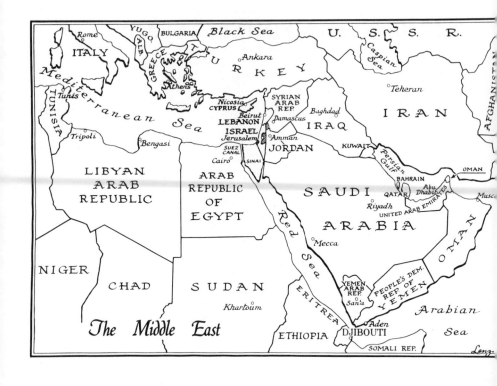

The Middle East

10

The Eradication of Israel?

For a quarter of a century, Iran and Israel were two of the major supporters of American policy in the Middle East. Iran and Israel shared with the United States the strategic goal of resisting the expansion of Soviet power and influence in the Middle East. Thus, the Shah's alignment with Israel reflected this common strategic interest of the two countries rather than a common concern with the Arab states. The Shah's regime opposed Nasser's Egypt, therefore, not because of its hostility toward Israel, but largely because its antimonarchical radicalism was reinforced by its close identification with the Soviet Union.

The Iranian Revolution brought many changes. No longer did the Shah police the Persian Gulf; gone was his discreet alignment with Israel. To Israel, that alignment had been useful not only against the Soviet Union but also against the hostile Arab states that encircled Israel. Tel Aviv's connection with Tehran, like its connection with Ankara, breached the Israeli wall of isolation in the Middle East. The Iranian Revolution, however, enlarged the hostile circle around the Jewish state.

The revolutionary regime in Iran has been one of the most implacable enemies of Israel. It aims at the "eradication" of the state of Israel through the establishment of a Palestinian state by means of armed struggle. Its crusade against Israel extended to Lebanon and was a factor in the Shias' resistance to the Israeli occupation forces in Lebanon; eventually the Israeli forces had to withdraw. Iran's crusade threatens to spill over into Israel proper.

THE TEHRAN–TEL AVIV ALIGNMENT

Beginning in 1953, when he overthrew the nationalist government of Muhammad Musaddiq, the Shah forged an alignment with Israel that lasted until 1979, when he lost his throne. To understand both the nature of this alignment and the destruction of it by the revolutionary regime, we need to examine the troubled origins of Iran's connection with Israel. As early as 1941, when the Shah ascended the throne, he wished to ally himself with the United States.[1] With the forced abdication of the Shah's father, Reza Shah, in that year, previously suppressed political forces burst on the scene with a vengeance. In addition to the assistance of his father's old civilian and military supporters, the young Shah needed the backing of an external power like the United States. He wished to resist both the pressure of domestic forces of opposition and the perceived threat of the Soviet Union—as much a bête noire for him as for his father. The Shah hoped that an Iranian connection with the new nation of Israel (which attained statehood in 1948) would help him achieve his goal of forming an alliance with the United States.

Of the three major political forces in Iran at the time, however, two were clearly opposed to an alliance between Iran and the United States as well as to any Iranian connection with Israel. These were the pro-Soviet and anti-Zionist Tudeh Communist party, on the extreme left, and the Shia fundamentalists, on the extreme right. The centrist nationalists were preoccupied with a crusade against British domination of Iran through the Anglo-Iranian Oil Company. The liberal intellectuals in this group did not oppose either the United States or Israel, although they were sensitive to Arab nationalist sentiments regarding the recognition of Israel.

Nevertheless, through his loyal prime minister, Muhammad Sa'ed, the Shah managed to grant de facto recognition to Israel in 1950. The Israelis had sought Iranian recognition for their own reasons; one reason was their desire to breach the wall of isolation which had been built around them by hostile Arab states after the Arab states' humiliating defeat in the 1948 war.[2] They also wanted to facilitate the immigration (Aliyah) of persecuted Iraqi Jews through Iranian territory. But they worried from the outset about the durability of the Iranian recognition. Leftist and rightist extremists in Iran tried to pressure the government of Ali Mansur and Ali Razmara to rescind the recognition given by Sa'ed. Shia fundamentalists assassinated General Razmara.

Prime Minister Muhammad Musaddiq was also confronted with the demand that Iran withdraw its recognition of Israel. He, however, was more susceptible than his predecessors had been to the pressure of the anti-Israeli Shia fundamentalists and the Tudeh communists. Musaddiq's all-absorbing crusade was against British policies in Iran, and his coalition government relied on the support of the same religious and leftist forces that demanded the cancellation of the recognition. As a liberal intellectual, Musaddiq did not oppose the recognition of Israel, but as a nationalist leader, he was vulnerable to the pressure of Arab nationalists, especially those of Egypt. As a compromise, he closed down the Iranian Consulate-General in Jerusalem in 1951—"for the time being"—but did not withdraw recognition.

In 1953 an American-supported coup against Musaddiq returned the Shah to power. Having suppressed all the forces of opposition, he resumed his courtship of both the United States and Israel. He developed relations with Israel in great secrecy, for he had to take into account the adverse impact such ties would have on Iran's relations with the Arab world. In every other way, his interests ran parallel with those of both the United States and Israel. Externally, they all opposed the Soviet Union and the extension of its power and influence in the Middle East. Israel was no longer a nonaligned state, as it had been before 1950, and the United States was waging a cold war with the Soviet Union everywhere. Furthermore, the Shah hated the Soviet Union more than ever, because in August 1953, through the Tudeh Communist party, it had tried to establish a "people's democratic republic" in Iran on the ruins of the Pahlavi dynasty.[3] Internally, the three countries seemed to have overlapping interests, as well. The Shah wanted to modernize Iran's military and economy as a means of maintaining his regime, the Pahlavi dynasty, and Iranian independence. To him these goals were fused, and the United States and Israel could help him achieve them. Iran could pay for the assistance with its oil. The Americans had acquired a 40 percent share in the Iranian oil industry as early as 1954, and the Israelis purchased all the oil the National Iranian Oil Company could sell them.

The identification of the United States and Israel with the Shah's regime over a quarter of a century resulted in two internal developments of relevance here. First, although Jews had lived in Iran for 2,500 years, they had seldom, if ever, been treated as well as they were during the Shah's regime. The essentially secular thrust of the Shah's policies favored all religious minorities in Iran, in spite of occasional aberrations. One of the most gifted Iranian minorities, the Jews took full advantage of the Iranian economic boom. Like the Muslim middle classes, they prospered as merchants, lawyers, pharmacists, doctors, and so on. The 600 members of the Tehran Association of Jewish Physicians, for example, exerted a strong influence. Most of the 200,000 Jews who lived in Iran during the Shah's regime settled in major cities such as Tehran, Shiraz, and Isfahan.

Second, the growing hatred of the Shah's policies among his opponents was transferred to Israel and the United States. The Shah's strategic alignment with Israel was low key. Few Iranians knew that "house number 10" in Tehran was the large, unidentified Israeli mission. And the Shah always blamed the Iranian oil sales to Israel on foreign oil companies. Yet, these aspects of the Shah's policy toward Israel would not have caused much resentment if they had been well known. It was the regime's association with the Israeli intelligence service, Mossad, which angered the public. Mossad was totally identified with the Shah's CIA-created SAVAK. This was the principal instrument of the regime's repressive measures, which included physically punishing religious and secular political dissidents by electric shock, tearing out of fingernails and toenails, rape, and genital torture.[4]

Just as the Shah's alignment with Israel was not anti-Arab, but anti-Soviet, it was not anti-Palestinian, either.[5] Even before the birth of Israel, Iran had favored the Arab position on the question of Palestine. In 1947 Iran, with Egypt, Iraq, Lebanon, Saudi Arabia, and Yemen, voted in the United Nations for a federated state of Palestine composed of two autonomous Jewish and Arab states, and against the partition plan. After the state of Israel came into existence in 1948, Iran endorsed the principle of "the legitimate rights of the Palestinian people," whether this was interpreted to mean their "repatriation" to their homeland in Palestine, as in United Nations Resolution 2535 of 10 December 1969, or their "self-determination," as in the joint Irano-Egyptian communiqué of 12 January 1975. After the Rabat conference, the Shah's Iran also accepted the notion that the Palestine Liberation Organization (PLO) must participate in the peace process, for United Nations Resolution 242 talked only about Arab refugees. Long before, Iran had consistently pressed for Israel to withdraw from the West Bank and the Gaza Strip on the basis of this resolution. The Shah's government also opposed Jewish settlements in occupied territories and the control of Muslim holy sites by non-Muslims.

The Shah's principal concern about the Palestinians was their radical factions, which trained and armed his Iranian opponents. For example, the head of the Marxist Popular Front for the Liberation of Palestine (PFLP), George Habash, and a leader of the Iranian Marxist-Leninist *Fada'eyin-e Khalq,* Hamid Ashraf, joined in opposing the Shah's regime. They formed the leading terrorist group in Iran, which began its "armed struggle" against the Shah's government as early as 1971. Caught between his general support of the Palestinian cause and the enmity of radical Palestinian factions to his regime, the Shah used to say: "We know how to discriminate between the justness of the Palestinian question and the wrongdoing directed against us by some Palestinians."[6]

"TODAY IRAN, TOMORROW PALESTINE"

The Iranian Revolution totally destroyed the Shah's longtime alignment with Israel. Iran's relations with no other country in the world, even the United States, were so quickly and drastically overturned as its relations with Israel were. The revolutionary regime's relations with the United States and all the Gulf states, including Iraq, did not deteriorate until after the so-called second revolution that destroyed the provisional government of Mehdi Bazargan. The only country besides Israel with which Iran broke relations was Egypt, and the principal reason for that break was Egypt's signing of the peace treaty with Israel.

This display of enmity toward Israel from the very outset reflected more than Ayatollah Khomeini's alleged anti-Semitism—although he had said harsh things about the Jews. For the Iranian revolutionary leader, the roots of the animosity lay elsewhere. "What informed individual does not know," he asked rhetorically, "that one of the areas of our difference with the deposed shah concerned his friendly relations with Israel? Who does not know that for over 20 years now we have in our statements and sermons regarded Israel as equal to the United States in oppression and [as] its follower in aggression and looting, and [that] we have condemned it as such?"[7]

This close identification of Israel with the Shah's regime and its repressive policies was widely held and largely accounted for anti-Israeli sentiments. Even before the revolutionary forces took power, the Shah's alignment with Tel Aviv was condemned by his last prime minister, Shahpour Bakhtiar. In seeking a vote of confidence by the *Majlis* on 11 January 1979, Bakhtiar called for Iran to "fully support" its Arab neighbors, "especially the Palestinian people, in the goal of achieving their legitimate rights." In an apparent demonstration of that support, he added that Iran would not resume oil shipments to Israel once oil production, which had been disrupted by oil strikes during the revolutionary upheaval, started up again.[8] Iran had provided 60 percent of Israel's oil imports. In anticipation of this serious blow to its economy, Israel had already negotiated long-term supply agreements, certainly with Mexico, and possibly with Nigeria and Gabon, as well. Israel had also built up a six-month reserve of oil supplies and had received the guarantee of the United States, under the 1975 Sinai agreement, to meet Israeli oil needs.

Nothing in the personal or political background of Prime Minister Bakhtiar indicated an anti-Israeli predisposition. Quite the contrary. Like many other liberal intellectuals, he would probably have left the matter alone had anti-Shah sentiments not been transferred to Israel. He was making a popular decision in the hope of distancing himself from the Shah's past policies, and at the same time he was trying to put to rest popular suspicions against his own government.

Even the moderate, low-key prime minister Mehdi Bazargan could not resist the public pressure to break totally from Israel. Only a week after the revolutionary forces took power, his government severed all relations with Israel. On 18 February 1979, Iran broke off diplomatic relations with the Jewish state and recalled Iranian diplomats. The announcement of the decision was timed to transmit a symbolic message, for the decision was made public only hours after Yasser Arafat met with the Bazargan cabinet. The prime minister was quoted as saying that the break was "fully in keeping with the policy announced before we came to power of cutting all ties with Israel."[9]

The popularity of the Palestinian cause in Iran was nothing new. As noted above, as early as 1947 the Iranians had sided with the Arab states on the Palestinian question in the United Nations, and both the nationalist government of Muhammad Musaddiq and the Shah's regime had consistently supported the Palestinians' cause. Furthermore, the Shah's government had opposed the Jewish settlements in the West Bank, had supported United Nations Resolution 242, and had insisted on the participation of the Palestinians in the peace process. The Shah believed that if "the rights of the Palestinian nation [were] not fulfilled, there [would] be no peace in the area."[10]

Yet, support for the Palestinian factions by the revolutionary regime was quite a different matter from Iran's earlier endorsements of the Palestinian cause. In effect, the Khomeini regime, or at least the leftist radical forces, wanted somehow to repay the Palestinians for their moral and other support. Reputedly, the PFLP had helped train the Iranian *Fada'eyin-e Khalq,* and the *Fatah* had done the same for the other major Iranian armed guerrilla group, the so-called Islamic Marxists or *Mujahedin-e Khalq.* Although Yasser Arafat played coy and while he was in Iran said nothing that would divulge the nature of the Palestinian aid to the Iranian revolutionary forces, he said enough to indicate that the Palestinians had helped them and probably expected aid from the revolutionary regime in return. He said: "It is enough that we are here, and no matter how much we have helped we can not offer as much back as the Iranian people have offered us." His slogans were also revealing. He called Iran his "second home," after Palestine. He hailed the "common goals" of the Iranian and Palestinian revolutions and throughout his visit to Iran, which began with a meeting with Khomeini on 17 February 1979, parroted Khomeini's slogan Today Iran, Tomorrow Palestine.

REPLACING ISRAEL WITH PALESTINE BY FORCE

Notwithstanding the pervasiveness of the anti-Israeli and pro-Palestinian sentiments in Iran and the prerevolutionary alignment between the Iranian and Palestinian revolutionary factions, it is doubtful that Iran would have taken such an extremist position against Israel had the Bazargan government not fallen. In taking over the American embassy on 4 November 1979, thereby precipitating the downfall of the Bazargan government, the student militants pointed out repeatedly that their action aimed at forestalling the return of both Israel and the United States to Iran "through the back door." In the minds of the extremist factions on both the right and the left, the normalization of relations with the United States by the Bazargan government would invite Israel back into Iran. They accused "the liberals" of conspiring in fact to bring Israel back, despite the formal break in relations with Tel Aviv.

Indeed, the triumph of the leftist and rightist radicals over the nationalist moderates meant a total break with the state of Israel. Suddenly, the followers of the "Khomeini line" discovered the Iranian nationalist leader Muhammad Musaddiq's "original sin" of having failed to withdraw the de facto recognition of Israel when he closed down the Iranian Consulate-General in 1951. To them, Bazargan and his technocratic cabinet members, including, at first, his foreign minister, Karim Sanjabi (the leader of the National Front), and then Foreign Minister Ibrahim Yazdi, were all cut from the same cloth. At heart they were supporters of both Israel and the United States, it was alleged.

The subsequent victory of the religious right over the secular left further doomed any chances for a more tolerant attitude toward Israel. It also threatened, for the first time, the Jewish community in Iran. Historically, that community had suffered during periods of ascendancy of Shia extremists, such as during the Safavid and Qajar dynasties. Although the liberal nationalists as well as enlightened Shia clerics had found it desirable to provide for the right of representation of the Jewish minority in the Iranian *Majlis* at the turn of the twentieth century, improvement in the treatment of Jews by the Muslim majority had occurred mainly during the reign of the modernizing, secular Pahlavi Shahs after 1925, particularly during the 1960s and the 1970s, before the Iranian Revolution.

After the second revolution, the Khomeini regime developed goals far beyond the earlier goal of destroying the Shah's alignment with Israel. The regime seemed to aim at exterminating the Israeli state itself. The revolutionary rhetoric depicted Israel as the "illegitimate offspring" of the Great Satan, and the United States as "the godfather" of the "twin evils of Zionism and American imperialism." Beyond the virulent anti-Israeli rhetoric, however, the revolutionary leaders seemed to have concluded that under no circumstances could Iran compromise with Israel, and that Iran should oppose any nation or non-state actor that tried to do so. The most often repeated "reason" offered for this totally hostile attitude was that "Israel will never make any concessions" to the Arabs. These were the words of the influential Speaker of the Iranian *Majlis*, Hojatolislam Hashemi-Rafsanjani. They reflected a view that was widely held by Iranian revolutionary leaders.

On the basis of this assertion, the revolutionary leaders argued that the Israelis would never accept the creation of a Palestinian state on the West Bank and the Gaza Strip. Even assuming that the Israelis were prepared to concede such an "impossibility," said Speaker Hashemi-Rafsanjani, the creation of such a state would not resolve the Palestinian problem. The "densely populated area already holds more than the [absorptive] capacity of the region" and could not absorb "3 or 4 million other Palestinians," he said. Hence, the Palestinians would necessarily "remain as refugees all around the world." Under such circumstances, the Speaker concluded, "if we recognize the validity of Israel's existence, we will be losing everything."[11]

While depicting the Palestinian problem in such apocalyptic terms, Speaker Hashemi-Rafsanjani suggested his own solution. "Go and take a place with force and say our government will be established here," he instructed his Arab and Muslim listeners. To put it differently, he was advocating the resolution of the Palestinian problem through armed struggle. This advocacy of the use of force to resolve the Arab-Israeli conflict did not, in the view of revolutionary officials, rule out the use of political means. But the more effective means was considered to be armed force. Even the relatively moderate foreign minister, Ali Akbar Velayati, suggested that the way "to face Israel is not only with political action[;] rather[,] all Muslims, Arabs in general and Palestinians specifically should take action based on armed struggle."[12]

Whereas Velayati seemed to want the Arabs and the Palestinians to launch an armed struggle against Israel, the more radical Iranian leaders seemed to wish to extend the struggle against Israel to the entire Muslim world. They advocated what may be called the "Islamization" of the Arab-Israeli conflict. Speaker Hashemi-Rafsanjani's words clearly support this proposition: "The means of eradicating the Zionist regime and the establishment of another government to replace it in Palestine lie in massing all powers of the Islamic world, foremost of which will be the capabilities of the Islamic Republic of Iran, Syria, Libya and Algeria."[13]

Unlike Syria and Libya, Algeria has been little involved with the Iranians in their anti-Israeli crusade. Perhaps with the exception of Libya, no Muslim state other than Iran—not even Syria—would go so far as to advocate the "eradication" of the state of Israel by force. Iranian leaders certainly opposed every peace initiative, including the Camp David Accords, the Fahd Peace Plan, the Fez Plan, and the Reagan Plan. Following the resumption of diplomatic relations between Jordan and Egypt, and especially the 11 February 1985 agreement between Yasser Arafat and King Hussein, the Syrian, Iranian, and Libyan tripartite alignment was emphasized as a counterweight to this initiative in the peace process. The *Majlis* Foreign Policy Committee issued a statement that, among other things, denounced the Hussein-Arafat agreement:

> The new agreement between the Jordanian regime and the PLO on extending recognition to the Zionist regime as well as entering into a lasting peace with it with regard to the territories occupied in 1967, including the establishment of a Palestinian government within the context of a confederal government with the Jordanian Monarchy are a rash step along the Camp David path; it is, moreover, aimed at moderating the consequences and repercussions of successive defeats suffered by the United States and the Zionist regime in Lebanon.[14]

IRANIANS FIGHTING ISRAELIS IN LEBANON

The Israeli invasion of Lebanon in June 1982 seemed to provide an opportunity for revolutionary Iran to give substance to its virulent crusade against Israel. In fact, as it turned out, strife-torn Lebanon was an ideal battlefield for the Khomeini regime to challenge simultaneously the ideological "twin evils of Zionism and American imperialism." Khomeini depicted the Israeli invasion as an "American plot" that was designed to divert the attention of Iran from its war against Iraq, and he warned the Iranians not to fall into this American trap, but at the same time he condemned the "deathly silence" of the Arab states that failed to come to the aid of the beleaguered Palestinians. He also called for the use of the Arab oil weapon. Against the backdrop of an apparent paralysis of the Arab and Soviet friends of the Syrians and the Palestinians, the only courageous words seemed to emanate from revolutionary Iran.

Khomeini did not offer to use Iran's oil weapon; presumably he needed it in the ongoing war with Iraq.

As friends of the PLO and Syria since the revolution, Iranian free-lance militants had all along wanted to join the PLO and Syria in Lebanon in the fight against Israel. As early as December 1979, an agitating cleric, Hojatolislam Muhammad Montazeri, led two hundred to three hundred "volunteers" to Syria, where they intended to join their "Palestinian brothers" in southern Lebanon for the fight against Israel. They were taken, instead, to the military camp of Al-Fatah, about fifteen miles from Damascus, after the Lebanese protested to Syria, after which Hafiz Assad assured President Elias Sarkis that the Iranian volunteers would not be permitted to enter southern Lebanon.[15] At the time, reportedly, both the PLO leader and the Syrian president were embarrassed by the episode.

By the time the Israelis invaded Lebanon, however, Iran was more than just a friend to Syria; it was an ally. Only two months earlier, the two countries had formalized their alliance. Iran had to show some kind of support for Syria, which was helping Iran in the war against Iraq.

One day after the Israeli invasion, a high-ranking Iranian military and political delegation arrived in Damascus. It included the commander of the Islamic Revolutionary Guards Corps, Colonel Sayyed Shirazi, who revealed that the Iranian delegation was there to plan "a religious war [*jihad*] against the Zionist enemy" in coordination with the Iranian Supreme Defense Council. To stress the seriousness of their purpose in fighting against Israel in Lebanon, other Iranian leaders made many statements that fell just short of a formal declaration of war against Tel Aviv. Under the constitution, such a declaration was solely the prerogative of Khomeini. Prime Minister Musavi unfurled the banner of "victory to Al-Quds" (Jerusalem) in asking his cabinet to approve a budget for the war against Israel.[16] He was also the first Iranian leader to say that Palestine was "a part of [the] Islamic homeland." In response to a question from a correspondent, Iranian Foreign Minister Ali Akbar Velayati said: "Yes, we announced our readiness to start fighting against Israel. . . . Naturally, one of the consequences [of declaring war against Israel] could be an Israeli attack against the Islamic Republic of Iran. We will be completely prepared for an engagement with Israel at any price."[17]

In effect, Iran was declaring a new form of armed conflict—not a regular war, but a "volunteers' war" against Israel. The decision to wage this kind of war against territorially remote Israel had been made about one year before the Israelis invaded Lebanon. According to a statement made by 138 *Majlis* deputies on 8 June 1981, the decision was

made jointly by two organs of the Iranian government, the Iranian Supreme Defense Council and the Islamic Revolutionary Guards Corps.
The decision, said the parlimentary deputies, had its "roots in the international Islamic revolution."[18] Subsequently, the Iranian government
also decided to make public its "plan for an Islamic front" worldwide,
which, according to Musavi, would be "followed up" by the Iranian
ministry of foreign affairs, "because the fight against imperialism
should take place all over the world."[19]

From this point on, details of how the plan for the Islamic front was to
be implemented became murky, probably for reasons of secrecy and
deniability with respect to the operations of Iranian volunteers and Islamic front groups. Nevertheless, there is little doubt that something
like an Islamic Revolutionary Council was established as an umbrella
organization, and that it included such groups as the Supreme Assembly
of the Islamic Revolution in Iraq and such "movements" as the Islamic
Revolution Movement of the Arabian Peninsula and the Islamic Liberation Movement of Bahrain. A "liberation" group was probably created
or already existed for Syria and Lebanon. There is also no doubt that
these liberation groups were linked to the IRGC through its Islamic
liberation movement unit. This unit and the liberation movements met
in November of 1981 in Tehran and unanimously condemned the Fahd
Peace Plan.[20]

The revolutionary group for Syria and Lebanon probably became the
conduit for the Iranian presence in Lebanon with the blessing of Hafiz
Assad. The Iranian delegation that visited Damascus formalized the
arrangements, and subsequently Syria allowed between eight hundred
and one thousand revolutionary guards to enter Lebanon. More than
three hundred guardsmen were initially stationed in the Syrian-con-
trolled Bekaa Valley, largely in the town of Baalbek. In addition to the
Iranian volunteers and guardsmen, there were stationed in this same
area a large number of the followers of Islamic Amal, a pro-Iranian
group that separated from the moderate mainstream Shia Amal movement in Lebanon after the Iranian Revolution. The interconnections of
these groups and the revolutionary regime in Iran will be examined
more closely in chapter 13.

The Israeli Defense Force (IDF) in Lebanon believed that the Iranians had been responsible for a suicide truck bomb attack on the Israeli
military headquarters in Tyre which killed twenty-nine Israeli soldiers.
They decided to retaliate. In November 1983, they mounted two air
raids on barracks housing Iranians in the area of Baalbek, killing
twenty-three Iranian Revolutionary Guards. This was the first incident
of armed conflict involving Iranians and Israelis. The revolutionary

leaders, who for years had poured out vitriolic anti-Israeli rhetoric, now had a chance to show the Arab and Muslim world concrete evidence of their willingness to make an "Islamic sacrifice." Prime Minister Hussein Musavi depicted the dead guardsmen as the first group of Iranian "martyrs" in the fight against Israel. The day before their bodies were returned to Iran for burial, he also predicted that Israel's "desperate move against the Islamic Revolution" would have the effect of "the Islamization of the struggle against Zionism and imperialism in the region."[21] He believed that the Arab-Israeli conflict had been transformed into an Islamic-Israeli struggle involving "all Muslims against Israel."

IRANIAN JEWRY

How did Iranian Jewry fare during this revolutionary move to promote the "eradication" of the state of Israel? As mentioned previously, although Jews had lived in Iran since before the destruction of the First Temple in Jerusalem nearly 2,500 years ago, they had rarely been so well treated as they were during the Pahlavi dynasty, and particularly in the heyday of oil prosperity. Harking back to Cyrus the Great, the first Persian monarch, who freed the Jews from Babylonian captivity in 538 B.C., the Pahlavi Shahs, who idealized pre-Islamic Persian history and culture as a formula to legitimize their rule, had no trouble easing ancient legal, social, and political restrictions on the Jews.

Iranian Jews felt threatened by the revolution for a number of reasons. First, historically, an increase in the influence of the Shia clergy in the affairs of the state, such as during the Safavid and Qajar periods, had been associated with anti-Jewish restrictions, just as the opposite had been true during the liberal constitutional period as well as during the era of secular, although dictatorial, modernizing Pahlavi monarchies. The revolution ushered in not just the influence, but also the actual rule, of the clerical class in a newly established Islamic Republic presumably committed to the reestablishment of Islamic law (shariah) as the central value guiding Iranian behavior. Second, Iranian Jewry evoked an unpleasant image for the Iranian revolutionary militants; Iranian Jews had been pro-Shah, pro-American, and pro-Israeli. Third, the ancient hatred of the Shia fundamentalists for the "heretic" followers of the Bahai faith could be extended to the Jews, for many of them had associated actively with the Bahais in business and professional pursuits. Fourth, and finally, Khomeini made enough anti-Semitic remarks prior to the revolution to fuel the Jewish fear of intolerance by his regime.

On the other hand, there were at least some reasons for the Jews to temper their fear. No matter how the Ayatollah might view the Jews, or how intolerant his zealous supporters might be, the Jews were, after all, one of the "peoples of the book," and their monotheistic faith, like that of the Christians, had been recognized by Islam. They, also like the Christians and the Zoroastrians, had enjoyed the right of representation in parliament under the 1906–07 Iranian Constitution. As a religious legist, or *faqih,* Khomeini would be bound by the *shariah* to abide by the precepts of Islamic law, if not the old constitution. Despite such rational indications of a hopeful future, however, the revolutionary upheaval unleashed passions that frightened all religious minorities. The Jews were horrified to note, for example, at the time of the bloody demonstrations in Tehran on "Black Friday" (8 September 1978), the menacing slogan Death to the Jews and Bahais. Subsequently, the militant Shias and the communists charged that some Israeli soldiers and Jews had participated with the Shah's troops in the brutal killing of the unarmed demonstrators on that day.

Iranian Jews, like other religious minorities, had high hopes about the government of Mehdi Bazargan. As soon as he took office, the representatives of Iranian Jewry presented their demands. These included constitutional guarantees of religious freedom and autonomy in private laws, the continuation of the Jewish school, the continuation of Jewish representation in parliament, and the promotion of Jews to senior positions in government. In the meantime, the rash of summary executions took the lives of some Jews; the Shia militants had taken the law into their own hands. The Bazargan government helplessly complained about the multiplicity of power centers amid revolutionary chaos and criticized summary executions, which took place without due process of law. On 9 May 1979, a multimillionaire Jewish industrialist, Habib Elghanian, was executed on charges, among others, of "spying" for Israel. Iranian authorities stressed that his execution had nothing to do with his religious faith. About a year later, the execution of another Jew sent shock waves through the Jewish community. Albert Danielpour was charged with the "murder" of factory workers, collaboration with the American CIA, and "cooperation in establishing the State of Israel." Reportedly, after the Elghanian execution, Khomeini had told a delegation of Iranian Jews that they would be treated fairly under the revolutionary regime, but many Jews had reluctantly left their homeland because they were afraid of mistreatment.[22] By June 1980, the exodus of some 30,000 Jews was reported, reducing the remaining Jewish community to 40,000 to 50,000, including at least 70 Iranian Jews who were held in jail at the time.

Iranian Jews were also concerned about the implications of Islamization for their lives in revolutionary Iran. The enactment of the so-called Islamic law of punishment and retribution and its regulations in 1982 frightened many religious minorities as well as modern Muslim intellectuals. Although it would appear that the law was enacted only "experimentally for five years," some of its provisions were found to be shocking to the recognized religious minorities such as the Jews. Article 152 of the law, for example, which prescribed one hundred lashes as punishment for sodomy (*lavat*) if the offense was committed by two Muslim men, in a related note stipulated that if the "active offender" (*fa'el*) was a non-Muslim, he would be executed.[23]

IRAN'S ISLAMIC CHALLENGE TO ISRAEL

Given the pre-Islamic Iranian tolerance of the Jews, and the continuous residence of Jews in Islamic Iran despite mistreatment during periods of ascendancy of clerical influence, the Iranian recognition of the state of Israel and the Shah's discreet alignment with it might appear quite natural. But the truth is that the Shah's relationship with Israel was motivated much less by these historical and cultural experiences than it was by political and strategic considerations. In tandem with this alignment and in keeping with the secular and modernizing thrust of the Shah's policies, the status of Iranian Jewry also improved. The Iranian Revolution destroyed the Tehran–Tel Aviv alignment, and Iranian Jews felt threatened by the implications of Islamization for their future.

The Khomeini regime's virulent anti-Israeli stance has primarily reflected the resentment of the revolutionary leaders over Israel's close identification with the Shah and the United States. More specifically, the close working relationship between Israeli intelligence and SAVAK led to the surge of anti-Israeli feelings.

The campaign to eradicate the Israeli state was supported by many Iranian revolutionary leaders, and it would be logical to conclude that the campaign would be a durable feature of the regime's foreign policy. Yet, the physical distance between Iran and Israel, the lack of territorial conflict between the two countries, the human ties between them, the potential strategic utility of Israel to Iran vis-à-vis the Soviets, and the continued attraction to Iranians of Israeli technological and medical know-how and facilities, among other factors, could some day temper the current ideological hostility of Iran toward Israel. In the meantime, however, revolutionary Iran has made the solution of the Palestinian problem, especially the "liberation of Jerusalem," one of the fundamental goals of its foreign policy. As stated earlier, the importance of one small and indirect arms purchase from Israel should not be exaggerated;

this was an isolated incident that occurred under unusual circumstances.

The Iranian campaign of Islamization of the Arab-Israeli conflict has so far spread propaganda more than any thing, but that is not all it has done. The example of the Iranian Revolution has undoubtedly deepened the Palestinian resolve to resist the Israelization of the area through Jewish settlements. In the absence of a peaceful solution to the Palestinian problem, the armed struggle that revolutionary Iran has been advocating as the only effective way to resolve the Arab-Israeli conflict might indeed become the instrument of resistance to Israeli occupation in the West Bank, and on a scale unimagined before.

As a result of the Iranian Revolution, Israel has suffered one of the greatest strategic setbacks of its history. It has lost a staunch and powerful ally in non-Arab Iran. Elsewhere in this book, I will suggest that even the Israeli decision to invade Lebanon might be better understood if the impact of Israel's strategic loss of Iran is taken into account. Similarly, Israel's costly defeat in Lebanon can be better understood by recognizing the enormous psychological impact of the Iranian example on the Shia resistance movement in south Lebanon.

11

The "Excommunication" of Egypt?

The challenge of revolutionary Iran has been as traumatic for Egypt as it has been for the Arab states of the Persian Gulf region. Egypt's distance from Iran, its position as the leading military power in the Arab world, and its strategic importance to the world—rivaling that of Iran—did not immunize it to the reverberations of the Iranian Revolution. The Khomeini regime not only has destroyed the Shah-Sadat strategic alignment in the Middle East but has also challenged the Islamic credentials of both the Sadat regime and the Mubarak regime as a means of keeping Egypt out of the Arab and Islamic fold as long as possible.

The Mubarak regime, like the Sadat regime before it, has tried to respond to the Iranian challenge mainly through diplomatic counteroffensives. The Mubarak regime has also sided with Iraq in the war against Iran and has provided men and arms in support of the Iraqi war effort.

The Iranian ideological crusade against Egypt has been tempered by Iran's interest in seeing its exports and imports pass unimpeded through the Suez Canal. It has also been tempered by the legacy of mutual cultural and intellectual respect between the two countries.

The cutting edge of the Iranian challenge to Egypt and to other states in the Middle East, however, has been Iran's Islamic fundamentalist ideology. Egypt's response to that challenge has been greatly influenced by the significant problems of the Egyptian economy, politics, and society.

THE SADAT-SHAH ALIGNMENT

The death of Gamal Abd al-Nasser in 1970 ended the cold war between Tehran and Cairo that had begun with the Shah's return to power in 1953. The American-supported coup against the nationalist government of Muhammad Musaddiq did more than return the Shah to power. It marked the beginning of the fulfillment of the Shah's oldest dream: an alignment with the United States.[1] He gave the United States a 40 percent share in the Iranian oil industry for the first time. He also obtained membership for Iran in the American-sponsored alliance of the Baghdad Pact. The Shah's basic purpose in forming an economic and strategic alliance with America was to insure the survival of his regime and the Pahlavi dynasty, which were being challenged by the Shah's domestic and foreign enemies. Domestic foes consisted mainly of nationalist, communist, and Muslim fundamentalist forces. The principal foreign adversaries were the Soviet Union and Nasser's Egypt.

The Nasser-Shah cold war characterized the relationship between Egypt and Iran during most of the 1950s. The Shah suspected an alliance between Egypt and the Soviet Union, especially after Moscow sold arms to Cairo. Presumably angered by the Shah's recognition of the state of Israel, the Nasser regime broke diplomatic relations with Iran in 1960. A continually escalating propaganda war between Cairo and Tehran raged throughout the 1960s until the Arab-Israeli war of 1967. The humiliating defeat of Nasser was no doubt welcomed in Tehran. The Shah's discreet ally, Israel, had cut Nasser down to size. In the postwar years before his death, Nasser appeared to be moving away from Moscow and toward Washington; this movement was welcomed by the Shah. Finally, after a decade, diplomatic relations between Egypt and Iran were resumed in 1970, shortly before Nasser's death.

Yet, the great opportunity for rapprochement between Egypt and Iran arrived only after President Anwar al-Sadat took power. Sadat's troubles with Moscow were as welcomed by the Shah as was his friendship with the conservative Arab states of the Persian Gulf region, especially his alignment with King Faysal before the 1973 October war. During the war, the Shah called for Israel to withdraw from occupied territories. He airlifted medical supplies to Jordan, sent pilots and planes to Saudi Arabia to help solve logistical problems, and permitted some Soviet supply planes to fly over Iran en route to Arab countries. After the war, the Sadat-Shah alignment was reinforced by a "pathbreaking" billion-dollar economic agreement that stipulated Iran's participation in the reconstruction of Port Said, the widening of the Suez Canal, and the construction of a pipeline to transport oil from Suez to Port Said. In addition, Egypt granted to Iran the use of port facilities on the Mediterranean which Iran would use as an outlet for commercial and industrial activities.[2]

The Tehran-Cairo alignment was further aided by the Shah's unconditional support of Sadat's approach to peace with Israel. As an old ally of Israel, the Shah welcomed the 1975 Sinai agreement. He also applauded the historic visit of Sadat to Jerusalem in 1977. Behind the scenes as well as publicly, the Shah's regime supported the prolonged, tedious peace negotiations between Cairo and Tel Aviv all the way to the Camp David Accords in 1978. By this time, the revolutionary process in Iran had begun to gain momentum. The future of the Shah's regime, and hence his strategic alignment with Egypt, were both threatened.

KHOMEINI AND SADAT

During his marathon negotiations with Menachem Begin in the seclusion of Camp David, President Sadat managed to put a telephone call through to the beleaguered Shah. The revolutionary forces had just shaken the very foundation of the Shah's regime, on 8 September 1978 launching the largest demonstration ever. Sadat conveyed to his "brother Muhammad Shah" the unswerving support of Egypt for his regime. On that day—known in the annals of the Iranian Revolution as Black Friday—the Shah's troops fired into unarmed crowds, killing many thousands of innocent demonstrators. Neither Sadat nor the Shah could have known that this was the beginning of the end. The Egyptian leader subsequently sent Vice-President Husni Mubarak to Tehran in order to brief the Shah about the Camp David Accords and to reaffirm his personal friendship with the Shah as well as the common "strategic interests between their two countries."[3]

The revolutionary storm forced the Shah out of his homeland. He landed first in Egypt, on 16 January 1979, and Sadat welcomed him warmly. By this time the Egyptian president himself was getting into deep trouble with his fellow Arabs. He had been censured by the Arab states for signing the Camp David Accords in September 1978. Iraq had taken the lead in the Arab campaign against Egypt, as Saddam Hussein hosted the first Baghdad Conference against Sadat in November 1978. Egypt was also threatened with sanctions if it went through with the signing of a peace treaty with Israel. Receiving the Shah under such circumstances would add to Egypt's isolation in the Middle East, because revolutionary Iran would join the Arab ranks against Egypt.

Sadat paid no heed to these considerations. His officials insisted that the reception of the Shah did not imply a specific Egyptian political stand on the revolution in Iran. Sadat emphasized his personal friendship for the 59-year-old monarch. He also kept saying how grateful he was for the Shah's aid to Egypt during the 1973 October war. The Egyptian press took a slightly different tack. The leading semiofficial newspaper, *Al-Ahram,* seemed to regret that everyone else had deserted the Shah and expressed the opinion that the people of Iran would remember him in the future for the good things he had done for them.[4] Of course, what must have concerned Sadat most of all did not figure in any of this public discussion. Sadat had just lost his staunchest Middle Eastern ally and was worried about the new shape of political alignments in the Middle East.[5]

The attitude of the provisional government of Prime Minister Mehdi Bazargan toward Egypt seemed cautious, and some even expected it to be conciliatory. Egypt had received and honored Bazargan's old friend, the nationalist leader and prime minister Muhammad Musaddiq, in the 1950s. The modern-educated middle class in Iran had always felt a historic and cultural attraction to Egypt. The Bazargan government had based its foreign policy in the Middle East on equality, reciprocity, and neighborliness. Bazargan was pursuing this approach with the Gulf states and wished to pursue it with Egypt, as well. But the single most important obstacle in his way was Sadat's signing of the Camp David Accords. The denunciation of the Egyptian leader by the Arab world did not help matters. Furthermore, Yasser Arafat was the first Arab leader to be received by the Bazargan government, only a week after the revolutionary forces seized power. The same domestic forces on the extreme right and left that favored cutting off all ties with Israel and building an alliance with the PLO also pressured the Bazargan government to break off diplomatic relations with the Sadat regime quickly.

These pressures became difficult to resist after the second Baghdad Conference, in late March 1979. Vice-President Saddam Hussein truly ran the show. Sadat was condemned for betraying the Palestinian cause, and even the moderate Saudis and other conservative Gulf states, except Oman, went along with imposing both diplomatic and economic sanctions on Egypt. Bazargan finally yielded to a combination of pressures from inside and outside Iran. The religious and secular extremists took heart in the ostracism of Sadat by nearly all Arab states, moderates and radicals alike. On 30 April 1979, Bazargan's government finally broke diplomatic relations with Egypt. But even then, Bazargan would not go as far as his critics wanted him to go. They demanded that economic sanctions be imposed on Sadat's Egypt, in accordance with the decision reached at the Baghdad Conference. But Foreign Minister Ibrahim Yazdi indicated that no such sanctions were being contemplated by the Iranian government.[6]

The fall of the Bazargan government in November unleashed the ideological crusade of the Khomeini regime against Egypt, just as it was unleashed against the Gulf states. Khomeini's brand of Islam was considered by Khomeini's supporters to be superior to that of Egypt, and the Iranians' traditional respect for Egypt as the center of Islamic thought and culture seemed to vanish overnight. A devout modern Muslim leader himself, Sadat tried to take up the challenge of Khomeini's brand of Islam. In dealing with the Iranian question, he juxtaposed Egypt's "true Islam" against Khomeini's fundamentalist Islam. Although the Islamic tradition lacks the institution of "excommunication," beginning at that point, the campaign of the Khomeini regime against Egypt seemed to take on the characteristics of that institution.

Even before the clerics gained control of Iranian foreign policy, they attacked the kind of Islam that Sadat represented in Egypt. They characterized as "un-Islamic" his grant of political asylum to the ill Shah and his homeless family in Egypt. But Sadat took the opportunity to respond in his own Islamic terms. He told the Peoples Assembly on 23 June 1979: "In the name of the Egypt of Islam, in the name of the Egypt of civilization, in the name of the Egypt of ethics, I say we would welcome the Shah and his family in political asylum."[7]

Not until March 1980, however, did the Shah take up Sadat's offer to return to Egypt. Even moderate revolutionaries such as President Bani-Sadr and Foreign Minister Ghotbzadeh were furious over Sadat's reception of the Shah. They had worked hard to have him extradited by Panama, the last of the five countries the Shah visited in exile. Now gravely ill, the Shah went back to Egypt, where he had first stopped as a guest in January 1979, and where he finally died in political asylum. Just before he died, the Shah expressed his personal bitterness against Khomeini, calling the Ayatollah "an evil man, an illiterate and a mad fellow who lives in the past."[8] The Shah's friend President Sadat took an equally dim view of the Iranian revolutionary leader. Continuing to feel defensive about the Iranian propagandist attacks on his Islam, Sadat stated that Khomeini did not know the "true Islam which is not a religion of hatred." He also considered the Iranian leader to be a "loony" who was carrying his country into "disaster."[9]

Yet, after the Shah's death, Sadat soft-pedaled his criticism of the Khomeini regime and tried to distance himself from its opponents. The best example of this was his response to the activities of the royalist opponents of the revolutionary regime. While in Cairo, the Shah's young son "Crown Prince Reza" laid claim to his father's throne on 31 October 1980, his twentieth birthday. The next day, Sadat declared forcefully in public that Egypt had recognized the revolutionary regime as the lawful government of Iran and would not change its position in the light of the Shah's son's claim.[10] This friendly gesture toward the Khomeini regime seemed to have little effect on the militant Iranians. For all practical purposes, they had already condemned Sadat to a violent death. On 24 March 1979, Ayatollah Sadeq Khalkhali, the leader of the old extremist Islamic group known as *Fadaiyan-e* Islam and better known at the time as Iran's "hanging judge," had condemned Sadat's extension of political asylum to the Shah and his family, saying that the Egyptian leader "would have to pay for his dirty act."[11]

Sadat's reiteration of Egypt's recognition of the revolutionary regime in Iran did not help him with his domestic critics, either. They, too, had been angered by his grant of political asylum to the Shah. For example, on the same day that Sadeq Khalkhali blasted Sadat, the leader of the small, leftist Nationalist Progressive Union party of Egypt, Khaled Mohieddin, repeated his stiff opposition to the Shah's stay in Egypt. Egyptian rightist forces were even more critical of Sadat's friendship with the Shah. The spokesmen of the Muslim Brotherhood charged that his support of Israel was not the Shah's only sin. He had actually "fought Islam." They urged the Egyptian president to give support to the Khomeini regime instead of pampering the oppressive Shah. Rightist and leftist students alike demonstrated at Cairo University, denouncing Sadat's policies toward Iran. They charged that the Shah was "a dictator, an alcoholic and an adulterer who [was] not worth a mosquito."[12]

What role his friendship with the Shah played in Sadat's death cannot be known. But only months before Sadat's brutal murder, a surge of Islamic fundamentalist sentiments and rhetoric was clearly evident in conversations not only on university campuses, but also in mosques. The impact of the revolutionary changes in Iran was felt even in Egypt despite that nation's longtime experience with Islamic extremism. The Iranian Revolution was perceived as the first successful contemporary Islamic resurgence that was aimed against both domestic oppression and foreign domination. Incited by goals similar to those driving the revolutionary forces in Iran, the 1952 revolution in Egypt, like other secular, nationalist movements, seemed to have failed, at least in the eyes of those Egyptians who saw salvation in Islamic radicalism. At the time of Sadat's murder, analogies between the Shah and Sadat seemed to have had enormous appeal to the religious and secular critics of the Egyptian leader.

The Shah issue was but one of four major issues bedeviling Sadat-Khomeini relations. First, Iran's rupture of diplomatic relations with Egypt seemed to be regarded by Egyptian officials as a demonstration of ingratitude. On the occasion of the establishment of the Islamic Republic of Iran on 1 April 1979, the Egyptian prime minister sent a warm congratulatory message to the Iranian government. Nevertheless, on the thirtieth of that month, Iran broke off diplomatic relations.

The Egyptian press reacted with a chorus of criticism in which *Al-Ahram* took the lead. In an "open letter" addressed to Ayatollah Khomeini, its chief editor told the Iranian leader that many Egyptians had at first respected his role in the revolution, but that they then had had second thoughts. This change of Egyptian attitude was attributed to several factors. The revolutionaries of Iran had vilified Egypt. The Khomeini regime had launched a merciless campaign of summary executions, resulting in the death of many innocent Iranians. The editor posed these questions: "Is this the Islam [of which] you made yourself its new prophet?" "Are these [summary executions] compatible with the teachings of Islam and its laws?" The reasons Iran gave for breaking off diplomatic relations with Egypt were trumped-up. Iran decried Egypt's relations with Israel and its abandonment of the Palestinian cause, but Iran's refusal to sell oil to Israel, the editorial said, was not that important, and the Iranian pronouncements in support of the Palestinians were empty gestures. In conclusion, the editorial called on the "Imam to return to the Qur'an in order to understand true Islam."[13]

Second, the Egyptian position on the hostage crisis alienated the new Iranian government. Like most other Arab states, Egypt denounced the takeover of the American embassy and the seizure of the hostages, but unlike any other Arab state, Egypt went out of its way to condemn the incident publicly on various grounds. First, once again Egypt assailed the "un-Islamic" character of the revolutionary regime's behavior. The Egyptian representative at the United Nations, for example, condemned the Iranian action because it violated not merely the principles of the law of nations, but also the tenets of Islam's holy Qur'an, which, he said, prescribed that "you who believe do not enter houses other than your own [reference to the U.S. embassy in Tehran] until you ask permission and you greet its people." Second, as one of the greatest centers of Islamic learning in the world, Egypt feared that the "actions of Iranians would project a wrong image of Islam to the rest of the world." And third, the Egyptians were said to believe that in the end the Iranians would be the real losers for their "thoughtless action against the Americans."[14]

From the revolutionary perspective, the Sadat regime rubbed more salt into Iran's wound with its enthusiastic support of the American military intervention in Iran. Sadat blamed the failure of the American rescue mission on mere "bad luck." His uncritical attitude was opposed to the stance taken by nearly all the other Arab leaders in the Persian Gulf. Subsequently, Sadat revealed that he not only had offered the United States help with the rescue operation, but had also promised Washington Egypt's assistance in efforts "to stop any aggression against any Gulf state." "That is my policy," he said.[15]

Third, and finally, in anticipation of increasing Egyptian isolation in the Arab world after the signing of the Camp David Accords, Sadat tried to make common cause with the Arab states whenever possible. The earliest such opportunity presented itself with the uproar in the Persian Gulf over the Iranian cleric Ayatollah Sadeq Ruhani's threat to annex Bahrain to Iran. The Egyptians vehemently denounced the threat, declared their preparedness to help, and generalized from their offer of help in this incident a protective posture vis-à-vis all the Gulf Arab states. In spite of ruffled feelings over the Camp David Accords, the Egyptian overtures must have been welcome during the first year of the Iranian Revolution, when the specter of the spread of revolutionary fervor loomed large in the region. The Egyptian press addressed Iran in bellicose terms. "Iran must understand," reported *Al-Ahram,* "that Egypt will come to the aid of any Arab state against any Iranian stupidity."[16]

Despite continued anti-Egyptian rhetoric, the Arab ostracism of Egypt began to weaken, but the Iranian campaign to "excommunicate" Egypt picked up momentum. The closer Egypt edged toward improved relations with fellow Arab states, the more the Khomeini regime stepped up its campaign of vilification. Only at one point during the Sadat regime—when Sadat condemned the Iraqi invasion of Iran—did it appear that Sadat-Khomeini relations might improve. He was quoted as saying on 1 November 1980 that Iraq had been the "aggressor" in the war with Iran.[17] Reportedly, Sadat said that Saddam Hussein had launched the war because he wanted to be the leader in the Gulf region and the Arab world. Sadat also charged that the Iraqi leader had provoked the war as a means of correcting his own error of judgment five years earlier, in 1975, when he gave the Iranians control of the Shatt al-Arab. Sadat was in effect hitting back at Saddam Hussein for having spearheaded the anti-Sadat campaign at the Baghdad Conference in March 1979, when the Arab states had imposed diplomatic and economic sanctions on his regime.

KHOMEINI AND MUBARAK

Husni Mubarak's succession to Egyptian leadership might have eased the poisoned relations between Iran and Egypt had it not been for the new president's aid to Iraq in the war against Iran. Mubarak was determined to breach the wall of Egyptian isolation, and felt that siding with Egypt's old Iraqi rivals might help him do so. The timing of the rapprochement was influenced by the interlocking needs of the two leaders. First, Mubarak had needed all along to return Egypt to the Arab fold, but his campaign got under way in earnest only after the recovery of the

Sinai in April 1982. Second, by then Saddam Hussein also needed Egypt as a friend and ally. Iran's successful March offensive had turned the tide of war against Iraq. Now that the two leaders needed each other, they buried the hatchet. As a first move toward reconciliation, the Iraqis resumed air links between Baghdad and Cairo. Then Iraqi military delegations began to visit Egypt. As a former recipient of Soviet arms, Egypt could provide the kind of military equipment that the Iraqis were accustomed to using. No less important, Egypt could provide the manpower that the Iraqis needed in their economy in order to be able to spare the increasing number of men needed for the war fronts.

From the Iranian perspective, this Egyptian aid to Iran's enemy was the straw that broke the camel's back. No matter what Mubarak did to distance himself from Israel and the United States, especially after the Israeli invasion of Lebanon, Mubarak's aid to Iraq's war effort, including some Egyptian troops, was considered by Iran to be almost an act of war by Egypt. From this point on, the acrimony between Tehran and Cairo deepened. The two countries always found themselves on opposite sides on every major issue. Other than intensifying its campaign of propaganda, there seemed to be little the Khomeini regime could do. The propaganda, however, could be directed against what, presumably, could most hurt the Mubarak regime: its ardent efforts to reenter the Arab and Islamic fold. The Iranian excommunication campaign, therefore, aimed at defeating these Egyptian efforts.

No one less than Khomeini himself set the stage for condemning any and all efforts aimed at returning Egypt to the Arab and Islamic fold. When the Islamic Conference Organization decided to reinstate Egypt in January 1984, Khomeini lamented the efforts of the United States and its "avowed supporters" to return Egypt to the "Arab League" (as he mistakenly called the ICO). He then criticized the Arab leaders for reversing the anti-Egyptian position they had taken in Casablanca by deciding in favor of Egypt's return. This act, Khomeini charged, constituted "a concerted endorsement" of Egypt's "betrayal of the aspirations of the Palestinians."[18]

President Ali Khamene'i seemed to take the campaign to excommunicate Mubarak's Egypt further than Khomeini did. For example, during his 31 August 1984 speech on Iranian efforts to expel Israel from the United Nations, he said:

We do not consider the present Egyptian regime, which was innovator of the tragic Camp David incident, as being part of the community of Muslim and Arab nations. Those who hatched the Camp David plot are traitors to the Islamic nation and Islamic aspirations. The United States attempts to bring the present boss of the Egyptian regime out of isolation, but we believe that the Muslim nations should [not] allow this task to be carried out. The Egyptian regime specializes in working out ignominious peace plans. We do not accept the Egyptian regime and the stifling country of Egypt.[19]

Not unlike other governments that found themselves the objects of Iranian vilification, the Egyptian government tried to blame most acts of terrorism, subversion, and general destabilization of the Middle East on the Khomeini regime, although Colonel Qadhafi of Libya remained Egypt's number one bête noire. When the news of the mysterious mining of the Suez Canal and the Red Sea emerged in the summer of 1984, the Egyptians at first blamed both Iran and Libya. Briefly, the sequence of events was as follows. On 6 August an unattributed radio commentary in Tehran seemed to applaud the mining by the Islamic Jihad Organization. On 8 August Prime Minister Musavi and Foreign Ministry officials condemned the mining operations. More important, however, on 9 August Ayatollah Khomeini denounced the radio announcement from Tehran and condemned the mining in these terms:

How is it possible that we can support an issue which is against the sentiments of the world, against Islam, and against common sense? Laying mines in a place is tantamount to wiping out a group of innocent people. How can Islam allow such a thing? How can Iran permit this? How can the Jondollah [army of God] allow such a thing? But you should know what problem we are facing. Whatever happens is attributed to us.[20]

Despite these denials, on 10 August President Mubarak named Iran as the primary suspect and threatened to retaliate in any way "we think proper." Field Marshal Abu Ghazala thought at the time that it was "almost 70 percent sure that Iran and Libya could be responsible." In threatening retaliation, Mubarak said that Egypt would "prevent any country which may have participated in the explosions that took place in the Gulf of Suez from crossing the Suez Canal."[21] Reportedly, the Egyptian government also sent a "specific warning" to Tehran through a "third, unidentified party."

As it turned out, however, Mubarak himself in effect confirmed Khomeini's claim that Iran was blameless. Saying he hoped Iran was not involved in the mining operations, he added, "I believe the Libyans did it."[22] Subsequently, it appeared that the Egyptians were backpedaling their earlier charges against the Libyans, as well. All that Mubarak's hasty overreaction in this incident seemed to achieve was to aggravate

Egyptian-Iranian relations. In this case the Egyptian president did not seem to have in his possession even circumstantial evidence to back up his charges. The charges resulted from the cold war atmosphere that had developed between the Khomeini regime and Egypt since April 1979.

REVOLUTIONARY IRAN, EGYPT, AND ISLAMIC FUNDAMENTALISM

Between 1960 and 1985, diplomatic relations between Egypt and Iran were broken off twice. The first break, during the Nasser regime, lasted a decade. The second one so far has lasted about six years during the Sadat and Mubarak regimes. The first one was in effect a result of the changes brought about by the Egyptian Revolution. The second one was a product of the Iranian Revolution. Of twenty-five years, in other words, sixteen years have been characterized by a cold war between Tehran and Cairo.

The asymmetry between the interests of the two countries has persisted since the destruction of the Shah-Sadat alignment as a result of the Iranian Revolution. The essentially secular, pro-American, and pro-Israeli orientation of the Egyptian regime has clashed with the basically religious, anti-American, and anti-Israeli thrust of the Khomeini regime. The Egyptian alignment with Iraq has further poisoned relations between Cairo and Tehran.

Recently there has emerged a new, wider, alignment pattern that also has placed Iran and Egypt at opposite ends of the Middle Eastern political spectrum. An alignment is being formed among Jordan, Egypt, and Iraq which is supported by Saudi Arabia, and other GCC states, and Yasser Arafat. On the other hand, a tripartite alignment has been struck among Iran, Syria, and Libya which enjoys the support of South Yemen and Ethiopia, both of which have, since August 1981, allied themselves with Libya in yet another tripartite alignment. For all practical purposes, the PLO has tilted toward the moderate alignment, while the extremist factions of the Palestinians side with the radical alignment. Abu Musa, for example, sides with both the Syrians and the Iranians.

Yet, none of these alignments has been carved in stone in the volatile Middle East. The turbulence of the area's politics has always resulted in sensational changes in regimes and political alignments. The Khomeini regime's campaign to excommunicate Egypt will become a matter of the past as surely as did the acrimonious campaign of Nasser against the Shah's regime. Despite all the antipathy toward Nasser, the Shah never lost sight of the importance of the Suez Canal to Iran. About 73 percent of Iran's imports and 76 percent of its exports depended on the canal.

And, despite the Iranian campaign to excommunicate the Mubarak regime, Iran continues to consider the waterway to be of vital importance to its interest. The Khomeini regime sends some three hundred ships through it each year.

As it is to all the Gulf Arab states discussed earlier, the all-pervasive and powerful example of Iran's Islamic revolution is that country's greatest challenge to Egypt. Even if the ideological crusade of excommunication against the Mubarak regime should die out and relations between the Egyptian and Iranian governments begin to move toward a degree of mutual tolerance and coexistence, Egyptian leaders would still have to face the political consciousness of their own masses who, because of the Iranian Revolution, have never been wider awake politically. Perceived as rejecting foreign domination and domestic repression, that consciousness inspires modern-educated, secularly oriented Egyptians as much as Muslim fundamentalists. For now, however, the most vocal and militant spokesmen of that political movement have been the extremist Egyptian fundamentalists.

Despite Egypt's longtime experience with Islamic fundamentalism, the Iranian model has had great appeal to the Egyptian Muslim extremists. They have continued to press for the complete establishment of *shariah* as the source of legislation and policy in Egyptian society. Yesterday's radical Muslim Brotherhood has by comparison become today's most moderate of the fundamentalist groups, working now inside the New Wafd and other parties. Those Muslim extremists who were responsible for the assassination of Egyptian President Anwar Sadat in 1981 acted as if they were carrying out Iran's Ayatollah Sadeq Khalkhali's words of March 1979, when he said that Sadat "would have to pay for his dirty act" of giving the Shah political asylum. In June 1985, when a huge pro-*shariah* demonstration was first planned and then called off, the men of the Egyptian Jihad Organization decried the Mubarak government's efforts to mollify them by selectively implementing Islamic law. They demanded, instead, "an Islamic republic led by religious men, like Ayatollah Khomeini's government in Iran."[23]

The Iranian Revolution has deepened the ancient division between sacred and secular politics in Egypt, as it has elsewhere in the Muslim world. Each approach has its followers, irrespective of nationality, sect, or class. Of course, the Muslim fundamentalists reject the very idea of separation of the sacred and the secular, for that, they charge, is an alien idea implanted in their societies by the superpowers. Yet other equally devout Muslims, both modern- and *shariah*-educated, reject the fundamentalist approach, believing that it is incapable of providing solutions to their deep-rooted social, economic, and political problems. These problems continue to haunt the people in revolutionary, fundamentalist Iran as much as in moderate, pragmatic Egypt. But even the firebrand Iranian fundamentalists, tempered by the exigencies of the real world, have begun to move toward a more pragmatic policy.

The most awesome reality that will bedevil any future Egyptian government is the grinding poverty of large segments of the Egyptian populace. Without minimizing the significance of the divisions between the Muslim majority and the Coptic Christian minority in Egypt, one can say that Egyptian society is comparatively homogeneous. Moreover, like the Iranians and unlike most other Middle Eastern peoples, the Egyptians enjoy a greater sense of national identity. Nevertheless, these relative advantages seem outweighed by the endemic pressure of an ever-increasing population on resources. Today Egypt imports between 50 and 70 percent of its food, and it has to feed one million more people every nine months. It is no wonder that underlying economic problems often erupt into political disturbances in Egypt, such as the bread riots in January 1977 and the policemen's rebellion in February 1986. Whether the Mubarak government finally blames the police riots on Islamic fundamentalism or on Nasserism, it will not in the end be able to disregard the unremitting economic malaise of Egypt. Mubarak's policemen were among the last people he would have expected to turn against him, but they did so to vent their anger over their pay ($4 a month) and their dismal working conditions.

Mubarak appears to be facing a continuing problem of Egyptian masses protesting an abysmal standard of living. If anything, the protests will intensify, even in the face of a diminished appeal of the Khomeini brand of Islam, as Mubarak and his successors will be unlikely to succeed in meeting the demands for a better standard of living. Early in 1986 the major sources of Egypt's domestic income were being eroded rapidly because of the fall in oil revenues, the fall in dues from shipments through the Suez Canal, and the fall in remittances from Egyptians working in the Gulf region. Under these circumstances, U.S. aid to Egypt, particularly nonmilitary aid, will have to be increased and systematized to avert economic disaster and political disarray.

12

The Islamization of Lebanon?

Who would ever have imagined that, of all the countries in the Middle East, it would be in Lebanon that American power and influence would suffer most from the effects of the Iranian Revolution? Factors such as the country's geographic distance from Iran; its historical, cultural, and commercial ties with the United States; and its jealous and powerful neighbors, Syria and Israel, all were impediments to an Iranian intrusion into Lebanon.

But the Iranian Revolution destroyed these protective shields for Lebanon vis-à-vis Iran. The effects of the Iranian Revolution combined with the aftermath of the Camp David Accords and the Egyptian-Israeli peace treaty to give rise to an unprecedented alliance between Syria and Iran. Iran's new access to Lebanon through Syria effectively shortened the distance between Iran and Lebanon. The alliance also diminished Syria's resentment over Iranian influence in Lebanon, especially after the Israeli invasion. The invasion, which was prompted in part by the Iranian Revolution, provided a unique opportunity for the Khomeini ideological crusade against the "twin evil" of America and Israel.

More important, the invasion presented an extraordinary opportunity for the Iranian revolutionaries to try to export their Islamic revolution to Lebanon. The ideological appeal of the Khomeini regime could have found no more fertile soil in which to flourish than in the sense of victimhood festering among the Shia masses in Lebanon. As yet, the outcome of this extraordinary microcosm of Middle Eastern malaise is uncertain, but understanding Lebanon without considering the Iranian factor is no longer possible.

THE SYRIAN-IRANIAN AXIS

The Iranian Revolution, which destroyed the Shah's alignments with Israel and Egypt, produced an alliance between Syria and Iran. Earlier, I analyzed aspects of this axis in connection with the Iraq-Iran war and Iran's hostility toward Israel. In what follows, I will examine the genesis of this alliance closely, because this factor is essential for developing an understanding of the Iranian involvement in Lebanon.

The alignment between Syria and Iran developed after the eruption of the Iranian Revolution as a result of five major factors. First, the hostile relations between the Shah's regime and Syria provided a strong impetus for the postrevolutionary development of the Syrian-Iranian axis. The Shah's relations with the Syrians were embittered during most of the 1960s. The pro-American Iranian and the pro-Soviet Syrian orientations in foreign affairs clashed. Syria's strident Pan-Arab claim to the oil-rich Iranian province of Khuzistan as "an integral part of the Arab Nation" made matters worse. Because of Iran's logistical, medical, and other nonmilitary aid to the Arab states during the 1973 October war, however, the relations between Damascus and Tehran improved for a short while thereafter. The Shah even gave financial aid to Syria.

Yet, by the late 1970s, the relationship between the two countries was again conflict-ridden. Given the Shah's close ties with Sadat, the rift between Sadat and Hafiz Assad after the 1975 Sinai agreement between Egypt and Israel contributed to the strained relations between Tehran and Damascus. The Shah's support of Sadat's bold peace initiative toward Israel produced more tension between the Shah and Assad.

Second, the hostility between Saddam Hussein and Hafiz Assad helped lead to the building of a Damascus-Tehran axis. This hostility between Baghdad and Damascus had recently erupted; it was not simply a continuation of old bad feelings. In fact, when the revolutionary forces took power in Iran, Syria and Iraq were on the best of terms and were committed to the establishment of an alliance between themselves. Against the backdrop of a decade of internecine hostility between the two Ba'thist regimes, this commitment seemed out of place. As early as 1966, Ahmad Hassan al-Bakr and Saddam Hussein had been ousted from the Ba'th National Command, an event that prompted them to establish a rival National Command in Baghdad when they took power in Iraq in 1968. For years the Iraqi regime had demanded that Syria dissolve its National Command, but suddenly the Iraqis withdrew their age-old demand.

This sudden show of good will between the old enemies was due principally to Egypt's signing of the Camp David Accords in September

1978. The southern Arab confrontation front facing Israel had, as a result of the accords, collapsed, and the need for a new counterforce against Israel on the eastern front seemed more pressing than ever. King Hussein of Jordan would not play the Syrian game, and Syria's military presence in Lebanon would not by itself be a sufficient force to counter Israel's threat. Now that Egypt, the primary Arab military power, had overturned the old strategic balance against Israel, Syria and Iraq needed to combine their forces to establish a new strategic equilibrium. In Baghdad in October 1978, Hafiz Assad and Hassan al-Bakr signed an agreement for Joint National Action, providing for political, economic, cultural, and military cooperation between Syria and Iraq.

Yet, in less than a year, this merger plan had broken down. Allegedly, Syria supported a "plot" for a coup that was to have been enacted on 16 July 1979, when President Hassan al-Bakr resigned and Saddam Hussein succeeded him. The revival of the old enmity in the new regional context meant an unprecedented increase in Iraq's interest in the Gulf region and a leap in Syria's interest in Lebanon. The fall of the Shah from power and Sadat from Arab grace had opened up new opportunities for the assertion of Iraqi leadership in the Gulf area. Egypt's separate peace with Israel had intensified the Syrian strategic stake in Lebanon. When Israel annexed the Golan Heights, Hafiz Assad seemed to have only one friend: Khomeini. Assad warmly welcomed the Iranian Revolution from the outset, and revolutionary Iran dispatched "volunteers" to support Syria against Israel.

Third, the Khomeini regime and the Assad regime needed each other for both external and internal reasons. By taking the Americans hostage, the Khomeini regime had brought down on itself international economic and diplomatic sanctions. Left out of the Egyptian-initiated peace process, the Assad regime nevertheless could not easily make common cause with other Arab states that were also angry with Egypt. Internally, the Khomeini regime faced chaotic revolutionary politics and Kurdish, Baluchi, and other ethnic unrest and insurgency. Hafiz Assad was not much better off than Khomeini. The Muslim Brotherhood, who had haunted him for a long time, nearly killed him in July 1980. The Syrians suspected the Iraqis in the assassination attempt, just as the Iraqis had suspected the Syrians in the coup plot against Saddam Hussein about a year earlier. In addition to Iraq, Jordan, Saudi Arabia, and even some factions of the PLO were suspected of supporting the anti-Assad Muslim Brotherhood. Given these internal and external concerns in Damascus and Tehran, a connection with the religiously based Khomeini regime could aid the image of the secular Ba'thists, just as one with the Alawite Shias in Syria could help the Khomeini regime.

Fourth, although their resentment against Israel and the United States was due to very different reasons, the Khomeini and Assad regimes could join hands in their common struggle against both Zionism and imperialism. This "twin evil" of Khomeini's ideological crusade furnished the perfect language for interaction and axis between Damascus and Tehran. Assad could use the alliance with Iran to undermine any American or other initiative for peace with Israel that ignored Syrian interests, and Khomeini could use it to fight any effort he perceived on the part of the United States to isolate and destroy his Islamic revolution.

Fifth, and finally, the Iraqi invasion of Iran provided an opportunity to transform the growing rapprochement between Damascus and Tehran into a formal alliance. As already noted, between 12 and 16 March 1982 Syrian and Iranian officials in Tehran signed a ten-year economic agreement, a closely related oil agreement, and (probably) a secret arms accord. After these agreements were signed, Syria closed its border with Iraq, on 8 April, and, more critically, shut off Iraqi oil exports through the Trans-Syrian oil pipeline, on 10 April. In return, the Syrians received not only some discounted oil, and some free oil, from Iran, but also an amount of oil in excess of what they could use, which the Syrians refined at Homs and Banias for foreign export and mixed with their own heavier, sulfur-laden oil to sweeten it.[1] As Foreign Minister Ali Akbar Velayati aptly observed when all these economic transactions were signed, they "are a means of strengthening and expanding political relations" with respect to the common Iranian and Syrian struggle against "imperialism."[2] Obviously, *imperialism* meant the United States, Israel, Iraq, and any other country or, for that matter, any political faction that happened to be on "the wrong side" of the Iranians and Syrians, including, of course, the anti-Iranians and anti-Syrians in Lebanon.

THE IRANIAN FACTOR IN THE ISRAELI INVASION

The Israeli invasion of Lebanon on 6 June 1982 and its aftermath provided the ideal opportunity for the Syrians and Iranians to use their axis to serve their interests in the Eastern Mediterranean. The Iraq-Iran war had provided the occasion to formalize that emerging alliance and to use it in the context of the conflict in the Persian Gulf. As noted, only after the Israelis invaded Lebanon were the Iranian Revolutionary Guards allowed to enter Lebanon for "the fight against Israel." The Israeli invasion also gave the Iranians a unique arena in which to try to create an Islamic republic. Blood-splattered Lebanon seemed like a haven for the zealous exporters of the Islamic revolution. However, the Israeli invasion itself stemmed partly from the Iranian Revolution.

Needless to say, there are myriad theories about the Lebanon war, but it seems that none so far has paid much attention to the impact of the Iranian Revolution. This is no place to catalogue the theories on the Lebanon war, but I will briefly describe a few of them to demonstrate the general neglect of the Iranian factor and to provide a backdrop for my own explanation.

First is the ideological theory, which focuses on the effect of New Zionism on Israel's decision to initiate the war in Lebanon. According to this theory, the invasion aimed at preventing any peace process that might lead to the surrender of the West Bank and Gaza, for New Zionism claims that "the God of Israel promised the entire country to the sons of Israel. This divine title deed pre-empts any other claim to either bank of the Jordan River. Giving up Judea and Samaria would constitute a moral sin by interfering with the unfolding process of redemption."[3]

Second is the demographic theory, which emphasizes changes in Israeli society. These societal changes reinforce the ideological commitment to the wholeness of *Eretz Yisrael.* By the time of the Lebanon war, according to this theory, the Israelis of oriental origin, the Sephardim, made up more than half of Israel's total population.[4] These Jews, as opposed to those of European descent, the Ashkenazim, beginning with the 1977 electoral victory had voted more and more with each electoral campaign for the Likud bloc, the main political base of New Zionism. Their "hawkish" attitudes toward the Arabs were reflected in the Israeli invasion of Lebanon.

Third, and most prominent, is the political theory of the Lebanon war. Zeev Schiff, the defense and military editor of the Israeli *Haaretz,* contends that "the Israeli-American complicity was not—as some Arabs charge—a conspiracy to send the Israeli army into Lebanon in order to expel the PLO and the Syrians. It was, instead, an implicit Israeli-American partnership. The Americans—having received advance information about Israeli intentions—chose to look the other way, making ambiguous comments about Lebanon that the Israeli government could interpret any way it liked." And the Israeli government interpreted Washington's "vague murmurings and apparent indifference as a green light for Operation Peace for Galilee."[5]

The account of former U.S. Secretary of State Alexander Haig, Jr., makes it difficult indeed to support the assertion that Washington's statements to Tel Aviv amounted to no more than "vague murmurings and apparent indifference." His account seems to support Schiff's statement that the United States had "advance information," but it also contends that Israel had been given, in Haig's words, "the strongest possible warnings by the United States."[6] "In a strenuous argument with Sharon," Haig says, he repeated what he had told the Israeli leaders earlier: "Unless there was an internationally recognized provocation, an attack by Israel into Lebanon would have a devastating effect in the United States." "No one has the right to tell Israel," Haig says Sharon replied, "what decision it should take in defense of its people."[7]

Whether "murmurings" or "warnings," the difficult question is why Israeli leaders decided to invade Lebanon in spite of Washington's misgivings. In the light of this study, I suggest that they did so because they believed that they could invade Lebanon without doing too much harm to Israel's relations with the United States. This belief was based on their perception that Israel's strategic value to the United States had increased mainly because of the Iranian Revolution. As noted earlier, for a quarter of a century, Iran and Israel had been two of the major supporters of American policy in the Middle East. The revolution destroyed one support and thereby necessarily increased the strategic value of Israel to the United States. After the fall of the Shah, Israeli leaders watched the panicky Americans search for a new "security framework" that would team Israel with such unlikely partners as Saudi Arabia and other Arab states. They watched the growing American concern over the Soviet invasion of Afghanistan. They observed America's strong commitment to defend the Gulf oil supplies. And they observed the creation of the Rapid Deployment Force. They rejoiced in Haig's obsession with the concept of "strategic consensus" and, at least initially, in the U.S.-Israeli agreement on a Memorandum of Understanding (MOU).

Given all this, it was only to be expected that Sharon would unfurl his own concept of the "safety valve," which he did in January 1982. This concept called for a preemptive strike before any threat anywhere could materialize. It was to be expected that Israel, about a month later, would tell Haig that a "large-scale force would advance from the Israeli border to the southern suburbs of Beirut."[8] Would not such a feat more than compensate for the loss of Israel's ally Iran by providing a political foothold in Lebanon under an Israeli-dominated Maronite Christian government and by destroying, in the process, the PLO and the Soviet-supported Syrian air force, if it dared to fight?

Even the timing of the Israeli invasion of Lebanon was influenced by the Iranian factor. The impressive Iranian offensive of March 1982 against Iraq was followed by the landmark success of Iranian arms at Khorramshahr on 24 May. Secretary Haig's overriding concern at the time seemed to be that Iran might succeed in its military offensives in the Iraq-Iran war. Would not Ariel Sharon recognize that concern? Why would this time—when Washington was preoccupied with the prospect of Iranian forces carrying the war into Iraqi territory—not be the best time to strike into the heart of Lebanon? The truism that all things in the Middle East are interconnected is one that statesmen and scholars alike ignore at their own peril. Ignoring the all-important fact of Israel's withdrawal from the Sinai in April 1982 was not wise.

SHIA VICTIMHOOD

The Israeli invasion was only the most recent of the foreign incursions into Lebanon over the previous four centuries. The Ottoman Turks, Egyptians, French, Syrians, and Palestinians had preceded them. In fact, the military presence of the Syrians and particularly the Palestinians was responsible in part for the Israeli invasion. Driven out of Jordan in 1970 during King Hussein's bloody crackdown on the Palestinian commandos, the Palestinians had arrived, settled, and, for all practical purposes, created a state within a state in Lebanon. By the time of the Israeli invasion, the PLO had been transformed from a guerrilla force into a conventional army that had assembled long-range heavy artillery, tanks, and mobile launchers that "could pepper northern Israel with salvos of deadly rockets."[9] Having arrived in Lebanon in the wake of the Lebanese civil war of 1975–76 at "the request" of the Arab League, the Syrian forces were the strongest Arab military ally of the PLO by the time the war came. But the Syrian air force fought to protect the Bekaa Valley, Syria's strategic "soft underbelly," rather than the Palestinian fighters who were being pounded by Israeli forces.

Foreign intervention and invasion had always in some measure been the product of the fragmented conditions of Lebanese society. Anything resembling e pluribus unum, one national community out of many, had always eluded Lebanon's grasp. The unhappy country had been torn apart repeatedly by communal, subcommunal, clannish, and personal conflict. Domestic factions had often welcomed foreign powers to protect them against their rivals. In the essentially Muslim-Christian conflict situation of 1958, for example, Maronite Christian President Chamoun invited American intervention, just as in 1975–76 President Franjieh relied on Syrian military intervention.[10] And later, when the bitter struggle between the Syrians and the Christian Phalangists developed, the Maronites welcomed Israel's support in perpetuating themselves in power in spite of the ever-present and ever-growing demand of the Muslim communities for political reforms and a more equitable division of power.

Muslim complaints had their roots in the charter drawn up for the new state of Lebanon. Based on a census conducted by the French in 1932, the National Charter gave most of the power to the Christians, presumably because they were slightly more numerous than the Muslims. The charter fixed the parliamentary representation at a constant ratio of six to five and stipulated that the most powerful office, president, be filled by a Maronite Christian. The premier was to be a Sunni Muslim, and the Speaker of the Chamber of Deputies a Shia Muslim. The same sectarian ratio was applied to every appointment for public office; more important, the army's commander in chief was a Maronite Christian, and many senior officer cadres were solidly Maronite Christian.

Over the decades the Shia Muslims grew in number to become the single largest community in Lebanon (30 to 40 percent of the population), but they remained the least powerful and most deprived community there. Like all the Shia communities in Arab countries of the Middle East, they were dominated by Sunni Muslims, but, unlike any other Shia community in the region, they were also subjected to the control of the Maronite Christians. Like all the other Lebanese, they suffered from foreign incursions, but unlike the Sunnis and the Christians, they became the main target of foreign subjugation and attack. In the Shia Muslims' traditional homeland in south Lebanon, the Palestinians oppressed the Shias for more than a decade, as did the Israelis for three years, and in 1982 and 1983 the Americans stood by President Amin Gemayel, a Maronite Christian, and his army, when the Shia suburbs of Beirut were pounded by Lebanese heavy artillery. The battleship USS *New Jersey* fired its heavy guns into Shia positions in support of the Lebanese army.

Everywhere in the Arab Middle East, the best-known appellation applied to the Shias is *mahroomin* (deprived or dispossessed), but only in Lebanon was the Shia protest movement designated initially as the *Harakat Mahroomin* (Movement of the Deprived). Several years before the creation of this movement, its founder, Musa al-Sadr, described the longtime "sufferings" (*massa'ab*) of the Shias from poverty, disease, and Sunni and Christian prejudice and mistreatment.[11] As the politicization of the Shia community increased and the Shias' birth rate burgeoned, the movement Musa al-Sadr founded expanded and gained strength. But in those days he did not seem to envisage anything like the *Harakat Mahroomin,* which later became popularly known as the *Harakat Amal* (Movement of Hope). Although Musa al-Sadr, who later became known as Imam al-Sadr, did not seem to be planning any political organization, he obviously carried the burden of the sense of victimization of the Shia community in Lebanon.

It was this longtime sense of being the underdog that underpinned the Lebanese Shia population's radical and moderate political movements as well as the political violence that captured worldwide attention in the 1980s. And it was the Shias' psychological state that made the ideological foray of the Khomeini regime into Lebanon possible. As noted earlier, the concept of the deprived masses is basic to the Khomeini ideology, as is an implacable enmity toward the United States and Israel. The Iranians use these concepts to appeal to the Muslims of Lebanon, and, as just noted, there is much in the experience of the Shia Muslims to fit these concepts perfectly.

The revolutionary regime has a commitment to the export of Khomeini's brand of Islamic fundamentalism, and Lebanon has a special role in the exportation. According to the former Iranian ambassador to Beirut, Hojatolislam Fakhr Rouhani, for example, Lebanon "is the most important hope for the export of the Islamic revolution." On 9 January 1984 he was reported to have said that the "likelihood of the establishment of an Islamic Republic in Lebanon is just as much as it was in Iran [in] late 1978, and . . . the Muslim masses of Lebanon, whether Shi'ites or Sunnis, look . . . towards Iran and the Islamic Revolution as their brother and saviour."[12] The former ambassador had even grander visions concerning the role of a unified Islamic movement in Lebanon. "If we concentrate," he said, "on the point that Lebanon is considered the heart of the Arab countries in the Middle East, has been serving as one of the most important information centers of the world for years, and has been serving as a platform from which different ideas have been directed to the rest of the Arab world, we can conclude that the existence of an Islamic movement in that country will result in Islamic movements throughout the Arab world."[13]

THE MEANS OF EXPORTING ISLAMIC REVOLUTION

Toward the achievement of its three major goals—to triumph over the United States, to eradicate Israel, and to Islamize Lebanon—the Khomeini regime has used a variety of means. First, despite fluctuations in the relationship between Iran and Lebanon since the Iranian Revolution, Tehran has maintained diplomatic relations with Beirut. Tehran has also consistently monitored and commented on Lebanese developments. For example, the Iranian Foreign Ministry condemned the veto by the United States on 6 September 1984 of the United Nations Security Council resolution for the withdrawal of Israeli forces from Lebanon. It was subsequently believed that this veto led to the bombing of the U.S. embassy annex in Beirut on 20 September. The Foreign Ministry also called for "the expulsion of the Zionist regime from the United Nations and the isolation of that illegitimate regime."[14]

The Iranian parliament has also closely watched the Lebanese situation and, in tandem with the Ministry of Foreign Affairs, has sometimes expressed its views on Lebanese issues. For example, it hailed the cancellation of the 17 May 1983 troop withdrawal agreement between Israel and Lebanon; the cancellation, it claimed, was "the direct result of the bloody struggle of the Muslim nation." It called the subsequent discussions between the two countries on the same subject "a treason to the martyrs." The Foreign Ministry added that "the continuation of these negotiations was another plot to expand Camp David [accords] despite the annulment of the agreement of 17 May," and it warned the Lebanese nation to be fully prepared "to combat this dangerous conspiracy which will only result in the destruction of the precious gains of the heroic struggle of the Muslim nation of Lebanon."[15]

Second, the Revolutionary Guards Corps has been widely used as an instrument of Iranian foreign policy in Lebanon. As noted, Revolutionary Guards arrived in the Bekaa Valley shortly after the Israeli invasion. Other than the Israeli retaliatory air attacks on IRGC bases which killed more than twenty guardsmen in November 1983, apparently there have not been any military clashes between the guardsmen and Israeli forces. But there is ample evidence that Lebanese Muslims are being indoctrinated and trained by guardsmen. The guardsmen themselves have been more than a paramilitary force in the Iranian military structure; they have been propagators of the Khomeini ideology, as well. In contrast to the regular Iranian armed forces, the Revolutionary Guards are considered to be the *Jondollah* (army of God) and to represent deep ideological commitment rather than professional military competence. Furthermore, both the regular and the paramilitary armed forces of Iran are subjected to intensive ideological indoctrination through a special secretariat in the Islamic Republican party (IRP).[16]

The Revolutionary Guardsmen have forged an informal but close alliance with the Lebanese *Hezbollah* (party of God) and the Islamic Amal Organization. The party of God is reputedly "Iran's mainstay" in Lebanon. The spokesman for the party is a 32-year-old cleric, Sheikh Ibrahim Amin, who makes no secret of the fact that the party receives "aid" from Iran. He also confirmed, on 28 June 1985, that the Iranian Revolutionary Guards were "helping to carry the Iranian experiment to Lebanon."[17] A better-known cleric, Sheikh Muhammad Hussein Fadlal-

lah, is regarded as the "supreme guide" of the party, but Sheikh Fadlallah denies that he is the leader of the *Hezbollah*. He depicts his ties with
Iran in terms of "an old relationship with the leaders of Islamic Iran
which started long before the Islamic Republic. It is a relationship of
friendship and mutual confidence."[18]

The Islamic Amal is led by Hussein Musawi, a Lebanese of Iranian
origin. His brother, Abbas Musawi, is one of the leaders of the party of
God, and his cousin was the Iranian chargé d'affaires in Beirut in 1983.
Hussein Musawi's faction is a breakaway group from the mainstream
Amal, which is led by the well-known, modern-educated Nabih Berri,
who helped free the American hostages of TWA flight 847. Hussein
Musawi had been the chief military commander in the parent Amal
movement before the organization split in 1982. The triumvirate—made
up of Amin, Fadlallah, and Musawi—closely follows the Khomeini line,
but Nabih Berri does not. He is regarded by the Iranian media as "too
Westernized." He does not visit Iran, as do Fadlallah and Musawi, and
the Iranian clerics seem to ignore him when they visit Lebanon.

Third, Iran considers clerics to be vitally important to the export of
the Islamic revolution to Lebanon. As noted earlier, the *ulama,* foreign
and native, are assigned a major role by the Khomeini regime in exporting the Islamic revolution. The interaction between Iranian and Lebanese clerics has been intensive over the years, as has the interaction
between these clerics and the Islamic Amal and the *Hezbollah.* The
Lebanese cleric who is most revered among the Iranian leaders is
Sheikh Muhammad Hussein Fadlallah. He has repeatedly visited Iran
and met with all the major Iranian leaders, including Khomeini, Montazeri, Rafsanjani, Khamene'i, and Velayati.

A crucial ideological-political question is whether Fadlallah sub-
scribes to the idea of establishing an Islamic republic in Lebanon. In his
meeting with Ayatollah Montazeri in Tehran on 18 February 1985,
Fadlallah reportedly said: "Lebanon is an Islamic country and is com-
prised of a majority of Muslims. Hence the Islamic movement must be
reinforced in this country. The objective of the struggle of the Lebanese
Muslims will be toward an Islamic system based on and relying on the
Koran and the injunctions of Islam so that by using the Islamic system,
the rights of the minorities may be safeguarded and implemented."[19]

Few Iranian leaders have expressed their views about the kind of
"Islamic system" they want for Lebanon. Consider Iranian Prime Minister Mir-Hussein Musavi's vague statement of 8 February 1984: "Lebanon is an Islamic country and its president should be elected from
among the majority of the people constituted by the Muslims. The entire world should understand that no Muslim in Lebanon would be pre-

pared to accept a Phalangist president allied to Israel."[20] There were rumors after Fadlallah's visit to Iran in early 1985 that he and the Iranian leaders disagreed regarding the creation of an Islamic republic in Lebanon. Fadlallah's view on the subject was as follows:

> The Iranian leaders are not thinking of an Islamic Republic in Lebanon in the least as the media reported. There are some differences. There are some Iranian scholars and some officials who are perhaps not fully aware of the situation in Lebanon. They spoke about it, but not the leaders. We told them that Lebanon was different, that we do not have sufficient and necessary conditions for an Islamic Republic. These discussions were with people outside the decision-making circles, with intellectuals and scholars.[21]

Until the Iranian leaders and Fadlallah explicitly state their views, the political order they envisage for Lebanon will remain unclear. But there is a widely shared perception that the *Hezbollah* and the Islamic Amal would like to have an Islamic republic resembling Iran's in Lebanon. This could be a misconception, because no one seems certain of the views of these two groups. If it is true that the *Hezbollahis* follow the guidance of Fadlallah, then they seemingly would also believe that the Lebanese "do not have necessary and sufficient conditions for an Islamic Republic." But such a logical conclusion is not guaranteed in the fluid, complex, and chaotic conditions of Lebanon.

Fourth, and finally, there is little doubt that Iran uses financial aid as an instrument of exporting the Islamic revolution to Lebanon. According to the Iranian chargé d'affaires in Beirut, Iran does provide aid, but "not through Hezbollah."[22] And according to Sheikh Ibrahim Amin,. "Iran supports [the *Hezbollah*] as well as all the downtrodden people in the world and [forces] fighting for freedom. This is something that is evident and not a secret."[23] The Iranian chargé also revealed for the first time in January 1985 that Iran had "underwritten all the expenses of the families of martyrs in the south [Lebanon]. . . . This form of support is continuing, not through any specific organization, because we are not trying to support in order to gain publicity. We consider this a binding duty that the Republic must discharge. We will not disclose [the amount of our] support until the victory of the revolution, God willing, in the south."[24] On 25 June 1985 an Amal activist told Thomas L. Friedman of the *New York Times* that the party of God seemed to have more money than the mainstream Amal. Western officials told Friedman that Iranian money enabled the fundamentalists to recruit militiamen with an offer of twenty-five hundred Lebanese pounds (one hundred and sixty dollars) a month for part-time service.[25]

The difficult question is whether Iranian money supports terrorists. On 27 June 1985 U.S. Senator Jesse Helms reportedly asserted that more than $30 million had been transferred from Iran to Lebanese Shias in the weeks just before the TWA hijacking. Helms reportedly claimed that the transfer had been made through the Iranian Martyrs Foundation, whose chairman, Hojatolislam Mahdi Karrubi, visited Lebanon twice, in early and late May, to meet with pro-Iranian Lebanese clerics in Beirut and Baalbek.[26] Although the senator implicated Iran in the hijacking, the evidence indicates that Karrubi's visit to Lebanon was not necessarily made in preparation for the hijacking operation.[27]

Karrubi arrived in Damascus on 31 May at the head of a high-ranking Iranian delegation that had been commissioned specifically by Ayatollah Montazeri "to explore ways and means for ending clashes in Palestinian camps." On 2 June (not in late May, as Senator Helms asserted) he arrived in Beirut, where he conferred with Sheikh Muhammad Hussein Fadlallah, Sheikh Hassan Khalid (Lebanon's Sunni mufti), and Sheikh Mahdi Shams al-Din (vice-president of the Supreme Council of Shia Muslims). He also traveled to south Lebanon, where he met with other clerics, including Sheikh Abbas Harb, who had been released from Israeli jails after sixteen months of imprisonment, and Sheikh Muharram Arif, who had also been released from jail—facts that are missing in Senator Helms' account. Another important omission in the Helms account is that an Iranian delegation headed by Hussein Lavasani, general political director at the Ministry of Foreign Affairs, arrived in Beirut on 31 May 1985. The Lavasani delegation, like the Karrubi delegation, was sent to Lebanon to help stop the fighting between the Amal militiamen and the Palestinians. Iran's primary objective was to stop the ever-growing power of the moderate mainstream Amal movement of Nabih Berri, whom Iran did not like and who was winning the fight with the Palestinians. Having already gained control of West Beirut, Berri forces had launched an offensive on 19 May to gain control of the Palestinian settlements of Sabra, Shatila, and Burj al-Brajneh in southern Beirut. The Karrubi and Lavasani Iranian delegations were sent to Lebanon, in my judgment, to prevent Berri's Amal movement from becoming an even greater force in Lebanon.

ACCUSATIONS OF TERRORISM AGAINST IRAN

Suspicion about Iran's sponsorship of terrorism as an instrument of its foreign policy has continued, despite the evidence to the contrary. The fact that no forcible measures against Iran have yet been taken as a matter either of preemption or of retaliation seemingly indicates that identifying the source and location of terrorist acts in Lebanon, as in the Persian Gulf region, has proved difficult. As noted, in the spring of 1985 U.S. Secretary of State George P. Shultz warned Iran, through the Swiss embassy, that Iran would suffer consequences if Americans held in Lebanon were executed. Furthermore, National Security Adviser Robert C. McFarlane linked Iran to the Shia extremists in Lebanon and threatened a U.S. military response against military targets in a state directing terrorist actions against the United States. On 2 April 1985 Iranian Prime Minister Musavi warned the United States not to bring about another American hostage crisis in the Middle East. Neither then, nor two years earlier, when for the first time the American embassy in Beirut, and then the U.S. Marine headquarters and the American embassy annex, were bombed, did the United States find it possible to implement the so-called Shultz Doctrine of "active prevention, pre-emption and retaliation."[28] Nor could it do so when the TWA plane was hijacked. The secretary of state called on the American public on 25 October 1985 to "reach a consensus" on the kind of antiterrorist response stipulated in his doctrine, a call that has been debated ever since, both inside and outside the Reagan administration.

Defense Secretary Casper Weinberger came up with his "six tests" on 28 November 1985 in response to the Shultz Doctrine, although the so-called Weinberger Doctrine is concerned not only with terrorism, but also with the use of U.S. combat forces abroad. These tests are: (1) The commitment must be deemed vital to our national interest or to that of our allies. (2) It should be made "wholeheartedly, and with the clear intention of winning." (3) Political and military objectives and the ways to meet them must be clearly defined. (4) As conditions change, the commitment's relation to the national interest must be reassessed. (5) Before a commitment is made, there must be "some reasonable assurance" of popular and congressional support. (6) A commitment to arms must be a last resort.[29]

Notwithstanding these doctrines and National Security Adviser McFarlane's explicit threat of military action against Iran, when TWA Flight 847 was hijacked, President Reagan said: "I've pounded a few walls myself" (wanted to hit someone but not known who or where to strike). The central difficulty in this case, as in all previous cases, was identifying the actor and the sponsor—although Senator Jesse Helms pointed his finger at Iran. In addition to the nation's inability to reach a consensus on an acceptable response to terrorism, therefore, the practical problem of where to assign blame also haunted the United States. A major part of these difficulties was that the question of the exact nature of Iran's involvement in terrorist acts remained controversial and unre-

solved. In parts 1 and 2 of this book, Iran's alleged complicity in terrorist acts in the Gulf was discussed. In what follows, three major cases of
terrorism in Lebanon in which Iran also has been accused of complicity
will be examined.

The U.S. embassy in Beirut had been of interest to Iranian militants
for a long time. After the seizure of the U.S. embassy in Tehran on 4
November 1979, about fifty militant Iranian students planned to march
on the U.S. embassy in Beirut, and other Iranians staged a sit-in on the
embassy's grounds. Al-Fatah militiamen rounded up the Iranian students and whisked them out of Beirut, and Syrian peacekeeping forces
evicted the Iranians who were occupying the U.S. embassy premises.
When the U.S. embassy in Beirut was bombed on 18 April 1983, the so-
called Islamic Jihad Organization took responsibility for the bombing.
An anonymous caller, presumably from this shadowy organization, told
the Beirut leftist daily newspaper *Al-Liwa* that the attack was "part of
the Iranian Revolution's campaign against imperialist targets throughout the world." Added the caller: "We shall keep striking at any imperialist presence in Lebanon, including the multinational force."[30] The
group suspected was Hussein Musawi's Islamic Amal. As always, the
Iranian government denied, in the words of Foreign Minister Ali Akbar
Velayati, "any involvement," claiming that "this allegation is another
propaganda plot against us."[31]

Iran was also blamed for the car-bomb attacks on U.S. and French
military installations in Beirut on 23 October 1983 which resulted in the
deaths of 241 Americans and more than 50 Frenchmen. Once again the
pro-Iranian Islamic Amal was suspected of involvement. Although Musawi denied the charges, he said that the French and American military
units in Lebanon were "aggressors and oppressors." He cited the Qur-
'an and the teachings of the first Shia Imam, Ali, as evidence that "it is
right to fight evil with evil," and he declared: "We have been prepared
to face the Israelis and Americans for years. We have prepared our
weapons and we have prepared our shrouds. We are willing to be killed
in the name of God and in defense of our country and our dignity."[32] In
addition to Musawi, Sheikh Muhammad Hussein Fadlallah was suspected of complicity. He told a *Washington Post* correspondent that he
was "mystified by the charges; he was a peaceful man; and he harbored
no grudges against either the U.S. Marines or the French."[33]

Although the Iranians denied the charges, the statements originating
in Iran varied. For example, the Iranian Foreign Ministry spokesman
denied, on 24 October, the "allegations of the U.S. defense secretary on
Iran's possible involvement," but then he added: "The United States
and the Multinational Force [have] entered Lebanon, supported by the

Zionist regime, with the object of usurpation and without the permission of [the] Lebanese nation. It has incurred heavy losses and difficulties due to the heroic resistance of the Lebanese people."

On the day of the bomb attacks, the chief justice of the Supreme Court of Iran, Musavi-Ardabili, told a group of clergymen that the Muslim people of Lebanon had learned "the lesson of revolution from Iran." The Iranian example taught the Americans and the French the lesson "not to embark on aggressions and attacks on oppressed nations."[34] On the other hand, the influential Speaker of the Iranian parliament, Hojatolislam Hashemi-Rafsanjani, while surmising that Iran's "resistance to imperialism" might have caused some people to involve Iran's name in this incident, stated categorically that "it is impossible that Iran was behind these bombing incidents. Iran, in fact, does not support terrorist acts. Iran supports popular movements in the struggle against occupation forces. We do not consider it just to interfere in such things. We have enough problems of our own."[35]

The third example of terrorism in Lebanon in which Iran was the suspected culprit is the hijacking of TWA flight 847. It was hijacked by Lebanese Shia Muslims on 14 June 1985, while carrying 153 passengers from Athens to Rome. Its subsequent odyssey took it to Algiers (twice) and Beirut (three times). On 15 June one American was killed, and his body was thrown onto the tarmac in Beirut. Other passengers and crew were released in batches. By 18 June, 36 passengers and 3 crew members (all of them American men) remained hostages, most of them dispersed in Beirut. The day before, the Shia Amal leader Nabih Berri said he had ordered the hostages taken off the plane to discourage a U.S. rescue attempt, and he assumed negotiations on behalf of the hijackers. Prolonged, agonizing negotiations recalled the 444-day Iranian hostage nightmare of 1979–81. But finally, on 27 June, Nabih Berri expressed optimism that the crisis could be resolved soon. In spite of a last-minute hitch on 29 June, the hostages were freed from captivity after seventeen days, on 30 June, arriving in Damascus in a Red Cross convoy on their way to the United States.

Those who held the hostages demanded the release of 766 prisoners who were being held at Atlit Prison in Israel. The prisoners were mostly Shia Muslims who had been arrested by the Israeli army as a means of protecting its withdrawal from southern Lebanon. According to the American interpretation, and more or less by the admission of some senior Israeli soldiers, Israel had put itself on the wrong side of the Geneva convention by transferring the Lebanese detainees to its own territory from a country with which it was not, technically, at war. Both Israel and the United States insisted on publicly unlinking the hostage crisis from the Israeli detention of the Lebanese prisoners.

The pro-Iranian *Hezbollahis* were believed to have commandeered the hijacking. An estimated one thousand of them demonstrated on 21 June near the hijacked plane. The throngs of young men and women—the women wearing Iranian-style chadors—who shook their fists, waved posters of Ayatollah Khomeini, and chanted "Death to America, the Great Satan" provided bitter reminders of earlier, Iranian, scenes. Also, the main targets of protest in this demonstration, as in the Iranian demonstrations, were the United States and Israel. One protest leaflet, for example, said: "Let us declare support for the plane hijackers. Let us declare solidarity with our imprisoned brethren in Israel's Atlit prison. Let us condemn America's crimes and global terrorism."[36]

Here, near the Lebanese coast in 1985, as near the Persian Gulf coasts in 1979-81 during the Iranian hostage crisis, the United States seemed to prepare to intervene militarily. Plans for a rescue operation in Iran had been drawn up as early as November 1979, when the hostages were first captured in the U.S. embassy in Tehran, although the rescue was not attempted until April 1980. During the incident in Lebanon, the aircraft carrier *Nimitz* and the guided-missile destroyer *Kidd* were ordered to positions off the coast. The Delta Force (the U.S. anti-terrorist squad) had also been dispatched to the Middle East.

Despite the many similarities between the embassy takeover in Iran and the TWA hijackings, it is only fair to ask whether the Iranians were guilty of complicity in the latter case. As startling as it may seem, the answer appears to be this: not only was Iran not involved in the hijacking at its inception, but Iran actually helped to resolve the hijacking crisis. To understand this proposition more fully, it is necessary to examine the visit to Libya and Syria of a delegation led by Speaker Hashemi-Rafsanjani; the visit was made at this time in connection with the intensified cooperation among Iran, Libya, and Syria in response to developments in the Arab-Israeli peace process.

Ever since the 11 February 1985 Yasser Arafat–King Hussein agreement to search for a new peace formula, the Iranians, Syrians, and Libyans had become progressively closer diplomatically. Apparently the three countries were equally interested in seeing that the formula, which enjoyed the blessings of Egypt and Washington, failed. The Iranians in particular wanted it to fail, since Iraq seemingly had joined Egypt and Jordan to form what Iranian Foreign Minister Ali Akbar Velayati called the Cairo-Amman-Baghdad "axis."[37] Rafsanjani's visits to Tripoli and Damascus were made partly to discuss this new axis in the Middle East, and partly to ensure that support for Iran's number one priority—the war with Iraq—continued. Iran was also actively involved at the time in building a better image for itself in the world so that it could pursue its new open-door foreign policy. Although these were the main purposes of the visits, by the time the Rafsanjani delegation arrived in Damascus, Syria had become involved in the hijacking crisis, and hence the crisis figured prominently in the discussions among the Iranians, Syrians, and Lebanese in Damascus.

Although not all the evidence about Iran's attitude and role is presently available, the evidence that is available warrants scrutiny. Iran's policy on the matter must be extracted from the statements of Speaker Rafsanjani. In a press conference in Damascus on 24 June 1985, he said: "In general, we do not approve of any acts that terrorize innocent people. But we must not forget the events that occurred in Lebanon such as Antoine Lahad's acts and the explosions in Tripoli and look upon the hijacking operation as an act of terror, but we must also regard the Elysée Palace and the Pentagon as centers of terrorism."[38] He denied the existence of a link between Iran and the hijacked airliner, saying that if "the United States wants to exploit the incident in order to clash with Iran, then I believe that experiences taught it that such a clash would not be in its interest. I believe it will not clash with us so long as it has agents like Saddam." More importantly, this report by the Syrian wire service SANA quoted Rafsanjani as saying: "I have no knowledge about the identity of the individuals who hijacked the plane. If we had such knowledge, we would have prevented it. But the United States is accustomed to considering Islam and the Islamic Republic responsible for everything that is happening in Lebanon."[39]

This rather conciliatory statement was not published in Tehran when, the following day, the Tehran domestic service reported Rafsanjani's remarks. Instead, the Iranian wire service added a paragraph that did not exist in SANA's report. Rafsanjani was quoted as saying: "Prisoners in Israel or elsewhere naturally have friends who work for their freedom and we cannot deny these martyr-loving persons from getting their rights through force or propaganda."[40] The explanation for the difference between the Syrian and Iranian versions is domestic politics in Iran. The *Hezbollahis* back home still needed to receive heavy doses of militant rhetoric.

But evidence began to surface indicating not only that Speaker Rafsanjani wished he could have prevented the hijacking, as he said, but also that Iran actually helped obtain the release of the hostages. The first indication of this help was reported on 1 July 1985 by respected *Washington Post* correspondent Don Oberdorfer, who wrote: "U.S. officials said [that] hints exist that Iran acquiesced in the settlement."[41] On 3 July he reported more fully: "Some administration officials said they believe that Iranian authorities, who have a close relationship with the most militant Shiite groups, used their influence late last week to persuade the extremist Hezbollah, or Party of God, to submit to Assad's authority and release four TWA hijacking hostages the group was holding."[42]

Iran's help may well have extended beyond simply persuading the *Hezbollahis* to submit to Assad's authority. Reports from Tehran indicate not only that Rafsanjani listened carefully on 24 June to a *Hezbollah* member's "comprehensive report" in connection with the *Hezbollahis'* points of view about their fight against Israel, the United States, and other Western forces, but that he also talked to a number of Palestinians; "Amal movement officials"; the pro-Iranian Sunni cleric Sheikh Sa'id Sha'ban, the leader of the Islamic Unification Movement in Tripoli; Sheikh Muhammad Mahdi Shams al-Din, vice-president of the Supreme Council of Shia Muslims; Sheikh Muhammad Hussein Fadlallah; and a group of Shia and Sunni *ulama* from the Lebanese group of *ulama*.[43] Having decided for their own reasons to try to secure the release of all the hostages, Rafsanjani and Assad were trying to reach a consensus on the release of the hostages on 24 June. The following day, Assad sent a message to Washington proposing the artful diplomatic formula that broke the logjam. He offered to bypass the main obstacle to the settlement, the "linkage problem," by giving the hijackers a guarantee of his own that Israel would release its Lebanese prisoners. He simply asked Washington, "Is it okay?" and Washington replied that there was no objection to the course he proposed to take.[44]

President Reagan and Secretary of State Shultz were not forthcoming about Iran's contribution to the freedom of the hostages. The secretary admitted that the United States had "no direct evidence of Iran being directly involved in the inception of the hijacking," but he did not mention any specific Iranian role in helping Syria gain the release of the thirty-nine hostages, either. Other U.S. officials, however, did. They characterized Rafsanjani's discussions with the various groups of Muslims in Damascus as "tough talk" in favor of the release of the hostages. They also interpreted Rafsanjani's denunciation of the hijacking after he arrived in China as a message to *Hezbollah* holdouts who were refusing to turn over four hostages to Amal on 29 June, the day before the final hostages were released. *Washington Post* correspondent David B. Ottaway's front-page column on 5 July 1985 about Iran's "moderation" was the first such news Americans had read in a long time.

Nevertheless, the American public was not at all aware of the emerging pragmatic trend in Iran's foreign policy. It was referred to for the first time in Robin Wright's 23 June article in the *Washington Post*.[45] The public was equally uninformed of the plain but important fact that Iran closed all its airports, as a "preventive measure," to the hijacked jetliner. The Iranian civil aviation organization said that "the decision was taken after it was heard that the said plane had left Beirut airport for the Persian Gulf region . . . and that the hijacked plane would [absolutely] not be permitted to land at any Iranian airport."[46] This statement was made on 15 June, the second day of the hijacking crisis, when the plane had landed in Beirut for the second time before taking off again for Algiers and then returning to Beirut for the third and last time.

NO ISLAMIC REPUBLIC FOR LEBANON

Nowhere in the Middle East did the ideological crusade of Khomeini seem to have a better chance for success than it did in Lebanon by the time Israel withdrew its forces. Despite the physical distance between Iran and Lebanon, the Iranian and Lebanese extremists' chiliastic goal of establishing an Islamic republic in Lebanon seemèd more accessible in Lebanon than in any other part of the Middle East. The Syrian-Iranian axis in effect lengthened the arm of revolutionary Iran, which extended from the Persian Gulf to the Eastern Mediterranean.

The combination of Iran's political access to Lebanon and the ideological and psychological appeal of Iran to the Lebanese Muslims in general, and to the traditionally aggrieved Shia community in particular, seemed to preordain the establishment of an Islamic Republic of Lebanon. Shia resistance played a major part in silencing the heavy guns of the battleship *New Jersey* which had pounded Shia positions. The humiliated American forces were "redeployed." This was the price that America paid for the Reagan administration's essentially misguided policy, which had been predicated more on strategic greed than on an understanding of the quagmire in Lebanon. Ariel Sharon's Operation Peace for Galilee failed to bring the long-promised peace to northern Israel, just as it failed to bring Israeli ideologues any closer to realizing the dream of *Eretz Yisrael.*

The invasion of Lebanon, which was expected to compensate for the great strategic loss of the Shah's Iran by providing a new foothold for both Tel Aviv and Washington in Lebanon, in effect did exactly the opposite. Syria emerged from the Lebanon war stronger than it had been before the war. Revolutionary Iranians roamed over Lebanon in defiance of the Lebanese government—if there was a Lebanese government. And the historically downtrodden underdog Shia Muslims emerged as the most powerful single community in Lebanon. Even Palestinians seemed to be rising from the ashes. But what most concerned the Israelis was the possible extension of the Shia movement into Israel.

Now no longer concerned with securing a foothold in Lebanon, the Reagan Administration hoped to maintain at least a toehold in the strife-ridden country. But of the old American influence in Lebanon, little was left: a handful of American captives and the beleaguered American University of Beirut.

Yet, none of this necessarily assures either the establishment of an Islamic republic in Lebanon or a long-lived American "hands-off" policy in Lebanon. In fact, neither of the two causes of the present debacle seems durable. The Syrian-Iranian axis could collapse just as quickly as it was erected, and the forward march of the extremist Shia movement could end just as quickly as it began. These two causes are interconnected.

The current and potential differences between Iran and Syria could destroy their axis, and the war between Iraq and Iran cannot go on forever. The common Syrian-Iranian enmity for Saddam Hussein will not be sufficient to maintain the axis. The secular Syrian Ba'thists despise theocracy and do not want there to be an Islamic republic in Iraq or in Lebanon. The Syrians may be said to accept United Nations Resolution 242, whereas the Iranians say they want to eradicate Israel. The list could easily be extended, but what is most relevant here is that the Syrians will tolerate no rival for influence and power in Lebanon, including the Iranians.

The pro-Iranian *Hezbollah* and Islamic Amal flourished in Lebanon during the Israeli occupation. If Syria withdraws its support of Iran, the two groups' chances for further success will be limited. Syria will tolerate these groups only as long as they serve its interests. The mainstream Amal controls West Beirut. It has some 12,000 men under arms and more or less enjoys the support of Syria. Nabih Berri enhanced his position by helping settle the TWA hijacking crisis—although he had to share the spotlight with Hafiz Assad.

Most important of all, the new Iranian open-door foreign policy will continue to erode the doctrinal commitment of Iran to the export of the Islamic revolution. The brakes were applied, with Iran's help, in the TWA hijacking crisis. The emerging pragmatic orientation of Iran's foreign policy will be more compatible with the views of the Iranian leaders' own influential Lebanese friends, such as Sheikh Muhammad Fadlallah, who believes that Lebanon does not have "sufficient and necessary conditions" to become an Islamic republic.

Part Four

OIL, REVOLUTION, AND WAR

13

Oil and the Iranian Revolution

When the revolution erupted, Iran seemed destined once again to occupy the pioneer's role in the oil politics of the Middle East. Iran had been the first country to grant a foreign oil concession, the first to produce commercial quantities of oil, and the first to try to nationalize its oil industry. Now it was the first nation in the region to destroy a conservative monarchy largely by means of oil strikes. Oil revenues had been the heartbeat of the Shah's regime, and oil strikes were his death knell.

In the previous instances, Iran had been at the forefront of widespread change on the oil scene; this time, however, the Iranian example alarmed the Arab monarchies throughout the Gulf region. Could potential and active dissident groups in the other Gulf monarchies use oil workers to topple regimes? Would the Shia oil workers in Saudi Arabia, for example, emulate oil workers in Iran?

This was not the only aspect of the revolution that concerned the Arab monarchies. The revolution's challenge to oil politics in the region also stemmed from the oil policies that were being actively pursued by the Khomeini regime within and outside the Organization of Petroleum Exporting Countries (OPEC). To examine the dual aspects of this challenge of the Iranian Revolution, the challenge must first be placed within its historical context—that is, it is necessary first to examine the effects of the oil factor on Iranian politics before the revolution.

OIL AND POLITICS: THE HISTORICAL PATTERNS

As the lifeblood of the Iranian economy, oil has affected every aspect of life in Iran since 1908, when the first geyser of oil burst forth in the province of Khuzistan. Iranian domestic politics and foreign policy have been greatly affected by Iran's oil. In fact, the grant of the first oil concession in Iran to William Knox D'Arcy, an adventurous British millionaire, in 1901 involved both domestic and international politics. Since at the time the Russians had a great influence on some Iranian officials, the British minister in Tehran, Sir Arthur Hardinge, intervened in behalf of D'Arcy in order to circumvent the expected Russian opposition to the grant of the concession. His intervention took the form of the time-honored British practice of bribing targeted officials. In collusion with Iranian Prime Minister Atabak, Hardinge used a ruse to acquire the concession for D'Arcy without the knowledge of the Russians.[1] The Iranians believed that Reza Khan was brought to power in 1921 in order to insure that the British government's majority share in the Anglo-Persian Oil Company—the outcome of the 1901 concession—was fully protected. They also believe that later, in 1933, Reza Shah gave a new concession to the newly named Anglo-Iranian Oil Company (AIOC) which did indeed help British oil interests more than it helped Iranian national interests.

From the perspective of the counter-elite in Iran, despotic shahs had always mortgaged the nation's economy to foreign interests as a means of maintaining themselves in power. This perception dates back to 1872, when a naturalized British subject, Baron Julius Reuter, was granted an economic concession that surprised even the British arch-imperialist Lord Curzon, who said that the concession was "the most extraordinary surrender of the entire industrial resources" of Iran.[2] Successful Russian opposition nullified the concession, but the same ruling monarch, Nasser ad-Din Shah, granted another sweeping concession to another British subject in 1890. The Iranian *ulama,* led by Haj Mirza Muhammad Hasan Shirazi, considered this tobacco concession contrary to the Qur'an and enjoined the people to abandon smoking until the concession was canceled. The popular support for the cancellation of this concession is generally regarded as the beginning of Iran's national awakening.

Reza Shah's twenty-year repressive rule did not allow any such expression of popular dissatisfaction with the AIOC; only after he was forced to abdicate the throne in 1941 as a result of the Anglo-Russian invasion were Iranians able to voice their opinion on such matters. The Soviets tried, as had the tsarist Russians, to match the British oil monopoly in southern Iran by acquiring a concession in the northern part of the country in 1944. The opposition to the Soviet pressure for an oil concession while Red Army troops occupied part of the country was led successfully by Muhammad Musaddiq, who is better known for his crusade against the AIOC before and, especially, after he took office as Iran's prime minister in 1951.

The nationalization of the Iranian oil industry under Musaddiq's leadership also involved issues of domestic policies and foreign policy. Domestically, the young Shah, who succeeded his father to the throne in 1941, wanted to increase the meager Iranian oil revenues by supplementing the 1933 oil concession. He needed the extra income for the economic and, especially, military modernization that was to help him maintain his power. On the opposite side, the counter-elite, including the Musaddiq-led National Front, the Tudeh Communist party, the fundamentalist terrorist faction known as *Fada'eyin-e Islam,* and the activist cleric Ayatollah Kashani, more or less shared the common goal of the nationalization of the oil industry, despite otherwise conflicting motives. The Shah's desire for a quick settlement of the oil nationalization dispute with Britain and Musaddiq's insistence on "complete" nationalization became intertwined with the struggle for power between them. The nationalist leader insisted unflinchingly, as he had throughout his life, that any monarch must reign according to the Iranian Constitution rather than rule in the way the Shah's dictatorial father had. Musaddiq's efforts to wrest control of the army—the backbone of the court—from the Shah led to a head-on collision between the two men in July 1952; as a result, Musaddiq returned as premier after a brief interruption. In the end, however, in collusion with the CIA, the Shah overthrew the Musaddiq government in August 1953, ending the oil nationalization crisis.

To Musaddiq and his followers, the struggle against the British oil interests in Iran was not an economic or a financial question, it was a struggle for Iran's political independence. The reason for this nationalist belief, in Musaddiq's words, "has been sure knowledge of the Iranian people . . . that the source of all the misfortunes of this tortured nation is only the oil company. The telling evidence for this is to be found in the events and miseries of this nation during the last fifty years."[3] His longstanding doctrine of "negative equilibrium" between the Russians and the British aimed at the removal of the power and influence of both in Iran. Toward this end, during the early phase of his nationalist struggle against the British in 1951–53, he did not hesitate to play an American "card," one of which involved accepting President Truman's mediator, Averell Harriman, in the hope that he would put pressure on the British. But Musaddiq's inability to compromise with the British disappointed the Americans, who, during the Eisenhower administration, accepted the British Conservative government's idea that the Musaddiq government must be overthrown because his flirtations with the Soviets and, particularly, the rising power of the Tudeh party threatened a "communist coup," which was unacceptable to both London and Washington at the height of the cold war.

THE SHAH'S OIL POLICY

The influence of the oil factor in Iranian domestic and foreign policy was no less pervasive during the next quarter-century, between the overthrow of the Musaddiq government in 1953 and the eruption of the Iranian Revolution in 1978–79. In the hands of the Shah, the oil industry became, over time, the single most important instrument of his domestic and foreign policy, although gaining control over it proved to be a protracted and arduous task. Immediately after Musaddiq was overthrown, the Shah was too weak to drive a hard bargain on behalf of Iran with the British and American governments and the Western oil companies, which then, as before, dominated world oil markets. Iran was nearly bankrupt because the British, by refusing to market Iranian oil supplies, had forced the oil industry to close, and the Musaddiq government had been unable to sell Iranian oil in the cartel-controlled world markets. Furthermore, the Shah was politically weak at home at the beginning. Overthrowing Musaddiq made the Shah's rise to power more difficult; he tried to consolidate his position by eliminating all sources of potential and active opposition, nationalist and communist alike. Yet, the underground opposition burst into the open even a decade after his return to power, when the clerics led a popular uprising against both the Shah's regime and the United States under the leadership of Ayatollah Khomeini in 1963. The bloody suppression of this crisis and the exile of Khomeini the following year is regarded today by Khomeini's followers as the dawn of their Islamic movement.

From a position of relative weakness, the Shah in August 1954 signed an oil agreement creating a Western Consortium that included five U.S. oil companies and British Petroleum.[4] Although the British monopoly was thus broken, the British did possess 40 percent of consortium shares. The American companies, with the full help of the U.S. government, also acquired a 40 percent share in the consortium, thereby realizing an old goal of controlling some Iranian oil resources. Notwithstanding the legal euphemisms of the provisions of the agreement, in effect the Iranian oil industry was "denationalized." The agreement gave Iran only 50 percent of the profits, was to last twenty-five years, and compensated British Petroleum too generously. The Shah let President Eisenhower and other American leaders know that he had signed the agreement only "under the circumstances," implying his dissatisfaction with its terms.

Circumstances had to change substantially before the Shah could flex his muscles against the consortium.[5] Domestically, he more firmly established his political control after the suppression of the religiously inspired uprising in 1963. He intensified efforts to implement the reform programs of the "White Revolution," which he had launched in January 1963 presumably as the antidote to both clerical reactionaries and communist radicals. But the nationalist elements drawn from the modern middle classes, especially the students and teachers who had challenged the Shah's regime since January 1960, were equally targeted. The Shah hoped to win over the peasant masses through land reform, and at the same time placate modernized intellectuals, whatever their ideological persuasion, with his own revolutionary rhetoric. The combination of this essentially tactical revolution and SAVAK's repressive measures was designed to insure the Shah's regime greater control of the polity. It did that, but in the process it also radicalized dissident political forces, some of which committed terrorist acts in the 1970s against Iranian and, especially, American officials in Iran.

In several respects, external circumstances changed even more dramatically in favor of the Shah's muscle-flexing vis-à-vis the consortium. The American influence in Iran diminished somewhat in the late 1960s because U.S. economic and military aid programs were phased out as Iran's rapid economic growth and ability to pay for its own military hardware were recognized. A second factor was an unprecedented improvement in Iran's commercial and economic relations with the Soviet Union. A third factor was the historic decision of the British to withdraw their forces from the Persian Gulf region by the end of 1971; the Americans were reluctant to fill the power vacuum, and, furthermore, President Nixon saw in the region at the time the ideal conditions for regional security by regional powers. Fourth, and most critically, by 1970 the market in the oil industry had been transformed from a buyer's to a seller's market. The State Department estimated that by 1980 the United States would consume 24 million barrels of oil a day, that domestic production would provide only 12 million barrels a day, and that two-thirds or more of imported oil would, of necessity, come from the Eastern Hemisphere.

Under the circumstances, the Shah was encouraged not only to pressure the consortium to take more Iranian oil at higher prices, but also to lead other OPEC oil producers in the region against twenty-two major Western oil companies. Together with the other two oil giants of the Gulf region, Saudi Arabia and Iraq, he drove a hard bargain in the Tehran agreement of 1971, increasing the price of Persian Gulf crude an average of forty-six cents per barrel and building in an annual increase of 2.5 percent in order to offset inflation in the West. On the home front, the Shah pressured the consortium in 1973 to sign a new oil agreement, presumably cementing Iranian control over its oil industry by making the Western oil companies mere purchasers of Iranian oil. Although the St. Moritz agreement enhanced Iran's ownership and control of operations, the Western oil giants and the Western industrialized countries in reality had a greater say in the oil industry, because they controlled the world oil markets.

In the same year, however, the industrialized world witnessed the "first oil shock" as OPEC was transformed into the biggest single macroeconomic force in the world in the wake of the Arab-Israeli October war. OPEC quadrupled the price of oil, and in the process wrested control of oil prices from the seven major oil companies. Today, as OPEC faces the worst crisis of its quarter-century history because of falling oil prices, it is hard to imagine that in the 1970s OPEC managed to raise oil prices fifteenfold. Despite his efforts throughout the 1950s and the 1960s to increase Iranian oil revenues, the Shah could not even obtain an annual income level of $1 billion. In 1974, however, Iran's oil income jumped spectacularly to $22 billion. Regardless of how unhappy the United States was about the Shah's hawkish oil-price stance, U.S. dissatisfaction was tempered because the United States had many interests in common with the Shah's regime. The Nixon administration made the Shah's regime the "policeman" of the Persian Gulf region so that parallel American and Iranian interests would be protected. It also promised, in 1972, to sell the Shah all the conventional weapons he wanted. The explosion of oil prices enabled the Shah to make massive purchases of military hardware from America and to dream of transforming Iran into one of the world's major conventional military powers.

KHOMEINI'S OIL POLICY

This, however, was not the way the Shah's steadfast opponents saw Iran under his rule. Against the backdrop of a legacy of perceived foreign economic and political domination, the Shah's twenty-five-year alliance with the United States was considered the apogee of the longtime monarchical betrayal of the national interest. The Shah's oil and military policies, more than anything else, his opponents believed, subordinated the Iranian-Islamic personality of the nation to the worldwide economic and political interests of the United States; hence the opposition's designation of the Shah as the American king. For Ayatollah Khomeini, even the nationalists of the 1950s did not go far enough in restoring Islamic-Iranian rights. He seemed to suggest this when he said: "During Musaddiq's time . . . they called for oil, but now—for Islam." Khomeini's disciples vehemently expressed their views on what they considered to be the Shah's ruinous oil policy. An early Khomeini disciple, Bani-Sadr, for example, charged that the Shah's regime deliberately used oil to subjugate the entire underdeveloped Iranian economy to the dominant economy of the Western industrialized world, particularly the United States. In the hands of the Shah's regime, therefore, "oil became the instrument of the destruction of the foundations of Iran's independent economy," stated Bani-Sadr in his book *Oil and Domination* (*Naft va Saltih*). He added that "Iran was forced to travel in a direction that would end in its losing control over its own destiny, and its people would not be able to earn their livelihood without exporting their wealth."[6] Although he belonged to a very different ideological universe, Khomeini entertained similar views. For example, the day after he triumphantly returned to Iran from exile, he expressed his favorite oil theme in these words:

> As for our own oil, it was given away to America and the others. It is true that America paid for the supplies it received, but that money was spent buying arms and establishing military bases for America. In other words, first we gave them our oil, and then we established military bases for them. America, as a result of its cunning (to which that man [the Shah] was also a party), thus benefited doubly from us. It exported weapons to Iran that our army was unable to use so that American advisers and experts had to come in order to make use of them. If the Shah's rule had (God forbid) lasted a few years longer, he would have exhausted our oil reserves in just the same way that he destroyed our agriculture.[7]

The oil factor, however, was more than the fuel that kept the Iranian Revolution boiling; it became the most important instrument of the seizure of power in the hands of the revolutionary forces. As the revolutionary crisis deepened, the forces of opposition resorted to oil strikes to topple the Shah's regime. The first street demonstration was held on 9 January 1978; after some thirty-one street demonstrations, the first oil strike was launched on 31 October in the wake of the 8 September massacre on Black Friday, in which many thousands of unarmed people in Jaleh Square were killed by the Shah's troops. Oil strikes, thus started, disrupted both oil production and exports, and the disruption fluctuated with the vicissitudes of the revolutionary crisis. At first the Shah's government tried to negotiate with the oil workers while at the same time threatening dismissals, deprivation of housing facilities, and the arrest of strike leaders. The oil workers' demands included the dismantling of the hated security police SAVAK, the release of political prisoners, termination of martial law, removal of foreign advisers—especially Americans—and punishment of corrupt officials. The Shah's government turned a deaf ear to all political demands, but it did try to meet most of the economic demands, including salary raises ranging from 40 to 60 percent.

As negotiations deadlocked and the crisis deepened, the oil strikes escalated and production dropped drastically; in November 1978, production dropped from 5 million barrels a day to just over 800 thousand barrels. The installation of a military government on 5 November was followed by a brief period of increased oil production—up to 2.3 million barrels a day. But the defiant resumption of oil strikes and work stoppages forced the production back down to just over 1 million barrels a day by 4 December. By the end of the month, however, oil exports completely ceased as a result of the resignations of some three thousand oil workers and a walkout by thousands of others. These paralyzing events followed the mammoth religio-political demonstrations staged on the observance of the occasion of the martyrdom of Imam Hussein on 10 and 11 December. Fuel shortages resulted; kerosene and gasoline were rationed. By then, major oil consumers of the world were becoming alarmed. According to U.S. Energy Secretary James R. Schlesinger, Americans might face gasoline rationing, price increases, and government allocation of fuel supplies if Iran's oil exports remained shut off for another three months.[8]

Prices did shoot up in 1979, resulting in the "second oil shock." These price increases, however, were not the result of the kind of shortages that had existed during the "first oil shock" in 1973, when the demand had far exceeded the supply of oil. In 1979, "oil was at the same time plentiful and short," according to Saudi Oil Minister Sheikh Ahmad Zaki Yamani.[9] In other words, in 1979 the oil market was not "tight," as it had been in 1973, because, according to GATT (General Agreement on Tariffs and Trade) sources, between 1973 and 1979 world petroleum consumption had increased by only 1.1 percent, and this slight increase had been offset by a worldwide surplus of crude oil.[10] The oil shortages and the rise in prices were caused by the panic buying of anxious consumers and the hoarding of oil by hopeful speculators.[11] Although the official price of oil was $13.34 per barrel, by the time the Shah left Iran on 16 January 1979, spot market prices had doubled and tripled. By late November 1979, Saudi Arabian light was trading at $41.00 per barrel on the spot market.

Having used oil strikes to seize power from the Shah, the Khomeini regime then used oil revenues, as its predecessors had, to consolidate domestic power and conduct foreign policy. Khomeini, who, before the downfall of the Shah, had considered the oil industry the tool of foreign domination in Iran, told the industry's manager and employees after the revolution: "The industry is the lifeline of the nation."[12] His first prime minister, Mehdi Bazargan, told oil industry workers after the resumption of oil exports in March 1979 that the Iranian Revolution itself would fail if oil exports were not resumed. The Shah had regarded oil as a "noble commodity"; Speaker Hashemi-Rafsanjani regards it as a "divine blessing" and "the foundation of the Iranian Revolution." The Shah had talked a great deal about eliminating Iran's excessive dependence on oil resources, and so do the revolutionary authorities. Foreign Minister Ali Akbar Velayati says that Iran is "anxious to assert its economic independence and not base its development solely on oil resources."[13] Oil Minister Muhammad Gharazi says that the objective of the Iranian Revolution is "to separate economy from oil and instead establish an economic system to stand on its own feet."[14] The Shah had talked tirelessly about the diversification of Iranian industry as a means to those same ends, but his regime, like the present one, had to face the fact of Iran's limited technical and marketing capability.

Despite the ideological onslaught of the revolutionaries against Iran's dependence on oil exports, the revolutionary regime, no less than the regime before it, sought to occupy a leading place in the international oil market. The immediate attainment of this goal, however, was impossible, largely because of the revolutionary regime's self-inflicted damages. The unruly anti-American forces stopped the operations of the consortium-controlled Oil Service Company of Iran, whose deputy chief was murdered. In addition, the exodus of many foreign and national oil experts, the Western economic boycott of Iran because of the seizure of American hostages, and the Iraqi invasion of Iran resulted in a drastic reduction of Iranian oil exports during 1979–80. Some revolutionary authorities rationalized the dramatic loss of oil export markets, saying that since they could not buy foreign goods because of Western trade sanctions, they did not need petrodollars. Others rationalized the Iranian fall in production by harping on the revolutionary theme of keeping the oil in the ground for future generations.

The reality, of course, was something else. Because of the circumstances just mentioned, Iran could not export much oil. But after the hostage crisis was over and Western trade sanctions were terminated, after President Bani-Sadr's government fell and the pro-Khomeini forces consolidated their power, Iran's bid to recapture its share of the oil market surfaced unambiguously. Before the revolution, Iran had been second only to Saudi Arabia in oil exports. In 1975, when Saudi Arabia produced 26 percent of all OPEC oil, Iran produced almost 20 percent, but in 1980 the figures were 36.8 percent and 5.5 percent respectively. Iran's production began to pick up in 1981, and a year later it amounted to 10.5 percent of all OPEC production, while Saudi Arabia's production amounted to 36 percent.[15] Iran was not yet producing as much oil as it wanted to, but it was moving rapidly to recapture its leading place in OPEC despite the war. The drop in oil exports entailed an enormous cut in revenues: in 1977, the year before the start of the revolution, Iran's income from oil was $21.6 billion, but in 1981 it dropped to a mere $8.6 billion.[16]

Just as Iran has asserted its intention to recapture a leading position in the world oil market, it has revived its oil rivalry with Saudi Arabia with a vengeance. The new ideological, political, and strategic conflict between Tehran and Riyadh seems to have intensified the oil rivalry. Iran is now using its oil as a "political weapon" to attain ideological and political superiority over Saudi Arabia. "With an increase in our country's activities in the international scene," states Prime Minister Mir-Hussein Musavi, "including the oil market, using oil as a political weapon weakens Arabia's role."[17] Even the oil battle lines of the revolutionary regime are similar to those of the Shah's government. In 1976, for example, the Iranian oil-price hawks and Saudi oil-price doves were once again at one another's throats, and their differences split OPEC at a meeting in Doha (Qatar); Saudi Arabia favored a 5 percent, and Iran a 15 percent, increase in oil prices.

Except for giving price discounts to increase exports or to compensate buyers for the rising insurance costs because of the war, the revolutionary regime in today's Iran is no less hawkish on oil prices than the Shah was. The ideological posturing only makes Iran's dealings in the oil market more colorful for observers and more painful for policymakers. Within OPEC, Iran is now the self-appointed leader of such indebted poorer oil producers as Nigeria and Venezuela, presumably the organization's "underprivileged" (mustaza'fin) nations, as opposed to the "privileged" (mustakberin) nations such as Saudi Arabia and other oil-rich GCC members.

Iran's production and price battles with Saudi Arabia and its associates continue, despite the momentous OPEC decisions of 1982 and 1983 in which the Iranian government participated. On 20 March 1982, for the first time in the history of OPEC, its thirteen members decided to set a formal limit on the level of their oil production as a means of reducing the worldwide surplus of oil and boosting oil prices. They settled on a total daily output of 17.5 million barrels. On 14 March 1983, they decided to cut overall oil prices down to $29 from a high of $34 per barrel. These decisions seemingly were confirmed at the OPEC meeting in Vienna on 10 July 1984; OPEC countries meant, presumably, to defend that price for "several years" in order to allow inflation to erode the real cost of oil, and so stabilize the demand for oil.[18] Although Saudi

Arabia had no formal quota, as the "swing producer" in OPEC it agreed to adjust its production to fill the gap between the rest of OPEC's production and the overall 17.5-million-barrel production level set by the organization. Actually, however, Saudi Arabia was expected to adhere to a quota of 5 million barrels a day, while Iran's formal quota was set at 2.4 million barrels.

These decisions in fact amounted to a reduction in production by both Saudi Arabia and Iran, but whereas Iranian authorities gloated over the drop in Saudi production, they remained unhappy about their own quota. Iranian Oil Minister Muhammad Gharazi, for example, triumphantly stated after an OPEC meeting in January 1983: "Saudi Arabia has lost its major role in OPEC." Gharazi added: "Iran's political strength has forced Saudi Arabia to cut its oil production from 5 to nearly 4 million barrels a day. Any reduction in Saudi production that is added to ours means victory."[19] After Iran's quota was set, Iranian Oil Minister Gharazi complained: "We can't live with 2.4 million barrels a day. . . . We need one million barrels of oil a day just for internal consumption. The current quota is too small for 42 million people fighting a war."[20] Iranian authorities continued to demand an increase in the Iranian quota, arguing that to be just, their quota must be based on "population, reserves and other factors, rather than [on] the present situation," as Speaker Rafsanjani said. Rafsanjani also said: "Although our country's population is several times that of Arabia, the latter's quota is several times greater than ours."[21]

Revolutionary Iran not only complained of Saudi Arabia's "imposed" production level and demanded an increase in its own quota from 2.4 to 3.2 million barrels of oil production a day, it also advocated an increase in prices from $29 per barrel to the previous $34, and linked the two demands. The Iranians did not seem to believe in 1984 that production and price limits aided the consumers, much less the OPEC nations. "Despite the views of Saudi Arabia," according to Oil Minister Gharazi, "which imposed the $29 price instead of $34 per barrel, the market conditions show that the reduction in the price of oil instead of being in the interest of the true consumers of oil has gone into the pockets of oil companies and the treasuries of the big countries. Only in Japan and in the United States has it led to a slight reduction in the price of oil for consumers."[22] According to the oil minister, at most, the price of oil should be set at $60 to $70 per barrel—presumably the price of substitute forms of energy such as coal—and at least, "the price of oil should increase according to the rate of world inflation."

All along the Iranians had blamed Saudi overproduction for the worldwide "oil glut," and they seemed outraged when, for six months early in 1984, the Saudis produced 500 thousand barrels a day over their quota of 5 million barrels. Independent observers agreed with this assessment, charging that "the Saudis have been among the main cheaters on their quotas."[23] In July 1984, also according to independent analysts, the Saudis kept production levels high because of a deal they had made to exchange oil for Boeing 747s and Rolls Royce aircraft engines. The Iranians charged that by increasing its output of oil, Saudi Arabia, in addition to paying for Boeings, had paid a large portion of Iraq's debts for arms purchases from France and the Soviet Union. They complained that the ten Boeing 747s were to be used "for military purposes," and that, even so, given the Saudi "reserves of $120 billion," Saudi Arabia could easily have purchased the Boeings for cash instead of pouring "another 40 million barrels of oil onto the confused international oil market."[24]

OPEC'S CONTINUING CRISIS

These charges reflected a much more serious problem, one that was engulfing all OPEC producers. Between the disruption of Iranian oil supplies in 1979 and Iran's squabbles with Saudi Arabia over "the confused international oil market" in the early 1980s, OPEC's share of the noncommunist world's oil production had fallen from three-fifths to two-fifths. Even more revealing, its share of the world oil market had fallen from 53 percent in 1975 to 30 percent in 1984.[25] A few of the reasons for OPEC's escalating crisis need to be mentioned here. First, OPEC members, by increasing oil prices fifteenfold during the 1970s in their attempt to redress what they considered past injustices at the hands of the Western industrialized nations and their giant oil companies, in fact contributed to the world oil glut of the early 1980s. Second, non-OPEC oil production was soaring even as oil demand was sagging; production outside OPEC grew by 22 percent from 1979 to 1984. Third, industrial production had increased after 1973 without a concomitant increase in demand for oil. According to the *Economist,* in "1972, the (mostly) rich nations of the Organization for Economic Cooperation and Development (OECD) used 7% more oil to produce 5% more gnp than the year before. Last year [1984] the OECD's gnp also grew by 5%—but its oil demand grew by only 2%. Japan, which has always passed energy costs through to energy users, now uses less than half as much oil per unit of gdp [gross domestic product] as it did in 1973."[26]

The implications of this downward trend in demand for oil were grave for all OPEC members, particularly Saudi Arabia. As the "swing producer," it adjusted its production of oil upward in 1979–81, but downward afterward. In the wake of the disruption of Iranian oil supplies during the revolution, Saudi Arabia had increased its oil production to more than 10 million barrels per day, but by 1985 it had, reluctantly, reduced production to a mere 2.2 million barrels per day. This meant that its revenues from oil tumbled from $120 billion in 1980 to $43 billion in 1984. It was estimated in the summer of 1985 that Saudi oil revenues would decrease to less than $25 billion a year at the prevailing rate.[27] Although, as the swing producer, Saudi Arabia did not have a set quota, in effect it had a quota of 4.3 million barrels per day, the largest of all OPEC quotas. Given Saudi Arabia's actual output of only 2.2 million barrels per day by 1985, however, the fact that the Saudi quota was larger than Iran's (2.4 million barrels per day) was inconsequential. All the OPEC members were in the same situation—the seller's market had vanished, at least for the time being, and they were all scrambling for larger pieces of an ever-diminishing pie.

In 1985 this situation intensified the existing tensions within OPEC. The organization was divided not only between the richer and the poorer members, but also between the political radicals and the political moderates. Saudi Arabia and its GCC partners encountered Algerian, Libyan, and Iranian resistance to their proposals, first in their meeting in Vienna in July 1985, and then in Geneva. After haggling for three days in Vienna, OPEC representatives went home on 7 July without having reached an agreement on changes in pricing and production policies. The agreement that was finally formalized in Geneva on 25 July represented an unstable compromise. Largely to help Saudi Arabia produce more oil, the OPEC ministers agreed to cut 50¢ a barrel from the price of heavy crudes, and 20¢ a barrel from the price of medium crudes. These cuts fell far short of Saudi Arabia's original demand for an across-the-board cut of $1.50.[28]

The Saudis were disappointed. Algeria, Iran, and Libya, however, disassociated themselves from the Geneva agreement. These countries simply did not want the Saudis to increase sales at the expense of their light crudes. On the other hand, the Saudis worried that the fifty-cent cut in the price of heavy crudes might not be enticing enough to get the four ARAMCO (Arabian-American Oil Company) partners—Exxon, Mobil, Texaco, and Chevron—to resume their large purchases of Saudi crude.[29] Saudi Arabia was already running the world's second biggest current-account deficit (after the United States), and the prospects for improvement did not seem very bright when the Saudi oil ministers left for home after the Geneva meeting. By the 1990s, when the rest of the world's oil production is expected to decline, the OPEC states in general and Saudi Arabia in particular might be in better shape. But in 1985, no

OPEC country seemed to be faring very well. Yet, Saudi Arabia, with less than 10 million people and more than $100 billion of reserves, earned more from oil than did impoverished Nigeria, which had 90 million people to feed and heavy debts to service.[30]

THE IMPERATIVE OF COMPROMISE

The oil challenge of revolutionary Iran to the other Persian Gulf states involved both the potential impact of its example of oil strikes and the active pursuit of its oil policy. For the first time in the history of the Persian Gulf oil industry, in 1979 the forces of political opposition in Iran used oil strikes to destroy a monarchical regime in the Gulf region. The Shia uprisings in the Saudi Eastern Province in the same year raised questions about the impact of the Iranian example on the large number of Saudi Shia oil workers, whose protest included the demand that the oil be kept in the ground and the allegation that the royal family was using the oil revenues wastefully while the Shia community continued to suffer from socioeconomic disadvantages. Oil income was the Al-Saud's most important instrument of maintaining power; oil income could even be used to redress the social and economic grievances of the Shia community.

The other aspect of the Iranian oil challenge surfaced after the consolidation of domestic power by the Khomeini regime, the settlement of the hostage crisis, and the lifting of the Western trade boycott. Before then, the Saudis had boosted their oil output to more than 10 million barrels per day to counter the effects of the second oil shock, but afterward, they and the other GCC states had to face Iran's determination to recapture its place as the second largest oil producer in the region. By 1985 Iran was producing nearly as much as Saudi Arabia and was continuing to challenge the levels of oil production and price favored by Saudi Arabia and other GCC states within OPEC.

Neither aspect of the oil challenge of revolutionary Iran should be exaggerated. To be sure, the Iranian revolutionary rhetoric within as well as outside OPEC was abrasive, but in practice, neither the Iranian example of crippling oil strikes nor the oil policies of the Khomeini regime posed a threat to the Gulf states. Six years after the eruption of the Iranian Revolution, there was no sign of revolutionary ferment in Saudi Arabia; nor were Shia dissidents or any other dissidents trying to use oil strikes to topple the House of Saud. Iran's hawkish oil price and production policy was not solely responsible for the troubles of the Saudis and their GCC partners, either. After all, there was nothing new about the demand for higher oil prices being made by the Khomeini regime, whose oil policy in this respect significantly resembled the Shah's. The Saudis managed to live with the oil policies of the Shah's and Khomeini's Iran. The alarmists who believed that the Iranian revolutionaries would be able to dictate price and production levels to other OPEC members were disregarding the most important lesson of the post-1973 period, which is that world oil markets, rather than any one oil state or group of states, determines these levels.

This brings me to a final thought on the subject. Twenty-five years after its establishment in September 1985, OPEC continued to exist despite all the dire predictions of its imminent collapse. For thirteen years after OPEC's creation, it made little difference how aggrieved its members were over their past experiences with the Western oil giants; there was not much they could do about the past. But when world market conditions favored the sellers in the 1970s, OPEC members were able to gain control of the oil decision-making process. After 1981, they saw their oil power being chipped away by forces largely beyond their control.

Yet, revolutionary Iran, conservative Saudi Arabia, and other GCC states managed to cooperate. Regardless of the form of government, regardless of differences over price and production levels, regardless of ideological antagonism, as oil states they had to sink or swim together. Dependent for survival on their oil revenues, the Gulf states had no other alternative but to compromise, even when they did not seem to be doing so. The rivalries among the Gulf states of OPEC will probably intensify after the Iraq-Iran war, for both Iraq and Iran will probably try to increase their production for postwar reconstruction and development. In spite of the war, Iraq was already, in 1985, demanding an addition to its quota of 500 thousand barrels per day in anticipation of an increase in its oil exports through a new pipeline. Whether in fact by the 1990s the Gulf states will be back "in the driver's seat" remains to be seen, but in good years as in bad, they will have to work out their problems to satisfy their common interests.

14

Oil and War

When the Iraq-Iran war broke out, the world braced itself for a "third oil shock," expecting another sudden rise in oil prices. After all, the first oil shock had been associated with an armed conflict—the Arab-Israeli war of 1973, which had quadrupled oil prices. The second oil shock, which resulted from the disruption of oil supplies from Iran during the revolution, had increased oil prices another 200 percent. On the surface, the Iraq-Iran war presaged adverse effects on oil prices. The belligerents, both of whom were major oil producers, struck at each other's oil facilities from the start. Their war threatened to spread to the rest of the Persian Gulf, disrupting the flow of all vital Gulf oil supplies to world markets. By the time the Lebanon war erupted, the world was awash in oil, but that did not stop observers from asking why the Arabs did not impose an oil embargo on the United States as they had in 1973.

Yet neither the Iraq-Iran war nor the Lebanon war led to the explosion of oil prices. This seemed odd, considering that the war in the Gulf caused the largest and longest disruption of oil supplies in the history of the Middle East. In the Lebanon war, the Arabs universally regarded the United States as a partner in the Israeli invasion, yet they did not even consider imposing an oil embargo against America. Why? The conventional answer is simple. The world oil glut protected consumers against shortages caused by the Iraq-Iran war. It also discouraged the already troubled Arab oil producers from doing anything to lessen their dwindling share of the world oil market, despite their feelings about the Lebanon war. But in this chapter, I will in part argue that, although the oil market was an important factor, powerful political and strategic factors also controlled the flow of oil during the war between Iraq and Iran and during the Lebanon war, just as they had during the Arab-Israeli war of October 1973.

An overemphasis on the market factor has distracted attention away from another significant area of scholarly investigation, and in this chapter, I hope to correct that oversight. The oil factor has emerged in a new form in the relations among Middle Eastern oil-producing states. It has become what may be called an "instrument of war," in that it has been employed as part of the combatants' war strategy. It has been used to destroy the oil-producing capacity of the enemy, to launch an oil-spill offensive, and to wage a tanker war.

NO THIRD OIL SHOCK: THE IRAQ-IRAN WAR

The long war between Iran and Iraq has disrupted the oil supplies of the Persian Gulf but has not caused a new "oil shock." Market conditions helped protect consumers against shortages; because the oil market was "soft," no panic buying or hoarding took place, as they did in the wake of the Iranian Revolution. Partly because of the large inventories of oil that had built up after the Iranian Revolution, the market was not tight when the Iraq-Iran war began, but the basic worldwide fall in demand for oil was the major reason for the lack of oil shortages at the time. By 1980, both International Energy Agency officials and OPEC members believed that there was an oil surplus of up to 2.5 million barrels a day, and that there was enough oil stored throughout the world for 100 days of global consumption if a major and prolonged disruption of oil were to occur.[1]

Yet, 2.5 million surplus barrels of oil a day would not alone have offset the loss of oil supplies during the war. When war broke out, Iran was exporting only 700 thousand barrels a day, but Iraq was exporting about 3.5 million. Because of the war, less than 3.5 million barrels of oil—mainly Iraqi oil—a day were lost to the world market. To offset worldwide oil shortages, Saudi Arabia, Kuwait, the United Arab Emirates, and Qatar decided, on 10 October 1980, to increase their oil production by some 3 million barrels a day. Saudi Oil Minister Sheikh Ahmad Zaki Yamani was quoted as saying at the time that his country's output would increase by 1 million barrels a day, to 10.5 million.[2] These countries together were already producing a total of 14 million barrels of oil a day, and the increase of 3 million barrels was more than ample to offset the loss caused by the war. True, spot market prices for Arabian light crude oil increased from $31 to $41, but the official price of this oil, which is the OPEC "marker" crude, did not change immediately. And the subsequent increase to $34 of the official price lasted for only a short while before OPEC decided to reduce the price to $29; this price plum-meted to less than $13 by March 1986, when the Saudis warned that the price of oil could drop to as low as $8 a barrel. Even the tanker war of the spring and summer of 1984, which posed the most serious threat to the outflow of Gulf oil supplies to that time, did not cause the oil short-ages that had been feared.

To leave the discussion here simply because there has been no oil shock so far, however, is to forgo an analysis of the interrelationship between oil and the war from a broader political and military perspec-tive, an analysis that could reveal the unprecedented use of oil by the combatants as an instrument of war. Before the Iraq-Iran war, few ob-servers believed that the most precious natural resource of two major Gulf oil producers could become fair game in wartime.[3] Yet, it has, and so pervasively that the war itself has been characterized as the "oil war."

OIL: AN INSTRUMENT OF THE GULF WAR

First of all, as part of its strategy, each combatant has tried to destroy the other's oil-production capacity. Since the start of the war, Iraq and Iran have attacked oil targets of all kinds. Iraq attacked Iran's huge oil refinery at Abadan on 23 September 1980, the day after the outbreak of the war. This refinery is one of the largest of its kind in the world, and it supplies Iran with the bulk of its needs in kerosene, gasoline, heating oil, and other refined products. This first air raid on the refinery was fol-lowed up by other hits, in less than a month causing damage, according to the Iraqis, to all the 152 oil storage tanks at Abadan. No oil port or city was spared by the Iraqi forces once Saddam Hussein escalated the months-old border skirmishes into a full-scale war.

The port city of Khorramshahr was one of the earliest and most important Iraqi targets. The Iraqi objective in capturing the city was not only to deprive Iran access to it, but also to try to establish control over the border river, the Shatt al-Arab. Iraqi forces also targeted the oil cities of Ahwaz and Dizful. Ahwaz is the capital city of the oil-rich Iranian province of Khuzistan and a vital oil supply center, by virtue of being the junction of six major pipelines leading from the Iranian oil fields and refineries of Khuzistan to northeastern and southeastern Iran. Iraq's primary objective in Ahwaz was to cut the flow of oil to the rest of Iran. Had they captured the city, the Iraqis could have cut the supply of gasoline and aviation fuel to Iran's tanks and aircraft.[4] Dizful is another Iranian oil "nerve center" that the Iraqi forces attacked time and again. The city's strategic importance is twofold; it is the starting point of a major highway that leads into central Iran, and it is the site of a pumping station that sends oil from the Khorramshahr-Abadan complex of facilities to central and northern Iran. Had the Iraqi forces been able to cut the pipelines in this city, the supply of crude oil to the Iranian refineries at Isfahan and Tehran would have dried up, and the whole country would have run out of oil within a few weeks.[5] The Kharg Island oil terminal, the most highly valued Iraqi strategic target throughout the war, will be examined in more detail later.

The Iranians, for their part, tried to inflict damage on strategic Iraqi targets. On the same day that Iraq first launched air raids on the Abadan refinery, for example, Iranian forces attacked three Iraqi oil installations. Iranian warships and jet fighters later hit the Iraqi Khor al-Amaya and Mina al-Bakr oil terminals, capable, in peacetime, of receiving oil tankers of 270,000 and 350,000 tons, respectively. The Iranian attacks on these vital deep-water terminals as well as on the Fao terminal in the early weeks of the war stopped, for all practical purposes, Iraqi oil exports to world markets through the Persian Gulf. The Iranians also attacked the vital Iraqi oil cities of Kirkuk, Mosul, and Irbil.

Basra has been as vital to the Iranian war strategy as Kharg Island has been to the Iraqi war strategy. This vulnerable Iraqi port city lies within a few miles of the Iranian border, from whence 175-millimeter Iranian guns have shelled it throughout the war. Basra is the location of huge industrial projects, including a petrochemical plant, a natural-gas processing unit, and an oil refinery. It is also largely inhabited by Iraqi Shias, who are the main sociopolitical target of Iran's wartime strategy. Iran's capture of parts of the oil-rich islands of Majnoon placed the Iranian forces within striking distance of the strategic highway between Basra and Baghdad, but there the Iranian forces faced stiff Iraqi resistance as well as the natural barrier of the several-hundred-yard-wide Shatt al-Arab. As noted, Iranian forces did cross the river in the southernmost part of the war front in February 1986, captured the Fao oil port on the tenth of the month, and held their bridgehead west of the river as late as March.

THE OIL-SPILL OFFENSIVE

For a while, Iraq created oil spills as a part of its war strategy. The Iraqi objective was threefold: to threaten Iran directly with pollution, to force Iran to close its offshore oil field, and to induce the Arab Gulf states that were threatened by pollution to try to persuade Iran to accept a cease-fire in the polluted maritime zone in the hope that the cease-fire could, in time, be extended to the entire war front.[6] Iraq's decision to launch an oil-spill offensive stemmed, of course, from the country's exasperation over its crippled oil exports through the Gulf lanes. Conscious of this Iraqi desperation, the Iranians were determined to maintain the pressure on Iraq by avoiding making a commitment to any cease-fire that could be extended to all armed hostilities. Yet, because they were also conscious of the fact that the threat of pollution to the other Gulf states as well as to Iran could not be ignored, the Iranians looked for a solution to the oil-slick problem which would be unrelated to an overall peace settlement.

The facts of the case are disputed, but it is clear that the offensive was launched early in 1983. As early as January, a platform in the Iranian Nowruz oil field, about fifty miles northwest of Kharg Island, began to leak because of damage that had previously been caused, accidentally, by an oil tanker. Iran claimed, however, that as a result of Iraqi military actions against Iran on 27 January, 11 February, and 2 March, Iranian wells had been damaged.[7] Other sources indicated that the spillage "began about February 7 when a well that had been capped and that had been weakened by rusting blew out. The situation worsened on March 2 when Iraqi warships damaged six wells nearby."[8] Environmental officials in Manama, Bahrain, reported in late March 1983 that the oil slick contained more than 100 thousand barrels of crude and was floating about twenty-nine miles north of Bahrain and Qatar and forty-six miles from the Saudi Arabian coast. In addition to the exact date the oil spill began, the number of oil wells involved was also controversial; some officials claimed that only one well was spilling fuel into the Gulf waters, while others believed three or even seven were gushing crude oil as a result of attacks by Iraqi fighter planes.[9]

Having launched the oil-spill offensive, Iraq maneuvered to block all efforts to cap the leaking oil wells so that it could keep pressure on its Arab associates as well as on Iran. By contrast, Iran welcomed any effort to stop the oil spill which would avoid the "Iraqi trap." While agreeing at the United Nations on 5 April 1983 to cooperate in cleaning up the giant oil spill, the Iranian representative quickly rejected the idea offered by the Iraqis and their friends that Iran's agreement would lead to a general cease-fire in the war. He stated categorically: "This is not the first step in a ceasefire."[10] In keeping with this position, Iran decoupled its agreement to the clean-up operations from the overall problem of reaching a peace settlement.

The process of resolving the oil-spill situation began on 28 March 1983, when the Iranian ambassador to Kuwait, Ali Shams Ardakani, took the initiative and asked Iran's neighbors in the Gulf to help break up the huge oil slick, saying, "We are ready to send our team," and inviting other Gulf countries, except Iraq, to join Iran "to face this immense pollution threat."[11] Subsequently, Iranian officials even met officials from Iraq and the six GCC states to discuss the problems involved. After two meetings among the environmental ministers in April broke up in disarray, the Iranian and Iraqi representatives sparred at a third meeting. Iraq insisted on a link between efforts to stop the oil slick and efforts to end the war, whereas the Iranian representative rejected that idea, saying that the "oil leaking from oil wells and the pollution resulting from it is a technical and not a political issue."[12] All that came out of this meeting was an agreement among the Gulf states to place their well-capping and pollution-control facilities at the disposal of a regional technical committee; this agreement was in accordance with a Gulfwide convention on pollution control that had been signed by all the Gulf states on 24 April 1978.[13]

Revolutionary Iran missed no opportunity to use the Iraqi oil-spill offensive to ingratiate itself with the nonbelligerent Gulf states. It offered its "neighbors" drinking water in the face of the threat of water contamination and damage to Gulf state desalination plants. At the same time, it took the opportunity presented by the spill to show its neighbors an example of Iranian "Islamic self-reliance" by capping the oil wells by itself, without American assistance. Although an observer has said that the Iranian government first asked the well-known American Red Adair team for help in capping the leaking oil wells,[14] Iranian leaders made great political hay out of having capped an oil well without any foreign help.

For example, on 21 September 1983, President Ali Khamene'i claimed that the Iranians had capped a well themselves, disproving the assertions of those who claimed the Iranians could not do so alone. He said that the Iranians had been told "that only the United States could do this job. They were expecting Imam Khomeyni to personally ask the United States to help in this matter. Later the Americans themselves offered to cap the oil well. However, the Ministry of Petroleum, with the help of its faithful and determined workers, took up the work itself. After overcoming many difficulties, it was able to stop the oil spill threatening the region."[15] Ayatollah Khomeini praised Iranian self-reliance and at the same time disparaged the alleged Arab lack of self-reliance. He said: "O God, help us and make us reliant on our national strength, on our Islamic strength so we can promote our national interests. One should feel sorry for the so-called Islamic states that exist around us. They are ready to accept their slavery. [I do not understand this attitude.] But I do understand this much:—If they depend on their Islamic strength, it will do them good."[16]

In addition to propagandist purposes, Iran used the Iraqi oil-spill offensive to further two other ends. First, it seriously sought to advance its technical prowess by relying exclusively on Iranian experts. It capped Nowruz oil well no. 3 in 1983 and Nowruz oil well no. 10 in 1984. In the year before it was capped, no. 10 burned out about 1,000 barrels of oil a day and spewed about 5,000 barrels a day onto Gulf waters. The capping of Nowruz no. 10 ended all oil spills in the Iranian continental shelf, because the other three Iranian oil wells that had been attacked and damaged burned out, all together, about 10,000 barrels of oil a day without spilling. Iranian oil officials considered the successful capping of Nowruz no. 10 as a "technical victory," one that helped prevent pollution of Gulf waters and defended the interests of all the littoral states.[17]

Second, Iran tried to elicit international recognition of its technical efforts and, at the same time, to encourage international disapprobation of Iraqi behavior. An international conference organized by Tehran University called on the secretary-general of the United Nations on 26 May 1984 to study the impact of oil spills in the Gulf, and urged that measures be taken for the short- and long-term prevention of pollution in the region. The conference declaration also said that "the attack on the oil wells and related installations in the Persian Gulf by the Iraqi regime was strongly condemned." Interestingly, Iraq was listed among the eight "nongovernment" representatives at the conference, and the United States was listed among the fourteen "participating countries."[18]

THE TANKER WAR AND THE KHARG TERMINAL

The third component of Iraq's strategy consists of the tanker war that Iraq launched in February 1984 and its air raids on the Kharg oil terminal, which it escalated in 1985. Before April 1984 Iraq had attacked some sixty ships, but after April it started using Super Etendard planes, instead of helicopters, to fire Exocet missiles at oil tankers in a unilaterally designated fifty-mile "war zone" around the vital Iranian oil terminal on Kharg Island. Iraqi missiles hit two Saudi oil tankers, and the Iranians retaliated by striking at a Kuwaiti oil tanker and an oil tanker partially owned by Saudi Arabia. The tanker war, also called the shipping war, thus started in earnest, but not all the ships that were attacked were oil tankers—nor were they all struck by Exocet missiles fired from Super Etendard planes. By 24 June, when the oil tanker *Alexander the Great* was struck, it was believed that sixteen oil tankers had been struck by Iraqi Exocet missiles, but no more than ten had been seriously damaged, and there were few casualties.[19] The attack on *Alexander the Great* brought the tanker war close to the heart of the Iranian economy—the tanker was hit while berthed at Kharg Island.

By the end of May and early June, the tanker war's effects were showing on Iran. Exports from Kharg Island, which had been around 1.5 to 1.6 million barrels per day, dropped to as few as 600 thousand barrels per day, costing Iran about $25 million daily. At one point exports may have stopped altogether; if so, the stoppage lasted for a short while. The overall costs to Iran at this time were tolerable. First of all, Iran continued to export 200 thousand barrels a day from its Sirri and Lavan ports. Also, it quickly recovered much of its Kharg terminal oil trade by enticing back its war-weary customers by offering them a discount of as much as $3.00 a barrel on its Kharg oil, an amount that more than compensated for the $2.33 per barrel increase in cargo insurance.[20] The recovery was apparently well underway by the July meeting of OPEC, when Iran was again demanding to increase its production to 3.2 million barrels of oil a day, up from the 2.4 million barrels it was allowed to export daily under the OPEC quota system.

Although the threat to Kharg terminal oil exports continued—and in fact became increasingly severe because of the massive shipments of Soviet and French arms entering Iraq—as of March 1986, Iraq seemingly had failed to achieve its primary objective. The Iraqi objective in launching the tanker war was to end the war. Iraq had hoped that its attacks on oil tankers would knock Iran out of the war by cutting off its oil revenues. Despite Iran's ten billion dollars in reserves, Iraq believed that Iran would quickly feel the financial crunch because of the high cost of the war and the rapidly deteriorating economic conditions inside Iran. Iraq had also hoped that by escalating the armed conflict, it would be able to goad Iran into closing the Strait of Hormuz, which would lead to Western military intervention and, possibly, an imposed peace. Finally, Iraq had hoped that it could force Iran toward a negotiated settlement with or without the mediation of other powers or international organizations. At the least, Iraq had hoped to maintain pressure on Iran not to launch its much-discussed "final offensive" on the ground. Iraq threatened to halt all Iranian oil exports from the Kharg terminal if Iran went through with its repeated threats to launch a decisive ground assault.

Two years after it was launched in earnest, the tanker war seemed to have failed. Iraq had sought to end the war of attrition quickly by escalating the conflict, but the tanker war itself seemed to have become stalemated. When it was first reported that the French had "loaned" Iraq five Super Etendard fighter-bombers equipped with radar-evading Exocet missiles, there was much talk about the example of their "devastating" effect against British ships in the war in the Falkland Islands. But only months after the Iraqis began using the missiles against oil tankers, the effectiveness of the Exocet missiles was questioned by some observers on various grounds, including the appropriateness of their use against large oil tankers. Apparently the heavy tanker hulls and the thick crude oil they carried slowed the missiles down. Other reasons for the failure of the tanker war included mistakes the Iraqi armorers made in loading the missiles onto the Super Etendard aircraft, the use of only a relatively few Exocets, and the availability of hundreds of spare tanker hulls in the world at the time.[21]

While the effectiveness of the Exocets against oil tankers was being questioned in the summer of 1984, the assessment of the Iraqis' ability to destroy the Kharg terminal was being upgraded. The effectiveness of the Exocets against the Kharg installations had always been in doubt, but in 1984 it was believed that the overall military balance had swung so far in Iraq's favor that Iraq had the capability to inflict severe damage on the vital Iranian oil terminal. "Because of recent French and Soviet arms sales," stated a U.S. Senate Foreign Relations staff report issued on 27 August 1984, "Iraq now had the capability to inflict severe damage on Kharg Island's oil terminal."[22]

The Iraqi escalation of attacks on Kharg Island's oil terminal beginning in August 1985 seemed to bear out this assessment. Two relatively effective hits on 15 and 25 August contrasted significantly with many ineffective previous air raids. The Iraqi government claimed that its fighter bombers had "demolished" Iran's oil shipping terminal on Kharg Island on 15 August and that the bombers' "crushing" blows to the island had "changed it into ashes."[23] By 19 September, when Iraq launched its tenth attack on the island, it was widely believed that all but two of the island's fourteen loading berths had been damaged.[24] By this time it was also believed that the attacks had cut Iran's oil exports by 25 percent. Considering that Kharg is the main outlet for Iran's oil exports, and therefore the source of 95 percent of its foreign exchange and 80 percent of its government revenue, it appeared that Iraq would finally be able to achieve its principal objective of knocking out Iran's oil exports, and thereby force Iran to negotiate peace.

By the end of 1985, however, after four and a half months of persistent attacks, it was evident that Iraq was no closer to its long-sought objective than it had been previously. Only a handful of a total of approximately fifty Iraqi air raids had by then been effective, for overall Iraq had continued its pattern of cautious, high-level—and, hence, ineffective—bombing. Although at one point the raids virtually shut down Iran's oil exports, as they had during the height of the tanker war in

1984, they proved ineffective in the long run. Before the Kharg attacks escalated in August, Iran was selling 1.9 million barrels of oil per day, and by the end of 1985 it was selling about 1.5 million barrels per day. The terminal had been damaged, but, overall, the effect of the air strikes on oil exports was limited, partly because Iran made nighttime repairs, installed temporary buoys, and used other makeshift arrangements.[25]

More than makeshift arrangements were needed, however, if Iran's overwhelming dependence on Kharg was to be reduced or eliminated. This was a lesson of Iraq's momentary success that was not lost on Iran, for it, too, entered what may be called the pipeline war. Iraqi oil exports, which had dropped to a low of 700 thousand barrels per day from 3.5 million after the war started in September 1980, seemed destined, at the end of 1985, to reattain the prewar level in two years. By the end of 1985, Iraq's oil-exporting capability had already reached 1.5 million barrels per day because it had increased the capacity of the Turkish pipeline from 700 thousand to 1 million barrels per day, and also because it was using the new pipeline (with a capacity of 500 thousand barrels per day) across Saudi Arabia to the port of Yanbu. To avoid further disruption of its oil exports from the Kharg Island terminal, in November 1985 Iran invited eleven Asian and European companies to bid on a twin pipeline from Gurreh, the underground pumping station from Kharg Island, to Asaluyeh. The completion of this plan in a year or so would enable Iran to transport its oil farther south in the Persian Gulf, out of range of Iraqi planes.[26]

In the meantime, Iran demonstrated as much restraint in its retaliations against the attacks on Kharg as it had against the strikes on oil tankers. While Iran's leaders repeated their familiar threat to close the Strait of Hormuz, they confined themselves to carrying out a measured two-track strategy. First, they threatened to bomb oil installations well inside Iraqi territory, and President Ali Khamene'i claimed, on 6 September 1985, that Iranian jet fighters had in fact struck installations at Ayn Zalah, one of the major oil fields in northern Iraq.[27] This claim was not confirmed, but there was little doubt about the other aspect of the Iranian strategy. On this same day, Iran began to stop, search, and, sometimes, seize vessels suspected of carrying arms and other supplies destined for Iraq. Beginning on 20 June a Kuwaiti ship had been detained by Iran for several days, but this was an isolated incident. The search of the Italian container ship *Merzario Britannia* on 6 September 1985, however, was part of Iran's broader retaliatory strategy against the Iraqi escalation of attacks on Kharg. Iranian troops boarded the ship thirty miles off the Saudi Arabian coast and searched it for five hours in what shipping industry sources saw as an "ominous new phase" of the war. Yet, although by the end of 1985 more than 150 ships had been searched, Iran, according to Western and Japanese sources, had been "pretty correct" up until then about "observing the rules of war."[28]

Iran's restraint in retaliating against the Iraqi attacks on Kharg should not simplistically be attributed to the effectiveness of Western naval deterrence. For example, the ability of the French container ship *Ville d'Anvers* to defy the Iranian navy's order to stop in November 1985 may be attributed to the French naval presence in the area.[29] Yet, such an assessment would ignore the fact that the purpose of the Iranian strategy was more to intercept arms and other war-related supplies headed for Iraq than to restrain traffic in the area.

Even more important, it would overlook the importance of political factors in the behavior of both combatants in regard to the tanker war and the Kharg terminal attacks. The tanker war did not fail simply because of technical and military limitations. Nor could Iraq's failure throughout the war to knock out the Kharg installations be attributed simply to a lack of military capability or to Iran's ability to defend Kharg Island. All sorts of political considerations also contributed to the military stalemate.

First, Iran was determined not to be pushed into a hasty attempt to close the Strait of Hormuz. It told all users of the strait that it would do so only as a matter of last resort. Closing the Strait of Hormuz could lead to consequences that Iran wished to avoid as long as possible. It could provoke American military intervention in the strait and possibly even American air strikes against Iranian airfields. Having all along believed that the United States was determined to destroy the Islamic revolution, the revolutionary regime wished to deny the Americans the opportunity to do so.

Second, regardless of Iran's paranoia, the United States was also determined not to be goaded into military intervention by Iraq's military escalation. Washington officials repeatedly stated their determination to maintain freedom of navigation through the Gulf, but the United States had no intention of plunging into direct military intervention, unless no other option was available. The recent searing experience in Lebanon, on the one hand, and the presidential elections, on the other, also made the American reaction to the tanker war a restrained one. Washington supplied Stinger missiles and other military equipment and personnel to Saudi Arabia over the 1984 Memorial Day weekend only because they were urgently needed; no U.S. military intervention had been planned at the time. In short, the restraint of the United States also made the tanker war less effective.

Third, Saudi Arabia was no less anxious than Iran and the United

States to limit the spread of the war. Saudi Arabia sought the mediatory help of the Syrians in telling Tehran that if Iran ceased attacking oil tankers, Saudi Arabia would ask Iraq to do the same. Iraq in effect aborted the Saudi offer by continuing its attacks on tankers. Riyadh also shunned all of Iraq's propagandist efforts to portray the war as an "Arab-Iranian war" after the 5 June air fight between Saudi and Iranian bombers.

The failure of the tanker war also had implications for the supply and the price of oil worldwide. The tanker war, like the Iraq-Iran war generally, failed to cause a "third oil shock." Despite the disruption of oil supplies from the Gulf beginning in September 1980 when the war broke out, and despite the escalation of the war in the spring of 1984 through the attacks on oil tankers, oil prices did not by any means increase the way they had during the Arab-Israeli war in 1973 and after the eruption of the Iranian Revolution in 1979. Although at the start of the Iraq-Iran war prices went up to $5 a barrel in three weeks, that level was not maintained, and OPEC had to cut the price per barrel from $34 to $29 and even lower as the war continued. The impact of the tanker war on oil prices was simply inconsequential. Even on the spot market, the price of Saudi light crude rose only 20¢ a barrel after three weeks of attacks on oil tankers.

Oil experts attributed the absence of a third oil shock to world oil market conditions. Oil markets, they believed, could handle supply shortages of more than 1 million barrels a day, and perhaps as much as 4 million barrels.[30] The problem with this kind of analysis was that it failed to take note of the political and military factors just analyzed. These factors severely limited Iraq's and Iran's ability to disrupt the flow of Gulf oil supplies. It would therefore make more sense to suggest that, in addition to favorable world oil market conditions, a complex of political and military factors helped prevent the advent of a third oil shock as a consequence of the Iraq-Iran war, at least through 1985.

NO FOURTH OIL SHOCK: THE LEBANON WAR

The Israeli invasion of Lebanon, like the Iraq-Iran war, did not result in an oil shock. In this case, too, the primary reason seemed to be soft market conditions. In other words, the Arab states failed to use their "oil weapon" in the Lebanon war in 1982 because they knew it would have no effect on the targeted states in the oil glut conditions of the time, whereas they used it in the Arab-Israeli war because the international oil market was tight in 1973, and, hence, their oil embargo against the United States would be effective.

It is reasonable to assume that market conditions had a part in the decision of the Arab states to resort to an oil embargo in 1973 and in their decision not to in 1982. Nevertheless, a comparison of the dominant political and strategic factors in the two wars leads to a more comprehensive and satisfying explanation for Arab behavior in these two armed conflicts with Israel. Such a comparison requires weighing not only the conditions of the world oil market during the two wars, but also the political and military conditions and interests that were of the greatest concern to the most important actors in both cases.

World Oil Market

In the 1973 war, the world market was a seller's market. President Nixon had warned that America's oil supplies were running out, and President Carter later called on the United States to regard the oil situation as the "moral equivalent of war." Reality matched the rhetoric. Prior to 1973, the United States had imported negligible amounts of Arab oil, but by the time the Arabs raised their prices, cut back their production, and, finally, imposed an oil embargo, Americans were importing about 2.5 million barrels of oil daily. By then, also, America's capacity to produce surplus oil had disappeared, because production had gone to 100 percent of capacity in order to supply demand. Beyond America, the specter of an ever-tightening oil market haunted the advanced industrialized nations, which consumed about 38 million barrels per day in 1973 and were expected to consume as many as 71 million barrels per day by 1982. This estimate subsequently proved to be high, but it had a profound effect on consumer behavior.

In the 1982 war, the oil market was, in contrast, a buyer's market. The oil shock was working in reverse by 1982; that is, 1973 had seen the consumers' first shock, whereas 1982 saw the producers'. The consumers' second shock, caused by the Iranian Revolution in 1979, had been more a function of panic buying by consumers and hoarding by speculators than of a tight market situation. Market theorists considered the oil glut in 1982 to be the only reason for the Arabs' reluctance to try to impose an oil embargo. One leading analyst, for example, said that an embargo "might undercut the efforts by moderate producers to stabilize the markets for oil and might hasten the flight from OPEC oil produced by Arabs."[31] But there were equally, if not more, powerful factors for the Arab states' decision to forgo an oil embargo during the Lebanon war, and these factors were not economically derived.

Egypt

Egypt, the leading Arab military power, and Saudi Arabia, the premier Arab oil producer, agreed before the Arab-Israeli war of 1973 to use oil as a "political weapon." In Henry Kissinger's words, Anwar al-Sadat was "the godfather of the oil embargo." Sadat launched the war, in his own words, "to challenge the Israeli security theory."[32] Sadat's purpose in the war, according to Kissinger, "was psychological and diplomatic, much more than military." Sadat believed that the shock of war would enable Israel to show a flexibility that was "impossible while Israel considered itself militarily supreme and Egypt was paralyzed by humiliation."[33] King Faysal agreed with Sadat, in principle, on the necessity of wielding the "oil weapon," but there is no evidence that before the war either leader envisaged the imposition of an "oil embargo" against the United States.

In the Lebanon war of 1982, Saudi Arabia and Egypt could not possibly have been interested in using the oil weapon in any way. Nor could they have cooperated to that end, as they had in 1973. Egypt was at peace with Israel; Egypt was a close friend of the United States, not a "semiadversary" as it had been in 1973; and Egypt was estranged from Saudi Arabia because of the peace treaty between Egypt and Israel. Saudi Arabia, on the other hand, was America's best friend in the Gulf now that the Shah's regime had fallen; Saudi Arabia felt threatened by revolutionary Iran; and Saudi Arabia feared the spread of the Iraq-Iran war more than ever, because Iran had just turned the tide of war against Iraq.

Syria

During the Arab-Israeli war of 1973, Syria was a beneficiary of the Arab oil embargo, because the Sadat-Faysal political alliance intertwined with the Assad-Sadat military axis. Sadat told Assad: "I have decided to fight my battle this year [1973] and have issued the relevant instructions to Marshal 'Ali. What do you say to this?" "I will be with you," said Assad. "We are going to fight and are preparing for it."[34] Syria could not fight Israel alone; Syria did not have the requisite military power. But Egypt's crossing of the Suez might help Syria at the Golan Heights, because Israel would have to fight on both fronts. Faysal would use the oil weapon in support of Egypt's war effort, whereas he would not resort to it for Syria alone.

In the Lebanon war of 1982, Saudi Arabia had even less interest in using the oil weapon for the sake of Syria. Syria was not truly at war with Israel. To be sure, the Syrian-Israeli air fight in the skies of Lebanon was "one of the biggest air battles in the more than three decades of Middle East hostilities," but it was a short-lived military engagement.[35] Syria fought it only to protect its interest in the strategic Bekaa Valley; the battle had nothing to do with the recovery of the Golan Heights. Nor had Saudi Arabia any interest in using the oil weapon in support of the PLO forces, which were truly at war with Israel. In order to help extricate the Palestinian forces trapped in Beirut by Israel, Saudi Arabia needed all the diplomatic help it could get from the United States. This was no time to use an oil embargo against Washington.

Saudi Arabia

In the Arab-Israeli war of 1973, Saudi Arabia would not have used an oil embargo against the United States had King Faysal not been put squarely on the spot. He had agreed with Sadat, in principle only, to use the oil weapon. The two had made no prior agreement to impose an oil embargo. In his war order of 1 October, therefore, Sadat talked only in general terms about the use of "Arab pressure exerted in propitious circumstances."[36] King Faysal had warned long before the war began that Saudi Arabia would "cut back its oil production unless the United States changed its pro-Israeli policies."[37]

During the first week of the war, when everyone, including Golda Meir and Henry Kissinger, was surprised by the successful Egyptian crossing of the Suez Canal, the Arabs had no thoughts of using the oil weapon.[38] The Egyptians were winning on the battlefield. But once the Israelis obtained the upper hand, the idea of using the oil weapon became increasingly attractive to the Arab states. The perfect excuse was furnished on 13 October by the massive arms supply to Israel which the United States presumably made in response to the Soviet arms airlift to Syria, but which Israel, in fact, had requested before the Soviet move. Led by Saudi Arabia, the OAPEC decided, on 17 October, to cut back oil production. This decision did not amount to an oil embargo against the United States, although the American press is confused on this point to this day.

The Saudi-led decision to impose an oil embargo on the United States was made on 20 October, the day after President Nixon requested that Congress provide $2.2 billion in arms assistance to Israel. Contrary to Henry Kissinger's claim that he "can find no record that anyone warned of an Arab reaction," on 12 October the executives of the chief ARAMCO shareholders warned the president that further U.S. action in support of Israel would result in a major interruption of oil supplies; their memorandum said, in part: "The Saudis will impose some cut-back in crude oil production as a result of the United States position taken thus far. A further and much more substantial move will be taken by Saudi Arabia and Kuwait in the event of further evidence of increased U.S. support of the Israeli position."[39] It is clear that, during the Arab-Israeli war of 1973, the Saudis had not been easily moved to impose an oil embargo on the United States.

By the time of the Lebanon war, not only were Saudi-American security ties too close for Riyadh to contemplate imposing an oil embargo
against America, but there was no arms aid to Israel to provoke Saudi
action. The Soviet Union seemed to be in no hurry to supply arms to
Syria in any way comparable to the way they had during the 1973 war,
and the United States neither received a request for arms from, nor gave
any arms to, Israel. In fact, relations between Washington and Tel Aviv
had seldom been as strained as they were during the Lebanon war. The
entire American diplomatic effort was directed against the excessive
use of military force by Israel, as evidenced by President Reagan's
decision to halt a new shipment of cluster-type artillery shells to Israel
(19 July) and his warnings to Israel (2 and 4 August) against "escalating
violence." The implication was that the United States might have to
resort to an arms embargo against Israel if Israel continued its "dispro-
portionate" assault on West Beirut.

Hence, in addition to world oil market conditions, powerful political
and strategic factors also explain why the Arab governments decided
against an oil embargo in the Lebanon war. There was no new oil shock
because, in the words of the Arabs themselves, in the overall political
and strategic circumstances, as well as the world oil situation, in 1982,
their "oil weapon" (*salah al-bitrol*) had been transformed into a "wooden
sword" (*al-saif al-khashabi*).

INCOMPETENCE, RESTRAINT, OR BOTH?

The foregoing analysis of the interrelationship of oil and war adds up
to two major propositions. First, although the market factor is very
important, it cannot fully explain the absence of oil price shocks during
the Iraq-Iran war and the Lebanon war. To be sure, the oversupply of oil
in the world cushioned customers during disruptions such as the cutoff
of Iraqi oil exports, but this was possible because the amount of disruption was limited by nonmarket factors. Had the war spread to Saudi
Arabia and crippled oil exports from Ras Tanura, or had Iraq been able
to knock out Iranian oil exports for four to six months, and had Iran, in
retaliation, been able to close the Strait of Hormuz to international oil
traffic for the same length of time, the situation, of course, would have
been wholly different.

But unbearable shortages did not occur, because powerful political
and strategic factors limited the disruption of oil supplies enough to
allow the existing oversupply of oil to make up the difference. In the war
in the Gulf, Saudi Arabia, the United States, and the combatants played
major roles in limiting the disruption. By every impartial observer's
admission, Iran "underresponded" in retaliating against Iraq in the

tanker war. Moreover, it made its threat of closing the Strait of Hormuz almost hypothetical by saying that, even if more than half of its oil exports were crippled, it would still probably not close the strait. Whether self-interest, incompetence, American deterrence, or all three influenced the Iranian stance, the fact remains that Iran exercised a significant degree of restraint in practice, despite its strident rhetoric.

Whatever accounts for Iraq's failure to destroy Iranian oil exports, the fact remains that this was another nonmarket factor that limited the disruption of oil supplies. Whether the Iraqis were too incompetent to knock out Kharg Island or were pressured by the Saudis and their other Arab friends to refrain from doing so or were incompetent as loaders of missiles on the Super Etendard aircraft—or whether Exocet missiles were simply ineffective in hitting oil tankers—it was these technical, military, and political factors that limited the disruption of the Gulf oil supplies.

The Saudis also contributed significantly to the curtailment of the disruption of oil supplies. They made every effort to dissuade the Iraqis from disrupting Iranian oil supplies beyond acceptable limits. When their own and Kuwait's oil tankers were targeted by Iran, they sought Syrian mediation in persuading the Iranians to deescalate. They also downplayed the air fight with Iran and, subsequently, made an unprecedented gesture of friendship through Foreign Minister Saud's visit to Iran. The policy of containment by political conciliation and military deterrence pursued by the Saudis and their GCC partners, individually and together, throughout the Iraq-Iran war significantly helped confine the disruption of oil supplies to Iraqi oil exports.

Finally, the United States also helped curb the disruption of oil supplies. The American commitment to defend the uninterrupted flow of Gulf oil under the Carter Doctrine, and the creation of the United States Central Command (USCENTCOM), helped to keep the disruption of oil supplies from expanding beyond the northern sector of the Persian Gulf region. No doubt the Reagan administration's fourteen-billion-dollar annual expenditure on the command, the emergency military aid the United States gave to Saudi Arabia, and the usual military support by the United States of all Gulf monarchies, including Oman (where the United States had access to Omani facilities), were equally helpful.

Nonmarket factors also played an important role in the Lebanon war. The military and political situation militated against any consideration of an oil embargo against the United States. Egypt, the leading Arab military power, was at peace with Israel during the Lebanon war. Sadat, in alliance with Saudi Arabia, had been "the godfather" of the Arab oil embargo in the October war, whereas Mubarak was anxiously awaiting entry into the Arab fold in 1982. In fact, the Lebanon war was not an "Arab-Israeli" war, despite brief, though devastating, Syrian air battles with Israel; it was an Israeli-Palestinian war. Yasser Arafat complained that he kept expecting his Arab and other friends to help, but no one did. Unlike during the October war, the Soviet Union did not rush to supply arms to the Arabs, nor the United States to the Israelis, during the war in Lebanon.

The second proposition is related to the first one. For the first time in the history of the Middle East, the conventional notion of an "oil weapon" became inadequate. In the Arab-Israeli wars of the past, an oil embargo had been used by the Arab states as a means of pressuring the United States to reduce its support of Israel. Because of the vastly different political and strategic circumstances that existed during the Lebanon war, that weapon had been turned into a "wooden sword." In the Iraq-Iran war, however, oil has been elevated from a "weapon" into an "instrument of war." The combatants have used this instrument in three major ways in their war strategy. They have made efforts to destroy each other's oil-production capacity by attacking oil facilities on land, offshore oil wells, and oil tankers.

Yet this apparent all-out offensive on strategic oil targets has, in effect, been limited by the mutual vulnerability of the combatants. The extent to which their incompetence or their self-restraint has kept them from striking at each other's most vital oil-producing facilities cannot be known. But a degree of restraint on the part of the combatants has been evident throughout the war. For example, it was reported early in the war that the Iranians bombed Iraqi oil-storage tanks for the psychological effect of the fire and smoke rather than to destroy the catalytic converters that are vital for oil production. Incompetence and restraint are not necessarily incompatible. In the Iraq-Iran war, they often go hand in hand.

Part Five

THE UNITED STATES AND
THE MIDDLE EAST

15

The Changing Situation in the Middle East: Guidelines for U.S. Policy

Clearly, the Iranian Revolution has had a major influence on the situation in the Middle East over the past half-dozen years. Although the Iraq-Iran war is the most obvious outcome of the revolution in the area, it is not necessarily the best understood. Iran's influence on Saudi Arabia's unprecedented military buildup and unusually active diplomacy, and on the founding and policies of the GCC, has been considerable. The destruction of the Tehran–Tel Aviv and Tehran-Cairo alignments and the formation of the Tehran-Damascus axis were the direct results of Iranian policies. The Lebanon war, the Arab-Israeli conflict, and the Palestinian problem have all been touched by the Iranian Revolution. Oil supplies have never fueled the conduct of war and the eruption of revolution more than in these instances; nor has the flow of oil ever been more disrupted by war and revolution. For the Arabs at war with Israel, oil was a weapon of political pressure against the United States, and now, for Iran and Iraq, oil is an instrument of war.

Furthermore, the effects of the Iranian Revolution have exposed and intensified many of the preexisting domestic problems. The ancient economic, social, and political grievances of the people—especially the Shias—against their rulers have come to the surface as never before, and the old sectarian, cultural, and ideological feuds between the Shias and Sunnis, the Iranians and Arabs, the Muslims and Christians, and religious and secular groups and individuals have sharpened. Although the phenomenon of Islamic revivalism is nothing new, the force of Islamic fundamentalism has never been as widespread in the Middle East as it is today. Although the symbols of Islam are as old as Islamic history, seldom have they been so effectively used by rulers to govern people, or employed by political dissidents against governments. Yet, it would be a mistake to view the Middle Eastern situation solely in terms of the resurgence of Islamic ideology. First, nationalism—Arab and Iranian—continues to coexist and compete with Islam as a focus of identity. Second, the Islamic ideology has no more provided solutions to the endemic problems of the area than any other ideology has. In short, despite the effects of the Iranian Revolution within Iran and other countries in the region, the basic structural problems of Middle Eastern societies continue.

This mixture of change and continuity adds to the complexities of the Middle Eastern situation and has far-reaching implications for U.S. policy in the area. I do not believe that these implications have so far been adequately understood. In fact, I contend that largely because they have been poorly understood, the United States has been unable to avoid disastrous policies, as in Lebanon, or wrong-headed ones, as in Iran. We are also making erroneous assumptions about the security of Gulf oil supplies which may well come to haunt us in the near future. Above all, because of our poor understanding, we have been inclined to impose a mythological dichotomy on the countries in the Middle East of "the good guys" and "the bad guys"—a dichotomy that is empirically indefensible.

On the basis of what I have presented thus far in this book, I would like to suggest that there are implications in the changing situation in the Middle East which we would do well to acknowledge if we are to develop a comprehensive, coherent, and effective U.S. policy in the region. Obviously, these suggestions are not intended to constitute policy blueprints. I hope they will serve as useful guidelines.

Tempering the Containment of Iran

To retain the option of reestablishing relations with the revolutionary regime in Iran, the United States will have to temper its stern containment policy. There is a real danger that it will fail to do so, effectively ruling out the option of a future reconciliation with Iran, because of the widespread sense that the United States has been victimized at the hands of the Khomeini regime. Considering the virulent anti-American crusade Tehran has been waging since the Iranian hostage crisis, American resentment and frustration are perfectly understandable. Americans, nevertheless, should remind themselves of the dictum they like to preach to the Iranians: passion is not policy.

An examination of Iran's Middle Eastern policies since the revolution should encourage the United States to temper its containment policy toward Iran. This book has revealed that with respect to every major issue, including the war with Iraq, Iranian policy has consistently contained elements of self-restraint, pragmatism, and even, occasionally, helpfulness. The revolutionary regime's bark has been worse than its bite, its rhetoric more strident than its actions, its declared policies more belligerent than its intentions. President Ali Khamene'i has characterized this emerging realism as Iran's "open-door policy" (*siyasat-e dar-ha-ye baz*). Its premise is the growing conviction that the very survival of the revolution is at stake. In Khomeini's words, Iran will face "defeat and annihilation" (*shekast va fana*) if it fails to establish relations with other governments. Although he has excluded Israel, South Africa, and the United States from this requirement, he has left the door slightly ajar for the United States: relations with America could be resumed if it "behaves itself" (*agar adam beshavad*). Speaker Hashemi-Rafsanjani has reportedly said: "We have no intention to keep our diplomatic relations severed forever but it will be difficult to restore relations under the present [Reagan] administration." He did not say it will be impossible.

This increasingly pragmatic orientation has been reflected in the newly initiated dialogue between Riyadh and Tehran, in Iran's intensified interaction with the United Arab Emirates, and in the improved political climate between all the GCC member states and Iran. Because Iran is strategically the most important Gulf state, its improved relations with its Gulf neighbors is bound to redound to the benefit of our Arab friends. The revolution has not changed the fact that Iran is still the strongest buffer against Soviet and communist expansionism in the Arabian Peninsula; in fact, the revolution has made the Iranian buffer all the more resistant, ideologically, to communism. This emerging sense of the need for coexistence between revolutionary Iran and its conservative Gulf neighbors takes on added significance in the wider context of Southwest Asia, where Iran, Turkey, and Pakistan are developing close economic relations, both bilaterally and collectively, through the newly created Economic Cooperation Organization (ECO), and where Iran and Pakistan are the states that are most likely to offer resistance to Soviet-occupied Afghanistan.

Beyond the Middle East, too, the results of the emerging pragmatic trend in Iranian foreign policy benefit our friends and allies. Iran buys 70 percent of its imports from Canada, Japan, and western Europe, and sells about half of its exports to the same areas. Iran regards Japan as the power in East Asia capable of filling the "technical and industrial vacuum" left by the United States, according to Speaker Hashemi-Rafsanjani, and at the same time, Iran seeks to expand relations with China, not only for economic, technical, and commercial reasons, but for political reasons, as well. China is viewed, in effect, as a great third-power counterweight to both superpowers.

In spite of all this, the Iraq-Iran war and the alleged Iranian involvement in terrorism would appear to prevent the United States from tempering its stiff containment policy toward Iran. Yet, there are grounds for optimism regarding these issues, as well. I shall deal with the war in detail later; the question of terrorism can be examined here. The accusations against Iran have overwhelmingly been based on circumstantial evidence. Furthermore, there are definite signs that Iran is trying to distance itself from terrorist groups because they are uncontrollable and, even more important, because supporting them would hinder its determined efforts to expand relations with other nations in pursuit of its new open-door policy.

These are the main indicators of the shift in the Iranian attitude toward terrorism. The day after the hijacking of the TWA plane, Iran closed its airports to the hijacked plane; its leaders condemned the act; and, more critically, Speaker Hashemi-Rafsanjani actually aided the process of freeing the American hostages. No less important, Iran put on trial the two South Yemeni hijackers who on 5 November 1984 seized a Saudi Arabian jetliner en route from Jeddah to Europe. On 29 December 1985 the Tehran Penal Court, although it acquitted one of them, sentenced the other hijacker to twelve years in prison. They were tried in compliance with not only relevant Iranian laws, but also the Hague and Montreal Accords. The trial was said to have been "the first of its kind in Iran's judicial history." These constructive acts against terrorism promise to help remove the blemish of terrorism from Iran's reputation, but Iran can further improve its image by trying, for both the crime of hijacking and the cold-blooded murder of two innocent American passengers, the hijackers of a Kuwaiti airliner who have been in its custody since December 1984.

Adopting an Active Peace Strategy in the Gulf

No matter how justified the U.S. "tilt" toward Iraq, the U.S. Middle Eastern formula has become rancid. Although Iran still insists on the punishment of Iraq's Ba'thist regime, we should now be pursuing an active peace policy, because there are indications that peace is attainable. Both combatants trust the United Nations secretary-general; Speaker Hashemi-Rafsanjani has mentioned the use of an "international court"; Khomeini has ordered the government to conduct a "defensive holy war"; and, as mentioned, the trend of Iranian foreign policy is toward a pragmatic orientation, for, as President Khamene'i said, such a stance will serve both Iran's "needs" (*niaz-ha*) and its "message" (*payam*)—that is, both its national interest and its Islamic ideology.

Our peace strategy must be both comprehensive and substantive. In addition to encouraging all other third-party mediation efforts, the United States should actively support the unprecedented efforts of Saudi Arabia and the active mediatory role of the U.N. secretary-general. Encouraging mediation by others, which we have done sporadically, is not enough, however. The belligerents should not simply return to the status quo. Whether the parties would agree to renegotiate the 1975 Algiers agreement or to conclude a new one, they must be encouraged to establish a third-party peacekeeping force on their most sensitive border areas. In spite of its elaborate security provisions, the present agreement fails to provide for such a permanent on-site security mechanism.

Anticipating an Iranian Victory

Washington should not rule out the possibility of an unconditional Iranian victory. Iraq's staying power is not absolute. Iran is convinced that it will eventually win the war, not simply because of its "faith power," but also because the overall geostrategic balance in the Gulf is in its favor, despite its greatly diminished air power. It is also determined to deprive Iraq of the principal targets of its superior air power by moving Iranian oil terminals farther south in the Gulf, beyond the reach of Iraq. By using its present footholds in the Majnoon Islands and in the Fao Peninsula, it will continue to nibble away at Iraqi staying power until it achieves its "final victory," the fall of the regime of Saddam Hussein.

Given the possibility of an Iranian victory, the United States would be in a better position to influence the subsequent course of events if it was not exclusively identified with Iraq, as it is now. This is an added reason for tempering the present stern containment policy toward Iran. It would leave considerably more room for America to maneuver in postwar Gulf affairs without appearing to be jumping on the bandwagon only after what may be an unconditional Iranian victory. Our overidentification with the Shah's regime effectively destroyed our access to Khomeini before he triumphantly returned to Tehran, as well as our chances of reconciliation with the powerful anti-Shah forces.

The United States might do well to borrow a page from French diplomacy. Iran broke off all commercial and financial ties with France in 1983 in retaliation for the delivery of five French Super-Etendard aircraft to the Baghdad government. But by early 1986, France was seeking to repair its badly damaged relations with Iran. Some pundits believe that the French thought that such a move was then timely because neither side could win the war. But I believe the French government made the strategic judgment that Iraq's ability to stay in the war was eroding, and acted accordingly.

Complementing Military Deterrence with More Diplomacy

Undoubtedly, the Soviet invasion of Afghanistan prompted the initial U.S. commitment to defend, if necessary by military means, the uninterrupted flow of Persian Gulf oil supplies against any outside force. But it was the Iranian Revolution that gave rise to the early ideas and courses of action that finally led to the Carter Doctrine and the formation of a multiservice force, which has had a unified regional command as the United States Central Command since 1 January 1983 and on which the Reagan administration has spent billions of dollars each year. This deterrent force, in effect, supplements the unprecedented Saudi buildup of a credible military deterrence and GCC efforts to create an integrated air defense system. In practice, the force seems to be directed more at containing revolutionism and the spread of war than at Soviet expansionism, just as America's "over-the-horizon" presence in the Indian Ocean has been strengthened to cope with such threats at the Strait of Hormuz.

No matter how justifiable our military efforts are, they have, over time, left the distinct impression that military muscle is the centerpiece of U.S. Gulf policy. This impression may indeed have acted as a deterrent to Iranian adventurism, although it is impossible to say to what degree. It may have discouraged Iran from trying to close the Strait of Hormuz (a move that Iranian leaders have considered most unlikely), although Iran's self-interest or incompetence may have boosted the effect of the U.S. military deterrence.

No matter how useful a strategy military deterrence may be, the United States must recognize the political and psychological side-effects of such a deterrence. The perception of American military domination of the Gulf region, unilaterally or in collusion with friendly regional rulers, can only intensify the already widespread anti-American sentiments in the area. It can only enhance Iranian anti-Western appeal and embolden both Sunni and Shia extremist dissidents—in short, fuel a sociopolitical explosion in the region even more disastrous than any of the incidents experienced since 1979. Regardless of how the peoples of the region feel about the Khomeini government, the fact is that the Iranian Revolution has awakened an unprecedented consciousness of an inchoate and yet powerful sense of selfhood. It has also increased a general sense of skepticism about the sincerity of incumbent regimes regarding ever-promised and always postponed political reforms.

Although the United States can encourage such reforms, it is in no position to dictate them. What it can do is prominently complement its military deterrence with diplomatic efforts. With respect to Iran and the Gulf, two fundamental principles deserve active American support. They are especially timely now, because of the improved attitude of the Khomeini regime toward the GCC states and the landmark dialogue between Riyadh and Tehran that was inaugurated during Prince Saud's visit to Iran. The first principle is nonintervention. For our part, we must declare unequivocally that the United States is not interested in destroying the Islamic revolution. Although the Iranian leaders might appear paranoid to us, they continue to believe that every American military effort is aimed at that objective. We must also insist that the principle of nonintervention be observed by Iran in its relations with all regional states, and that would include any peace settlement with Iraq. Ayatollah Khomeini has said time and again that export of revolution by "the sword" is no export at all, and Hojatolislam Hashemi-Rafsanjani has invoked the Qur'anic precept "No compulsion in religion" to assure the regional states of Iran's good intentions. What is more critical is that Iran's behavior has shown that the regime has begun to distance itself from suspected terrorist groups because it realizes that the perception of Iran as a renegade nation blocks its determined efforts to expand friendly relations with other nations.

Second, we must clean up our muddied position on the all-important principle of freedom of navigation throughout the Gulf region. Until 1 June 1984, when we endorsed the United Nations Security Council Resolution 552, our position on that principle was crystal clear. Regardless of legal technicalities, this resolution was one-sided in that it failed to criticize both combatants; by implication, it criticized only Iran. We ought to rectify this lack of evenhandedness by encouraging the council to reaffirm its more balanced resolution 540 of 31 October 1983 on the principle of freedom of navigation throughout the Gulf. Resolution 552 intensified Iranian grievances not only against the United States but also against the council, which Iran has never forgiven for its failure to condemn the Iraqi invasion. By sponsoring a new resolution on the war itself, the United States could kill two birds with one stone. It could regain Iran's trust in order to retain more assuredly the option of improving relations with Iran in the future, and it could increase Iran's confidence in the U.N. Security Council in the hope of strengthening the council's peacemaking role in the Iraq-Iran war. Such a resolution would deplore both Iraq's escalation of armed hostilities on 22 September

1980, when the war started, and Iran's extension of the war into Iraqi territory for the first time on 13 July 1982. Although the council's 24 February 1986 resolution deplored, for the first time, inter alia, the "initial" aggression that started the war in 1980, it failed to mention Iraq by name.

Encouraging a Confederation of the GCC

The formation of the GCC may turn out to be one of the most significant long-term developments in the Gulf region in recent years. It is not, as some of its misguided supporters maintain, an anti-Israeli group, nor is it, as its detractors charge, an "arm of NATO," a "tool of the United States," a "stalking horse of Saudi Arabia," or a "latter-day CENTO." Contrary to conventional wisdom, it was not originally created simply as a reaction to the Iraq-Iran war, although, subsequent to its formation and especially after the coup attempt in Bahrain, security concerns emerged prominently. Rather, the GCC was initially created partly to protect the conservative monarchies against the tremors of the Iranian Revolution in their own societies. It is not an alliance against Iran. The fact that the creation of the GCC was also influenced by the Soviet invasion of Afghanistan has encouraged some circles in the Pentagon to try to attain all kinds of military "hookups" with the group. In spite of years of concern over the security of its members, the group has effectively resisted associating too closely with the United States, particularly in terms of the grant of base rights, and the pre-GCC Omani-U.S. facilities agreement has remained an anomaly.

We should obviously extend military aid such as transferring naval craft to the GCC or to its individual members (such as the sale of five AWACS and E-3A planes to Saudi Arabia) when requested, but we should emphasize our nonmilitary assistance. If indeed the overarching long-term goal of the GCC is "confederation," as Secretary-General Abdallah Bisharah says it is, that goal would deserve U.S. support. But, in the short run, we should aid the GCC strategy aimed at economic integration, political coordination, and social, cultural, and educational "approximation." More critically, the United States must insist that the GCC leaders broaden and deepen the basis of social support for the organization. Otherwise, the GCC will be viewed as nothing but a collective tool in the hands of the rulers of the six states for the preservation of the status quo.

We must also encourage the GCC-Iran dialogue. As seen, Iranian leaders (although not lower officials and those in charge of the propagandist machinery) have been cautious in their pronouncements on the GCC. The conciliatory tone was set by Speaker Hashemi-Rafsanjani, who made the Iranian attitude toward the organization contingent on whether it served the interests of its members or of outside powers. In spite of the fact that the revolutionary regime is unhappy about Oman's facilities agreement and joint military exercises with the United States, and about Kuwaiti and Saudi logistical and financial aid to the Iraqi war effort, it has not used these grudges as a basis for an attack on the GCC as a whole. On the contrary, Iran has received GCC mediation missions and has welcomed offers of postwar help in rehabilitating Iranian "institutions" destroyed by the war. After the exchange of visits by Prince Saud and Foreign Minister Velayati, hope for even greater dialogue between the GCC and Iran soared. The brisk Iran-Dubai reexport trade and close Iran-Sharjah economic ties will in this improved atmosphere aid, deepen, and strengthen the dialogue between the GCC and Iran, despite the setback after the Iranian capture of Fao.

The United States should anticipate and prepare for a surge of interest in regional cooperation in the Gulf region after the war. The GCC states conveniently bypassed the question of membership for the Arab country of Iraq and did not even think about including Iran. These countries were at war. After the war, the question of their membership will probably come up. When it does, Washington should take a neutral position while continuing its support for the GCC. It will be up to the GCC members to decide this internal issue. They might, for example, offer Iran or Iraq or both some kind of an "associate" membership, or pursue some other formula. On the other hand, the problem of building a consensus among the six original members might surface with a vengeance after the war, once the perceived threats of the contagion of the revolution and the spread of the war subside. Their ability to cope with that problem will significantly depend on their success in working out their internal differences. It will also depend partly on the extent to which they are able to institutionalize their multifaceted functions between now and when the war ends.

Preventing the "Islamization" of the Arab-Israeli Conflict

The United States needs to develop a much more sophisticated understanding of the implications of the Iranian Revolution for the Arab-Israeli conflict. For a quarter of a century, the Shah's discreet alignment with Israel helped advance American, Israeli, and Iranian interests, especially against Soviet expansionism, but also in favor of American peacemaking processes. While the Khomeini regime is no less distrustful of the Soviets than the Shah was, it has distinguished itself as the most radical anti-Israeli state in the entire Middle East, opposing every major peace initiative. It has set for itself the goals of eradicating the

Jewish state—replacing it with a full-fledged Palestinian one—and "liberating Jerusalem." Dozens of its Revolutionary Guardsmen have been killed by Israeli forces in Lebanon, where the Iranian anti-Israeli and anti-American crusade contributed to the withdrawal of both American and Israeli forces.

It would be a mistake for the United States to underestimate the Iranian determination to Islamicize the conflict, just as it would be a mistake to exaggerate that determination. For Israel, the stark strategic fact remains that, just when it won a peace with Egypt, the greatest Arab military power, it lost Iran, its most steadfast strategic partner in the Middle East. Israel had cultivated Iran's friendship since Israel's birth as an independent state, largely in order to breach the wall of hostile Arab encirclement. For the United States, a main setback is the formation of the tripartite alliance between Iran, Libya, and Syria against Israel. This radical axis complicates the peace process. It is also an anti-Egyptian, anti-Jordanian, and anti–Yasser Arafat grouping. The United States and Israel must also face the fact that Iran's message among the desperate Palestinians in the West Bank and Gaza Strip is increasingly powerful. That message—that the only effective way to solve the Palestinian problem is to destroy Israel by armed struggle— has begun to sound like sweet music to their ears.

The Iranian factor has made the resolution of the Arab-Israeli conflict in general and the Palestinian question in particular more complicated, acute, and urgent. The U.S.-Israeli agreement on a Memorandum of Understanding, and like agreements, would hardly compensate Israel and the United States for the loss of strategic Iran or help to resolve the Arab-Israeli conflict. On the contrary, the overidentification of Israel with the United States that such strategic links signify can intensify Arab and Iranian resentment against both.

Going Easy on Syria

Building bridges to Syria will help the United States in four major ways. First, although Khomeini and Hafiz Assad nurse a common enmity toward Saddam Hussein, Hafiz Assad has no interest whatever in seeing an Iranian-installed Ayatollah in Baghdad. Nor does Washington. On the basis of this common interest, the United States could help to stiffen Hafiz Assad's opposition to Iranian efforts to form an Islamic republic to Iran's liking in Iraq. Second, Hafiz Assad resents the intrusion of Iranian Revolutionary Guardsmen, mullahs, and volunteers in Lebanon. So does Washington. Now that the Israeli forces have withdrawn from southern Lebanon, the Syrian leader might be even more anxious to ask the Iranians to leave Lebanon. Iran has promised to honor such a request.

Third, neither the extremist Iranian-supported Islamic Amal of Hussein Musawi nor the pro-Iranian *Hezbollah* faction is palatable to Hafiz Assad. Nor to Washington. The departure of Iranian Revolutionary Guardsmen from Lebanon would go a long way toward pulling the props out from under these groups. Washington should encourage Syria's support of the "moderate" mainstream Amal, which has already become the brawniest force in Lebanese politics. Tehran's distaste for Nabih Berri is not shared by Damascus.

Fourth, and finally, in spite of all their similar anti-Israel rhetoric, Damascus and Tehran essentially differ over the acceptable methods of resolving the Arab-Israeli conflict. The Iranian goal of "eradicating" Israel by armed struggle collides head-on with the position of Syria, which may be said to accept United Nations Resolution 242 as a basis for a peace settlement with Israel. Syria's principal objective is the recovery of the Golan Heights, an objective that, unfortunately, Washington has failed—both in the Camp David Accords and in the Reagan Plan—to take seriously into account. For the time being, the Syrian-Iranian axis is held together mainly by a common enmity toward Saddam Hussein. The larger the rift between Washington and Damascus, the stronger that axis can become, and vice versa.

Relaxing the U.S. Embrace of Egypt

When Anwar al-Sadat visited Jerusalem and then followed the path that led to the Camp David Accords, the Shah's Iran was the only country in the Middle East which publicly supported his move. By the time Sadat signed the peace treaty with Israel, the Shah had lost his throne. Added to the destruction of the Tel Aviv–Tehran alliance, the destruction of the Cairo-Tehran alignment was a great strategic setback for the United States. The Khomeini regime's breaking of diplomatic relations with Sadat's Egypt and its denunciation of the Egyptian grant of political asylum to the Shah and his family are the basis for the cold war between America's most powerful Arab friend in the Middle East and the Khomeini regime. Ayatollah Sadeq Khalkhali's brutal prediction that Sadat "would have to pay for his dirty act," and Sadat's public support of the American rescue mission in Iran, contributed to the freeze, as did Mubarak's erroneous and precipitous accusation of Iranian involvement in the mysterious mining of the Suez Canal and the Red Sea.

What should concern the United States more than this strategic loss, however, is the intensified surge of Islamic fundamentalism. Ayatollah Khalkhali's prediction about Sadat's fate came true because of bullets fired by Egyptian Muslim fundamentalists a great distance from Tehran. But near or far, there is absolutely no doubt that the Khomeini symbol of successful defiance of the United States in Iran will continue to enthrall peoples throughout the region as long as the perception of American domination, particularly military domination, persists. Beneath the wave of anti-Americanism in Egypt, as elsewhere in the Middle East, there is also the perception of U.S. opposition to popular demands for the redress of grievances, for genuine social and economic betterment, and for political participation, because of American over-identification with regimes that are considered to be uninterested in sharing real power with their people.

No longer is it the Islam of the Muslim Brotherhood that is invoked to protest the underlying socioeconomic and political problems. Rather, it is the Khomeini model of Islamic fundamentalism. Although Mubarak managed to have a huge pro-Islamic law demonstration called off in June 1985, the Jihad Organization decried nevertheless the selective implementation of Islamic law, even demanding unequivocally "an Islamic republic led by religious men, like Ayatollah Khomeini's government." Before Sadat was murdered, the phenomenon of Islamic resurgence perhaps was not as fully appreciated as it should have been by U.S. officials and the modernized Egyptian elite. Anything the United States could do to downplay its great presence in Egypt might reduce the kind of cultural as well as political revulsion that led to the destruction of the Shah's regime.

No Durable U.S. Exodus from Lebanon

Strife-ridden, blood-splattered Lebanon seemed permanently hostile to America six years after the Iranian Revolution, a revolution that I suggest influenced Israel's decision to invade Lebanon in the first place. Among the victimized Shia Muslim community, the Khomeini ideological foray could penetrate more deeply than it could anywhere else in the Middle East. Oppressed over the centuries by waves of foreign and domestic enemies—Turks, Egyptians, French, Syrians, Palestinians—the Shia Muslims were battered in 1983 by the heavy guns of the U.S. battleship *New Jersey.* In Beirut, hundreds of American servicemen paid with their lives for the foolish decision that was made in Washington in utter disregard of local circumstances and against the expert advice of many both in and out of government. Not since the fall of Saigon in 1975 had America been so badly shaken. The ignominious "redeployment" of U.S. forces, the scrapping of the Lebanese-Israeli withdrawal agreement of May 1983, the merciless murder of Malcolm Kerr, the president of the American University of Beirut, the continued captivity of U.S. citizens, and the repeated destruction of U.S. embassy buildings were caused by a strategic greed that considered an Israeli-American foot-hold in Lebanon compensation for the loss of the Shah's Iran. This was the unspoken consideration that prompted all of the blunders made by the United States in Lebanon.

Yet the ancient Shia rage in Lebanon, as elsewhere in the Middle East, was conveniently seen as nothing but the product of Iranian agita-tion, just as our debacle was largely blamed on revolutionary Iran and its local allies. No one asked where these pro-Iranian Shia enemies of Israel and America were before the Israeli invasion. When did the Iranian Revolutionary Guardsmen show up in Lebanon? Why could Iranian cler-ics freely roam the Lebanese landscape? And what happened to Israel's proverbial Lebanese Shia friends after the invasion?

The honest answer was stated by Yitzhak Rabin in a moment of candor: Israel let the Shia genie out of the bottle. The way to put it back in is not for the United States to talk about bombing the Iranian holy city of Qom or Jamaran, Khomeini's residence. To be sure, the revolutionary zealots of Iran (and not its top leaders) dream about establishing an Islamic republic in Lebanon. But both Nabih Berri, leader of the main-stream Amal, and Sheikh Muhammad Hussein Fadlallah, the "spiritual guide" of the radical *Hezbollah,* oppose such a goal. Moreover, the grow-ing Syrian impatience with the Iranian Revolutionary Guardsmen and the withdrawal of the Israeli forces from Lebanon, among other factors, will reduce the chances of anything resembling an Islamic republic be-ing created in Lebanon. That in itself, however, will not guarantee the return of the United States to Lebanon's favor. A just and workable political order must be hammered out by the Lebanese political forces themselves, and this is the overriding goal that the United States must continue to support. Our current exodus is the price we paid for an avoidable blunder. It must remain a temporary aberration in that long historical association with Lebanon which is so nobly symbolized by the American University of Beirut.

U.S. Complacency about Oil Supplies

Like so many other aspects of the manifold challenge-response phe-nomenon in the Middle East since the Iranian Revolution, the complex-ities of the oil issue have escaped the attention of analysts and govern-ment officials. Contrary to conventional wisdom, the reason for the lack of a "third oil shock" during the Iraq-Iran war—which, incidentally, has caused the largest and the longest disruption of Gulf oil supplies in history—is not simply the soft market situation. A complicated web of political, strategic, and technical factors has limited the oil supply disruption enough to allow the existing oversupply of oil to compensate for shortages. In other words, the political and strategic policies of the GCC states and the United States have prevented a drastic and durable disruption of oil supplies. Just as significantly, the warring parties' own incompetence and self-interest, or a combination of both, have limited the extent of the disruption.

During the Lebanon war, the Arab oil producers also failed to impose an oil embargo against the United States because of the political and strategic interests and policies of regional states and superpowers rather than simply because of the Arab oil producers' concern with the oil glut. To be sure, when the Arabs imposed an oil embargo in 1973, the market was a seller's market, whereas in 1982 it was a buyer's market. But neither in 1973 nor in 1982 was the market the sole determinant of the Arabs' actions. Arab and non-Arab political and strategic interests, which were also drastically different in the two periods, helped determine the actions of the oil producers.

The configuration of political and strategic factors which has so far kept the size of the oil disruption within acceptable and absorbable limits could change and thereby destroy the advantage presented by the existing oversupply. Suppose Iran managed somehow to knock out the Ras Tanura terminal, or Iraq knocked out the Kharg Island installations and the Strait of Hormuz was closed in retaliation—what would then happen to the cushion provided by the surplus? A mammoth disruption could result from factors other than the spread of the war. One of the major lessons of the Iranian Revolution has been that oil strikes can be used to destroy a conservative monarchy in the Persian Gulf. Although there are many differences between the conditions in, for example, Saudi Arabia and the conditions in Iran, the toppling of a monarchy elsewhere in the Gulf through oil strikes is not out of the question. In 1979, we may do well to recall, the Saudi Shia oil workers demanded, among other things, that the oil be kept in the ground.

It would be a serious mistake for the United States to let its guard down because of the existing oversupply situation, although OPEC is obviously undergoing an oil shock today and will probably continue to suffer from dwindling oil prices for some time. Saudi Arabia is running the second largest current-account deficit after the United States, but the situation could change and prompt sudden major disruptions. Conditions for domestic convulsions are ripe, the Iraq-Iran war rages on, the Arab-Israeli conflict and the Palestinian problem are no closer to resolution today than they were before the Iranian Revolution (in fact, they both have become less solvable), and the crisis in Lebanon shows no sign of abating. Just as political and strategic conditions could change in ways that would make the disruption of oil supplies unbearable, market conditions could change in ways that would reduce the surplus cushion. If the expected decline in non-OPEC oil production by the 1990s does occur, the world might find the OPEC producers back in the driver's seat.

Finally, contrary to conventional wisdom, the challenge of revolutionary Iran with respect to oil price and production issues has not been any more hawkish in practice than those, for example, of Libya and Algeria. The Saudis have managed quite well to live with Khomeini's hawkish oil price policy, as they did with the Shah's. In spite of all their tough rhetoric, the Iranians have managed to abide by the 1982 and 1983 OPEC landmark decisions on price and production levels.

Noting the Deeper Challenge and Response

The American public in general and the policy community in particular must avoid becoming part of the Middle Eastern problem. We can begin to do this by shedding our stereotypical, superficial, and facile characterizations of Middle Eastern issues, policies, and peoples. Our perceived adversaries are not simply "fanatical" or "terrorist" or "anti-American," and our perceived friends are not purely "rational," "moderate," and "pro-American." These characterizations are factually unfounded and reflect a failure to understand the nature of the deeper challenge and response that Middle Eastern societies face. They also reflect a profound dilemma for U.S. policy in the Middle East.

An understanding of the deeper challenge and response facing Middle Eastern societies has been bedeviled since the Iranian Revolution by numerous monistic theories about the resurgence of Islam and allegedly related problems, especially terrorism. But the resurgence of Islam can hardly be explained by the Arab defeat at the hands of Israel beginning with the 1967 war or by the rise of Arab oil power yesterday—or, ironically, by the demise of that power today—or by the Muslim rejection of Western imperialism and Western values or by the lack of novelty of the phenomenon of Islamic revival in Islamic history. Nor can terrorism be explained by asserting that it is a "characteristic" of Islam simply because an extremist Shia sect known as the *hashishiyya* (the Assassins) existed in the twelfth century.

By and large, these theories fail to promote our understanding of the resurgence of Islam. Muslim societies everywhere face the challenge posed by the modern world. According to Lucian Pye, the developing world in general faces the challenge of such modern values as the spirit of science and advanced technology, a rational view of life, a secular approach to social relations, justice in public affairs, and primary loyalty to the nation-state. But these are not simply "Western" values, except historically. They are now worldwide values and are in a process of constant diffusion. For more than two hundred years the Muslim Middle East has tried to respond to the challenge of these modern values not only by imitating a variety of secular ideologies ranging from liberal and integral nationalism to socialism and communism, but also by formulating such "religious" ideologies as Islamic modernism, Islamic socialism, and Islamic fundamentalism.

Muslim thinkers have been engaged since the nineteenth century in the enterprise of trying to provide answers to the challenge posed by the rapid diffusion of the values of "world culture." This is evidenced by the examples of Jamal al-Din al-Afghani, Muhammad Abduh, Muhammad Iqbal, Abdul Ala Maududi, Sayyid Qutb, and Hasan al-Banna in the past, and by Ayatollah Khomeini and Ali Shariati in recent years. Muslim political groups have been equally involved in that same enterprise—the Muslim Brotherhood and Fada'yyan Islam of the past, and the Egyptian Muslim Brotherhood and Islamic Jihad, the Lebanese mainstream Amal or Islamic Amal or *Hezbollah* or *Tawhid,* and the Kuwaiti *Salafi, Jama'at Islah,* and *Jama'at Saqafah* of today.

Even the official ideologies of Middle Eastern rulers have not been devoid of prescriptions for ways to meet the challenge of the actualities of the modern world. Secular ideologies such as Kemalism, Musaddiqist nationalism, Nasserite Arab socialism, and Iraqi and Syrian Ba'thism coexist and compete today, as they did in the past, with religious ideologies. Khomeini's *mustaza'fin* Islam or the Saudi *muwahhidun* Islam equally exemplify a search for answers to the problems posed by modern life, even though their answers are essentially traditional in nature. To be sure, secular and religious ideologies are often used by rulers to legitimize their hold on power, just as they are used by political dissidents to wrest that power from the rulers. But to limit the function of Islam to this particular aspect of the Middle Eastern political process is to distort reality by indulging in reductionism. As zealous as the Khomeini regime has been, its experience nevertheless shows that pragmatism is as much in evidence in Islam in the twentieth century as it was in the seventh. In trying to cope with the challenge of the realities of modern life, even Khomeini cannot build a Wall of China around Iran in an ever-interdependent world.

Beyond its uses in the Middle Eastern political process, Islamic resurgence has a deeper meaning in the life of the peoples of the region. By equating modernism with crass materialism, an equation that is by no means confined to Middle Easterners, a harking back to traditional values signifies, to a great extent, a demand for spiritual and moral values by which the inevitable new material values of the modern world can be tempered, humanized, and harmonized with the old values. It also signifies a demand for a better standard of living and more social justice, a demand that is rapidly spreading among the masses. But because this demand is not being satisfied, the revolution of rising expectations is often transformed into what may be called "the revolution of rising alienation." Such alienation underpinned the eruption of the Iranian Revolution as much as moral outrage and political dissatisfaction with the Shah's regime.

Thus, the challenge of Iran and the response of other Middle Eastern nations cannot be captured by the prevailing notions about the resurgence of Islam. Even more critically, the challenge-response dialectic actually represents the different ways by which rulers and peoples of the area, in their fundamental search for self-realization, are trying to respond to the larger and deeper challenge presented by the values of the modern world. Given the complexity of the Middle Eastern situation, I have warned against easy characterization of the governments and the peoples of the region as "pro-American" and "anti-American," or "rational" and "fanatical," in formulating U.S. policy, and have urged instead that we assess the issues and problems of the area in terms of indigenous perceptions and conditions.

Yet, of all areas of the Third World, the Middle East seems to be the most difficult region for us to consider in its own terms. The Middle East has been, in George Ball's words, "a point of strategic significance from the earliest days when Alexander the Great cast envious eyes on this area. It's the bridge between Europe and Africa. It's an area which dominates the whole southern littoral of the Mediterranean and therefore is key to the defense of Western Europe. It's an area in which the Soviet Union has had a long interest, ever since the days of the Czar . . . it also happens to contain the greatest pool of energy in the world." This perception of the area's strategic importance lies beneath a longtime tendency in the American policy community to view the Middle Eastern problems primarily from the perspective of U.S. competition for power and influence with the Soviet Union. From the Truman Doctrine in 1947, through the Eisenhower Doctrine and the Nixon Doctrine to the Carter Doctrine in 1980 and its Reagan corollary to date, that perspective has been part of the dilemma of American policy in the Middle East.

To compete with the Soviet Union successfully, we insist on the objective of "political stability" in the countries of the region. Our insistence is based on the assumption that political instability would automatically redound to the benefit of the Soviet Union, enabling the Kremlin to fish in the troubled waters of the Middle East. The contrary evidence of the fate of the Soviet Union in Egypt and Iran after the revolutions in these countries is usually disregarded. As a result, we are prone to perceiving political stability in terms of the preservation of the status quo in an area of the world which is profoundly in need of basic change if it is to respond effectively to the challenge of the modern world. Caught on the horns of such a dilemma, we often find ourselves talking about encouraging "peaceful change," whereas in practice we are trying to maintain the status quo. To this extent we have, in fact, become part of the Middle Eastern problem.

But the larger part of the problem lies in the Middle Eastern societies themselves. In this respect, the conservative and the revolutionary regimes are in the same boat. The evidence is to be found in the records of the two major revolutionary regimes of the region. More than thirty years after the Egyptian revolution and seven years after the Iranian, the fundamental problems of social injustice, political repression, and abysmal standards of living of the masses of the people still cry out for solution. Alas, it appears likely that past cycles of quietude imposed by authoritarian governments (rather than genuine political stability) and negative societal convulsion (rather than purposeful revolution) will continue into the future. For a young and impatient nation such as ours, this is deeply discouraging. But we must understand that there is neither a simple explanation for the Middle Eastern situation nor an easy solution to its problems. Nevertheless, we must reverse the past patterns of our policy if, instead of being part of the Middle Eastern problems, we are to become a major catalyst toward their solution. We must encourage basic changes in practice rather than preserving the status quo in the name of peaceful change.

Epilogue

Iran's America Initiative

More than a year before the disclosure of the U.S.-Iran arms affair, I detected an emerging pragmatic tendency in the foreign policy of revolutionary Iran and urged that the United States retain the option of eventually improving relations with Iran. Such relations, I suggested, might best be improved by means of "non-strategic trade" and by working through the United Nations to end the war between Iran and Iraq.[1] The National Security Council and the Central Intelligence Agency, in usurping control of American foreign policy toward Iran, not only undermined the popularity of President Reagan at home and the credibility of the United States abroad but also destroyed any short-term opportunities to explore a constructive relationship between the two countries.

Just as this arms-for-hostages deal, or "Iran folly," has jeopardized such opportunities in the short run, the "Gulf folly" seems to threaten them in the mid term. The American reflagging of the Kuwaiti oil tankers and the U.S. naval escort have begun to have major political consequences. The increased U.S. military presence in the Persian Gulf, in the name of preserving free navigation, has played right into the hands of the extremist factions in Iran's domestic revolutionary politics and is threatening its open-door foreign policy. Whereas President Reagan's preoccupation with the release of American hostages was the driving force behind the secret arms deal with Iran—despite all the talk about a "strategic opening" to Iran[2]—his obsession with the crusade against the Soviet Union was the primary reason for plunging into the treacherous waters of the Persian Gulf.

Despite the difference in motivations, both U.S. initiatives share one major feature—a poor understanding of Iranian domestic and foreign policy. I hope to improve that understanding by critically examining

Iran's "America initiative" and its immediate aftermath. Toward this end, I shall speculate on the origins of this initiative and scrutinize its channels, its objectives and means, and its broader significance for the foreign policy of revolutionary Iran, especially in light of its factional domestic politics.

ORIGINS

The converging effects of Iran's domestic revolutionary politics and its protracted war with Iraq were the source of Iran's America initiative. Having effectively eliminated their "liberal" ideological and political rivals by destroying the government of Mehdi Bazargan and the presidency of Abolhasan Bani-Sadr, the followers of the "Khomeini line" or ideology managed to consolidate power and monopolize legitimacy in the name of Islam. Having driven the Iraqi invaders from Iranian soil and then carried the war into Iraqi territory, they appeared to match success on the domestic political scene with triumph on the battlefield. Taking note of this perceived twofold gain, Ayatollah Khomeini declared on 15 December 1982 that the revolution had ended and that from then on Iran needed "stability" and "reconstruction."[3] A week later, he called, for the first time, for an end to Iran's "hermit" status in world affairs,[4] a pronouncement that ran counter to his earlier call for Iran's international isolation as a necessary condition of its "real salvation." Khomeini himself had changed the "Khomeini line."

The Iranian Ministry of Foreign Affairs took up the cue in 1983. In a series of seminars, the Institute for Political and International Studies (IPIS) began to examine some of the basic tenets of Iranian foreign policy, including the doctrine of "neither East, nor West, but the Islamic Republic." In keeping with Khomeini's new guideline, this slogan was interpreted to mean that Iran must reject domination by both the East and the West rather than refrain from establishing relations with either. It was also determined that, in order not to jeopardize the survival of the "Islamic citadel,"[5] the pursuit of Iran's national interest should be accorded a higher priority than the export of the Islamic revolution.

Meanwhile, further changes in the revolutionary political process created new pressures on Iranian leaders. Tipped off by the CIA that KGB agents had penetrated the Iranian civilian and military bureaucracy, the Khomeini government destroyed the pro-Soviet Tudeh Communist party and expelled eighteen Soviet diplomats in 1983.[6] As if the Soviet resumption of large-scale arms supplies to Iraq were not bad enough, the discovery of Soviet infiltration of the Iranian government compounded Iran's historical distrust of Russia and its fear of the threat presented by Soviet military occupation of neighboring Afghanistan.

The suppression of the Tudeh party marked the successful elimination of all major forces of opposition to the Khomeini regime, but the Iranian government encountered an ideological challenge from within the ranks of Khomeini loyalists. Ironically, this challenge was the product of Khomeini's own hard-line rhetoric. Such extremist factions as the *Hezbollah* lined up to the right of even Khomeini. They clung to Khomeini's earlier calls for Iran's isolation and aggressively pressed for the export of the Islamic revolution by any means, including the use of force. I call these factions "transnationalist." They completely reject the idea of the nation and instead subscribe to the classical Islamic concept of *'Umma,* or the Islamic community, which transcends the existing modern international system. I call "internationalist" the other revolutionaries, those who emphasize the importance of the nation-state over the *'Umma* and hence accept the existing international system pragmatically. This group is by and large in political ascendancy at this time. If there are "moderates" or "radicals" in Iran with respect to foreign policy, they are moderate or radical only in terms of these two major coexisting revolutionary tendencies.

The description of these factions is not written in stone; it fluctuates. This fluctuation reflects the ancient problem of factionalism in Iran. Contrary to conventional wisdom, factionalism in Iranian politics, as I have argued elsewhere, stems not from sociocultural divisions but from the lack of a normative consensus. Over their long and troubled history, Iranians have faced such fundamental questions about their organized existence as what they are as a society, as a nation, and as a state and where their place is in the world. It is not that Iranians have no answers to these questions; it is that they have too many.

This is exactly why political factions in Iran are extremely fluid, why today's moderates may be tomorrow's radicals and vice versa, and why a moderate on one set of issues may be radical on another. On economic issues, for example, there are those who believe in a free market and those who favor state intervention in the economy. The "free marketeers" are not all necessarily moderate on foreign policy issues, nor are all "etatists" radical. The opposite may well be true: With respect to foreign policy issues, Ayatollah Montazeri is a transnationalist, but regarding economic issues, he is a free marketeer. Rafsanjani, on the other hand, is an internationalist on foreign policy issues and an etatist on economic matters. Both are revolutionaries.

By the summer of 1984, in addition to the potential threat of the transnationalists on the extreme right and the communists on the extreme left, there was a dramatic increase in the threat of Iraqi disruption of Iranian oil exports. The tanker war was taking a heavy toll; in one instance when Iran tried to retaliate against Iraq by attacking Saudi Arabia, Iraq's perceived supporter, it failed dismally. The Saudis, we may recall, downed an Iranian F-4 plane in June 1984. Khomeini vigorously revived his 1982 call for Iran to abandon its "hermit" status in world affairs. Under the combined pressures of extremist activities at home and the failure of Iranian arms abroad, President Khamene'i declared on 31 July that Iran would pursue an "open-door" foreign policy as a means of serving both its "needs" and its Islamic "message."[7] In an obvious rebuke to the transnationalists, Ayatollah Khomeini on 29 October 1984 warned that Iran would encounter "defeat and annihilation" if it failed to establish relations with other governments.[8] More important, he hinted for the first time at the possibility of a future relationship with the United States.

While it took about two years, between 1982 and 1984, for the idea of a possible opening to the United States to germinate, once sprouted it grew quickly into Iran's America initiative of 1985. The catalyst was the hijacking of TWA flight 847 on 14 June 1985. According to the CIA Inspector General, Israeli officials asked Manuchehr Ghorbanifar to use his influence in Tehran to obtain the release of the hostages on the plane. On 19 June, "Iran sent the United States a message to the effect that Tehran wanted to do as much as it could to end the TWA crisis."[9] On 24 June, Rafsanjani condemned the hijacking while on a visit to Damascus, stating unequivocally that "if we had such knowledge, we would have prevented it." He helped free the thirty-nine American hostages on 30 June. Equally important, on 3 July 1985, for the first time, he publicly called on the United States to take the initiative in resuming relations with Iran. He said, "We have no intention to keep our diplomatic relations severed forever but it will be difficult to restore relations under the present administration."[10] The Tower Commission board could not resolve "conclusively" whether President Reagan gave "prior approval to Israel's transfer of arms to Iran," but it is interesting to note that it was on 30 August 1985 that Israel delivered 100 TOW missiles to Iran, the first of the six arms shipments to Iran in the course of the secret dealings.

CHANNELS

Through what channels did Iran deal with the United States? Iranian leaders considered it absolutely necessary to deal with Washington as secretly, indirectly, and cautiously as possible. They feared the public's response to open and direct contacts with the United States government, a pervasive concern documented by both Americans and Iranians. For example, after meeting with an Iranian "senior foreign affairs advisor" during his visit to Tehran of 25–28 May 1986, Robert C. McFarlane reported by cable as follows:

> In the course of the 4-hour meeting it became evident that the three Iranian leaders—Rafsanjani, Musavi (Prime Minister) and Khamenei (President) are each traumatized by the recollection that after Bazargan met with Brzezinski in the Spring of 1980 [sic], he was deposed (so strong was popular sentiment against doing business with the Great Satan). Today the force of events and self-interest has brought them to the point of realizing that we do have some common interests. . . . But they still cannot overcome their more immediate problem of how to talk to us and stay alive.[11]

In a meeting with the American delegation on 26 May 1986, the Iranian "foreign affairs advisor" reportedly said that the Iranian leadership both influenced people and was affected by people; it was an interactive condition. "It is not whatever the Imam [Khomeini] says. His word is accepted because he talks from the heart of the people. This is why the leadership of Iran is not something dogmatic. It is not a dictatorship, religious or otherwise. The leadership depends on wisdom of public opinion. After death of Brezhnev, Iran sent a delegation. The leadership was attacked by the nation for this act. No one went to Chernenko's funeral."[12]

It would be cynical to say that all this talk about fear was an Iranian ploy to fend off McFarlane's angry insistence on meeting with high-ranking Iranian officials. The pragmatist or internationalist leaders of Iran were genuinely afraid of the uncompromisingly hostile attitude toward the United States held by the xenophobic transnationalists, who insisted adamantly that the Khomeini line still required no relationship with foreign governments, especially the American government. In the same way that they had protested the dispatch of an Iranian delegation to Brezhnev's funeral, they raised cain when the Iranian government received the West German foreign minister, Hans-Dietrich Genscher. These transnationalists, centered in the holy city of Qom, challenged the Foreign Ministry for control of Iranian foreign policy. Some of them gathered around Mehdi Hashemi, who ran the unit of the Revolutionary Guards that had been established in 1981 to aid the Islamic liberation movements abroad. As will be seen, it was his constituency that eventually leaked McFarlane's secret visit to Tehran to a Lebanese magazine.

Iran dealt with the United States largely through arms dealers. The principal intermediary was an Iranian businessman living in Europe named Manuchehr Ghorbanifar. He was suggested to the Americans by Israeli officials, "who had maintained covert dealings with Iran for years."[13] He purportedly had extensive ties to the political leadership in Tehran. He was deeply involved in five of the six arms transactions with the United States and arranged the unsuccessful McFarlane visit to Tehran. The NSC and the CIA continued to rely on him, even though McFarlane had taken a dislike to him from the very beginning and Ghorbanifar had failed a CIA-administered polygraph test during a visit to Washington in January 1986.[14] Some have attributed the idea of exchanging arms for hostages to him, others to his Israeli friends. What's more, using highly questionable tactics of exaggeration, misrepresentation, and even outright fabrication, he kept the secret deals alive when they were about to collapse.

Another major intermediary was Albert Hakim, an Iranian-born American businessman who got involved with the U.S.-Iran dealings in January 1986. In June 1987 he told the House and Senate committees investigating the Iran-*contra* affair that he disagreed with the "approach" used by Ghorbanifar, because, he alleged, Ghorbanifar intended "to create a system through which he could continue to sell arms to Iran and release hostages and then for the Lebanese to go on and get more hostages and for the United States to sell more arms."[15] In contrast, he asserted, "I tried very hard to get to that layer of the Iranian Government that could see beyond exchange of arms for hostages." Hakim was linked to the "second channel," the "Relative" (presumably Rafsanjani's). Without even a security clearance, in a meeting in October 1986 in Frankfurt, Hakim discussed with Iranian officials an outrageous nine-point agenda. It provided, among other things, for the United States to exert pressure on Kuwait to release the seventeen *Da'wa* prisoners it was holding as a result of the 1983 bombings there.

By dealing with the U.S. government through such intermediaries, the Iranian leaders, in effect, built a two-layered scheme of deniability into their covert relations with Washington. As far as is known, the intermediaries did not have direct access to Iranian leaders. Ghorbanifar reportedly had access to a deputy in the office of Prime Minister Musavi, and Hakim was in touch with the "Relative," who continuously indicated that he had "a special mandate" from Rafsanjani to meet with U.S. government officials.[16]

American sources, however, indicate that U.S. officials met and talked directly with Iranian officials in Frankfurt in February and October 1986 and during McFarlane's visit to Tehran in May 1986. The same sources indicate direct telephone conversations between American and Iranian officials as well as a CIA-arranged trip of the "Relative" to Washington during 19–20 September, in which Hakim and Lt. Col. Oliver North gave him a tour of the White House and conducted two days of extensive negotiations with him. The Americans felt all along that they needed to have direct contact with Iranian officials rather than having to deal through intermediaries. That is why Oliver North seemed so excited over his first meeting with an Iranian official, in February 1986 in Frankfurt. He believed that the person he met from the office of the prime minister of Iran had "authority to make his own decisions on matters of great import" and that "this was first USG/GOI contact in more than 5 yrs [sic]."[17] McFarlane, on the other hand, was infuriated over having been allowed to meet only third- and fourth-ranking officials.

OBJECTIVES

The most important short-term objective of Iran's America initiative was the purchase of arms and spare parts. Iranian revolutionary leaders have repeatedly lamented what they see as the Shah's legacy of military dependence on the United States. The war with Iraq had only intensified their resentment of this dependency. President Carter had imposed an arms embargo on Iran in response to the taking of American hostages. After the hostage settlement of 1981, when economic sanctions were lifted, the arms embargo continued because of the declared American policy of neutrality. As the war with Iraq continued inconclusively and the Iraqis managed to surpass Iran in every major category of military equipment, the need for American arms became even more urgent. Neither the American-manufactured arms available in the international market nor the arms manufactured by other nations could adequately meet that need.

Although rumors had circulated about the flow of Israeli war material to Iran, the only arms sale acknowledged by the Israelis was a $27-million transaction early in the war.[18] But the disclosure of U.S. arms sales to Iran shows that Israel's involvement far surpassed that one transaction. During the course of those sales a total of six shipments went to Iran. Israel delivered 100 TOW missiles on 30 August 1985 and 408 TOW antitank missiles on 18 September. Because an Israeli charter aircraft encountered difficulty in obtaining landing clearance from a third country, the United States assisted the delivery of 18 Hawk missiles to Iran on 25 November 1985. These missiles, except for one that had been test fired, did not meet the Iranian needs and were returned to

Israel. The fourth shipment consisted of 1,000 American TOWs, 500 of which were delivered to Bandar Abbas in Iran on 17 February and the other half on 27 February 1986. The fifth shipment was Hawk spare parts, one pallet of which went to Iran on 25 May 1986 in the same plane that took the McFarlane delegation to Tehran. He later said that he did not know until he got to Tel Aviv that spare parts were being loaded onto his plane. Additional Hawk spare parts were delivered on 3 August 1986. The sixth and last shipment consisted of 500 Israeli TOWs delivered on 6 November 1986, three days after the news of the dealings had broken.[19]

Although Iran managed to buy millions of dollars worth of arms, it probably could not have bought as much as it had hoped. According to the "foreign affairs advisor," "there is [sic] $2.5 billion deal. No one knows what it is. Rafsanjani said officially Iran is ready to buy weapons from America." The Iranian adviser was saying this to the visiting American delegation, hoping to convince them that large-scale arms sales to Iran would favorably impress the Iranian military and public and eventually pave the way for public meetings between Iranian and American leaders. He also indicated an Iranian desire to have American military advice on such weapons systems as F-14 Phoenix and Harpoon missiles. No such advice ever materialized, and the intelligence information on the war front that the United States did provide was falsified or incomplete. And President Reagan's repeated urging that American arms sales to Iran not affect the balance of forces in the war against Iraq explains in part Iran's inability to buy the kind of military equipment it needed.

Did the weapons supplied to Iran affect its fighting capability? Iran's "Karbala Five" offensive, which was launched on 8 January 1987, might provide a clue. The use of Hawk antiaircraft missiles could account for the heavy losses suffered by the Iraqi air force, and perhaps for the subsequent decrease in Iraqi air raids on Iranian targets such as Ahwaz and Tehran. On the other hand, Iran's increased bombing of Iraqi targets might reflect the arrival of spare parts for American-made aircraft.[20] Yet, the Iranian leaders, who had repeatedly promised a decisive offensive by the end of the Iranian calendar year on 20 March, backpedaled. Rafsanjani said on 9 February 1987, "To tell the truth, we cannot see a bright horizon now, so far as ending the war in its present form is concerned."

Did Iran's America initiative have any objective other than buying arms? The Iranians were interested in broadening discussions with the United States to include Washington's cooperation in the defense of Iran against potential Soviet invasion and in assistance to the Afghan resistance movement. For example, the "foreign affairs advisor" told the McFarlane mission on 26 May 1986, "I am happy to hear you believe in an independent, sovereign Iran. We are hopeful that all American moves will be to support this dialogue. But we feel and see the Russian danger much more than you. You see the threat with high technology. We feel it, touch it, see it. It is not easy to sleep next to an elephant that you have wounded. To weaken Iran does not mean the Soviets want Iran. It means they want to reach the warm waters of the Gulf."[21]

To suggest that the Iranians were simply playing on the Reagan administration's preoccupation with the threat of the Soviet Union, with a view to buying more arms, would be excessively cynical. Apart from Iran's historical distrust of Russia and the fear created by Soviet military occupation of Afghanistan, there had been the recent shock of uncovering the Soviet Union's plot to penetrate the Iranian government; so the Soviet threat loomed especially large in the Iranian mind at this time. For their part, the Americans harped on the Soviet threat to Iran, demonstrating the Reagan administration's obsession with the "evil empire." Aside from this, the U.S. negotiators sought to persuade the Iranians that the United States and Iran had common strategic interests.

Most important, the Iranian leaders who were secretly dealing with the United States were also seeking to strengthen their power base at home. They were internationalists, within the ruling circle, who perceived the survival of the revolutionary regime to be partly dependent on the outcome of the war. As such, their interest in the continuation of the fighting was significantly different from that of the transnationalists, who saw the war primarily as a means of exporting the Islamic revolution. The internationalists considered the purchase of American arms vitally important to their goal of achieving a "decisive victory." Such a victory would ensure their control over the revolutionary government in face of the challenge of the transnationalists on the extreme right and the communists and other counterrevolutionaries on the extreme left. Given the internationalists' relatively greater mistrust of the Soviet Union, the "Great Satan" seemed, under the circumstances, the lesser evil with which to deal. The willingness to deal with the United States reflected a deeper pattern of behavior in the Iranian political culture. Historically, political factions in Iran have sought to overcome their political and ideological rivals by manipulating a great power. The Shah wooed the United States for decades in countering the threat of the nationalists, the communists, and the Islamicists at home and the Soviet Union abroad. He finally lost the United States, however, when the Islamicists seized power during the course of the revolution.

MEANS

What means did Iran employ in implementing its America initiative? The most obvious one was making payments for arms. Subsequent to the outbreak of the scandal, Iranian leaders discovered, to their horror, that the Americans had diverted their money to the *contras* fighting Iran's Nicaraguan friends.[22] Iranian officials perceived their dealings with the United States more in terms of arms for money than arms for hostages. They claimed they had used their influence with the Lebanese captors for the release of American hostages for "humanitarian" reasons.

Ghorbanifar unabashedly used scaremongering tactics to pressure the Americans to sell arms to Iran. He told the Americans, for example, that if the United States failed to deliver arms, the hostages would lose their lives. He further claimed that he himself and other Iranian officials involved would be killed. This kind of tactic left a strong impression that Iranians were in complete control of all American hostages. Only the "Relative" told the Americans plainly that not all Lebanese captors responded to Iranian influence.

Many were led to believe that Iran had total control over all American hostages simply because there seemed to be a direct relationship between hostages released and arms delivered.[23] The Islamic Jihad (holy war), which is reputedly the cover name for the pro-Iranian Lebanese captors, released the Reverend Benjamin Weir on 14 September 1985, the Reverend Laurence Martin Jenco on 26 July 1986, and David P. Jacobsen on 2 November 1986. Arms were delivered to Iran on the same day that Weir was released, and on 30 and 31 October shortly before Jacobsen was released. No arms were delivered before Jenco was released. North believed that Jenco's release was the result of McFarlane's mission, a mission in which North participated.

The evidence, however, calls for caution. First, according to the Farsi-speaking retired CIA expert on Iran, George Cave, who went on the McFarlane mission to Tehran, the "serious problem we must address is whether the Iranians can gain control of the hostages. . . . This could be our real problem. The Iranian side may be most willing, but unable to gain control."[24] Second, having debriefed Father Jenco immediately after his release, North reported, "The captors themselves are increasingly disenchanted with the Iranian relationship." He then added, "The continued reluctance of the Hezballah [*sic*] itself to follow precise Iranian instructions on *how* [italics in original] to release the hostages is seen as an indication of efforts by Hezballah to demonstrate at least partial independence."[25]

Third, according to the testimony of Under Secretary of State John Whitehead, the influence of Iran over the Lebanese captors seems to have been limited:

> MR. BROOMFIELD: What direct and indirect influence does the Government of Iran or do factions thereof have over the groups holding United States citizens kidnapped in Lebanon?
>
> MR. WHITEHEAD: We don't know. We think that they may have some influence. They probably do not have direct influence, but we think they may have some influence, and we have some evidence that they have the ability to influence those who do actually hold the hostages, and so we try to put that influence to work to attain our ends of getting the hostages released.[26]

Whitehead also told the Committee on Foreign Affairs of the House of Representatives what he thought about the effects of the arms sales on the release of Weir, Jenco, and Jacobsen: "Three hostages were released, but whether that release had anything to do with the effort [the Reagan administration's Iran initiative], no one knows."[27]

Fourth, and most important, the factional nature of Iran's politics seriously limits the ability of the Iranian government to influence the release of U.S. hostages. There is no doubt that the taking of American hostages in 1979 in Tehran reflected domestic factional strife. At the time, the extremists both right and left of the political spectrum combined forces to drive the centrist government of Bazargan out of power. The American hostages were pawns in Iran's faction-ridden game of politics. Robin Wright, a leading expert on international terrorism, believes that Iran's factional strife today is spilling over into the chaotic Lebanese situation, making American hostages once again victims of Iran's domestic politics.

THE AFTERMATH

Just as factionalism influenced the *making* of Iran's America initiative, it also destroyed it. As seen, the internationalists, led by Rafsanjani, were instrumental in developing and implementing Iran's America initiative, while the transnationalists had all along opposed Iran's open-door foreign policy. From their base in Qom, the transnationalists sought to control Iran's foreign policy. On 2 October 1986 the faction of Mehdi Hashemi (the brother of Ayatollah Montazeri's son-in-law, Hadi Hashemi), who headed the office of the Islamic Liberation Movement, kidnapped the Syrian chargé d'affaires, Ayad Mahmood. The Iranian government dispatched the Minister of Revolutionary Guards (Mohsen

Rafiqdust) to Damascus to apologize officially to the Syrian government.[28]

The internationalists now moved decisively. Khomeini's son, Ahmad, immediately intervened to release the Syrian envoy from the clutches of the Revolutionary Guards, who had apparently roughed him up. More important, soon after the kidnapping, Mehdi Hashemi and Montazeri's son, Saeed, and many of the followers of Hashemi were arrested. The office of the Islamic Liberation Movement was shut down. The feared Intelligence Minister Hojatolislam Mohammad Rayshahri wrote to Khomeini on 26 October that, with Khomeini's "knowledge and concurrence," Mehdi Hashemi and his associates had been arrested. He charged them with murder, kidnapping, illegal possession of arms, forgery, and attempting to cause divisions in the country. In his response on 27 October, Khomeini said that the "line" (ideology) of Hashemi and his associates had "deviated from the revolution and from Islam." This was his most severe criticism of the foreign policy orientation of the transnationalists. He also entrusted Rayshahri with the responsibility "to investigate all aspects of this matter with utmost care and fairness" and instructed him that "since this is an issue connected with the country's security and is against Islam and the revolution, only the intelligence Ministry should investigate."[29] Eight days later, on 3 November 1986, *Al-Shira'*, a Lebanese magazine, disclosed the McFarlane visit to Tehran on the basis of a leak from pro-Hashemi elements. The transnationalist zealots thus retaliated against the pragmatic internationalists by spoiling their secret dealings with the United States.

On twenty-seven different occasions over a period of nine months after the disclosure of the U.S.-Iran secret dealings, the Iranian leaders denied that they had made any deals with the United States. Rafsanjani, who did most of the talking, explained that Iran had dealt only with arms dealers. It had purchased arms in the international market regardless of the country of origin, except that Israel was specifically excluded.

Besides issuing denials, Iranian leaders strove to outdo each other in denouncing Washington. Khamene'i's rhetoric was harsher than Rafsanjani's; so was Musavi's. Rafsanjani mocked the McFarlane visit, telling perhaps one of the tallest Persian tales of his career! Embellishing the facts of the visit, he claimed that the Americans had arrived in Tehran without Iran's permission, carrying Irish passports and bringing a cake and a Bible. They were allegedly arrested and held during their stay in Iran. He also claimed that Khomeini told Iranian leaders, "There should be no talking with these people and do not receive their message, but find out who they are, what their designation is, and who sent them."[30]

Khomeini personally intervened to quash an eight-man parliamentary demand for an investigation. On 17 November 1986 the evening newspaper *Resalat* reported that Foreign Minister Ali Akbar Velayati had been asked to explain to the public what exactly had transpired regarding Iranian-U.S. relations. It added that the Iranian parliament, which held "anti-Americanism" to be one of its most important revolutionary principles, "wanted to know which officials and authorities decided to establish links" with Washington.[31] Three days later, on 20 November, Khomeini declared that Americans had come back to Iran and "presented themselves meekly and humbly at the door of this nation wishing to establish relations. They wish to apologize for their mistake, but our nation rejects them. This is an issue, an issue greater than all your other victories." Without naming the deputies, he admonished them saying, "You should not set up radicals and reactionaries. You should not create a schism. This is contrary to Islam. It is contrary to faith and contrary to fairness. Do not do such things."[32] Three days later, Rafsanjani characterized Khomeini as a "skilled physician" whose statement served as "a healthy medicine drying out the roots of sedition." Also, a majority of deputies wrote Khomeini, expressing regrets about the "irresponsible acts" of their colleagues and stressing their own allegiance to Khomeini and his line.[33] That was the end of the matter.

Despite all his mocking, belittling, and denouncing of Washington, Rafsanjani managed to imply sympathy for the beleagured American president. He repeatedly said Iran would try to use its influence to free American hostages under certain conditions and held out the possibility of improving relations with the United States. His conditions ranged from the unfreezing of Iranian assets to effecting changes in U.S. support of Israel. It is difficult to say whether Rafsanjani, in talking about the future, was trying to discourage questions about past dealings with the United States or genuinely trying to retain the option of future relations. He may have intended to do both, but he was not alone in talking about the future relationship of Iran and the United States. Even Ayatollah Montazeri, having quickly distanced his son and himself from the Hashemi group, changed his tune about a possible rapprochement. He was quoted as saying: "If the United States truly changed its policies and methods, then it would be possible to establish ties. In this case relations would be between two independent countries and not between an oppressor and the oppressed."[34] The semiofficial newspaper *Kayhan* (in Persian) took up the question of rapprochement on 16 November 1986:

First of all we must see what the United States is hoping to achieve by announcing its readiness to open negotiations with Iran. Is the United

States really ready to correct its past mistakes? Is it ready to honor Iran's right in defending its interests? Is it ready to enter into honest and equal negotiations with Iran? If the United States is able to assure Iranian officials of these things, we must not run away from dealing face to face with this or that U.S. official.[35]

THE BURDEN OF PRAGMATISM

Before the disclosure of the secret dealings between the U.S. and Iran, this study, in its central thesis, identified a pragmatic streak in the foreign policy of revolutionary Iran. The foregoing analysis of Iran's America initiative and its immediate aftermath seems to confirm that thesis. No one could have predicted that revolutionary Iran would be ready to go so far as to deal with the United States, even if secretly and largely through intermediaries. Nor could any one have foreseen that immediately after disclosure of such dealings Iranian leaders would continue to indicate that they retained the option of improving relations with the United States.

What are the implications of Iran's America initiative for the future of Iran's foreign policy in general and its relations with the United States in particular? The answer largely depends on the character of Iran's foreign policy. From the fall of the Bazargan government in 1979 until the summer of 1984, Iran's foreign policy was characterized by ideological confrontation. In Khomeini's words, "We must settle our accounts with great and superpowers, and show them that we can take on the whole world ideologically, despite all the painful problems that face us." But this ideological crusade poisoned Iran's relations not only with the United States but also with most countries of the Middle East. Moreover, it provoked the ambitious Iraqi invasion of Iran. In December 1982, however, Khomeini himself called for an end to Iran's "hermit" status in the world and finally, in October 1984, made the expansion of Iran's relations with the rest of the world the *sine qua non* of revolutionary Iran's survival. This open-door policy was associated with a more pragmatic and less ideological thrust. Iran's relations with its nonbelligerent neighbors in the Persian Gulf began to improve. At the same time Iran launched its secret America initiative.

But pragmatism is not an end in itself. It must be viewed from the broader perspective of the ends and means of Iran's open-door policy. Assuming that this policy is not merely a tactical device—and I don't believe it is—then it is beset with two major problems, war and terrorism. The war with Iraq is a major obstacle to the goal of expanding and improving Iran's relations with the rest of the world. No matter how mistaken Iraq may have been—and I believe it was—to invade Iran, from the moment Iran carried the war into Iraqi territory in July 1982, Iran's persistence in fighting has foreclosed the possibility of a negotiated peace. In addition to causing the loss of a million human lives and the destruction of billions of dollars worth of property, the continuation of the war by Iran has fueled international disapprobation of the Iranian government and as a result has significantly impeded the attainment of the objectives of its open-door foreign policy.

Terrorism has also been an impediment to Iran's improving its relations with other countries. Every Iranian leader has denounced hijacking, kidnapping, and other terrorist acts. Iran has tried to distance itself from such acts and has sought to help gain the release of hostages when possible. Yet, suspicious attitudes toward Iran as a renegade state continue. To be sure, Iran does not completely control the captors of foreign hostages in Lebanon. But its open support of the *Da'wa* and its moral, material, and financial support of the *Hezbollah* in Lebanon and other Islamic liberation fronts continue to feed suspicion about its motives. Can Iran afford to be viewed as a pariah state while seeking to normalize relations with other states? As the Persian saying goes, one cannot have both "God and dates" (*ham khoda va ham khorma*).

The war and terrorism interlocked with Iran's American initiative. American arms were purchased to continue the fight against Iraq. Granted the limitations on Iran's influence over the captors of American hostages and that Iran paid exorbitantly for the arms, Iran did indirectly trade innocent hostages for arms. For these important reasons Iran's America initiative was as flawed as America's Iran initiative.

As long as these activities, contradictory to the objectives of Iran's open-door policy, continue, the true character of Iran's foreign policy will remain ambiguous. Only Iran can clarify it. The best way to do so would be for it to seize upon the unprecedentedly equitable resolution of the United Nations Security Council, which was passed unanimously on 20 July 1987. This resolution demands "an immediate cease-fire on land, at sea and in the air" as a first step toward a negotiated settlement. It also contains, among other things, a provision that should appeal to Iran. The Council has requested that the Secretary General "explore, in consultation with Iran and Iraq, the question of entrusting an impartial body with inquiring into responsibility for the conflict." This provision, it seems to me, is compatible with Rafsanjani's idea of creating an "international court," which he first mentioned on 19 June 1985 in his address to a group of Islamic ambassadors.

Iran's acceptance of such a cease-fire would also help clarify its position on terrorism. There is little doubt that Iran's support of the *Da'wa* group is primarily a by-product of the war. A negotiated settlement would help remove the suspicion that Iran uses dissident Iraqis for terrorist acts in Kuwait and elsewhere and would help alleviate the fear of the Gulf Arab states that Iran plans to impose an Iranian-style Islamic republic in Iraq. In Lebanon, Iran's support of the *Hezbollah* will continue to foster the suspicion of Iran's involvement in terrorist acts. One might view the Imam Khomeini Hospital and the Martyr Foundation in Lebanon as medical, social, educational, and recreational services compatible with Khomeini's exhortation that the Islamic revolution be exported only by the example of "Islamic ethical behavior." But the presence of Revolutionary Guards in Lebanon and their military training and mobilization of the Shia population is not in keeping with Khomeini's admonition that "the export of ideas by force is no export."

Removal of the problems of war and terrorism—the primary obstacles in the way of realizing fully the objectives of Iran's open-door policy—would also facilitate the establishment of a constructive relationship between Tehran and Washington based on mutual interest and respect. Neither Iran's America initiative nor the Reagan administration's Iran initiative ever really aspired to this end.

Yet, in the immediate future the prospects of better U.S.-Iran relations seem bleak, and Iran's open-door policy appears to be in a shambles. The American reflagging of the Kuwaiti oil tankers and U.S. naval escorts triggered the escalation of anti-American rhetoric, culminating in Ayatollah Khomeini's acrimonious message of 30 July 1987. He instructed Iranian pilgrims to Mecca to "echo the crushing slogan of the disavowal of pagans and apostates of world arrogance, headed by the criminal U.S.A."—the harshest language he had used against America in years. As a result of clashes between the Saudi police and demonstrating Iranian pilgrims in Mecca on the following day, hundreds of persons were killed, most of them Iranians. Two days later, on 2 August, the architect of Iran's open-door policy seemed to be pulling down one of its main pillars, Iranian reconciliation with Saudi Arabia. Speaker Rafsanjani, addressing more than a million angry Iranians massed in front of the Majlis in reaction to the Mecca violence, said, "We, as soldiers of God and implementers of divine principles, oblige ourselves to avenge these martyrs by uprooting Saudi rulers from the region." Such a threat had not been made by any Iranian leader since the dawn of the Iranian revolution. Interior Minister Ali Akbar Mohtashemi, as expected, outdid all other Iranian leaders in making inflammatory statements. He promised "revenge on U.S. forces for the pure blood of the pilgrims of the house of God" and predicted that "the Muslim nation and the Party of God all over the world will give an appropriate response by direct attacks on U.S. interests and their presence all over the world."

This explosion of emotions blurred the distinction between pragmatic internationalists and xenophobic transnationalists in Iran. The latter's actions matched the former's rhetoric. Iranian crowds went berserk; they attacked the Saudi and Kuwaiti embassies and also threatened to avenge the bloodshed in Mecca by retaliating against the United States. The star of the most revolutionary factions seemed to be on the rise. Clearly, the nascent pragmatic streak in Iran's open-door foreign policy had suffered a dramatic setback.

Whether or not this setback will be transformed into a long-term reversal of revolutionary Iran's open-door policy will depend in part on those internationalist leaders who wield power in Iran today. Iran's open-door policy, like any other policy, can only endure if it is broadly supported by the Iranian people rather than by any particular faction. In turn, such support will depend largely on the willingness of Iranian leaders to allow for the kind of genuine political freedom that is required for developing a normative consensus about such fundamental questions as what the Iranian people are as a society, as a nation, and as a state, and where they fit in the society of modern nation states. Failure to provide such leadership would only reinvigorate one of the most ancient and persistent tendencies in Iran's political culture—the adoption in foreign affairs of unrealizable goals and inappropriate means.

APPENDIXES

NOTES

SELECT BIBLIOGRAPHY

INDEX

Appendix A

Tables of Arms, Oil, and Population in the Middle East

TABLE 1 The OPEC Countries, 1983

Country	Daily Oil Exports (thousands of barrels)	Revenues from Oil (millions $ U.S.)	Daily Crude Oil Production (thousands of barrels)	Population (thousands)
Algeria	260.4	9,765.00	660.90	20,500
Ecuador	126.3	1,473.00	237.50	9,250
Gabon	120.2	1,447.00	151.80	1,130
Indonesia	858.3	13,475.00	1,245.30	155,310
Iran	1,718.7	19,014.00	2,441.70	41,640
Iraq	725.4	9,650.00	1,098.80	14,550
Kuwait	544.4	8,720.00	1,054.10	1,670
Libya	937.4	11,080.00	1,104.90	3,340
Nigeria	935.2	10,762.00	1,235.50	93,597
Qatar	268.3	3,112.00	269.00	280
Saudi Arabia	3,701.7	47,815.00	4,539.40	10,370
United Arab Emirates	1,077.3	12,577.00	1,149.00	1,210
Venezuela	962.4	13,839.00	1,800.80	15,120

Source: OPEC Annual Statistical Bulletin, 1983 (Vienna: OPEC, 1985).

TABLE 2 The Gulf Countries, 1983

Country	Daily Oil Exports (thousands of barrels)	Revenues from Oil (thousands $ U.S.)	Daily Crude Oil Production (thousands of barrels)	Estimated Proven Reserves[a] (1,000 bbl[b])	Population (thousands)
Bahrain	160.0	2,080,000	176.00	170,000	370
Iran	1,718.7	19,014,000	2,441.70	48,500,000	41,640
Iraq	725.4	9,650,000	1,098.80	44,500,000	14,550
Kuwait	544.4	8,720,000	1,054.10	92,710,000	1,670
Oman	128.6	1,653,720	389.00	3,500,000	1,000
Qatar	268.3	3,112,000	269.00	3,350,000	280
Saudi Arabia	3,701.7	47,815,000	4,539.40	171,710,000	10,370
United Arab Emirates	1,077.3	12,577,000	1,149.00	32,490,000	1,210

Sources: OPEC Annual Statistical Bulletin, 1983 (Vienna: OPEC, 1985); OAPEC Annual Statistical Bulletin, 1983 (Kuwait: OAPEC, 1985).
[a]From Oil and Gas Journal 85, no. 52 (31 December 1984): 71, 114 (figures as of 1 January 1985).
[b]bbl = billions of barrels.

TABLE 3 Selected Persian Gulf Ports and Terminals for Large Tankers

Country	Port	Fully Laden (Max. DWT)[a]	Part Laden (Max. DWT)	Max Draft (ft.)
Iran	Kharg Island	500,000	—	106
Iran	Ras Bahrgan	250,000	—	79
Iran	Sirri Islands	350,000	—	79
Iraq	Khor al-Amaya	270,000	330,000	68
Iraq	Mina al-Bakr	350,000	—	96
Kuwait	Mina Al-Ahmadi	500,000	—	91
Qatar	Halul Island	500,000	—	100
Qatar	Umm Said	250,000	300,000	65
Saudi Arabia	Ju'aymah	540,000	—	93
Saudi Arabia	Ras Tanura	200,000	400,000	72
United Arab Emirates	Das Island (Abu Dhabi)	300,000	—	73
United Arab Emirates	Jebel Dhania (Abu Dhabi)	90,000	250,000	49
United Arab Emirates	Fateh (Dubai)	300,000	350,000	150

Source: Bryan Cooper, ed, OPEC Oil Report, 2d ed., November 1979 (London: Petroleum Economist, 1979).

Note: This table contains only loading terminals and ports named in the April 1979 OPEC Oil Report (ed. Bryan Cooper [London: Petroleum Economist, 1979], pp. 107–8).

[a]DWT = deadweight tons.

TABLE 4 Major Oil Pipelines in the Middle East

Pipeline and Route	Length (miles)	Diameter (inches)	Capacity (barrels per day)	Potential Capacity (barrels per day)
Pipelines to the Eastern Mediterranean				
Iraq to Turkey (Kirkuk to Dortyol)	652	40	600,000	1,200,000
Iraq to Syria (Kirkuk to Baniyas, Syria, and to Tripoli, Lebanon)	407	48	1,200,000	No increase planned
Saudi Arabia to Lebanon (Tapline)	754	30 / 31	470,000	No increase planned
Pipelines to destinations south of Suez				
In service				
Trans-Arabian (TAPS-1, Abqaiq to Yanbu)	789	48	1,850,000	—
Trans-Arabian (TAPS-2, Abqaiq to Yanbu)	725	26 / 28 / 30	—	—
Under consideration				
Iraq to Saudi Arabia			5,000,000	
Iraq to Jordan			1–2,000,000	
Saudi Arabia to Oman (GCC project)			—	

Sources: Compiled and adapted from *OPEC Annual Statistical Bulletin, 1983* (Vienna: OPEC, 1985); Anthony C. Cordesman, *The Gulf and the Search for Strategic Stability* (Boulder, Colo.: Westview Press, 1984).

TABLE 5 Shia Muslims in Persian Gulf Countries

Country	Total Population, 1981[a]	Citizen Population, 1981[a]	Shia Population, 1983[b]	Shias as a Percentage of Total Population	Shias as a Percentage of Citizen Population
Bahrain	350,798	238,420	171,900	49.00	71.98
Kuwait (1982)	1,562,190	606,800	141,000	9.02	23.23
Oman (1980)	984,000	805,000	56,000	5.69	6.95
Qatar[b] (1980)	243,357	65,357	52,500	21.57	80.32
Saudi Arabia	9,229,107	7,079,107	350,000	3.79	4.94
United Arab Emirates[b]	1,040,275	289,892	120,000	11.53	41.39
Total	13,409,727	9,084,576	891,400	6.64	9.81
Iran[b]	41,000,000	40,000,000	38,000,000	92.00	95.00
Iraq	14,400,000	13,500,000	8,100,000	56.00	60.00

[a]For Bahrain: (Kuwait) Arab Times, no. 5498, 24 August 1982, p. 7.
For Kuwait: Middle East Economic Digest: Kuwait and the Middle East, May 1982, p. 35.
For Oman, Qatar, Saudi Arabia, and Iraq, Demographic and Related Socio-Economic Data Sheets for Countries of the Economic Commission for Western Asia (ECWA), no. 3 (Beirut: UN-ECWA, May 1982), pp. 131, 115, 147.
For the UAE: Quarterly Economic Review for the UAE: Annual Supplement, 1981 (London: Economist Intelligence Unit, 1981), p. 8.
[b]Compiled from The Middle East Military Balance, 1983, ed. Mark Heller (Tel Aviv: Tel Aviv University, Jafee Center for Strategic Studies, 1983). There is a great difference in the percentages of Shia populations based on Heller's figures and those given by James A. Bill in "Islam, Politics, and Shi'ism in the Gulf" (Middle East Insight 3, no. 3 [January/February 1984]: 6). This discrepancy is especially serious in regard to Qatar and the UAE (16 and 18 percent respectively in Bill's table).

TABLE 6 Iranians in Persian Gulf Countries

	Total Population, 1981[a]	Foreign Population, 1981[a]	Iranians[b]	Iranians as a Percentage of Total Population	Iranians as a Percentage of Citizen Population
Bahrain	350,798	112,378	.7,700	2.19	3.22
Kuwait (1982)	1,562,190	955,390	80,000	5.12	13.18
Oman (1980)	984,000	179,000	2,335	0.23	0.29
Qatar (1980)	243,357	178,000	56,700	23.29	86.75
Saudi Arabia	9,229,107	2,150,000	12,500[c]	0.13	0.001
United Arab Emirates	1,040,275	717,475	40,000	3.84	13.80
Total	13,409,727	4,325,151	199,235	1.48	19.54

[a]For Bahrain: (Kuwait) *Arab Times*, no. 5498, 24 August 1982, p. 7.
For Kuwait: *Middle East Economic Digest: Kuwait and the Middle East*, May 1982, p. 35.
For Oman, Qatar, and Saudi Arabia: *Demographic and Related Socio-Economic Data Sheets for Countries of the Economic Commission for Western Asia (ECWA)*, no. 3 (Beirut: UN-ECWA, May 1982), pp. 131, 115, 147.
For the UAE, *Quarterly Economic Review for the UAE: Annual Supplement, 1981* (London: *Economist* Intelligence Unit, 1981), p. 8.
[b]Figures are estimates and are collected from Gulf newspapers, several issues of *Middle East Economic Digest*, and the ECWA, all in Joseph A. Kechichian, "Demographic Problems Facing the Gulf Cooperation Council," *International Demographics* 2, no. 4 (April 1983): 12.
[c]*New York Times*, 23 March 1981.

TABLE 7 Citizens and Foreigners in the GCC States

Country	Total Population[a]	Citizen Population	Foreign Population[a]	Citizens as a Percentage of Total Population	Foreigners as a Percentage of Total Population
Bahrain	350,798	238,420	112,378	67.9	32.1
Kuwait	1,562,190	606,800	955,390	38.8	61.2
Oman	984,000	805,000	179,000	81.8	18.2
Qatar	243,357	65,357	178,000	26.8	73.2
Saudi Arabia	9,229,107	7,079,107	2,150,000	76.7	23.3
United Arab Emirates	1,040,275	322,800	717,475	31.0	69.0

[a]For Bahrain: (Kuwait) *Arab Times*, no. 5498, 24 August 1982, p. 7.
For Kuwait: *Middle East Economic Digest: Kuwait and the Middle East*, May 1982, p. 35.
For Oman, Qatar, and Saudi Arabia: *Demographic and Related Socio-Economic Data Sheets for Countries of the Economic Commission for Western Asia (ECWA)*, no. 3 (Beirut: UN-ECWA, May 1982), pp. 131, 115, 147.
For the UAE: *Quarterly Economic Review for the UAE: Annual Supplement, 1981* (London: *Economist* Intelligence Unit, 1981), p. 8.

TABLE 8 U.S. Military Sales to the Gulf States, 1950–1984 (In Thousands of U.S. Dollars)

	Bahrain	Iran	Iraq	Kuwait	Oman	Qatar	Saudi Arabia	United Arab Emirates	Total
1950–1974	0	7,042,258	13,152	30,388	0	0	1,744,012	0	8,829,810
1975	15	1,211,018	0	352,112	1,610	0	1,063,608	0	2,628,323
1976	26	1,544,191	0	186,574	223	0	1,922,376	2,176	3,655,866
1977	76	1,300,594	0	16,614	740	0	1,260,541	268	2,578,833
1978	24	298,438	0	65,260	0	0	1,849,767	36	2,213,525
1979	33	14,329	0	10,774	51	0	5,609,903	2,745	5,637,835
1980	4,863	0	0	121,693	22,885	41	3,073,793	106	3,223,381
1981	55	0	0	43,857	48,869	234	1,048,138	5,817	1,146,970
1982	5,326	0	0	115,375	24,208	358	5,397,395	121	5,542,782
1983	6,563	0	0	148,155	583	176	1,939,192	663,180	2,757,849
1984	7	0	0	154,871	1,822	1,433	2,844,090	4,101	3,006,324
Total, 1950–1984	16,988	11,410,828	13,152	1,245,673	100,991	2,242	27,752,815	678,550	41,208,087

Source: Compiled from U.S. Department of Defense, Security Assistance Agency (DSAA), Foreign Military Sales, Foreign Military Construction Sales, and Military Assistance Facts (Washington, D.C.: Data Management Division Comptroller, September 1984).

TABLE 9 The Military Power of the Gulf States in the 1980s

| Country | Population | Troops | | | | Military Expenditures | |
		Active	Army	Air Force	Navy	1983 (millions U.S. $)	As a percentage of GNP[a]
Bahrain	400,000	2,800	2,300	200	300	253	8.1
Iran[b]	42,500,000	555,000	250,000	35,000	20,000	17,370	10.6
Iraq[b]	14,900,000	642,250	600,000	38,000	4,250	10,296	46.4
Kuwait	1,750,000	12,500	10,000	2,000[e]	500	1,360	6.0
Oman	1–1,600,000	21,500[c]	16,500	3,000	2,000	1,772	28.5
Qatar	270,000	6,000	5,000	300	700	166	9.1
Saudi Arabia	8–12,000,000	51,500[d]	35,000	14,000	2,500	21,952	15.4
United Arab Emirates	1,300,000	43,000	40,000	1,500	1,500	2,422	8.0

Sources: Adapted from The Military Balance, 1984–1985 (London: International Institute for Strategic Studies, 1984); World Military Expenditures and Arms Transfers, 1972–1982 (Washington, D.C.: United States Arms Control and Disarmament Agency, April 1984).

[a]Figures are for 1982, except the figures for Iran and Qatar, which are, respectively, for 1981 and 1980.
[b]Figures for Iran and Iraq are estimates.
[c]Including some 3,700 foreign personnel.
[d]In addition, there are 10,000 foreign contract military personnel.
[e]Excluding expatriate personnel.

Ayatollah Ruhollah Khomeini: A Biography

According to most sources, Ayatollah Ruhollah Khomeini was born on 24 September 1902. The title Ayatollah (the sign of God) reflects his scholarly religious standing in the Shia Islamic tradition. His first name, Ruhollah (the spirit of God), is a common name despite its religious meaning, and his last name reflects the name of his birthplace, the town of Khomein, which is about two hundred miles south of Tehran, Iran's capital city. His father, Mustapha Musavi, was the chief cleric of the town where he was murdered only five months after the birth of Ruhollah. The child was raised by his mother, Hajar, and Aunt Sahebeh, both of whom died when Ruhollah was about fifteen years old.

Ayatollah Khomeini's life from his childhood to the present has gone through three distinct phases. The first phase, from 1908 to 1962, was marked mainly by training, teaching, and writing in the field of Islamic studies. At the age of six, he began to study the Qur'an, Islam's holy book, and elementary Persian. Subsequently, he was taught Islamic jurisprudence by his older brother, Morteza Pasandideh, who is also an Ayatollah and is living in the holy city of Qom in Iran. Ruhollah completed his studies in Islamic law (*sharia*), ethics, and spiritual philosophy under the supervision of Ayatollah Abdul Karim Haeri-ye Yazdi, first in Arak, a town near Khomein, and later in Qom, where he also got married and had two sons and three daughters. His older son, Hajj Mustafa, died or, allegedly, was killed by the Shah's security agents, but the younger one, Ahmad, is now living in Tehran and is relatively active in revolutionary politics.

Although during this scholarly phase of his life Khomeini was not politically active, his studies, teachings, and writings reveal that he firmly believed from the beginning that clerics should practice political activism. Three factors support this view. First, his interest in Islamic studies surpassed the bounds of traditional subjects of Islamic law, jurisprudence (*fiqh*), principles (*usul*), and the like. He was keenly interested in philosophy and ethics. Second, his teaching often focused on the overriding relevance of religion to practical social and political issues of the day. Third, he was the first Iranian cleric to try to refute the outspoken advocacy of secularism in the 1940s. His well-known early book, *Kashfe Assrar* (Discovery of secrets) is a point-by-point refutation of *Assrar-e Hezar Saleh* (Secrets of a thousand years), a tract written by a disciple of Iran's leading anticlerical historian, Ahmad Kassravi.

The second phase of Khomeini's life, from 1962 to 1979, was marked by political activism. During this phase he carried his lifelong fundamentalist interpretation of Shia Islam to its logical and practical conclusions. In the 1970s, in contrast to the 1940s, he no longer accepted the idea of a limited monarchy under the Iranian Constitution of 1906–7, an idea that he clearly had accepted earlier, as noted in *Kashf-e Assrar.* In his book *Hokumat-e Islami* (Islamic government), a collection of his lectures in Najaf, Iraq, that was published in 1970, he rejected both the Iranian Constitution, as an alien import from Belgium, and monarchy, as an un-Islamic and illegitimate institution usurping the legitimate authority of the supreme religious leader (*faqih*), who should rule as both the spiritual and the temporal guardian of the Muslim community (*umma*). In 1962 he launched his crusade against the Shah's regime; this led to a religiopolitical rebellion on 5 June 1963. This date (the fifteenth of *Khurdad* in the Iranian solar calendar) is regarded by the revolutionary regime as the turning point in the history of the Islamic movement in Iran, for the Shah's bloody supression of the uprising was followed by the exile of Khomeini in 1964.

The radicalization of Khomeini's religiopolitical ideas and his entry into active political opposition in the second phase of his life reflected a combination of circumstances. First, the deaths of the leading, though quiescent, Iranian religious leader Ayatollah Sayyed Muhammad Burujerdi (1961) and of the activist cleric Ayatollah Abul Qassem Kashani (1962) left the way to leadership open to Khomeini, who had attained a prominent religious standing by the age of sixty. Second, since the rise of Reza Shah to power in the 1920s, the clerical class had been on the defensive because of his secular and anticlerical policies and those of his son, Muhammad Reza Shah, and these policies were most strongly expressed and enforced in the early 1960s. The Shah's so-called White Revolution in 1963 in particular was considered by the religious leaders as detrimental not only to the Shia cultural tradition, but also to their landed and educational interests. Third, the Shah's granting of diplomatic privileges and immunities to U.S. military personnel and their dependents in 1964 was viewed as degrading to the Iranian sense of national independence.

The third phase of Khomeini's life began with his return to Iran from exile on 1 February 1979 and will probably continue as long as he lives. The outstanding feature of this phase is the emergence of Khomeini as the founder and the supreme leader of the Islamic Republic of Iran. Throughout this phase, Khomeini has been preoccupied with the fundamental goal of engineering an ideal Islamic society in Iran. From the perspective of Khomeini and his leading disciples, the Iranian Revolution has so far gone through three major periods. The first one began when Khomeini appointed Mehdi Bazargan as the head of the "provisional government" on 5 February 1979 and ended with Bazargan's fall on 6 November, two days after the seizure of the U.S. embassy in Tehran. This, according to Khomeini, marked the beginning of the second revolution, which, in his view, was better than the first one (which had led to the departure of the Shah from Iran on 16 January 1979 and the seizure of power by revolutionary forces on 11 February). The hallmark of this so-called second revolution was the elimination of mainly nationalist forces from politics. As early as 2 June 1979, for example, the National Democratic Front accused Khomeini of "dictatorship," and as early as 20 August 1979, as many as twenty-two opposition newspapers were ordered closed. In terms of foreign policy, the landmarks of the second revolution were the destruction of any basis for U.S.-Iran relations and the Iranian defense against the Iraqi invasion of 22 September 1980. The admission of the Shah to the United States on 22 October 1979, Khomeini's instruction to Iranian students on 1 November to "expand with all their might their attacks against the United States" in order to force the extradition of the Shah, and the seizure of the American embassy on 4 November led to 444 days of agonizing dispute between the United States and Iran.

The so-called third revolution began with Khomeini's dismissal of President Abul Hassan Bani-Sadr on 22 June 1981. In retrospect, the fate of Bani-Sadr, as that of Bazargan, reflected Khomeini's single-minded determination to eliminate from power any individual or group that could stand in the way of his engineering the ideal Islamic Republic of Iran, which he had formally proclaimed into existence on 1 April 1979—according to Khomeini, "the first day of the Government of God." This government, however, has yet to be molded thoroughly according to his fundamentalist interpretation of Islam. In terms of foreign policy, the main characteristics of the third revolution were the continuation of the Iraq-Iran war, increasing rapprochement with the Soviet Union, and expanded efforts to export the Islamic revolution.

In my opinion, the revolution has been going through yet a fourth phase since late 1982. Domestically, the clerical class has consolidated its control, has prevented land distribution, and has promoted the role of the private sector in the economy. Internationally, Iran has launched an "open door" foreign policy as a means of ending its status as a pariah and has begun to distance itself from terrorist groups. It has expanded commercial relations with western Europe, China, Japan, and Turkey, has decreased the amount of interaction it has with the Soviet Union, and has left the door open for reestablishing relations with the United States.

Source: Written originally by R. K. Ramazani for *Encyclopedia of World Biography,* this article is reproduced here with permission.

Appendix C

Gulf Cooperation Council Charter

Cooperation Council for the Arab States of the Gulf: The States of the United Arab Emirates, the State of Bahrain, the Kingdom of Saudi Arabia, the Sultanate of Oman, the State of Qatar, and the State of Kuwait,

Being fully aware of their mutual bonds of special relations, common characteristics and similar systems founded on the Creed of Islam; and based on their faith in the common destiny and destination that link their peoples; and in view of their desire to effect coordination, integration and interconnection between them in all fields; and based on their conviction that coordination, cooperation and integration between them serve the higher goals of the Arab Nation; and, in order to strengthen their cooperation and reinforce their common links; and in an endeavor to complement efforts already begun in all vital scopes that concern their peoples and realize their hopes for a better future on the path to unity of their States; and in conformity with the Charter of the League of Arab States which calls for the realization of closer relations and stronger bonds; and in order to channel their efforts to reinforce and serve Arab and Islamic causes, have agreed as follows:

ARTICLE ONE, Establishment of Council
A council shall be established hereby to be named The Cooperation Council for the Arab States of the Gulf, hereinafter referred to as Cooperation Council.

ARTICLE TWO, Headquarters
The Cooperation Council shall have its headquarters in Riyadh, Saudi Arabia.

ARTICLE THREE, Cooperation Council Meetings
The Council shall hold its meetings in the state where it has its headquarters, and may convene in any member state.

ARTICLE FOUR, Objectives
The basic objectives of the Cooperation Council are:
1. To effect coordination, integration and interconnection between member states in all fields in order to achieve unity between them.
2. Deepen and strengthen relations, links and scopes of cooperation now prevailing between their peoples in various fields.
3. Formulate similar regulations in various fields including the following:
   a. Economic and financial affairs
   b. Commerce, customs and communications
   c. Education and culture
   d. Social and health affairs
   e. Information and tourism
   f. Legislation and administrative affairs.
4. Stimulate scientific and technological progress in the fields of industry, mineralogy, agriculture, water and animal resources; the establishment of scientific research centers, implementation of common projects, and encourage cooperation by the private sector for the good of their peoples.

ARTICLE FIVE, Council Membership
The Cooperation Council shall be formed of the six states that participated in the Foreign Ministers' meeting held at Riyadh on 4 February 1981.

ARTICLE SIX, Organizations of the Cooperation Council
The Cooperation Council shall have the following main organizations:
1. Supreme Council to which shall be attached the Commission for Settlement of Disputes.
2. Ministerial Council.
3. Secretariat-General.
Each of these organizations may establish branch organizations as necessary.

ARTICLE SEVEN, Supreme Council
1. The Supreme Council is the highest authority of the Cooperation Council and shall be formed of heads of member states. Its presidency shall be rotatory based on the alphabetical order of the names of the member states.

2. The Supreme Council shall hold one regular session every year. Extraordinary sessions may be convened at the request of any member seconded by another member.
3. The Supreme Council shall hold its sessions in the territories of member states.
4. A Supreme Council shall be considered valid if attended by two thirds of the member states.

ARTICLE EIGHT, Supreme Council's Functions

The Supreme Council shall endeavor to achieve the objectives of the Cooperation Council, particularly as concerns the following:
1. Review matters of interest to the member states.
2. Lay down the higher policy for the Cooperation Council and the basic line it should follow.
3. Review the recommendations, reports, studies and common projects submitted by the Ministerial Council for approval.
4. Review reports and studies which the Secretary-General is charged to prepare.
5. Approve the bases for dealing with other states and international organizations.
6. Approve the rules of procedures of the Commission for Settlement of Disputes and nominate its members.
7. Appoint the Secretary-General.
8. Amend the Charter of the Cooperation Council.
9. Approve the Council's Internal Rules.
10. Approve the budget of the Secretariat-General.

ARTICLE NINE, Voting in Supreme Council

1. Each member of the Supreme Council shall have one vote.
2. Resolutions of the Supreme Council in substantive matters shall be carried by unanimous approval of the member states participating in the voting, while resolutions on procedural matters shall be carried by majority vote.

ARTICLE TEN, Commission for Settlement of Disputes

1. The Cooperation Council shall have a commission called "Commission for Settlement of Disputes" and shall be attached to the Supreme Council.
2. The Supreme Council shall form the Commission for every case separately based on the nature of the dispute.
3. If a dispute arises over interpretation or implementation of the Charter and such dispute is not resolved within the Ministerial Council or the Supreme Council, the Supreme Council may refer such dispute to the Commission for Settlement of Disputes.

4. The Commission shall submit its recommendations or opinion, as applicable, to the Supreme Council for appropriate action.

ARTICLE ELEVEN, Ministerial Council
1. The Ministerial Council shall be formed of the Foreign Ministers of the member states or other delegated Ministers. The Council's presidency shall rotate among members every three months by alphabetical order of the states.
2. The Ministerial Council shall convene every three months and may hold extraordinary sessions at the invitation of any member seconded by another member.
3. The Ministerial Council shall decide the venue of its next session.
4. A Council's meeting shall be deemed valid if attended by two thirds of the member states.

ARTICLE TWELVE, Functions of the Ministerial Council
The Ministerial Council's functions shall include the following:
1. Propose policies, prepare recommendations, studies and projects aimed at developing cooperation and coordination between member states in the various fields and adopt required resolutions or recommendations concerning thereof.
2. Endeavor to encourage, develop and coordinate activities existing between member states in all fields. Resolutions adopted in such matters shall be referred to the Ministerial Council for further submission, with recommendations, to the Supreme Council for appropriate action.
3. Submit recommendations to the Ministers concerned to formulate policies whereby the Cooperation Council's resolutions may be put into action.
4. Encourage means of cooperation and coordination between the various private sector activities, develop existing cooperation between the member states' chambers of commerce and industry, and encourage the flow of working citizens of the member states among them.
5. Refer any of the various facets of cooperation to one or more technical or specialized committees for study and presentation of relevant proposals.
6. Review proposals related to amendments to this Charter and submit appropriate recommendations to the Supreme Council.
7. Approve the Ministerial Council's Rules of Procedures as well as the Rules of Procedures of the Secretariat-General.
8. Appoint the Assistant Secretaries-General, as nominated by the Secretary-General, for a renewable period of three years.

9. Approve periodic reports as well as internal rules and regulations related to administrative and financial affairs proposed by the Secretary-General, and submit recommendations to the Supreme Council for approval of the budget of the Secretariat-General.
10. Make arrangements for the Supreme Council's meetings and prepare its agenda.
11. Review matters referred to it by the Supreme Council.

ARTICLE THIRTEEN, Voting at Ministerial Council
1. Every member of the Ministerial Council shall have one vote.
2. Resolutions of the Ministerial Council in substantive matters shall be carried by unanimous vote of the member states present and participating in the vote, and in procedural matters by majority vote.

ARTICLE FOURTEEN, Secretariat-General
1. The Secretariat-General shall be composed of a Secretary-General who shall be assisted by assistants and a number of staff as required.
2. The Supreme Council shall appoint the Secretary-General, who shall be a citizen of one of the Cooperation Council states, for a period of three years which may be renewed for one time only.
3. The Secretary-General shall nominate the Assistant Secretaries-General.
4. The Secretary-General shall appoint the Secretariat General's staff from among the citizens of member states, and may not make exceptions without the approval of the Ministerial Council.
5. The Secretary-General shall be directly responsible for the work of the Secretariat-General and the smooth flow of work in its various organizations. He shall represent the Cooperation Council with other parties within the powers vested in him.

ARTICLE FIFTEEN, Functions of the Secretariat-General
The Secretariat-General shall undertake the following functions:
1. Prepare studies related to cooperation and coordination, and to integrated plans and programmes for member states' common action.
2. Prepare periodic reports on the Cooperation Council's work.
3. Follow up the execution by the member states of the resolutions and recommendations of the Supreme Council and Ministerial Council.
4. Prepare reports and studies ordered by the Supreme Council for Ministerial Council.
5. Prepare the draft of administrative and financial regulations commensurate with the growth of the Cooperation Council and its expanding responsibilities.
6. Prepare the Cooperation Council's budget and closing accounts.

7. Make preparations for meetings and prepare agenda and draft resolutions for the Ministerial Council.
8. Recommend to the Chairman of the Ministerial Council the convocation of an extraordinary session of the Council whenever necessary.
9. Any other tasks entrusted to it by the Supreme Council or Ministerial Council.

ARTICLE SIXTEEN, The Secretary-General and the Assistant
Secretaries-General and all the Secretariat-General's staff shall carry out their duties in complete independence and for the common interest of the member states. They shall refrain from any action or behavior that is incompatible with their duties and from divulging the secrets of their jobs either during or after their tenure of office.

ARTICLE SEVENTEEN, Privileges and Immunities
1. The Cooperation Council and its organizations shall enjoy on the territories of all member states such legal competence, privileges and immunities as required to realize their objectives and carry out their functions.
2. Representatives of the member states of the Council, and the Council's employees, shall enjoy such privileges and immunities as are specified in agreements to be concluded for this purpose between the member states. A special agreement shall organize the relation between the Council and the state in which it has its headquarters.
3. Until such time as the two agreements mentioned in item 2 above are prepared and put into effect, the representatives of the member states in the Cooperation Council and its staff shall enjoy the diplomatic privileges and immunities established for similar organizations.

ARTICLE EIGHTEEN, Budget of the Secretariat-General
The Secretariat-General shall have a budget to which the member states shall contribute equal amounts.

ARTICLE NINETEEN, Charter Implementation
1. This Charter shall go into effect as of the date it is signed by the heads of states of the six member states named in this Charter's preamble.
2. The original copy of this Charter shall be deposited with Saudi Arabia's Ministry of Foreign Affairs which shall act as custodian and shall deliver a true copy thereof to every member state, pending the establishment of the Secretariat-General at which time the latter shall become depository.

ARTICLE TWENTY, Amendments to Charter
1. Any member state may request an amendment of this Charter.
2. Requests for Charter amendments shall be submitted to the Secretary-General, who shall refer them to the member states at least four months prior to submission to the Ministerial Council.

ARTICLE TWENTY-ONE, Closing Provisions
No reservations may be voiced in respect of the provisions of this Charter.

ARTICLE TWENTY-TWO
The Secretariat-General shall arrange to deposit and register copies of this Charter with the League of Arab States and the United Nations, by resolution of the Ministerial Council.

This Charter is signed on one copy in Arabic language at Abu Dhabi City, United Arab Emirates, on 21 Rajab 1401 corresponding to 25 May 1981.

United Arab Emirates	Sultanate of Oman
State of Bahrain	State of Qatar
Kingdom of Saudi Arabia	State of Kuwait

Source: Gulf Cooperation Council Secretariat, Riyadh, n.d., n.p.

Revolutionary Iran at the Strait of Hormuz

[Excerpts] Hojjat ol-Eslam val-Moslemin Hashemi-Rafsanjani, provisional Friday Imam of Tehran, in the second sermon of this week's Friday prayers in Tehran, referring to the martyrdom anniversary of the fourth martyr-in-the-altar, Ayatollah Ashrafi-Esfahani, reminded the congregation of this martyr's efforts and self-sacrifices toward supporting the war fronts and paid tribute to these efforts. He said: This is an honor for the Islamic Republic and evidence revealing the discord among and terrorist nature of the hypocrites and other small groups.

Continuing his sermon with reference to the currents governing the war situation and recent propaganda, he said: At this stage and in these conditions, world arrogance does not wish the war to end, and all its noise is aimed at preventing an end to the war. When the United Nations, America, the Soviet Union, the West, and the region's reaction say that there must be peace, they lie. They precipitated the war to overthrow the Islamic Republic and to bring another shah to power so that he would protect the southern potentates. They intended to shape Saddam in this way, but their calculations went wrong and today there is nothing left of the Qadisiyyah hero but an aggressive and defeated straw man; those potentates are forced to tolerate a blow at the body of their exhausted economy for every shell or missile fired at Iran.

In contrast, our people adapted themselves to the war and made the impossible possible; our society became active and powerful. This irritates world arrogance because the Islamic Republic's policy has leaked across its borders and is being used as a model in Pakistan, the Philippines, Chile, El Salvador, and other parts of the world. World arrogance has to prevent us from achieving these victories, otherwise the world situation will change.

Hashemi-Rafsanjani said: They know well that their course is not a military one. Considering the long distance and unfamiliarity with the region, a few American divisions will not be able to act any better than 12 Iraqi divisions which knew the region and were familiar with it; nobody could fight in this region and achieve a better result than the Iraqis. Therefore, all their propaganda is aimed at putting us under pressure and giving credit to Saddam, so that both he and the war would continue so that world arrogance could sell its arms and so that countries such as France would be saved from crushing, economic bottlenecks.

Referring to the propaganda of world arrogance concerning Iran's oil wells and pollution of the Persian Gulf waters, Hashemi-Rafsanjani said the wells were capped by the powerful hands of oil industry workers and thus foiled this propaganda.

The provisional Friday Imam of Tehran, in connection with the new trick of world arrogance concerning the Super Etendard aircraft, said: [Begin recording] This issue will not solve any of their problems. It will eventually add another problem to their existing problems. Regarding propaganda, we have a tongue too and make these explanations to enlighten our nation. In the first place, the combat power of these aircraft is greater than the aircraft owned by Saddam. His aircraft are weaker because their speed is less. For instance, if our aircraft chase them, they will be able to shoot them. This will happen if they come; therefore, they will have no effect. Their speed is about the speed of sound, a bit more; their range, instead of 300 km is 600 km or a bit more; but if they fly deep inside our territory, they will be faced with danger. Compared with our F-14 aircraft, they are many times weaker. Our aircraft's missile range is great, and we have more missiles than Saddam. Five Super Etendard aircraft alone have no combat value; if one of their pilots falls sick, if a spare part is missing, they will not be able to fight. Having only 70 or 80 F-14 aircraft, we face restrictions defending our airspace, 70 or 80 F-14s . . . [chants of "God is great," "Khomeyni is the leader," "Death to the United States," "Death to the Soviet Union," and "Death to Israel"].

The only thing they can possibly do is this, the important point is this: They can do nothing on the ground. If you think that these aircraft will come to Tehran, Esfahan, or Tabriz, that is not the case, however, they carry a particular missile with flight characteristics making them work well over water. For hitting ships they are among the best arms in the Third World today. They can hit ships well; if they fire their missiles from 70 km—provided that they have aimed well—the missile may hit the ship. Of course, this is not something new—it is an Exocet missile.

The Exocet missile has such characteristics. They have used them before, firing them from helicopters from a distance of 40 km.

If Iraq received these aircraft, the Exocet's operational range would increase by 30 km, that is, from Iraqi territory they can hit any ships which we want to send, for instance, to Bandar-e Mahshahr. It is not easy to hit Khark [Kharg] because it is 150 km from us and we can guard the sea with our F-14s. From that distance, it is very difficult for them to come. I do not say they cannot come; they have to come by some trick.

Our pilots have said to us: Let them come; we hope they will come, with French pilots. Iraqi pilots are not competent enough to fly these aircraft. We will shoot them down over our territory and [rest of sentence interrupted by prolonged chants from the congregation, including "Death to France"].

They have not dared deliver them yet; they have made a noise; somebody says they have been delivered and another says they have not; a third says they are at the airport while a fourth says they have dismantled them and have given the parts to the Iraqis to assemble them themselves—they cannot assemble them. They have made up many stories and have made a noise to frighten us. What happens if they deliver them? That will be the end of the story; Iraq will possess five aircraft which do not have much military value. If they had military value, they would be able to hit some of our ships there. They claim that they will come to Khark Island and hit the ships there and will stop our oil. This is the ultimate danger they can cause. Of course, in my opinion, it is very unlikely. They have created the noise in a serious manner. They have created some for and some against it. Some say France's action is madness; others say France is acting in an irresponsible way; while some say France is engaged in trading death. Some say France is not paying attention to the responsibility of Western civilization, and some say France is bringing calamity to all of Europe. While others say Iran is not giving up, Iran must be brought to the negotiation table.

Both sides are talking and making noise so that we will believe that they are telling the truth. Imagine they are speaking the truth, there is no joke in war. If that is the case, we must be prepared. First of all, we are prepared to defend and are confident. It has Soviet Tupolevs, which are much more dangerous than the other aircraft. It has MIG-25s, which are much more dangerous. Some of the Mirages delivered by France before are much more dangerous. The Soviet [Scud?] missiles and the surface-to-surface Chinese and French missiles are much more dangerous, and they have achieved nothing. If that were the case and if they were brought into battle, there would be two possibilities—either we would shoot them down in midair or they would manage to hit some of our ships. Or, they could manage to close Khark pipelines. There cannot be more than these three possibilities. The first and second are nothing, that is, if they come and hit some ships, the situation would be as it is now—they hit them even now, even now they have Exocets and hit them—well, it is a war and there will be things like this, we tolerate them.

Of the West's provocations now that they are digging their own graves is that they say the Iranians have said from the beginning that they will block the Strait of Hormuz as soon as Iraq receives these aircraft, whereas they have not blocked it yet and they have retreated. Well, you have heard what we have said; they have heard it themselves; from the beginning, we have said it. We said it 2 or 3 months ago: We will block the Strait of Hormuz when we cannot export oil. Even if they hit half of our oil, it will not be in our interest to block the Strait of Hormuz. When we do not have oil, when we are unable to export oil, the Persian Gulf will be of no use to us since we will have no money, and the Strait of Hormuz will be of no use to us. That is when we will enter the arena and do what we like, although I consider such an eventuality to be very unlikely.

That day will be a very difficult one because, first, the world is not that mad to carry out such acts; there are only these noises at the moment. If the world went mad and risked this, then it would be evident that the world is prepared for a great disaster. It would be evident that the Western world has realized that life is not possible for it like this and wants to pin the blame on the war. On that day, we must prepare ourselves for aggression; if we do not want it, they will make it happen. The world will carry out this measure only if it is prepared for an unprecedented crisis in which the price of one barrel of oil would reach 100 dollars. This is not rhetoric.

About 7 million barrels of oil are currently passing through this strait daily. After the victory of our revolution, world oil production suddenly dropped by 5 million. Saudi Arabia, Kuwait and others began to compensate for this because the strait was open. But because of shortages for 6 months, the price of oil jumped from $12 to $36. We saw this happen. Today, if the same thing happens, Saudi Arabia, Kuwait, Qatar, Dubayy, and others would not be able to compensate for the shortage, because we will close the strait. They should not say that it is impossible to block it. They have been talking nonsense. For instance, a Kuwaiti shaykh said: If the Iranians decide to block the strait, they would require 240 ships to place in the strait. They think that we will place them in such a way that there is no room to pass! There is no need to close it this way. We can create a wall of fire with 103-mm guns, and you know how many we had and how many we have captured from the Iraqis so far. And you are aware that we are manufacturing the ammunition ourselves in our own factories here.

We could create a wall of fire over the Strait of Hormuz twice a day. On the island of Qeshm, we are very near the strait. Larak Island is right on the strait. Even from Bandar 'Abbas itself, we can use our 175-mm guns with with a range of 48 km. Who would be able to approach the strait if we were to shell it with such guns from Bandar 'Abbas? You yourselves know that our planes are armed with many air-to-sea missiles. Our underground depots are full of such missiles, which we have not yet used. The Americans themselves know; the Americans are aware that we have not yet even used the planes that they gave us in the shah's era. These planes are more powerful than Exocets and have a longer range. We have not used them yet. There are many other things that they know we have. We can even close the Strait of Hormuz with Kalashnikovs. Our children can sit in small boats very close to the strait. Larak Island is right in the middle of the strait. What is the matter with you? All this is known. They think that we are going to block it with a fleet of ships, so that they can sink our ships.

Apart from that, if a 300,000-ton oil tanker were to be hit and sink in the strait, the oil slick would make it very difficult to ply the strait. There are many other methods, of which they are aware. For instance, we can use the port of Jask, or further east or west, or elsewhere. This sea is at our disposal. Generally, it would be easy to block the Strait of Hormuz, if we deem it necessary. Of course, I said we would block it if we think it would serve our interests. We do not want to block it now; but we could do it. I said that the security of the Gulf, in the first place, is in our interest. Saudi Arabia, Kuwait, Qatar, the Emirates, Oman and the rest of them use this area much less than we do. We use it much more. We will maintain the security of this area as far as possible. When this area becomes useless for us, then the whole world will be deprived and nothing will go out of here.

What would happen then? Suppose we reach the point when the Strait of Hormuz is blocked, then at that time we will have to give a few martyrs. It would not be like previous wars when we suffered many martyrs, because we know that blocking it is easy. What would be the outcome of this blockade? They think that Iran is dependent on the strait itself because it has so many ships plying the waters and so many factories that are dependent on imports. They therefore think that it would be suicide for Iran to close the strait. Of course, it would be suicide for us if we were like you. But we are not like you. We are a nation that follows the line of Imam Husayn and Karbala. We are a people who have planned our lives and revolution on the basis of the model left to us by Imam Husayn. You have seen that we mean it. We are telling the truth and we have proved it. The events of Karbala are being repeated in our society today. Our nation is prepared to put up with 6 months of hardship if necessary. It is prepared to deprive itself of luxuries because it would not be necessary to be deprived of basic living requirements. Our bread and water, fuel and traffic would not be disrupted. For instance, we might be deprived of a refrigerator, because we would not be able to import a spare part.

It would not be hard for our nation to put up with such shortages. Of course, there are some pampered people who would not put up with such shortages. These pampered people might chant slogans. Then we would send them for hard labor in the desert. If the hard times were to come, they would not be allowed to stay in lines in Tehran and make us go to Sistan to grow wheat. No, we would send them to Kahnuj and we ourselves would stay here to run the country. [Cries of "Death to France."] On a day like that, our nation might take a giant step toward absolute self-sufficiency within 6 months. We have a place like Kahnuj where it is possible to sow wheat through all four seasons of the year. We have Jiroft which is a granary. We have a place like Jaz-Murian where it is possible to plant crops all the year round and its area could feed all the country if managed properly.

You others cannot put up with the shortages. If the 8 million barrels daily flow of oil to the West of Japan were to be stopped for 6 months, your greedy capitalists would put higher prices on the oil. Your capitalists are worse than ours. We also have such capitalists, who start hoarding products as soon as they hear of possible shortages. But your capitalists are worse than ours. They have started raising the price of oil even now. Yesterday, we heard that the price of oil had gone up by about $1, and nothing has happened yet. This is the nature of capitalists. Rich people are very frightened, first and foremost. They are cowards and frightened of the slightest trouble. Second, rich people are greedy and take advantage of every occasion to make money. This is the way they are. Capitalists are the same throughout the world and they cannot be changed. Of course, there are some exceptions where the rich are not greedy. Such people are not capitalists by nature; they have earned their wealth by being good managers.

It would not be possible for you others to put up with the shortages. Therefore, you would try to avoid it. You might resort to another option, that is, you might resort to force to open the strait in time. Well, this would culminate in war with arms. Are we afraid of being engaged in a war with you? See our examples of the Karbala martyrs and our own martyrs, then judge for yourselves whether we are afraid. In the history of mankind, our Imam Husayn is a symbol of martyrdom for the path of justice. The title of lord of the martyrs, given to this great personality of mankind, is indeed an appropriate title. The events of Karbala are an example today for us, for our women, children, young and old men. Those events are a guide for us to follow. [End recording.]

Continuing his remarks, Hojjat ol-Eslam val-Moslemin Hashemi-Rafsanjani referred to the crushing answers given by the Iranian youths in the Saddamists' prisons as an example of Karbala epic and added: These young men are the great men of history and the heirs of Imam Husayn. They might be small in stature but they are heroes of history. You would have to face such heroes.

Source: Tehran Domestic Radio Service in Persian (1030GMT), 14 October 1983; in Foreign Broadcast Information Service, *Daily Report, South Asia,* 17 October 1983, vol. 8, no. 201, pp. 11–13.

Notes

CHAPTER 1: THE GEOSTRATEGIC BALANCE

1. Gregory F. Rose, "Soldiers of Islam: The Iranian Armed Forces since the Revolution," Office of the Assistant Chief of Staff, G2/DSEC, 4th Infantry Division (Mechanized), Fort Carson, Colo. See also William F. Hickman, *Ravaged and Reborn: The Iranian Army, 1982* (Washington, D.C.: Brookings Institution, 1982).
2. Rose, "Soldiers of Islam."
3. *New York Times,* 21 June 1984.
4. *Economist* (London), 9 June 1984.
5. See, for details, R. K. Ramazani, "The Strait of Hormuz: The Global Choke-point," in *The Indian Ocean in Global Politics,* ed. Larry W. Bowman and Ian Clark (Boulder, Colo.: Westview Press, 1981), and idem, *The Persian Gulf and the Strait of Hormuz* (Alpen aan den Rijn, The Netherlands: Sijthoff & Noordhoff, 1979).
6. See Foreign Broadcast Information Service, *Daily Report, South Asia,* 23 September 1983, vol. 8, no. 130 (hereafter cited as FBIS/SA).
7. Ibid., 17 October, vol. 8, no. 201. The text is in appendix D.
8. Ibid., 29 May 1984, vol. 8, no. 104.
9. See Ramazani, "Strait of Hormuz," in Bowman and Clark, *Indian Ocean,* and idem, *Persian Gulf.*
10. *Washington Post,* 21 October 1984.
11. See FBIS/SA, 17 October 1983, vol. 8, no. 201.
12. Ibid.

CHAPTER 2: THE IDEOLOGICAL CRUSADE

1. Raymond Aron, *Peace and War: A Theory of International Relations* (Garden City, N.Y.: Anchor Press/Doubleday, 1973), p. 325.
2. See Abdulaziz Abdulhussein Sachedina, *Islamic Messianism: The Idea of Mahdi in Twelver Shi'ism* (Albany: State University of New York Press, 1981).
3. FBIS/SA, 4 November 1981, vol. 8, no. 213.

4. Ibid., 14 February 1983, vol. 8, no. 031.
5. R. K. Ramazani, "Khumayni's Islam in Iran's Foreign Policy," in *Islam in Foreign Policy,* ed. Adeed Dawisha (Cambridge: Cambridge University Press, 1983), pp. 9–32.
6. See Haj Ruhollah Musavi Khomeini, *Kashf-e Assrar* (Tehran: Islamieh, 1363/1943).
7. My translation from *Sukhanraniha-ye Imam Khomeini dar Shish Mahe-ye Avval-e 1359* (Tehran: Nur, 1359/1980), p. 8.
8. FBIS/SA, 8 July 1981, vol. 8, no. 130, annex no. 015.
9. My translation, *Kayhan,* 26 July 1982.
10. FBIS/SA, 17 August 1983, vol. 8, no. 160.
11. Ibid., 19 September 1983, vol. 8, no. 182.
12. See, for details, R. K. Ramazani, "Iran's Islamic Revolution and the Persian Gulf," *Current History,* January 1984, pp. 5–8 and 40–41.
13. FBIS/SA, 24 March 1980, vol. 8, no. 058, supplement 070.
14. See *Soroush,* March 1981, pp. 4–5.
15. FBIS/SA, 25 August 1983, vol. 8, no. 166.
16. See ibid., 16 March 1982, vol. 8, no. 051.
17. My translation, *Kayhan,* 26 July 1982.
18. FBIS/SA, 9 March 1982, vol. 8, no. 046.
19. See *Soroush,* March 1981.
20. See the *Middle East,* 19 April 1984, p. 15.
21. For the text in Persian, see *Kayhan Hava'i,* 23 May 1984; in English, FBIS/SA, 14 May 1984, vol. 8, no. 094.
22. FBIS/SA, 23 September 1983, vol. 8, no. 188.
23. Hamid Algar, trans. and annotator, *Islam and Revolution: Writings and Declarations of Imam Khomeini* (Berkeley, Calif.: Mizan Press, 1981), p. 202.
24. See R. K. Ramazani, *The United States and Iran: The Patterns of Influence* (New York: Praeger, 1982).
25. See Ramazani, "Khumayni's Islam in Iran's Foreign Policy." On Khomeini's political thought, see the slender but solid study by Farhang Rajaee, *Islamic Values and World View: Khomeyni and International Politics* (New York: University Press of America, 1983).
26. See R. K. Ramazani, *The Persian Gulf: Iran's Role* (Charlottesville: University Press of Virginia, 1972).
27. FBIS/SA, 24 October 1983, vol. 8, no. 206.
28. Ibid., 10 November, vol. 8, no. 219.

CHAPTER 3: THE SOCIOPOLITICAL EXPLOSION

1. For the text of al-Hakim's interview in English, see *Impact International,* 25 April–8 May 1980. See also Batatu's "Iraq's Underground Shi'a Movements: Characteristics, Causes, and Prospects," *Middle East Journal,* Autumn 1981, pp. 578–94.
2. FBIS/SA, 13 March 1984, vol. 8, no. 050.
3. Ibid., 21 September 1983, vol. 8, no. 184.
4. Ibid., 11 July 1984, vol. 8, no. 134.
5. *Washington Post,* 20 and 27 March 1984, and the *New York Times,* 1 April 1984.
6. For the best report, see the *Washington Post,* 3 February 1984.

7. Ibid.
8. Ibid.
9. FBIS/SA, 14 December 1983, vol. 8, no. 241.
10. Ibid.
11. Ibid., 16 December 1983, vol. 8, no. 243.
12. Ibid., 29 December 1983, vol. 8, no. 251.
13. *Washington Post,* 28 March 1984.
14. FBIS/SA, 10 December 1984, vol. 8, no. 238.
15. Ibid., 18 December 1985, vol. 8, no. 244.
16. Ibid., 2 January 1985, vol. 8, no. 001.
17. *Economist* (London), 15 December 1984.
18. *New York Times,* 2 April 1985.
19. Ibid.
20. *Washington Post,* 3 April 1985. On 23 May 1985 the White House repeated the warning to Iran. A news report also said that President Ronald Reagan was prepared to order the bombing of the holy city of Qom. See the *Washington Post,* 24 May 1985.
21. *Washington Post,* 3 April 1985.
22. Ibid., 28 April 1985.
23. See *Kuwait Times,* 2 October 1979.
24. Ibid., 9 October 1979.

CHAPTER 4: THE CAUSES OF THE IRAQ-IRAN WAR: CONTAINMENT AND
AGGRANDIZEMENT

1. See *Baghdad Observer,* 14 March 1979.
2. Ibid., 6 April 1979.
3. See Ministry of Foreign Affairs, the Republic of Iraq, *The Iraqi-Iranian Dispute: Facts* v. *Allegations* (New York, October 1980), p. 65.
4. Ibid., p. 28.
5. *An-Nahar,* 6 April 1980.
6. *Baghdad Observer,* 25 April 1980.
7. Foreign Broadcast Information Service, *Daily Report, Middle East and Africa,* 23 September 1980, vol. 5, no. 186 (hereafter cited as FBIS/M&A).
8. As cited in the *New York Times,* 23 September 1980.
9. Ibid., 20 September 1980.
10. FBIS/M&A, 18 September 1980, vol. 5, no. 183.
11. *New York Times,* 22 September 1980.
12. Emphasis added. See FBIS/M&A, 26 September 1980, vol. 5, no. 189.
13. See Ministry of Foreign Affairs, the Republic of Iraq, *Iraqi-Iranian Dispute,* p. 4.
14. *New York Times,* 19 October 1980.
15. For the text, see the *New York Times,* 1 October 1980.
16. President Saddam Hussein's interview with *Al-Mostaqbal,* as reported in the *Baghdad Observer,* 16 October 1979.
17. FBIS/M&A, 29 September 1980, vol. 5, no. 190.
18. Ibid.
19. *Washington Post,* 28 March 1979.

CHAPTER 5: PERSISTENCE OF THE IRAQ-IRAN WAR

1. Gregory F. Rose, "Soldiers of Islam: The Iranian Armed Forces since the Revolution," Office of the Assistant Chief of Staff, G2/DSEC, 4th Infantry Division (Mechanized), Fort Carson, Colo., p. 21.
2. *Washington Post,* 31 July 1984.
3. Anthony H. Cordesman, "Lessons of the Iran-Iraq War: Part Two: Tactics, Technology, and Training," *Armed Forces Journal International,* June 1982.
4. *Arab News,* 16 April 1979, p. 2.
5. *New York Times,* 4 February 1981 and 12 October 1980.
6. Ibid., 12 October 1980.
7. This information is based on Anthony H. Cordesman, "Lessons of the Iran-Iraq War: The First Round," *Armed Forces Journal International,* April 1982, p. 42. See also appendix A, table 9 herein.
8. See Cordesman, "Lessons of the Iran-Iraq War."
9. *New York Times,* 16 October 1980.
10. FBIS/SA, 7 July 1982, vol. 8, no. 130; 9 July 1982, vol. 8, no. 132.
11. Ibid., 26 May 1982, vol. 8, no. 102.
12. Ibid., 3 June 1982, vol. 8, no. 107.
13. *New York Times,* 4 February 1981.
14. *Washington Post,* 2 October 1981.
15. *Economist* (London), 9 October 1982.
16. *New York Times,* 7 October 1980.
17. Ibid., 6 October 1980.
18. *Washington Post,* 30 January 1982.
19. *Economist* (London), 9 July 1983.
20. Ibid.
21. *New York Times,* 4 October 1982.
22. Ibid., 24 September 1980.
23. Ibid., 21 November 1982.
24. *Washington Post,* 30 July 1984.
25. *New York Times,* 21 November 1982.
26. Ibid., 16 May 1982.
27. *Washington Post,* 1 January 1984.
28. Ibid., 29 June 1984.
29. For details, see FBIS/SA, 17 March 1982, vol. 8, no. 052.
30. *Economist* (London), 30 April 1983.
31. *Washington Post,* 29 May 1982.
32. Ibid., 28 May 1982.
33. *New York Times,* 20 October 1981.
34. *Washington Post,* 19 July 1984.
35. Ibid., 5 January 1984.
36. For the text, see *L'Express,* 3 December 1982, p. 65.
37. *New York Times,* 24 September 1980.
38. Ibid., 16 January 1981.

CHAPTER 6: CONTAINMENT BY CONCILIATION: SAUDI ARABIA

1. *An-Nahar,* 25 August 1978.
2. *Al-Riyadh,* 7 January 1979.

3. Ibid., 1 February 1979.
4. Ibid., 12 February 1979.
5. Ibid., 14 February 1979.
6. *Arab News,* 3 April 1979.
7. *Al-Riyadh,* 22 April 1979.
8. Ibid., 11 November 1979.
9. *Arab News,* 20 May 1980.
10. *Al-Riyadh,* 23 February 1980.
11. FBIS/SA, 22 March 1984, vol. 8, no. 057.
12. Ibid., 6 September 1983, vol. 8, no. 173.
13. Ibid., 24 August 1983, vol. 8, no. 165.
14. Ibid., 13 October 1981, vol. 8, no. 197.
15. *Economist* (London), 18 September 1982.
16. *Washington Post,* 25 November 1982.
17. FBIS/SA, 22 July 1983, vol. 8, no. 142.
18. Ibid., 2 August 1983, vol. 8, no. 149.
19. Ibid., 17 August 1983, vol. 8, no. 160.
20. Ibid., 15 September 1983, vol. 8, no. 180.
21. Ibid., 11 July 1984, vol. 8, no. 134.
22. Ibid., 17 July 1984, vol. 8, no. 138.
23. *Washington Post,* 19 May 1985.
24. FBIS/M&A, 19 March 1985, vol. 5, no. 053.
25. FBIS/SA, 20 May 1985, vol 8, no. 097.
26. Ibid.
27. FBIS/M&A, 29 May 1985, vol. 5, no. 103.
28. FBIS/SA, 21 May 1985, vol. 8, no. 098.
29. FBIS/M&A, 20 May 1985, vol. 5, no. 097.
30. *New York Times,* 9 December 1985.
31. FBIS/SA, 2 December 1985, vol. 8, no. 231.
32. FBIS/M&A, 11 December 1985, vol. 5, no. 238.
33. Ibid.
34. Ibid., 9 December 1985, vol. 5, no. 236.
35. FBIS/SA, 11 December 1985, vol. 8, no. 238.
36. *New York Times,* 5 September 1985.

CHAPTER 7: CONTAINMENT BY DISAPPROBATION AND DETERRENCE: SAUDI ARABIA

1. *New York Times,* 12 October 1980.
2. Ibid.
3. Ibid., 24 May 1984.
4. FBIS/M&A, 5 June 1983, vol. 5, no. 109.
5. Emphasis added. FBIS/SA, 7 June 1983, vol. 8, no. 111.
6. Emphasis added. FBIS/M&A, 5 June 1984, vol. 5, no. 109. See also FBIS/M&A, 8 June 1984, vol. 5, no. 112.
7. For the text of this treaty, see R. K. Ramazani, *The Persian Gulf and the Strait of Hormuz* (Alpen aan den Rijn, The Netherlands: Sijthoff & Noordhoff, 1979), pp. 154–57.
8. *New York Times* and *Washington Post,* 15 March 1984.
9. FBIS/M&A, 5 June 1984, vol. 5, no. 109.

10. *New York Times,* 21 May 1984.
11. For related documents, see U.N. Security Council, S/RES/552 (1984), 1 June 1984; U.N. Security Council, S/PV/2546, 1 June 1984; and U.N. Security Council, S/RES/540 (1983), 31 October 1983.
12. For a valuable study made years before the war, see U.S. Congress, *Oil Fields as Military Objectives: A Feasibility Study* (Washington, D.C.: U.S. Government Printing Office, 1975).
13. This account is based on General Philip C. Gast's statement. He was director of the U.S. Security Assistance Agency. See the *New York Times,* 6 June 1984.
14. See U.S. Congress, House Committee on Foreign Affairs, *Developments in the Persian Gulf, June 1984, Hearing before the subcommittee on Europe and the Middle East* (Washington, D.C.: U.S. Government Printing Office, 1984), p. 27.
15. *New York Times,* 6 June 1984. For the text of the U.S. State Department's statement on the Stinger missile sale, see *New York Times,* 30 May 1984.
16. See U.S. Congress, House Committee on Foreign Affairs, *Developments in the Persian Gulf,* p. 32.
17. Ibid., pp. 31–32.
18. See *Aviation Week and Space Technology,* 26 October 1981.
19. FBIS/SA, 7 June 1984, vol. 8, no. 111.
20. FBIS/M&A, 13 June 1984, vol. 5, no. 115.

CHAPTER 8: CONTAINMENT OF REVOLUTION: THE GENESIS OF THE GCC

1. The text of the GCC Charter is in appendix C.
2. See R. K. Ramazani, "Iran's Search for Regional Cooperation," *Middle East Journal* 30, no. 2 (Spring 1976): 173–86.
3. See R. K. Ramazani, *The Persian Gulf and the Strait of Hormuz* (Alpen aan der Rijn, The Netherlands: Sijthoff & Noordhoff, 1979), pp. 107–12.
4. Gulf Information and Research Center, *Gulf Cooperation Council for the Arab States of the Gulf, 1983.*
5. Before the fall of the Bazargan government, Saudi leaders worried about a communist takeover because of the chaotic conditions in Iran. See, for example, Crown Prince Fahd's remarks in *Al-Riyadh,* 9 January 1979. But after the Soviet invasion of Afghanistan, Saudi leaders felt a new common bond of Islam with Iran against the Soviet and communist threat to the region. See, for example, Prince Saud's comments in *Arab News,* 8 April 1980, pp. 1 and 14.
6. See *Arab News,* 22 July 1979, and *Al-Riyadh,* 23 July 1979.
7. *An-Nahar,* 27 December 1979.
8. *Kuwait Times,* 27 April and 7 January 1980.
9. *An-Nahar,* 12 September 1979.
10. *Al-Riyadh,* 9 and 21 January 1980.
11. Ibid., 23 February 1980.
12. Ibid., 28 January 1980.
13. As reported in ibid., 23 February 1980.
14. *Kuwait Times,* 20 December 1979.
15. *Al-Riyadh,* 30 December 1979.
16. Emphasis added. As reported in *Arab News,* 3 March 1980.

17. Ibid., 22 September and 29 May 1979.
18. *Kuwait Times,* 17 November 1979.
19. For details, see R. K. Ramazani, *Beyond the Arab-Israeli Settlement: New Directions for U.S. Policy in the Middle East* (Cambridge, Mass.: Institute for Foreign Policy Analysis, 1977), pp. 7–16.
20. See R. K. Ramazani, "Genesis of the Carter Doctrine," in *Middle East Perspectives: The Next Twenty Years,* ed. George S. Wise and Charles Issawi (Princeton: Darwin Press, 1981), pp. 165–80.
21. *Arab News,* 3 March 1980.
22. Ibid., 2 April 1980.
23. Ibid., 5 May 1980.
24. *Kuwait Times,* 13 April 1980.
25. Emphasis added. *An-Nahar,* 29 October 1979.
26. FBIS/M&A, 28 May 1981, vol. 5, no. 102.
27. Gulf Cooperation Council, *Message from the Secretary-General* (Kent, Eng.: CW Printing, n.d.).

CHAPTER 9: CONTAINMENT OF SUBVERSION AND WAR: THE GCC
IN ACTION

1. FBIS/M&A, 28 May 1981, vol. 5, no. 102.
2. Ibid., 20 January 1982, vol. 5, no. 103.
3. Ibid.
4. Ibid., 12 November 1981, vol. 5, no. 218.
5. Ibid., 8 February 1982, vol. 5, no. 244.
6. *Times* (London), 29 March 1982.
7. FBIS/M&A, 25 February 1982, vol. 5, no. 028.
8. Ibid., 14 December 1983, vol. 5, no. 241.
9. Ibid.
10. Ibid., 10 September 1982, vol. 5, no. 176.
11. Ibid., 8 November 1983, vol. 5, no. 217.
12. *Aviation Week and Space Technology,* 26 October 1981.
13. *Economist* (London), 21 January 1984.
14. FBIS/M&A, 22 June 1984, vol. 5, no. 122.
15. Ibid.
16. Ibid., 25 June 1984, vol. 5, no. 123.
17. FBIS/SA, 17 May 1983, vol. 8, nos. 096 and 097.
18. Ibid., 23 August 1983, vol. 8, no. 164.
19. *Washington Post,* 11 November 1981.
20. Ibid., 9 June 1984.
21. *Khalij Times,* in FBIS/SA, 19 November 1982, vol. 8, no. 224.
22. FBIS/M&A, 21 May 1985, vol. 5, no. 098.
23. *Washington Post,* 7 November 1985.
24. Emphasis added. For the text of the communiqué, see FBIS/M&A, 6 November 1985, vol. 5, no. 215.
25. FBIS/SA, 1 November 1985, vol. 8, no. 212.
26. Ibid., 19 November 1985, vol. 8, no. 223.
27. Ibid., 13 November 1985, vol. 8, no. 219.
28. Ibid., 4 November 1985, vol. 8, no. 213.
29. FBIS/M&A, 13 December 1985, vol. 5, no. 240.

CHAPTER 10: THE ERADICATION OF ISRAEL?

1. For details, see R. K. Ramazani, *Iran's Foreign Policy, 1941–1973: A Study of Foreign Policy in Modernizing Nations* (Charlottesville: University Press of Virginia, 1975), especially pp. 25–90. See also idem, *The United States and Iran: The Patterns of Influence* (New York: Praeger, 1982), pp. 1–18.
2. For a solid treatment of the subject, see Uri Bialer, "The Iranian Connection in Israel's Foreign Policy, 1948–1951," *Middle East Journal* 39, no. 2 (Spring 1985): 292–315.
3. See, for details, Ramazani, *Iran's Foreign Policy,* pp. 219–50.
4. For details, see Ramazani, *The United States and Iran,* p. 73.
5. For details, see R. K. Ramazani, "Iran and the Arab-Israeli Conflict," *Middle East Journal* 32, no. 4 (Autumn 1978): 413–28.
6. Ibid.
7. FBIS/SA, 8 September 1981, vol. 8, no. 173.
8. *New York Times,* 13 January 1979.
9. *Washington Post,* 19 February 1979.
10. *Kayhan,* 1 December 1973.
11. FBIS/SA, 23 November, vol. 8, no. 225.
12. Ibid., 20 June 1983, vol. 8, no. 119.
13. Ibid., 17 July 1984, vol. 8, no. 138.
14. Ibid., 19 February 1985, vol. 8, no. 033.
15. *Washington Post,* 19 December 1979, and *New York Times,* 21 December 1979.
16. FBIS/SA, 10 June 1982, vol. 8, no. 112.
17. Ibid.
18. Ibid., 9 June 1981, vol. 8, no. 110.
19. Ibid., 28 October 1981, vol. 8, no. 208.
20. Ibid., 20 November 1981, vol. 8, no. 224.
21. Ibid., 21 November 1983, vol. 8, no. 225.
22. *New York Times,* 29 January 1980.
23. See *Ashena'i ba Majlis-i Shuray-i Islami* (Tehran: Chapkhanih-ye Majles-i Shuray-i Islami, Chap Avval, 1983), pp. 147–79.

CHAPTER 11: THE "EXCOMMUNICATION" OF EGYPT?

1. For details, see R. K. Ramazani, *Iran's Foreign Policy, 1941–1973: A Study of Foreign Policy in Modernizing Nations* (Charlottesville: University Press of Virginia, 1975), and idem, *The United States and Iran: The Patterns of Influence* (New York: Praeger, 1982).
2. For details, see R. K. Ramazani, "Emerging Patterns of Regional Relations in Iranian Foreign Policy," *ORBIS* 18, no. 4 (Winter 1975): 1043–69.
3. *Al-Ahram,* 24 October 1978.
4. Ibid., 18 January 1979.
5. *New York Times,* 18 January 1979.
6. Ibid., 3 May 1979.
7. *Washington Post,* 24 January 1979.
8. *New York Times,* 29 January 1980.
9. *Al-Ahram,* 23 December 1979.
10. *New York Times,* 2 November 1980.
11. Ibid., 25 March 1980.

12. Ibid., 27 March 1980.
13. *Al-Ahram,* 11 May 1979.
14. Ibid., 4 December 1979.
15. Ibid., 26 April 1980.
16. Ibid., 28 September 1979.
17. *New York Times,* 2 November 1980.
18. FBIS/SA, 14 February 1984, vol. 8, no. 031.
19. Ibid., 4 September 1984, vol. 8, no. 172.
20. Ibid., 10 August 1984, vol. 8, no. 156.
21. *Washington Post,* 11 August 1984.
22. *New York Times,* 14 August 1984.
23. *Washington Post,* 15 June 1985.

CHAPTER 12: THE ISLAMIZATION OF LEBANON?

1. *New York Times,* 3 January 1984.
2. FBIS/SA, 17 March 1982, vol. 8, no. 052.
3. See, for example, Ofira Selktar, "The New Zionism," *Foreign Policy,* no. 51 (Summer 1983), pp. 118–38.
4. See, for example, the *Economist* (London), 30 July 1983.
5. See Zeev Schiff, "The Green Light," *Foreign Policy,* no. 50 (Spring 1983), pp. 73–85.
6. See Alexander M. Haig, Jr., *Caveat: Realism, Reagan, and Foreign Policy* (New York: Macmillan, 1984), p. 317.
7. Ibid., p. 7.
8. Ibid., p. 332.
9. *New York Times,* 21 June 1982.
10. See R. K. Ramazani, *Beyond the Arab-Israeli Settlement: New Directions for U.S. Policy in the Middle East* (Cambridge, Mass.: Institute for Foreign Policy Analysis, 1977), pp. 56–62.
11. I held the Agha Khan Chair of Islamic Studies at the American University of Beirut in the academic year 1967–68, when this conversation took place.
12. FBIS/SA, 10 January 1984, vol. 8, no. 006.
13. Ibid., 2 February 1984, vol. 8, no. 023.
14. Ibid., 7 September 1984, vol. 8, no. 175.
15. Ibid., 9 November 1984, vol. 8, no. 219.
16. See Gregory F. Rose, "Soldiers of Islam: The Iranian Armed Forces since the Revolution," Office of the Assistant Chief of Staff, G2/DSEC, 4th Infantry Division (Mechanized), Fort Carson, Colo.
17. *Washington Post,* 29 June 1985.
18. For the best available account of Fadlallah's views, see his interview with editor George Nader in *Middle East Insight,* June/July 1985, pp. 12–19.
19. FBIS/SA, 19 February 1985, vol. 8, no. 033.
20. Ibid., 9 February, vol. 8, no. 028.
21. See Fadlallah's interview in *Middle East Insight,* June/July 1985.
22. FBIS/SA, 24 January 1985, vol. 8, no. 016.
23. *Washington Post,* 29 June 1985.
24. FBIS/SA, 24 January 1985, vol. 8, no. 016.
25. *New York Times,* 26 January 1985.
26. Ibid., 28 January 1985.

27. For evidence, see FBIS/SA, 3-6 June 1985, vol. 8, nos. 106-9.
28. For excerpts of Musavi's address, see the *New York Times,* 26 October 1984. For George Ball's criticism, see the *New York Times,* 16 December 1984.
29. For excerpts of Weinberger's address, see ibid., 29 November 1984. My summary is based on the *Washington Post's* version of 30 November 1984.
30. *New York Times,* 19 April 1983.
31. *Washington Post,* 20 April 1983.
32. *New York Times,* 28 October 1983.
33. *Washington Post,* 30 October 1983.
34. FBIS/SA, 24 October 1983, vol. 8, no. 206.
35. Ibid., 27 October 1983, vol. 8, no. 209.
36. *Washington Post,* 22 June 1985.
37. FBIS/SA, 21 March 1985, vol. 8, no. 055.
38. FBIS/M&A, 25 June 1985, vol. 5, no. 122.
39. Ibid.
40. Ibid.
41. *Washington Post,* 1 July 1985.
42. Ibid., 3 July 1985.
43. FBIS/M&A, 25 June 1985, vol. 5, no. 122.
44. *Washington Post,* 3 July 1985.
45. Robin Wright, with my permission, relied on the manuscript for my article that later appeared in the fall 1985 issue of *Foreign Policy* (no. 60), "Iran: Burying the Hatchet."
46. FBIS/SA, 17 June 1985, vol. 8, no. 116.

CHAPTER 13: OIL AND THE IRANIAN REVOLUTION

1. For details, see R. K. Ramazani, *The Foreign Policy of Iran, 1500–1941: A Developing Nation in World Affairs* (Charlottesville: University Press of Virginia, 1966), pp. 70–72.
2. Ibid.
3. For details, see R. K. Ramazani, *Iran's Foreign Policy, 1941–1973: A Study of Foreign Policy in Modernizing Nations* (Charlottesville: University Press of Virginia, 1975), p. 196.
4. For details, see ibid., pp. 264–72.
5. See R. K. Ramazani, *The United States and Iran: The Patterns of Influence* (New York: Praeger, 1982), pp. 21–36.
6. Abulhassan Bani-Sadr, *Naft va Saltih: Ya Naqsh-e Naft dar Tose'ah-ye Sarmayeh-dary dar Pahneh-ye Jahan va Zaman* (Tehran, 1357/1977), p. 5. For a reliable treatment of revolutionary Iran's oil policy in its early years, see Shaul Bakhash, *The Politics of Oil and Revolution in Iran,* a staff paper (Washington, D.C.: Brookings Institution, 1982).
7. Hamid Algar, trans. and annotator, *Islam and Revolution: Writings and Declarations of Imam Khomeini* (Berkeley, Calif.: Mizan Press, 1981), p. 258.
8. *Washington Post,* 8 January 1979.
9. Ibid., 19 December 1978.
10. Ibid.
11. Dankwart A. Rustow, *Oil and Turmoil: America Faces OPEC and the Middle East* (New York: Norton, 1982), p. 184.

12. FBIS/SA, 1 June 1982, vol. 8, no. 105.
13. Ibid., 25 February 1982, vol. 8.
14. Ibid., 30 August 1982, vol. 8, no. 168.
15. See the chart in *Petroleum Economist* 50, no. 10 (October 1983).
16. *Petroleum Economist* 50, no. 6 (June 1983).
17. *Wall Street Journal,* 25 January 1983.
18. *Economist* (London), 28 July 1984.
19. *Washington Post,* 25 January 1983.
20. *Wall Street Journal,* 9 November 1983.
21. FBIS/SA, 21 December 1982, vol. 8, no. 245.
22. Ibid., 6 July 1984, vol. 8, no. 131.
23. *Washington Post,* 6 August 1984.
24. FBIS/SA, 15 August 1984, vol. 8, no. 159.
25. *New York Times,* 8 July 1985.
26. *Economist* (London), 6 July 1985.
27. *New York Times,* 21 July 1985.
28. *Washington Post,* 26 July 1985.
29. *Economist* (London), 27 July 1985.
30. *New York Times,* 21 July 1985.

CHAPTER 14: OIL AND WAR

1. *Washington Post,* 21 November 1980, and *New York Times,* 24 September 1980.
2. *New York Times,* 12 October 1980.
3. See R. K. Ramazani, *The Persian Gulf and the Strait of Hormuz* (Alpen aan den Rijn, The Netherlands: Sijthoff & Noordhoff, 1979). Nevertheless, the combatants have shown some restraint.
4. *New York Times,* 16 October 1980.
5. Ibid., 7 October 1980.
6. *Economist* (London), 23 April 1980.
7. *New York Times,* 5 April 1983.
8. Ibid., 18 March 1983.
9. Cf. the *New York Times,* 8 April 1983, and the *Washington Post,* 22 September 1983.
10. *New York Times,* 6 April 1983.
11. Ibid., 29 March 1983.
12. FBIS/SA, 2 May 1983, vol. 8, no. 085.
13. For the text, see Ramazani, *The Persian Gulf,* pp. 163–71.
14. See William O. Beeman, "Gulf Oil Spill: Desperate Dilemma in the Persian Gulf," *Middle East Insight* 4, no. 3 (August/October 1983): 3–5.
15. FBIS/SA, 22 September 1983, vol. 8, no. 185.
16. Ibid.
17. Ibid., 21 and 29 May 1984, vol. 8, nos. 099 and 104.
18. Ibid., 29 May 1984, vol. 8, no. 104.
19. *Economist* (London), 30 June 1984.
20. *Washington Post,* 17 June 1984.
21. *Economist* (London), 30 June 1984.
22. *New York Times,* 28 August 1985.
23. *Washington Post* and *New York Times,* 16 August 1985.

24. *Economist* (London), 28 September 1985, and *Washington Post,* 21 September 1985.
25. *Wall Street Journal,* 6 December 1985.
26. *Washington Post,* 27 December 1985.
27. Ibid., 7 September 1985.
28. Ibid., 11 November 1985.
29. Ibid.
30. *New York Times,* 30 May 1984.
31. *Christian Science Monitor,* 18 June 1982.
32. For the text of the war order, see Anwar el-Sadat, *In Search of Identity: An Autobiography* (New York: Harper & Row, 1977), pp. 235–37.
33. See Henry Kissinger, *Years of Upheaval* (Boston: Little, Brown & Co., 1982), p. 460.
34. El-Sadat, *In Search of Identity,* p. 241.
35. *Washington Post,* 10 June 1982.
36. For the text, see the *Wall Street Journal,* 6 December 1985, p. 326.
37. *Newsweek,* 16 September 1973.
38. Golda Meir, *My Life* (New York: G. P. Putnam's Sons, 1975), pp. 420–27; and Kissinger, *Years of Upheaval,* p. 459.
39. See Richard Chadbourn Weisberg, *The Politics of Crude Oil Pricing in the Middle East, 1970–1975: A Study in International Bargaining* (Berkeley: Institute of International Studies, University of California, 1977), p. 100.

EPILOGUE: IRAN'S AMERICA INITIATIVE

1. The preview of this book was published on 8 September 1985. See R. K. Ramazani, "Iran: Burying the Hatchet," *Foreign Policy,* Fall 1985, no. 60, pp. 52–74.
2. See *The Tower Commission Report: The Full Text* (joint publication of Bantam Books and Times Books, New York, 1987), especially pp. 104, 215, 220, 274, and 295 (hereafter cited as *Report*).
3. See FBIS/SA, 16 December 1982, vol. 8, no. 242.
4. Ibid., 27 December 1982, vol. 8, no. 248.
5. See Daftar-e Motala'at-e Siyasi Va Baynalmellali, *Gozaresh-e Seminar,* especially vol. 2.
6. *Report,* p. 103.
7. For the text, see *Kayhan* (air edition in Persian), 8 August 1984, p. 5.
8. For the full text, see ibid., 7 November 1984, p. 4.
9. *Report,* p. 126.
10. *Washington Post,* 4 July 1985.
11. *Report,* p. 298.
12. Ibid., pp. 317–18.
13. *New York Times,* 14 November 1986.
14. *Report,* p. 40.
15. *New York Times,* 6 June 1987.
16. *Report,* p. 397.
17. Ibid., pp. 249–50.
18. See chapter 5, pp. 82–83.
19. *Report,* pp. 438–48.
20. See *Economist,* 14 February 1987.

21. *Report,* p. 313.
22. It is unclear whose idea it was to divert the Iranian money to the *contras.* Lt. Col. Oliver North told Attorney General Edward Meese on 23 November 1986 that he had discussed support for the Nicaraguan resistance with Amiran Nir, advisor to Israeli Prime Minister Peres, in January and that "Nir proposed using funds from arms sales to Iran for that support." See U.S. Congress, Senate Select Committee on Intelligence, *Report on Preliminary Inquiry* (Washington, D.C.: U.S. Government Printing Office, 1987), p. 43.

    Yet on 8 July 1987, in response to a question by House Select Committee counsel W. Nields, Jr., North said that Manuchehr Ghorbanifar had taken him into "the bathroom" and offered him several incentives to make the arms transactions work. North said, "the attractive incentive for me was the one he made that residuals could flow to support the Nicaraguan resistance." He then added, with apparent glee:

> I must confess to you that I thought using the Ayatollah's money to support the Nicaraguan resistance was a right idea. And I must confess to you that I advocated that. And I saw that idea of using the Ayatollah Khomeini's money to support the Nicaraguan freedom fighters as a good one. I still do. I don't think it was wrong period. I think it was a neat idea. (*New York Times,* 9 July 1987)

    Ghorbanifar fired back on 10 July. His denial was as vulgar as North's was flippant. (See *New York Times,* 11 July 1987.)
23. See, for example, *Current History,* February 1987, p. 81.
24. See *Report,* p. 334.
25. Ibid., pp. 381, 382.
26. See U.S. Congress, House Committee on Foreign Affairs, *The Foreign Policy Implications of Arms Sales to Iran and the Contra Connection* (Washington, D.C.: U.S. Government Printing Office, 1986) p. 23.
27. Ibid., p. 24.
28. FBIS/SA, 10 October 1986, vol. 8, no. 197.
29. Ibid., 28 October 1986, vol. 8, no. 208.
30. Ibid., 5 November 1986, vol. 8, no. 214.
31. Ibid., 18 November 1986, vol. 8, no. 222.
32. Ibid., 20 November 1986, vol. 8, no. 224.
33. Ibid., 25 November 1986, vol. 8, no. 227.
34. Ibid., 10 November 1986, vol. 8, no. 217.
35. Ibid., 21 November, vol. 8, no. 225.

Select Bibliography

ARABIC

al-Badri, Hassan. *Al-Ta'āwun al-'askari al-'arabi al-mushtarak: Mādiyuha, Hā-dirihu, Mustaqbaluhu* [Joint Arab military cooperation: Its past, present, and future]. Riyadh: Dar al-Marikh lil-nashr, 1982.

Bitār, Fuād. *Azmat al-dimuqrātiyat fil 'ālam al-'arabi* [Democracy in the Arab world]. Beirut: Manshurāt Dar Bayrut, 1984.

al-Fārisi, Fuād 'abd al-salām. *Qadāya Siyāsiyyah mu'āsarat* [Contemporary political problems]. Jidda: Tihama, 1982.

al-'iqād, Salāh. *Al-Tayārāt al-Siyāsiyyah fil-khalīj al-'arabi* [Political currents in the Arabian Gulf]. Cairo: Maktabat al-Anglo al-Masriyat, 1983.

al-Isha'āl, 'Abdallah. *Al-Itār al-Qānunī wal-Siyāsī li-majlis al-Ta'āwun al-khalījī* [The legal and political framework of the Gulf Cooperation Council]. Riyadh, 1983.

Kāzimi, Dia' Kāzim. *Al-Musna'āt al-sha'biyat fil-khalīj al-'arabiyyah* [Popular industries in the Arab Gulf states]. Basra, Iraq: Centre for Arab Gulf Studies, University of Basra, 1981.

Khāqi, 'Adil Amin. *Munazamat al-iqtār al-'arabiyyah al-musdirat lil-batrul, 1968–1977: Dirāsat muqārinat al-duwali* [The organization of Arab oil exporting countries, 1968–1977: A study in world organization.] Kuwait: Journal of the Gulf and Arabian Peninsula Studies, 1983.

al-kuwarah, 'Ali Khalifah. *Idārat al-mashru'āt al-'āmat fi dual al-Jazirat al-'arbiyyah al-mantājat lil-nafd* [Guide to projects in oil producing states on the Arabian Peninsula]. Riyadh: King Sa'ud University Press, 1982.

Muhammad, Muhammad Jāsim. *Man Yuhadidu Amn al-Khalīj al-'Arabiyyah?* [Who is threatening the security of the Arabian Gulf?]. Basra, Iraq: Centre for Arab Gulf Studies, University of Basra, 1982.

al-Nafissi, 'Abdallah Fahd. *Daur al-Shi'at fi tataur al-'Irāq al-Siyāsi al-Hadith* [The role of the Shi'a in the development of modern Iraqi politics]. Kuwait: Madba'at al-'asriyat, 1976.

————. *Majlis al-Ta'āwun al-Khalījī: Al-Itār al-Siyāsi wal-istrātījī* [The Gulf Cooperation Council: The political and strategic framework]. London: Ta-Ha Publishers, 1982.

Nasif, 'Ayad Taha. *Al-Istrātījīyat al-dawliyat fi mantaqat al-khalīj al-'arabiyyah* [International strategy in the Arab Gulf region]. Basra, Iraq: Centre for Arab Gulf Studies, University of Basra, 1982.

Rajab, Yahya Halimi. *Majlis al-Ta'āwun li-dual al-khalīj al-'arabiyyah: Ruyat mustaqbāliyat* [The Cooperation Council for the Arab states of the Gulf: Future developments]. Kuwait: Maktabat dar al-'arubat lil-nashr wal-Tawzi', 1983.

Ramādani, Ruhallah K. *Al-Khalīj al-'Arabi Wa Mudiq Hurmuz* [The Arab Gulf and the Strait of Hormuz]. Basra, Iraq: Centre for Arab Gulf Studies, University of Basra, 1984. Translated by 'Abd al-Sāhib al-Shaykh from the English original, titled *The Persian Gulf and the Strait of Hormuz.* Alpen aan den Rijn, The Netherlands: Sijthoff & Noordhoff, 1979.

al-Rumaihi, Muhammad. *Al-Khalīj laysa Nafdan: Dirāsat fi Ishkāliyat al-tanmiyat wal-wahdat* [The Gulf is not just petroleum: A study of cooperation]. Kuwait: Shārikat Kāzimat lil-nashr wal-tarjimat wal-tawzi', 1983.

Shafîq, Munîr. *Al-Islām wa Tahaddiyāt al-Inhitāt al-Mu'āsir* [Islam and the challenges of the contemporary decline]. London: Ta-Ha Publishers, 1980.

Shikāra, Ahmad 'Abdul Razzaq. *Al-Daur al-Istrātījī lil-wulāyāt al-mutahidat al-amirīkiyat fi mantaqat al-khalj al-'arabi hata muntasaf al-thamāniyāt* [The United States' strategic role in the Arabian Gulf till the mid-1980s]. Dubayy, United Arab Emirates: Madba'at Kāzim, 1985.

al-Sultān, 'Abdallah al-Muhsin. *Al-Bahr al-Ahmar fil-sira' al-'arabi al-Israīli* [The Red Sea in the Arab-Israeli conflict]. Beirut: Manshurāt Markaz Dirāsāt al-Wahdat al-'arabiyyah, 1984.

al-Tamimi, 'Abdel Mālik Khalaf. *Al-Tabshīr fi mantaqat al-khalīj al-'arabi: Dirāsat fil-tārikh al-ijtimā'iyat wal-siyāsi* [Human resources in the Arab Gulf region: A historic, social, and political study]. Kuwait: Shārikat Kāzimat lil-nashr wal-tarjimat wal-tawzi', 1983.

Wathāi'q Majlis al-Ta'āwun al-Khaījī [Documents of the Gulf Cooperation Council]. Doha, Qatar: Qatar News Agency, 1983.

al-Zayn, 'Ali. *Fusul min Tārikh al-Shi'at fi Lubnān* [Chapters of Shi'a history in Lebanon]. Beirut: Dar al-Kalimat lil-nashr, 1979.

ENGLISH

Abdulghani, Jasim M. *Iraq and Iran: The Years of Crisis.* Baltimore: Johns Hopkins University Press, 1984.

Ajami, Fouad. *The Arab Predicament: Arab Political Thought and Practice since 1967.* Cambridge: Cambridge University Press, 1981.

Alessa, Shamlan Y. *The Manpower Problem in Kuwait.* London: Kegan Paul International, 1981.

Aliboni, Roberto. *The Red Sea Region.* Syracuse, N.Y.: Syracuse University Press, 1985.

Alnasrawi, Abbas. *OPEC in a Changing World Economy.* Baltimore: Johns Hopkins University Press, 1985.

Amin, Samir. *The Arab Economy Today.* London: Zed Books, 1984.

———. *The Arab Nation: Nationalism and Class Struggle.* London: Zed Books, 1983.

Andersen, Roy R.; Robert F. Seibert; and Jon G. Wagner. *Politics and Change in the Middle East: Sources of Conflict and Accommodation.* New York: Prentice-Hall, 1982.

Arjomand, Said Amir, ed. *From Nationalism to Revolutionary Islam: Essays on Social Movements in the Contemporary Near and Middle East.* Albany: State University of New York Press, 1984.

El-Azhary, M. S. *The Iran-Iraq War: Historical, Economic, and Political Analysis.* New York: St. Martin's Press, 1984.

———, ed. *The Impact of Oil Revenues on Arab Gulf Development.* London: Croom Helm, 1984.

Bakhash, Shaul. *The Reign of the Ayatollahs: Iran and the Islamic Revolution.* New York: Basic Books, 1984.

Ball, George W. *Error and Betrayal in Lebanon.* Washington, D.C.: Foundation for Middle East Peace, 1984.

Batatu, Hanna. *The Old Social Classes and the Revolutionary Movement of Iraq: A Study of Iraq's Old Landed and Commercial Classes and of Its Communists, Ba'athists, and Free Officers.* Princeton: Princeton University Press, 1982.

Beblawi, Hazem. *The Arab Gulf Economy in a Turbulent Age.* New York: St. Martin's Press, 1984.

Beeman, William O. *Language, Status, and Power in Iran.* Bloomington: Indiana University Press, 1986.

Benard, Cheryl, and Zalmay Khalilzad. *The Government of God: Iran's Islamic Republic.* New York: Columbia University Press, 1984.

Berque, Jacques. *Arab Rebirth: Pain and Ecstasy.* London: Zed Books, 1983.

Bolling, Landrum R., ed. *Reporters under Fire: U.S. Media Coverage of Conflicts in Lebanon and Central America.* Boulder, Colo.: Westview Press, 1984.

Bradley, C. Paul. *Recent United States Policy in the Persian Gulf.* Grantham, N.H.: Thompson & Rutter, 1982.

Brown, L. Carl. *International Politics and the Middle East: Old Rules, Dangerous Game.* Princeton: Princeton University Press, 1984.

Clements, F. A. *Oman: The Reborn Land.* New York: Longman, 1980.

Connant, Melvin A. *The Oil Factor in U.S. Foreign Policy, 1980–1990.* Lexington, Mass.: D.C. Heath, for the Council on Foreign Relations, 1982.

Cordesman, Anthony H. *The Gulf and the Search for Strategic Stability: Saudi Arabia, the Military Balance in the Gulf, and Trends in the Arab-Israeli Military Balance.* Boulder, Colo.: Westview Press, 1984.

Daoudi, M. S., and M. S. Dajani. *Economic Diplomacy: Embargo Leverage and World Politics.* Boulder, Colo.: Westview Press, 1985.

Darius, Robert G., John W. Amos, and Ralph H. Magnus. *Gulf Security into the 1980s: Perceptual and Strategic Dimensions.* Stanford, Calif.: Hoover Institution Press, 1984.

Dawisha, Adeed, ed. *Islam in Foreign Policy.* Cambridge: Cambridge University Press, 1984.

――――. *The Arab Radicals.* New York: Council on Foreign Relations, 1986.

Dekmejian, R. Harir. *Islam in Revolution.* Syracuse, N.Y.: Syracuse University Press, 1985.

Dowdy, William L., and Russell Trood, eds. *The Indian Ocean: Perspectives on a Strategic Area.* Durham, N.C.: Duke University Press, 1985.

Ebinger, Charles K. *The Critical Link: Energy and National Security in the 1980s.* Cambridge, Mass.: Ballinger, for the Center for Strategic International Studies, 1982.

El-Ebraheem, Hassan Ali. *Kuwait and the Gulf: Small States and the International System.* Washington, D.C.: Center for Contemporary Arab Studies, 1984.

Esposito, John L. *Islam and Politics.* Syracuse, N.Y.: Syracuse University Press, 1984.

Farid, Abdel Majid, ed. *Oil and Security in the Arabian Gulf.* New York: St. Martin's Press, 1981.

Fesharaki, Fereidun, and David T. Isaak. *OPEC, the Gulf, and the World Petroleum Market.* Boulder, Colo.: Westview Press, 1983.

Fischer, Michael M. J. *Iran: From Religious Dispute to Revolution.* Cambridge, Mass.: Harvard University Press, 1980.

Grasz, Liesl. *The Omanis: Sentinels of the Gulf.* New York: Longman, 1982.

Grummon, Stephen R. *The Iran-Iraq War: Islam Embattled.* The Washington Papers, no. 92. New York: Praeger, 1982.

Guecioueur, Adda. *The Problems of Arab Economic Development and Integration.* Boulder, Colo.: Westview Press, 1984.

Hammond, Thomas T. *Red Flag over Afghanistan: The Communist Coup, the Soviet Invasion, and the Consequences.* Boulder, Colo.: Westview Press, 1984.

Hawdon, David, ed. *The Changing Structure of the World Oil Industry.* Dover, N.H.: Croom Helm, 1984.

Heard-Bey, Frauke. *From Trucial States to United Arab Emirates.* New York: Longman, 1982.

Heikal, Mohammad. *Autumn of Fury: The Assassination of Sadat.* New York: Random House, 1983.

Helms, Christine Moss. *The Cohesion of Saudi Arabia.* Baltimore: Johns Hopkins University Press, 1981.

Hiro, Dilip. *Iran under the Ayatollahs.* London: Routledge & Kegan Paul, 1985.

Horwich, George, and Edward J. Mitchell, eds. *Policies for Coping with Oil Supply Disruption.* Washington, D.C.: American Enterprise Institute for Public Policy Research, 1982.

Johns, Richard, and David Holden. *The House of Saud: The Rise and Rule of the Most Powerful Dynasty in the Arab World.* New York: Holt, Rinehart & Winston, 1981.

Keddie, Nikki R. *Roots of Revolution: An Interpretative History of Modern Iran.* New Haven: Yale University Press, 1981.

Kelly, Marjorie, ed. *Islam: The Religious and Political Life of a World Community.* New York: Praeger, for the Foreign Policy Association, 1984.

Khadduri, Majid. *The Islamic Conception of Justice.* Baltimore: Johns Hopkins University Press, 1984.

Khuri, Fuad I. *Tribe and State in Bahrain: The Transformation of Social and Political Authority in an Arab State.* Chicago: University of Chicago Press, 1980.

Kostiner, Joseph. *The Struggle for South Yemen.* New York: St. Martin's Press, 1984.

Kuniholm, Bruce R. *The Persian Gulf and United States Policy.* Claremont, Calif.: Regina Books, 1984.

Looney, Robert E. *Saudi Arabia's Development Potential.* Lexington, Mass.: Lexington Books, 1982.

Malik, Hafeez, ed. *International Security in Southwest Asia.* New York: Praeger, 1984.

El-Mallakh, Ragaei, and Berry Paulson. *OPEC and the United States: The Political Economy of Oil Supply.* Boulder, Colo.: Westview Press, 1985.

Marr, Phebe. *The Modern History of Iraq.* Boulder, Colo.: Westview Press, 1984.

Martin, Lenore G. *The Unstable Gulf: Threats from Within.* Lexington, Mass.: Lexington Books, 1984.

Nakhleh, Emile A. *Persian Gulf and American Policy.* New York: Praeger, 1982.

Neff, Donald. *Warriors for Jerusalem: The Six Days in 1967 That Changed the Middle East.* New York: Simon & Schuster, 1984.

Niblock, Tim, ed. *Social and Economic Development in the Arab Gulf.* London: Croom Helm, for the Centre for Arab Gulf Studies, University of Exeter, 1980.

Noyes, James H. *The Clouded Lens: Persian Gulf Security and U.S. Policy.* 2d ed. Stanford, Calif.: Hoover Institute for International Studies, 1982.

Peterson, J. E. *The Politics of Middle Eastern Oil.* Washington, D.C.: Middle East Institute, 1983.

Piscatori, James, ed. *Islam in the Political Process.* Cambridge: Cambridge University Press, 1983.

——. *Islam in a World of Nation States.* Cambridge: Cambridge University Press, 1986.

Quandt, William B. *Saudi Arabia in the 1980s: Foreign Policy, Security, and Oil.* Washington, D.C.: Brookings Institution, 1981.

Rajaee, Farhang. *Islamic Values and World View: Khomeyni on Man, the State, and International Politics.* New York: University Press of America, 1983.

Ramazani, Rouhollah K. *The Foreign Policy of Iran, 1500–1941: A Developing Nation in World Affairs.* Charlottesville: University Press of Virginia, 1966.

——. *The Persian Gulf: Iran's Role.* Charlottesville: University Press of Virginia, 1972.

——. *Iran's Foreign Policy, 1941–1973: A Study of Foreign Policy in Modernizing Nations.* Charlottesville: University Press of Virginia, 1975.

——. *Beyond the Arab-Israeli Settlement: New Directions for U.S. Policy in the Middle East.* Cambridge, Mass.: Institute for Foreign Policy Analysis, 1977.

——. *The Persian Gulf and the Strait of Hormuz.* Alpen aan den Rijn, The

Netherlands: Sijthoff & Noordhoff, 1979.

————. *The United States and Iran: The Patterns of Influence.* New York: Praeger, 1982.

Randall, Jonathan C. *Going All the Way: Christian Warlords, Israeli Adventurers, and the War in Lebanon.* New York: Viking, 1983.

Roy, Mottahadeh. *The Mantle of the Prophet: Religion and Politics in Iran.* New York: Simon & Schuster, 1985.

Rubinstein, Alvin Z. *The Great Game: Rivalry in the Persian Gulf and South Asia.* New York: Praeger, 1983.

Rustow, Dankwart A. *Oil and Turmoil: America Faces OPEC and the Middle East.* New York: Norton, 1982.

Said, Edward W. *Covering Islam: How the Media and the Experts Determine How We See the Rest of the World.* New York: Pantheon Books, 1981.

Sick, Gary. *All Fall Down: America's Tragic Encounter with Iran.* New York: Random House, 1985.

Al-Sowayegh, Abdulaziz. *Arab Petropolitics.* New York: St. Martin's Press, 1984.

Stempel, J. D. *Inside the Iranian Revolution.* Bloomington: Indiana University Press, 1981.

Tahir-Kheli, Shirin, and Shaheen Ayubi. *The Iran-Iraq War: Old Conflicts, New Weapons.* New York: Praeger, 1983.

Tibi, Bassam. *Arab Nationalism: A Critical Enquiry.* Translated by M. Farouk-Sluglett and P. Sluglett. London: MacMillan, 1981.

Wright, Robin. *Sacred Rage: The Crusade of Modern Islam.* New York: Linden Press/Simon and Schuster, 1985.

Yodfat, Aryeh Y. *The Soviet Union and the Arabian Peninsula: Soviet Policy towards the Persian Gulf and Arabia.* New York: St. Martin's Press, 1983.

Yoshitsu, Michael M. *Caught in the Middle East: Japan's Diplomacy in Transition.* Lexington, Mass.: Lexington Books, 1984.

PERSIAN

Afrasiyabi, Bahram. *Libi va Tarikh* [Libya and history]. Tehran: Zarin, 1363/1984.

Akhgari, Muhammad Reza. *Risheyabi-yi Mokhtasari az Tarikhche-yi Guruha* [A short account of the historical roots of the various groups]. Tehran, 1363/1984.

Amir'ala'i, Shams-al-Din. *Dar Rah-i Enqelab va Doshvariha-ye Ma'muriyat-i Man dar Faranseh* [On the path of the revolution and my difficulties in France]. Tehran: Dehkhoda, 1362/1984.

Ashena'i ba Majlis-i Shuray-i Islami [An introduction to the Islamic Consultative Assembly]. Tehran: Majlis, 1361/1982.

Asrar-i Jang-i Tahmili be Ravayat-i Osara-yi Araqi [The secrets of the imposed war as told by the Iraqi POWs]. Tehran: Surush, 1363/1984.

Ayat, Hassan. *Darsha'i az Tarikh-i Iran* [Lectures on the history of Iran]. Tehran: Hezb-i Jumhuri-yi Islami, 1363/1984.

Bazargan, Mehdi. *Bazyabi-yi Arzeshha* [The reviving of the values]. 3 vols. Tehran, 1361–62/1983–84.

———. *Enqilab-i Iran dar daw Harekat* [The Iranian revolution in two phases]. Tehran, 1363/1984.

Davari, Ali. *Nahzat-i Rawhaniyun-i Iran* [The movement of the 'ulama in Iran]. 11 vols. Tehran Bonyad-i Imam Riza, 1360/1981.

Davari-Ardakani, Riza. *Inqilab-i Islami va Vaz'-i Kununi-yi 'Alam* [The Islamic revolution and the contemporary world situation]. Tehran: Markaz-e Tabataba'i, 1361/1983.

———. *Nasionalism, Hakemiyat-e Milli va Isteqlal* [Nationalism, national sovereignty, and independence]. Isfahan: Poursesh, 1364/1985.

Dehnavi, Muhammad, comp. *Majmu'i-yi Mokatibat va Payamha-yi Ayatollah Kashani* [A collection of Kashani's letters and sermons]. 5 vols. Tehran: Chapakhsh, 1361–63/1983–85.

———. *Qiyam-i Khunin-e Panzdah-e Khurdad* [The bloody uprising of June 1963]. Tehran: Rasa, 1361/1982.

Fada'iyan-i Islam. *Rahnamay-i Haqayiq* [Guide to the truth]. Tehran, 1329/1950.

Farsi, Jalal-din. *Istrategy-i Bayn al-mellali* [International strategy]. Tehran: Markaz-i Intisharat-i 'Ilmi va Farhangi, 1361/1983.

Gozaresh-i Siminar [The report of the seminar]. 2 vols. Tehran: Vezarat-i Umur-i Khariji, 1362—63/1984–85.

Gozari bar daw Sal Jang [A review of two years war]. Tehran: Sepah-i Pasdar, 1361/1983.

Habibi, Hassan. *Jami'i, Farhang, Siyasat* [Society, culture, and politics]. Tehran: Amir Kabir, 1363/1985.

Haqshenas, S. N. *Dasa's va Jenayat-i Rus dar Afghanistan* [The Soviet crimes and intrigues in Afghanistan]. Tehran: Jam'iyat-i Islami-yi Afghanistan, 1364/1985.

Imam dar barabar-i Sahyunizm [The Imam confronting Zionism]. Tehran: Sepah-i Pasdar, 1361/1982.

Jonbish-i Mojahidin-i Araqi [The movement of Iraqi mujahids]. Tehran: 'Amaliyat-i Shahid Abu-Jihad, 1361/1982.

Madani, Seyyed Jalaudin. *Tarikh-i Mo'asir-i Iran* [The contemporary history of Iran]. 2 vols. Qum: Intisharat-i Islami, 1361/1982.

Majlis Shuray-i Islami az Didgah-i Imam Khomaini [Imam Khomeini's view of the Islamic Consultative Assembly]. Tehran: Hizb-i Jumhuri-yi Islami, 1361/1982.

Mokri, Mohammad. *Na Sharghi, Na Gharbi, Jumhuri-yi Islami: Asnad va Manab' Khabari Inqilab-i Islami Iran darbarey-i Ravabet-i Iran-o-Shawravi* [Neither East, nor West, Islamic Republic: The media of the Islamic revolution on the Iran-Soviet relations]. Tehran: Amir Kabir, 1362/1984.

Monzer, Ali. *Velayat-i Faqih va Democrasi-yi Irshad Shodi* [Valayat-i Faqih and the guided democracy]. Tehran: Sepah-i Pasdar, 1358/1980.

Movvahid, H. *Daw-sal-i Akhar: Riform ta Inqilab* [The last two years: From reform to revolution]. Tehran: Amir Kabir, 1363/1984.

Mutahari, Murteza. *Jahan Bini-yi Islami* [The Islamic world view]. 4 vols. Qum: Intisharat-i Islami, 1359/1980–81.

Najafabadi, Salehi. *Velayat-i Faqih, Hukumat-i Salihan* [Velayat-i Faqih, the government of the righteous men]. Tehran: Rasa, 1363/1984.

Naqavi, Muhammad-Ali. *Islam va Melligara'i, ya Nasionalizm az Didgah-i Islam* [Islam and nationalism, or the Islamic view of Nationalism]. Tehran: Nashr-i Farhang-i Islami, 1360/1981.

Notqhayi Qabl az Dastur-i Hojjat-ol Islam Rafsanjani [The speeches of Rafsanjani in the parliament]. 2 vols. Tehran: Majlis, 1363/1984.

Rouhani, Seyyed Hamid. *Barrasi va Tahlili az Nehzat-i Imam Khomaini* [A review and an interpretation of Imam Khomeini's movement]. 11th printing. Qum: Intisharat-i Islami, 1361/1982.

———. *Shari'at-mdari dar Dadgah-i Tarikh* [Ayatollah Shari'at-madari before the tribunal of history]. 3d printing. Tehran: Vezarat-i Irshad, 1361/1983.

Saberi, Kiyumars. *Mukatibat-i Shahid Raja'i ba Bani-Sadr va Chegunegi-yi Intikhab-i Avvalin Nakhust Vazir-i Jumhuri-yi Islami* [Martyred Raja'i's correspondance with Bani-Sadr and the story of the selection of the first prime minister of the Islamic Republic of Iran]. 2d printing. Tehran: Vezarat-i Irshad, 1362/1984.

Tahlili bar Jang-i Tahmili-yi Rejim-i Araq 'Alayhi Jumhuri-yi Islami Iran [An interpretation of the imposed war by the Iraqi regime on the Islamic Republic of Iran]. Tehran: Vezarat-i Umur-i Khariji, 1361/1982.

Yazdi, Ibrahim. *Akharin Talashha dar Akharin Ruzha; Matalibi Nagofti Piramun-i Inqilab-i Islami-yi Iran* [The last efforts in the last days; untold stories about the Islamic revolution of Iran]. Tehran: Qalam, 1363/1984.

———. *Barrasi-yi Safar-i Hoyzer be Iran* [An examination of Huyser's trip to Iran]. Tehran: Nehzat-i Azadi, 1362/1984.

Index

Abadan, Iraqi attacks on, 5–6, 72, 74, 102, 216–17
'Abdallah ibn 'Abd al-'Aziz, and Iranian Revolution, 88–89, 124
Abu Dhabi, 115–16. *See also* Gulf Cooperation Council; Iran; United Arab Emirates
Abu Musa Island, 14, 30, 66, 87, 90. *See also* Iran; Persian Gulf
Afghanistan, and Soviet occupation, 9–10, 27, 29, 67, 119–23. *See also* Gulf Cooperation Council
Airborne Warning and Air Control System (AWACS): and Kuwait, 10, 136; and Saudi Arabia, 9, 108–9, 135, 242
Air Defense Enhancement Package, 109–11
Algiers Agreement, abrogation of, 58, 60–63, 67, 116, 239. *See also* Hussein, Saddam; Iraq; Persian Gulf
'Ali, Imam, 39, 66. *See also* Hussein, Saddam
'Ali, Jamil, death of, in Bahrain, 50
Amal, 37, 157, 182–85, 189, 245. *See also* Berri, Nabih; Lebanon; al-Sadr, Musa
Arab-Israeli conflict. *See* Iran; Israel; Lebanon; Palestinians; United States
al-'Arabiyah Island, 8–9, 87, 104. *See also* Saudi Arabia
Arafat, Yasser, and Iran, 152–53, 155, 165, 231, 244. *See also* Egypt; Israel; Palestinians

'Ashura, commemoration of, in Saudi Arabia, 40
Assad, Hafiz, 81, 82, 157, 177, 193, 227, 244–45. *See also* Iran; Lebanon; Syria
AWACS. *See* Airborne Warning and Air Control System
'Aziz, Tariq, 38, 59, 78–79. *See also* Hussein, Saddam; Iraq

Bahrain, 12–13, 32, 39; and coup plot (1981), 49–53, 102, 131–33; and Gulf oil spill, 218–20; and Iran, 30, 49, 118; and Saudi Arabia, 132; and Shia Islamic Guidance Society, 53; and Shias, 48–53. *See also* Gulf Cooperation Council; Iran; Shia
Bakhtiar, Shahpour: and Gulf security, 30, 131; and Israel, 152; and Palestinians, 151
al-Bakr, Ahmad Hassan, 58, 176–77. *See also* Hussein, Saddam; Iraq
Baluchis, 4, 66, 177
Bani-Sadr, Abolhasan, 60, 73, 166, 207; and oil, 204–5
Baseej, 7, 19. *See also* Islamic Revolutionary Guards Corps
Basra, 4, 107, 217
Batatu, Hanna: on Da'wa party, 35; on al-Mujahidin, 36
Ba'th party. *See* Iraq
Bazargan, Mehdi, 35, 49, 57, 58, 59, 74, 107, 207; and Egypt, 165; and Israel,

Turkomans, 4
Turner, Stansfield, 102

Ulama (religious scholars), 26, 89, 94,
185; visits of Arab Gulf *ulama* to
Khomeini, 27
United Arab Emirates (UAE): and
Carter Doctrine, 125; and Iran, 34,
90, 115, 140; and Iraq-Iran war, 129.
See also Gulf Cooperation Council
United Nations: resolution on Palestine,
150; resolutions on Iraq-Iran war,
106, 130, 143, 238–39
United States, 22–23, 28, 53–54; and
anti-Americanism in the Middle
East, 245–46; and Arab-Israeli
conflict, 243–44; and Carter
Doctrine, 123–25; and challenges to
U.S. policies in the Middle East,
249–56; and freedom of navigation in
Persian Gulf, 224, 241–42; and Gulf
Cooperation Council states, 242–43;
and hostage rescue mission, 168;
influence of Iranian Revolution on
Middle East policies of, 236–52; and
Iran, 236–38, 240–42; and Iranian
Revolution, 241–42; and Iraq-Iran
war, 78–80, 238–40; and Kuwait,
136; military support of, to Iran,
82–83; and oil embargo, 226, 228;
and Oman facilities agreement, 123,
242; and Saudi Arabia, 107–11; and
Syria, 244–45; and terrorism in
Lebanon, 187–94, 244–47; and

terrorism in the Middle East,
235–52; and twin-pillar policy in the
Middle East, 87, 107
United States Central Command
(USCENTCOM): and Khasab air
base, 13; and Oman, 230, 240. *See
also* Gulf Cooperation Council;
Persian Gulf; United States
Union of Soviet Socialist Republics
(USSR). *See* Soviet Union

Velayati, 'Ali Akbar: and Iran's war
objective, 75; and Israel, 154–56;
and Kuwaiti airliner hijacking, 46;
and Kuwaiti bombings, 45; and
nonalignment, 22; and oil policy, 207;
and Syria, 178; and Syrian-Iranian
axis, 81; visits of, to Saudi Arabia,
98–100, 243. *See also* Iran
Vilayat-e Faqih, 19–21

Weinberger, Caspar W., and terrorism,
135, 188

Yamani, Ahmad Zaki, 206, 215
Yazdi, Ibrahim, 153, 165. *See also*
Bazargan, Mehdi; Iran
Yemen. *See* People's Democratic
Republic of Yemen

Zayed bin Sultan (President of the
UAE), 125. *See also* United Arab
Emirates